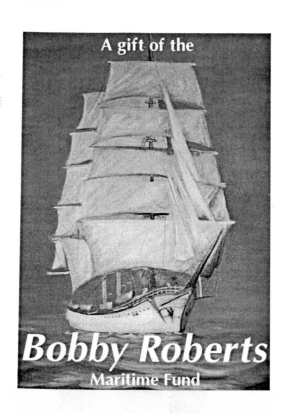

THE U.S. NAVY AGAINST THE AXIS

THE
U.S. NAVY
AGAINST
THE AXIS

THE U.S. NAVY AGAINST THE AXIS

SURFACE COMBAT
1941–1945

Vincent P. O'Hara

NAVAL INSTITUTE PRESS
Annapolis, Maryland

Naval Institute Press
291 Wood Road
Annapolis, MD 21402

Library of Congress Cataloging-in-Publication Data
O'Hara, Vincent P., 1951–
  The U.S. Navy against the Axis : surface combat, 1941–1945 / Vincent P. O'Hara.
    p. cm.
  Includes bibliographical references and index.
  ISBN-13: 978-1-59114-650-6 (alk. paper)
  ISBN-10: 1-59114-650-X (alk. paper)
  1. World War, 1939–1945—Naval operations, American. 2. United States. Navy—History—World War, 1939–1945. I. Title.
  D773.O35 2007
  940.54'5973—dc22

                                                                                    2006032627

Printed in the United States of America on acid-free paper ∞

14 13 12 11 10 09 08 07   9 8 7 6 5 4 3 2
First printing

Book design: David Alcorn, Alcorn Publication Design
All maps and figures in this book were created by the author.

Table of Contents

Tables

Figures

Maps

Preface

[I] heard the good news of the success of the raid, and I deeply felt the blessing of divine grace.

— Marquis Kido Koichi

On 2 September 1945 an Allied armada crowded Tokyo Bay: ten battleships, five small aircraft carriers, fifteen cruisers, fifty-seven destroyers of various types, and 162 other warships. Just forty-five months before at Pearl Harbor, Japan had devastated the battle line of the U.S. Navy's surface fleet. The American voyage from Pearl Harbor to Tokyo Bay was extraordinary, and it invites at least two questions: How did the U.S. Navy achieve such success in World War II, and what role did surface warships play in securing that success?

In the decades leading up to the conflict, the Navy considered its war-winning weapon to be the battle line, the fleet's big guns operating together in formation. The U.S. and Imperial Japanese navies spent decades developing doctrine, honing tactics, and gaming battles between their fleets. America's War Plan Orange envisioned battleships blasting their way across the Pacific, winning a climactic naval engagement and, through a naval blockade, compelling Japan's surrender. Japan built mammoth battleships and super torpedoes and trained its men to exhaustion to win the same naval Armageddon and knock its powerful, but presumably irresolute, foe out of the war. In 1941, after observing two years of conflict in the Atlantic and Mediterranean, most leaders of both navies still considered battleships their paramount naval weapons. Then, on 7 December 1941, Japanese carriers delivered a strike that instantly wrecked America's plan and its doctrine. Thereafter, according to one historian, "the few remaining old battlewagons retreated to California while the carriers and submarines held the line in the Pacific."[1] This assessment reflects the most widely held belief of how the Navy fought and won the Pacific War. "These great carrier battles, in which the rival Japanese and American fleets never saw each other and in which battleships became little more than embarrassing encumbrances, settled the outcome of the naval war in the Pacific," reads a typical analysis.[2] These conclusions are so deeply ingrained that they have become articles of faith. But are they valid? Did carriers really hold the line in the Pacific and then settle the war's outcome?

The Americans and Japanese fought five carrier-versus-carrier battles: Coral Sea in May 1942, Midway in June 1942, the Eastern Solomons in September 1942, Santa Cruz in October 1942, and the Philippine Sea in June 1944. However, Santa Cruz left the carrier forces mutually exhausted. This reflected the major limitation carriers suffered. They were few in 1942 and 1943 and vulnerable, and their aircraft, while powerful, were brittle. The best planes available relied upon surprise or overwhelming force to achieve their greatest successes, like at Pearl Harbor. Even under ideal conditions, flying close to a land base and enjoying air superiority, aircraft could only dominate an area during daylight hours—weather permitting. Even absent combat, air operations consumed men and machines voraciously. In the arsenal of mid-twentieth century sea power, aircraft were precision instruments. Navies often needed bludgeons to complete their missions. The old paradigm of surface warships slugging it out retained considerable application, even after Pearl Harbor.

Airpower, coupled with submarines armed with reliable torpedoes and skippered by aggressive commanders, new technologies such as radar, and the productive muscle of American industry were components of the Navy's victory. The surface fleet did not play the part envisioned by its prewar commanders, but, within the evolving environment of modern war, naval guns and torpedoes nonetheless played a crucial role. When victory seemed uncertain, the U.S. Navy prevailed in a series of confused, violent, and bloody battles fought by the fleet's cruisers and destroyers and even battleships, shrugging off an early series of sharp defeats inflicted by the ruthlessly efficient Imperial Japanese Navy. American, British, Dutch, and Australian warships fought the bitter defensive battles in the Dutch East Indies. Naval guns had the power to disrupt operations at Guadalcanal's Henderson Field, and, ultimately, naval guns had to protect it after attrition drove the carriers from the battle. The defeat of Japan's surface warships off Guadalcanal preserved victory in America's first significant offensive of the war. American cruisers and destroyers led the advance up the Solomon Islands that wasted Japan's naval strength, then, the surface fleet defended the beachheads in the Philippines against Japan's desperate attempts to avoid absolute defeat. In Europe, one major battle and a flurry of minor ones attended the success of the great American amphibious assaults at Casablanca, Normandy, and the French Riviera.

The most decisive battle of the Pacific War was a surface engagement, the Naval Battle of Guadalcanal. And, while the deadly combination of abundant fast carriers and submarines ultimately guaranteed American control of the sea, that control was a consequence, not a precondition, of the 1942 and 1943 campaigns. Even as late as October 1944, when the Japanese navy finally committed its full strength to the elusive "Decisive Battle," the American fast carriers and submarines failed to stop the Imperial battle fleet from successfully positioning itself to claim the victory it sought.

Instead, the obsolete U.S. battle line annihilated one prong of the enemy's advance and, incredibly, destroyers and destroyer escorts played a major role in repulsing the other prong. What do these events show? Simply that the value of surface warships as gun and torpedo platforms, and their ability to decisively influence events, continued well into the war's final year.

In the Atlantic Ocean and Mediterranean Sea, the U.S Navy faced conditions far different from those in the Pacific. Ironically, the largest U.S. naval battle in European waters occurred off the coast of Africa against the French. The victory at Casablanca, however, proved decisive in that a distinctly possible but unlikely defeat would have retarded American's war effort in the theater that leaders in Washington, D.C., deemed critical to the war's outcome. By the time the U.S. Navy faced the Germans in the English Channel and the Mediterranean, the German navy's surface forces, although active, were incapable of inflicting any significant setbacks to the Americans.

This book relates the story of the U.S. Navy's surface fleet at war between 1941 and 1945 and documents its role in securing America's victory. Every battle fought against the Japanese, the Germans, and the French is detailed, from minor episodes such as the destruction of the gunboat *Asheville* to the mighty battleship duels. Even if a campaign did not hinge upon a single battle, as it did at Casablanca or Guadalcanal, an examination of the campaign's surface engagements and their context reveals much about the functioning of seapower and the Navy at war, particularly because many engagements are so often ignored or painted over to provide a larger canvas for the "important" battles.

This book also relates how the fleet planned to fight; how the shock of defeat tested the U.S. Navy as an organization and revealed its institutional strengths and weaknesses; and how the stress of combat forged new doctrine, tactics, and attitudes. It examines how weapon systems performed, how prewar expectations colored wartime experiences, and how new technologies and capabilities were integrated into and expanded existing concepts of warfare.

This book does not relate the complete story of what the U.S. Navy did during World War II. The curious reader may refer to an abundance of general histories for that, or consult more focused discussions of airpower, amphibious warfare, or the submarine campaign to get a fuller picture. However, no work has ever specifically examined the U.S. Navy's surface forces and their unique contributions to America's victory or related how the conduct of surface combat affected the Navy's organization as a whole.

Difficult decisions attend the presentation of any historical narrative. In this book I use the English system of measurement, with metric distances converted to yards and rounded off. "Miles" always refers to nautical miles. Unless otherwise noted, all times are local. Japanese proper names are presented family name first, given name second. Japanese ranks and formations are rendered into their English equivalent, with the exception of retaining the term *Sentai* for units of Japanese battleships and cruisers. This term is retained because "cruiser division" or "battleship division" is slightly misleading and "battle division" seems clumsy.

As the author, I am the source of all opinions expressed in this work. I am responsible for all errors of fact, as well. That said, I would like to acknowledge the people who advanced my efforts to write *The U.S. Navy Against the Axis*. I thank my parents, Vincent P. O'Hara Sr. and Margaret H. O'Hara, for their unstinting support. I thank my editor, Thomas J. Cutler, for providing inspiration and advocating my work. I thank Enrico Cernuschi, my friend and collaborator, for his insight.

Many people have commented and improved portions of the manuscript, or otherwise helped, including Dr. Jeffrey Kacirk, Karl Zingheim, Carl Schaniel, Richard B. Frank, Robert von Mier, Richard Worth, Donald Kehn Jr., Randy Stone, Jesse Thompson, and the San Diego Pearl Harbor Survivors. Thank you, gentlemen. Thank you to Akio Oka for your translations, and to Ed Lamb for your assistance with the manuscript. I also thank the staff of the National Archives and Records Administration, most especially Barry L. Zerby and Jodi Foor, and the Naval Institute Press.

Finally, no one can write unless the people around him understand. Thank you to my children, Yunuen and Vincent, and to Maria, my wife.

CHAPTER 1

The Navy That Went to War

History books tell of the distain the U.S. Navy held for Japanese naval prowess. This may have been so, but not in the groups I had been with since graduation. We held them in great respect as seamen and naval officers.

—VICE ADM. EDWIN B. HOOPER

An orientation will ease the reader's passage before plunging into the maelstrom of surface naval combat. Therefore, this chapter briefly relates some of the important factors affecting the U.S. Navy's surface forces as they entered World War II, compares the American and Japanese navies, and provides background for this book's recurrent themes.

The Big Picture

Ever since the Spanish-American War and the emergence on the world stage of Mahan as the authoritative source on naval strategy, the U.S. Navy had been obsessed with the military aspect of sea power and the primacy of battle as the means of achieving command of the seas.

—H. P. WILLMOTT

In 1914 the measure of sea power, as expressed by its most influential advocate, the American naval officer Rear Adm. Alfred Thayer Mahan, was the ability to control maritime lines of communication; nations considered this the decisive factor in modern warfare. The Great Powers agreed that surface warships, particularly the mighty line of battle ships—the revolutionary, big-gunned, heavily armored dreadnoughts—were the means by which sea power could be gained, maintained, or disputed. Battleships were the premiere weapon system of the pre-atomic age and the principal measure of a nation's military power.

Following World War I the surviving Great Powers decided that the cost of sea power, as expressed by the unlimited construction of battleships, was prohibitively high and too disruptive to continued prospects for world peace. This led to a series of arms control treaties beginning with the Washington Naval Treaty of 1922. Under this agreement, the major navies consented to severely restricting battleship construction and limiting the design and numbers of other types of warships. From this process grew the new "treaty" cruisers, which were later called heavy cruisers. Meanwhile, "light" cruisers and destroyers grew in size and capability.

Despite the treaties, however, the impact of Germany's submarine campaign during World War I, and the nascent stirring of air power, certain assumptions about naval warfare survived unchanged. Nearly all naval war planners believed that the principal role of warships was to sink other warships in surface naval engagements. The planners believed that sinking the enemy's surface warships would lead to control of the maritime lines of communications and, thus, victory in war. Finally, at least the Japanese and U.S. commanders believed, this control could be obtained in a single naval engagement: "the Decisive Battle."

Tradition and Doctrine

Damn the torpedoes, full speed ahead!

—REAR ADM. DAVID FARRAGUT

In 1941 the U.S. Navy enjoyed a tradition of success. From its official founding in 1794, it had fought victorious naval wars against the French, the Barbary Pirates, the British, the Confederate States, Spain, and Germany. Its pantheon of heroes included Perry, Decatur, Farragut, and Dewey, and it had its aphorisms that captured the service's glorious spirit, such as "Don't give up the ship!" and "We have met the enemy and they are ours!" By the 1930s, after fifty years of growth, the U.S. Navy formed America's senior service. Indeed, in 1939 the U.S. Army ranked beneath those of Belgium and Bulgaria in terms of manpower, but the U.S. Navy stood second to none. The Navy was a mature and confident force, ready to fight its enemies, especially Japan.

U.S. Navy planners believed a single surface naval battle could decide a Pacific War. They, "like their peers in Japan and Britain, looked forward to waging one decisive battle between whole fleets. . . . Triumph in this duel would give the U.S. Navy control of the sea and ultimate victory ashore."[1] Recent history invited this belief. Naval victories settled the Sino-Japanese War of 1895, the Spanish-American War of 1898, and the Russo-Japanese War of 1905. Some experts concluded that Great Britain and Germany's failure to fight a decisive naval battle in World War I had doomed Europe to the horror of a protracted ground war. Thus the Navy believed the battle line constituted a war-winning weapon. Upon this foundation rested America's naval warfare doctrine. The Imperial Japanese Navy harbored similar beliefs based upon a shorter, but remarkably congruent tradition. Naval battles decided Japan's first two modern, foreign wars. The victory against Russia, in particular, provided a template for defeating the United States.

Thus, the concept of "the Japanese and the American navies [pitting] fleet against fleet and fighting out the whole war in one decisive stroke" likewise became the cornerstone of Japanese naval doctrine.[2]

Tactics

While many of the conditions of war vary from age to age with the progress of weapons, there are certain teachings . . . which remain constant, and being, therefore, of universal application, can be elevated to the rank of general principles.

—REAR ADM. A.T. MAHAN

Advances in weaponry and the science of fire control encouraged the U.S. Navy to regard long range gunfire as the key to victory. Navy strategists envisioned fighting in four range bands, with extreme range being beyond 27,000 yards and close as less than 17,000 yards. They believed that "the five battleships of the *Colorado* and *Tennessee* classes represented the most powerful collection of battleships with extreme range capability in the world. As a result, planners considered combat in the extreme range band very advantageous."[3] The Imperial Japanese Navy recognized this and, being outnumbered, focused on equalizers. Japan built a class of super battleships to out-range the Americans and also developed a super torpedo that was bigger, deadlier, faster, and effective from beyond the extreme range band. The Japanese fleet also practiced night fighting and attritional tactics, and it concentrated on quality, planning to defeat the Americans with better ships manned by better crews.

Weapons

Before World War II, most strategists thought that gun and torpedo fire had been developed to such a point that naval battles would be decided in a few minutes, at the end of which one side would either be annihilated or so crippled that it could fight no more.

—SAMUEL E. MORISON

The U.S. Navy went to war with some very good and some very bad weapons (Table 1.1). American naval guns proved generally robust and capable of sustaining excellent rates of fire. The 5-inch/38 guns equipping most destroyers and the newer battleships and cruisers "[were] probably the single most successful medium-calibre naval weapon of World War II."[4] After his flagship fired 2,464 six-inch rounds in battle without major malfunction Rear Adm. A.S. Merrill wrote, "The Bureau of

Ordnance is to be congratulated on the excellent ordnance equipment that is installed aboard these ships."[5] On the other hand, American torpedoes suffered from faulty detonators and irregular depth-keeping that rendered them nearly useless for the war's first eighteen months.

TABLE 1.1. U.S. GUNS AND TORPEDOES

GUNS						
Gun type (inches/ caliber)	AP Projectile Weight (lbs.)	Muzzle Velocity (ft./sec.)	Max. Range (yards)	Firing Cycle (secs.)	Approx. Barrel Life (rounds)	Ship(s) Carrying Ordnance
16/44.7	2,240	2,520	35,000	40	395	Maryland class
16/44.7	2,700	2,300	36,900	30	395	North Carolina and South Dakota classes
16/49.7	2,700	2,500	42,345	30	290	Iowa class
14/44.6	1,500	2,600	34,300	50	250	Texas, Nevada, and Pennsylvania classes
14/49.7	1,500	2,700	36,300	45	250	New Mexico and California classes
8/54.7	260	2,800	27,430	18	715	CA-24–36
8/54.7	355	2,500	30,050	15	715	CA-37–45 and Baltimore class
6/52.6	105	3,000	25,300	6–7	700	Omaha class
6/47	130	2,500	26,118	6–8	1,500	Brooklyn and Cleveland classes
5/50.6	50	3,150	18,850	10	900	Colorado, New Mexico, New York, and Texas classes, some CVEs
5/25	53.85	2,110	14,500	3–4	4,260	Old BBs, CA-24–37, Brooklyn class
5/38	55	2,600	18,200	3–4	4,600	Destroyers, new/ rebuilt BBs/CAs
4/51.6	33	2,900	15,920	5–6	500	Old destroyers
3/53.2	14	2,700	14,590	4	4,300	DMS, DEs, many others

					Range/Speed,	
					Min.–Mean–	Ship(s)
	Diameter	Length	Weight	Warhead	Max. (yards/	Carrying
Mark	(inches)	(feet)	(lbs.)	(lbs.)	knots)	Ordnance
TORPEDOES						
MK11	21	22.6	3,511	500 TNT	6,000/46–10,000/34–15,000/27	CAs, CLs, DDs
MK12	21	22.6	3,505	500 TNT	7,000/44–10,000/33.5–15,000/26.5	Improved MK11
MK15	21	24.0	3,841	825 TPX	6,000/45–10,000/33.5–15,000/26.5	DDs
MK13	22.4	13.4	2,216	600 TPX	6,300/33.5	PTs, some aircraft

Source: Campbell, *Naval Weapons of World War II*; Friedman, *US Naval Weapons*.
AP—armor piercing, BB—battleship, CA—heavy cruiser, CVE—escort aircraft carrier, DD—destroyer, DE—destroyer escort, DMS—destroyer minesweeper, PT—patrol torpedo boat, TPX—Torpex

Japanese's oxygen propelled Long Lance Type 93 torpedo was the world's most capable in terms of range, speed, and explosive power, but it was prone to premature detonation, had large "wander" values, and was difficult to handle. Lighter Japanese guns could not compare to their American counterparts in terms of rate of fire and barrel life (Table 1.2). The Japanese 8-inch/.49 gun, however, equaled or outmatched its American equivalent and proved effective, when given a chance.

TABLE 1.2. JAPANESE GUNS AND TORPEDOES

	AP					
	Projectile	Muzzle	Max.	Firing	Approx.	Ship(s)
Gun Type	Weight	Velocity	Range	Cycle	Barrel Life	Carrying
(inches/caliber)	(lbs.)	(ft./sec.)	(yards)	(secs.)	(rounds)	Ordnance
GUNS						
18.1/44.5	3,219	2,559	45,960	30	200	Yamato class
16.14/44.6	2,249	2,559	42,000	21.5	250	Nagato class
14/45	1,485	2,526	38,770	30–40	250	Other BBs
8/49.2	277.5	2,756	31,600	12–15	320	CAs

6/50	100	2,789	22,970	10–15	500	*Kongo, Fuso,* and *Agano* classes
5.51/50	83.8	2,789	21,600	10	500	*Nagato,* old CLs
5/49.3	50.7	2,986	20,100	6–12	550	Destroyers
5/40	50.7	2,362	16,075	4–7	800	CAs
4.7/45	45	2,707	17,500	12	700	Old destroyers
3.9/65	28.7	3,314	21,300	3–4	350	*Akizuki* class, *Oyodo*
3.9/65	28.7	3,314	21,300	3–4	350	*Akizuki* class, *Oyodo*

TORPEDOES						
Mark	Diameter (inches)	Length (feet)	Weight (lbs.)	Warhead weight (lbs.)	Range/Speed, Min.– Mean– Max. (yards/knot)	Ship(s) Carrying Ordnance
8thY	24	27.6	5,207	761	10,900/38– 16,400/32– 21,900/28	Old DDs and CLs
T90	24	27.8	5,743	827	7,650/46– 10,900/43– 16,400/35	*Fubuki* and some CAs
T93/1	24	29.5	5,952	1,080	21,900/48– 35,000/40– 43,700/36	Most CAs, modern DDs
T93/3[a]	24	29.5	6,173	1,720	16,400/48– 27,300/40– 32,800/36	

Source: Campbell, *Naval Weapons of World War II.*
a. The T93/3 torpedo became available in 1943.
BB—battleship, CA—heavy cruiser, CL—light cruiser, DD—destroyer

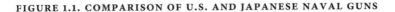

FIGURE 1.1. COMPARISON OF U.S. AND JAPANESE NAVAL GUNS

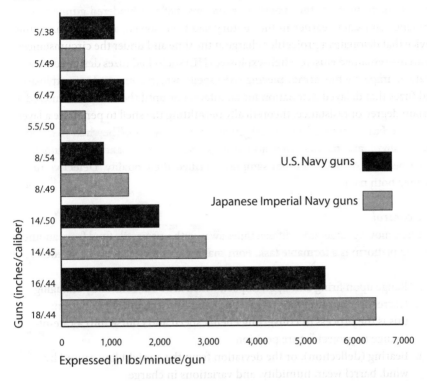

Some interesting relationships appear when comparing guns using the raw measure of pounds of shells fired per minute under ideal conditions. Figure 1.1 illustrates why the Japanese and Americans favored guns of 14 inches and above. The punch line to the story of the Second Naval Battle of Guadalcanal was that the USS *Washington* could sling nearly twice as much metal as the *Kirishima*, discounting each individual shell's greater hitting power. The true difference between American and Japanese artillery can be appreciated by comparing cruisers and destroyers—the ships that did most of the fighting. The 5/38 gun on U.S. destroyers had twice the "firepower" of its Japanese counterpart. The 6/47 gun on U.S. light cruisers enjoyed an output nearly triple that of the 5.5-inch/50 gun arming the old Japanese light cruisers. Only the Japanese eight-inch weapon excelled, at least by this standard. And, as the fates of the *Hiei* and the USS *South Dakota* demonstrated, the weight of metal delivered on a target did matter, regardless how heavily armored that target was.

Guns, however, do not sink ships. Projectiles do, and "as the Royal Navy discovered to its cost at Jutland, the details of projectile design, quite as much as those of guns and fire controls, could determine battle effectiveness."[6] Defective shells likewise plagued navies during the Second World War, the U.S. Navy as much as any. Although many of the explosives problems that had hindered gunnery performance and safety earlier in the century had been solved, a reliable fuze—the device that detonates a projectile's charge at the time and under the circumstances desired—remained elusive. High-explosive (HE) shells had fuzes designed to detonate on impact while armor piecing (AP) shells, which contained less explosive, had fuzes that delayed detonation for an interval or until the shell encountered a certain degree of resistance, theoretically permitting the shell to penetrate a layer of armor. Fuzes operated in a tough environment however. They had to survive launch, flight, and impact. They also sat in storage for years and had to function when needed. At best, random sampling verified their quality. Defective fuzes plagued both navies.[7]

Fire control

Hitting a moving target up to fifteen miles away with a projectile fired from another moving platform is a formable task. Four major variables need to be considered:

1. Range upon firing and upon impact, which are both constantly changing
2. Correction by observation (spotting) and by mechanical prediction; this is the process of converting enemy speed and course into a rate-of-change to project future position
3. Bearing (deflection), or the deviation from the straight line caused by wind, barrel wear, humidity, and variations in charge
4. Dispersion, which is the scattering of the shells from a salvo when they arrived at their destination

Generally, guns fired deliberately until spotters could observe shells splashing on either side of—straddling—their target. An observed straddle provided the best evidence the guns were on target. Only after spotters observed a straddle or hits would guns commence shooting at their maximum rate of fire ("for effect"). Up to that point, range, which determined the shells' time of flight, and the delay between a salvo landing and the calculation of new range information limited the rate of fire. When fire control radar became available to the U.S. Navy, it provided a means of obtaining initial range and calculating corrections more quickly. But even to the end of the war, many gunnery officers preferred visual over radar correction, at least during the day.

Ships

In the U.S. prewar fleet, the gun reigned as king. U.S. heavy cruisers, unlike those of other navies, did not carry torpedoes. Modern American light cruisers were an aberration, divided between torpedoless gunfire ships, the *Brooklyns* and *Clevelands* armed with 15 and 12 rapid-fire six-inch weapons, respectively, and the torpedo-equipped, anti-aircraft (AA) *Atlanta* class. U.S. destroyers, however, combined a happy blend of ruggedness, range, and capability and only got better in the first war class, the *Fletchers*.

Feeling that the treaties it signed unjustly restricted the size of its navy, Japan emphasized surface fighting capability. Nearly every major warship in the Japanese fleet underwent reconstruction during the 1930s, and by 1941 all of Japan's modern cruisers carried 8-inch guns, leaving the older, lighter vessels armed with 5.5-inch guns, like those in the *Nagara* and *Sendai* classes, as flotilla leaders. (In the test of combat, of which these vessels saw plenty, they proved capable and deadly.) Japanese destroyers compromised their antisubmarine and anti-aircraft roles to become deadlier ship killers. Key to this ability was a quick torpedo reloading system that doubled their torpedo armament.

Technology

[Radar] runs like a thread through just about all of our operational activities. Its impact on the Navy is nearly as heavy as the advent of steam or of modern shooting weapons.
—ADM. CHESTER NIMITZ, SEPTEMBER 1943

Radar was the new technology that had the biggest impact on surface warfare during World War II. The U.S. Navy began developing radar in 1930. The first air search sets became available in November 1939 and were installed shipboard in 1940. By 1941 the navy had developed adequate search and fire control radar for its larger vessels.[8]

Japan began experimenting with radar in the early 1930s, but considered it a defensive technology without immediate application and did not invest in the research required to develop an effective prototype. Japan only began a crash development program in August 1941, after seeing radar's applications in the European war. It completed its first crude production model, a land-based air-search set that November. However, a small electronics industry, uncoordinated research, duplication of efforts between the Imperial army and navy, and an obsession with secrecy handicapped Japan's efforts. Shipboard radar finally appeared operationally by mid-1943, but its introduction was far too little, far too late. As two leading historians of the Japanese navy concluded, "Without doubt, the prewar American advance in radar and the Japanese failure to match it were some of the principal reasons for American naval victory and Japanese naval defeat in the Pacific War."[9]

Aviation

Aircraft are fine as long as they are airborne, but they can not stay there indefinitely. They must come to earth sometime.
—ADM. ERNEST J. KING, FALL 1942

The critical role aviation, and particularly naval aircraft, played in securing America's victory in the Pacific War is unquestioned. However, the controversies arising from the use and function of airpower in the 1940s still color many interpretations of American's naval war.

The power of naval air was transitional throughout World War II. Some of its limitations were noted in the Preface, but bear repeating. Airpower was periodic. Planes could not dominate an area at night or in bad weather, and they were fragile and easily neutralized. Aircraft were evolving weapons, incapable of accomplishing what their most strident advocates claimed. The best argument against considering the Pacific War a "carrier war" however, was Vice Adm. Thomas C. Kinkaid's 1944 observation that the war in the Pacific had been "conducted generally along the lines visualized before the war"[10]—that is, before the concept of the fast carrier task force was ever conceived.

A team won the war. Air, surface, submarine, amphibious, and logistical forces and efforts integrated, and no part was decisive by itself.

Intelligence

It was like playing poker when opposition knows all about our hands.
—YOKOI TOSHIYUKI, "SPECIAL CHAMBER" OFFICER

The U.S. Navy was very successful in compromising Japanese codes and reading their radio traffic. The impact of this intelligence on the outcome of specific battles and campaigns certainly facilitated America's victory. Reflecting both the importance and success of American intelligence efforts, the Joint Intelligence Center, Pacific Ocean Area (JICPOA) had grown to 1,300 officers and men by the beginning of 1945. The Imperial Japanese Navy, however, following its doctrine of furious, brief war, employed just twenty-nine officers in its intelligence division, the "Special Chamber," by 1941. Staffing remained pretty much at this level until 1944, when additional manpower was finally assigned.[11] Historians have noted that "for the rest of the [Japanese] navy, below fleet level, intelligence was regarded as a secondary function; there existed no officers or officers whose sole responsibility was intelligence collection, analysis, and dissemination."[12] Japanese cryptanalysts never cracked the strip ciphers used by the U.S. Navy so they concentrated on radio traffic analysis and made a virtue of this necessity. One Japanese cryptographer recalled,

"As a result of studying the statistics on the enemy communications . . . we came to a stage where we could almost judge the enemy's next move correctly."[13] Despite warnings from their intelligence experts, Japan's high command never accepted that the enemy routinely compromised their most secure codes.

The impact of American's intelligence superiority should not be exaggerated, however. The Pearl Harbor attack and the Leyte Gulf battle stand as examples of Japan's ability to achieve surprise at any point in the war. Moreover, American naval intelligence suffered serious lapses, such as its failure to properly assess the capabilities of Japanese torpedoes and the limitations of U.S. torpedoes for nearly two years.

Tactical intelligence operated on a completely different level. For both the United States and Japan aerial reconnaissance provided the principal means for gathering information about enemy movements and shipping, followed by submarines, traffic analysis, and, in the Solomons, coast watchers. A redundant and vexing problem suffered by both navies was the tendency of aerial spotters to exaggerate or mistake the size and composition of enemy forces. As this book will clearly demonstrate, postaction damage assessment was another area in which both navies proved sadly inadequate with results damaging both the refinement of doctrine and even the formulation of strategic plans.

Logistics

Cross that threshold, and hold on straight along that passage, and you will come to the kingdom of death. But beware of pressing forward unprovisioned into those caverns of darkness.
—APULEIUS, *THE GOLDEN ASS*

An operational history relates how the guns were fired, at what range and bearing, and what havoc their projectiles' impact wrought. It does not tell how the shells fired in battle made their journey from the factory to Long Beach, California, then to an ammunition ship, and thence to Hawaii or Espiritu Santo, while all the way competing for valuable space with all other manner of matériel. Likewise, an operational history does not tell what accounting methods were used to ensure a sufficient supply of the right kinds of shells at the right location at the right time.

Logistics dictate grand strategy. Before World War II, Japan imported 90 percent of the oil it used annually. This dependency on foreign supply compelled Tokyo to conquer areas that contained the resources it required to fight a protracted war. The U.S. Navy faced different logistical imperatives in 1941 and successfully anticipated many of the requirements for campaigning across the grand expanse of the Pacific Ocean. These included ready-to-construct modular base units, realistic

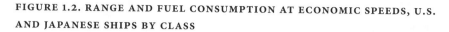

FIGURE 1.2. RANGE AND FUEL CONSUMPTION AT ECONOMIC SPEEDS, U.S. AND JAPANESE SHIPS BY CLASS

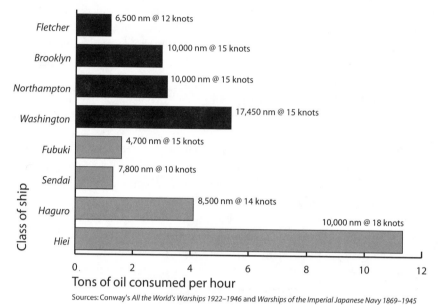

Sources: Conway's *All the World's Warships 1922–1946* and *Warships of the Imperial Japanese Navy 1869–1945*

logistic plans, and personnel to implement those plans. The Navy's development of underway replenishment enabled its task forces to greatly extend their reach.

Japan anticipated a short war. The Imperial navy began the conflict with insufficient stocks of ammunition. It was at least five years behind the U.S. Navy in the matter of underway replenishment, and it only organized its first specialty construction units in November 1941. "The problems of 'bullets, beans and black oil' could not hold the attention of either staff or line officers fixated on the dramatic strategies and tactics of the great encounter at sea," historians have noted.[14]

Operationally, logistics determined how ships would fight and, in large part, where. The nature of the steam turbine systems that propelled the vast majority of warships meant that the faster a ship sailed, the more oil-fired boilers it had on line, and the more fuel it consumed (see Figure 1.2). A *Benson* class destroyer could travel 5,580 miles at twelve knots. At twenty knots, this dropped to 3,880 miles. In terms of consumption, a destroyer sipped 1.25 tons of oil an hour at cruising speed. While at battle speed, it gulped nearly seventeen tons per hour.[15] The need to constantly refuel constrained operations. No ship ever carried enough fuel.

Logistics explains why apparently powerful units swung at anchor when ferocious battles raged just a day's sail away. Battleships consumed oceans of fuel. Task Force 1, the four old battleships available in the Pacific in 1942, required 40,000 tons of fuel oil a month, and the South Pacific Command did not have the storage capacity to deploy Task Force 1 until the end of 1942. The fuel requirements of one major sortie by Japan's Combined Fleet from Truk to Guadalcanal required as much as 15,000 tons against the entire navy's monthly requirement of 300,000 tons.[16]

American warships generally enjoyed better fuel economy than their Japanese equivalents as well as longer ranges. Given their limited resources, the Imperial navy did not undertake battleship operations lightly.

Leadership

A good naval officer has to be a son of a bitch.
— ADM. ERNEST J. KING

One of the U.S. Navy's strengths proved to be its ability to sift through its prewar commanders to discover and promote effective leaders. Admiral King was recommended to President Roosevelt as early as June 1940 as someone who could "[shake] the service out of a peace-time psychology."[17] This King did ruthlessly— and sometimes unfairly—discarding men who failed to measure up. For King, the greatest sin was a perceived lack of aggression. Vice Admirals Frank Jack Fletcher and Robert Ghormley lost their jobs on this account, as did many ship captains. Leaders such as Adm. William Halsey who erred on the side of over-aggression more often survived.

The higher levels of command generally gave leaders freedom to fight their battles without undue interference. King enunciated this policy from the very beginning, "[C]ommand shall be exercised by the issue of general operating plans and or directives and that pertinent direction and responsibility shall be vested in appropriate principal subordinates in charge of command."[18] This was a positive aspect of the U.S. Navy's system, and it stood in great contrast to the close supervision under which German, Italian, Soviet, and, sometimes, British naval officers operated.

The Imperial Japanese Navy did not value criticism, and some effective Japanese leaders got beached for being outspoken or disagreeing with their superiors. In the same spirit, leaders with undistinguished records, or even those guilty of serious command lapses, enjoyed promotion. Despite a propensity toward personal sacrifice, Japanese admirals, like their German and Italian counterparts, many times proved remarkably delicate about risking their ships, forced as they were to fight a war of poverty against a foe of (apparently) limitless resources. However, like the Americans, Japanese commanders were generally left free by the higher authorities to conduct their mission and fight their battles without interference.

Training and Personnel

A gun which never misses its target is the equal of a hundred guns which must fire a hundred shots before hitting their mark.

—ADMIRAL TOGO HEIHACHIRO

The individual sailors in American's prewar navy were generally long-term professionals. In 1939, as part of the process leading to a "Two Ocean Navy," the Navy began expanding from 7,900 officers and roughly 100,000 enlisted men. By the war's end, the U.S. Navy numbered 3.3 million.[19] The reserves, university ROTC programs, and a mass-production training system enabled the United States to man its fleet with relatively competent personnel.

The Navy's prewar training was designed to prepare the fleet for the type of war it expected to fight. The Navy refined its battle doctrine throughout the 1920s and 1930s in a series of maneuvers and fleet problems. Competition was the key to prewar training and winning was more important than anything else, for, "upon it hung prizes and promotion."[20]

In these war games, the Navy adopted conventions to represent deadly results. Overlapping circles on a chart equaled a deadly depth charge attack, while intersecting tracks represented a successful torpedo attack. Rules promoted conservatism, and the most successful prewar captains were those who could obtain desired results within the static structure of those rules. Needless to say, such captains did not always prove competent in combat.

The Japanese Navy had 9,749 officers and 97,718 enlisted personnel in 1936.[21] The Japanese priorities in all things were to emphasize quality over quantity and to win with the resources at hand. Even prewar, these priorities revealed their shortcomings, as the navy was understaffed by "at least two thousand combat and engineer officers."[22] At the beginning of 1943 the Imperial navy's personnel department reported, "We are now faced with a situation in which we cannot relieve fatigued men on the front lines and cannot fully replace men who are lost [in combat]. . . . Of all the nations fighting in this war, Japan has been the slowest and least thorough in mobilizing its men."[23] Nonetheless, the Japanese navy counted 1.7 million personnel in August 1945.

Japanese fleet training involved a long and nearly continuous process conducted under conditions that would keep any other nation in port. Casualties were common. As a member of the Japanese naval ministry described it postwar, "The severity of training was one of the prominent traditions of the Japanese Navy. . . . [A] saying became current among the crewmen that a week of the Japanese Navy consisted of 'Monday, Monday, Tuesday, Wednesday, Thursday, Friday, and Friday.'"[24] This harsh training regimen reflected a belief that "crews inured to the pace would be the most capable on the day of the Decisive Battle."[25]

Like the Americans, the Japanese staff used war games to develop tactics, predict outcomes, and evaluate performance. Results were honed in biannual competitive battle practices sandwiched between annual cruises. The effectiveness of this realistic, even dangerous training showed in the war's first year.

Force Structures

Boy, somebody's going to catch hell now. They hit the ship.
—COXSWAIN JAMES LEAMON FORBIS, USS *ARIZONA*

Table 1.3 presents a rough, and ready, comparison of the U.S., Allied, and Japanese navies on 7 December 1941.

TABLE 1.3. WARSHIPS AVAILABLE IN THE PACIFIC, 7 DECEMBER 1941

Type of Ship	Japan	U.S. Pacific	U.S. Other	British and Commonwealth Pacific and East Indies	Dutch Pacific	Allied Total Pacific
CV	6	3	4			3
CVL	3					
CVE	1					
BB old	10	9	7	1		10
BB new				1		1
CA	18	13	5	2		15
CL	20	9	10	10	4	23
DD	81	57	42		6	63
DD old	27	13	59	8		21
PB				5		5
SS	63	56	58		13	69

Sources: Conway's *Fighting Ships, 1922–1946*; Roskill, *War at Sea*, Vol. I, 560; Preston, *Navies of World War II.*
BB—battleship, CA—heavy cruiser, CL—light cruiser, CV—aircraft carrier, CVE—escort aircraft carrier, CVL—light aircraft carrier, DD—destroyer, PB—patrol boat, SS—submarine

Which navy had the better force for immediately going to war? The Imperial Japanese Navy did. Which navy had the organization, infrastructure, and national resources for fighting a long-term war? Unquestionably, the U.S. Navy did. The Japanese had one year to wrest victory from the U.S. Navy.

CHAPTER 2

Old Ships, Faulty Ammunition, Iron Men: The East Indies I

If ever students should, in the years to come, seek an example of the consequences of loss of maritime control over waters adjacent to countries in which world power held great interests, they will surely need to look no further than the events in the Pacific and Indian Oceans during the early months of 1942.

—STEPHEN ROSKILL

The Japanese carrier strike against Pearl Harbor destroyed the U.S. battle line sinking five battleships and damaging three. In the weeks following, shocked by its losses, unsettled by command uncertainties, and wanting to husband its remaining assets, the Pacific Fleet adopted a cautious attitude. It avoided the enemy's strength, even declining battle at the price of losing Wake Island. However, the U.S. Navy's Asiatic Fleet guarding the front line against Japan enjoyed no such luxuries. Headquartered at Manila and commanded by Adm. Thomas Hart, this "fleet" mustered just one heavy cruiser, two light cruisers, thirteen old destroyers, two gunboats, and sundry auxiliary ships. Its main strength supposedly resided in its twenty-three modern and six older *S* class submarines.

The Navy Department realized that when war arrived, the uneven collection of warships making up the Asiatic Fleet would stand no chance against Japanese carriers and battleships, and on 20 November 1941 the department directed Hart to withdraw his cruisers and destroyers south. Singapore, not Manila, would form the Allied bastion in East Asia.

When war began eight destroyers had already arrived in the Indies. The *Houston* and *Boise* sailed for the Indies on the evening of 8 December escorting a pair of tankers and the seaplane carrier *Langley*. But, in a harbinger of things to come, Japanese bombers destroyed the core of the gathering Allied fleet, sinking the British capital ships *Prince of Wales* and *Repulse* off Malaya on 10 December.

Allied submarines, handicapped by faulty torpedoes and cautious commanders, failed to slow the Japanese advance. Imperial troops landed on British Borneo on 16 December, and Davao fell on 20 December, followed by Menado in the Celebes on 11 January and Tarakan in Dutch Borneo on 12 January. Shocked by

Japan's audacious offensive, the Allies hurriedly reinforced Singapore and the East Indies. Washington ordered Hart to relocate to Java, and he did so by submarine. Arriving in Java on 2 January 1942, Hart left just a few patrol torpedo (PT) boats operating from Bataan. On 15 January the Allies established a joint American, British, Dutch, Australian (ABDA) command to coordinate their collective defense of Southeast Asia and the Dutch East Indies. Admiral Hart became ABDAFLOAT, the naval commander. However, ABDA's multinational command structure, hampered by different languages and deficient communications, proved inadequate. As one Dutch officer observed, "Nobody knew what anybody else was doing. You've never seen such a mixed-up thing as that headquarters."[1]

The conquest of the Dutch East Indies—an immense archipelago stretching 3,300 hundred miles east to west (the distance from Lisbon to Russia's Ural Mountains) and 1,200 miles north to south—was Japan's primary war goal. Taking the East Indies would give the mountainous island empire the resources it required to become a true world power.

In 1940 the East Indies had 70 million inhabitants, giving it the seventh largest population in the world. The island of Java alone was the equal of France or Italy in number of inhabitants. The wealth of the Indies lay principally in petroleum, but the archipelago is also rich in tin, magnesium, nickel, bauxite, rubber, copra, coal, and foodstuffs. Vice Admiral Kondo Nobutake, as commander of Japan's Southern Force, was charged with this conquest. He planned "an island-hopping, three-pronged simultaneous attack from the west, north, and east, pointed at and converging on the island of Java."[2] Kondo aimed the central prong of his advance at Borneo's oil-rich east coast, and the collapse of American resistance in the Philippines—except for Bataan—in early January 1942 cleared the way (see Map 2.1).

On 7 January 1942 the 56th Regiment and 2nd Kure Special Naval Landing Force departed Davao on sixteen transports bound for Tarakan in Dutch Borneo. Rear Admiral Nishimura Shoji commanding Destroyer Squadron 4, Minesweeper Divisions 11 and 30, and Submarine Chaser Division 31 escorted the convoy. Although Dutch troops had no realistic hope of repelling the attack, shore batteries sank a pair of Japanese minesweepers on 12 January. The Dutch minelayer *Prins van Oranje* attempted to escape that night, but she ran afoul of the Japanese patrol boat *P38* and destroyer *Yamakaze* north of Tarakan Island. Only sixteen members of the Dutch crew survived the ensuing battle.

Japanese planes began operating from Tarakan's airfield four days later. With air cover ensured, Nishimura sailed once again on 21 January, this time bound for Balikpapan, a port and important oil field two-thirds of the way down Borneo's east coast.

Allied aircraft and submarines had contested Japan's early advances, and they had inflicted some losses on the Imperial navy, especially at Kuching, where the

MAP 2.1. DEFENSE OF THE DUTCH EAST INDIES, JANUARY–FEBRUARY 1942

Surface Actions
1. Battle of Balikpapan, 24 January
2. Battle of Badung Strait, 19-20 February
3. Battle of the Java Sea, 27 February

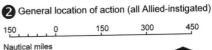 General location of action (all Allied-instigated)

150   0   150   300   450

Nautical miles

Scale: 1:13,500,000

NORTH

Japanese lost one destroyer, a minesweeper, and two transports. However, the Allies failed to defeat a single landing. While the Dutch and British reserved their warships to escort convoys, Hart formed Task Force 5 under Rear Adm. William A. Glassford Jr. The group comprised the heavy cruiser *Houston*, the light cruisers *Boise* and *Marblehead*, and eight destroyers of Squadron 29. Once formed, Task Force 5 eagerly sought to engage the enemy.

Glassford led the light cruisers and six destroyers north on 17 January, hoping to surprise a Japanese fleet reported off Kema, but his intelligence proved faulty. On 20 January, following Dutch reports of the anticipated enemy thrust down the Makassar Strait, the USS *Boise, Marblehead*, and six destroyers departed Kupang. While transiting Sape Strait into the Flores Sea on 21 January the *Boise* tore her bottom on an uncharted pinnacle in what should have been twenty-six fathoms of water. One account of the incident includes the complaint that it "was a difficult passage . . . made no easier by the inaccuracy of the English-language charts. The Dutch charts were better but none of the Americans could read them and the Dutch claimed they had no extra pilots available."[3] When Glassford heard once again that the sighting reports were false, he ordered Destroyer Division 59 to patrol off the Postillion Islands at Makassar Strait's southern exit while the *Boise* and *Marblehead*, which had burned out a turbine and could only reach a top speed of fifteen knots,) retired west toward Lombok Strait.

On 22 January the submarine USS *Pike* reported sighting twenty-six enemy ships escorted by fourteen destroyers advancing toward Balikpapan. For the fourth time Hart ordered Task Force 5 forward. Instead of three cruisers and eight destroyers, however, Glassford had only Division 59 available. He sent them north and transferred his flag to the *Marblehead*. Escorted by the USS *Bulmer*, which was suffering from salting in her condensers, Hart turned to support the division after its strike.

Battle of Balikpapan, 24 January 1942

Division 59 began its long run north on the morning of 23 January. Commander Talbot intended to arrive off Balikpapan and deliver a surprise attack two hours before dawn. The weather helped. The destroyers ran through massive seas that broke green over their forward mounts. While the *Pope* suffered a broken bridge window and buckled spray shields, the rough weather screened the American ships from enemy aircraft that searched Makassar Strait. Dutch aircraft, on the other hand, enjoyed better conditions to the north and found Nishimura's convoy.

Nishimura's force was nearly identical to the one that had captured Tarakan two weeks before. The fifteen transports were escorted by the *Naka* and ten destroyers of Divisions 2, 9, and 24, which were modern, first-line units that completely outclassed the elderly American "cans." Nishimura also deployed the patrol boats, minesweepers, and three sub chasers of Base Force 2.

At 1525 nine B-10 bombers attacked and lightly damaged the 7,070-ton *Tatsugami Maru*. At 1830 a single aircraft "suddenly appeared from a crack between thick clouds" and attacked the *Nana Maru* (6,557 tons).[4] A bomb hit the *Nana Maru's* aft bridge and engulfed the ship in flames, forcing her eventual abandonment.

TABLE 2.1. FORCES ENGAGED AT THE BATTLE OF BALIKPAPAN

	Type of Ship	Year Launched	Displacement, Full Load (tons)	Max. Speed (knots) a	Guns (number by inch/caliber)	Torpedoes (number of tubes by diameter in inches)	Damage
American Destroyer Division 5 (Cdr. Paul H. Talbot)							
John D. Ford (F)	DD	1920	1,308	30	4 x 4/51 & 1 x 3/76.2	12 x 21	D1
Pope	DD	1920	1,308	30	4 x 4/51 & 1 x 3/76.2	12 x 21	
Parrott	DD	1919	1,308	30	4 x 4/51 & 1 x 3/76.2	12 x 21	
Paul Jones	DD	1920	1,308	30	4 x 4/51 & 1 x 3/76.2	12 x 21	
Japanese Base Force 2 (Rear Admiral Nishimura Shoji)							
PC36	PB	1922	1,162	18	2 x 4.7/45		Sunk
PC37	PB	1922	1,162	18	2 x 4.7/45		
PC38	PB	1922	1,162	18	2 x 4.7/45		
W15	MS	1933	800	18	2 x 4.7/45		
W16	MS	1933	800	18	2 x 4.7/45		
W17	MS	1935	707	19	2 x 4.7/45		
W18	MS	1935	707	19	2 x 4.7/45		

Note. Gardiner's Conway's *All the World's Fighting Ships*, Jentschura et al.'s *Warships of the Imperial Japanese Navy*, Worth's *Fleets of World War II*, and the works of M.J. Whitley listed in the Bibliography are the principal sources for this and subsequent tables specifying ship's data.

a. In each of the tables of combatants, the maximum speed given is the designed speed unless the ship was damaged. Operationally, most ships would have top speeds several knots below designed speed, depending upon the condition of their machinery and the state of the sea and wind.

D1—light or superficial damage (including splinter damage, DD—destroyer, F—flagship, PB—patrol boat, MS—minesweeper

    Time: 0245–0400

    Weather: Overcast

    Visibility: Mixed to poor

    Sea state: Slight swells

    Surprise: Americans

    Mission: Americans—beachhead attack; Japanese—amphibious attack*

*Further details on what the missions entailed can be found in the Appendix.

With the coming of dark, the threat continued as at 1930 patrol boat *P36* reported a submarine attack. Nonetheless, the Japanese convoy arrived at 2015 and anchored in two rows; eight ships near the shore and six further out. The small Dutch garrison had torched the refinery, and the scene was spectral, with flames casting a reddish glow against the underside of dark thunderheads and the winds blowing thick, greasy smoke southeast out to sea.

At 2345 the Dutch submarine *K-XVIII*, attacking trimmed on the surface due to the weather, shot four torpedoes at the *Naka*. This volley missed, but, continuing past, one 21-inch weapon struck the *Tsuruga Maru* (6,987 tons). As *W17* and *W18* stood by to rescue survivors, Nishimura ordered Destroyer Division 9 to patrol 3,300 yards east of the convoy, deploying Sub Chaser Division 31, consisting of *Ch10*, *Ch11* and *Ch12*, to the west, the patrol boats to the south, and minesweepers to the north. *Naka* meanwhile joined Division 2 further out in the channel, where she dropped six depth charges on a contact spotted by the *Murasame* and incorrectly claimed a sinking based on an observed oil slick.

At 0010, as Japanese boats began shuttling troops and supplies to shore, Talbot's force raced unseen and unsuspected up the strait. At 0200 "the loom of gigantic fires became visible" to the American sailors. They "could smell burning oil 20 miles at sea."[5] An officer aboard the *Pope* memorialized the mood this way: "The canopy of smoke hung over us, lending a sinister touch to the proceedings. We seemed cut off from the rest of the world as we approached a misplaced corner of Hell."[6] Talbot had several close calls. At 0245 the *John D. Ford* reported four enemy destroyers passing ahead from starboard to port. She ignored a blue signal blinker flashed by the last ship and adjusted course slightly to starboard, benefiting from a fortunate resemblance to the *Naka* (see Map 2.2).

Then the *John D. Ford*'s lookout reported transports silhouetted against the lurid fires burning ashore about 9,000 yards off the port bow. Followed by the *Pope*, *Parrott*, and *Paul Jones*, the *John D. Ford* closed at twenty-seven knots.

Suddenly, the *John D. Ford* ran by an enemy destroyer close to starboard on an opposite course. This "destroyer" was the minesweeper *W15*. According to the Japanese ship's account, she was, "moving slowly in the northern part of the anchorage [and] sighted an unknown vessel which, because of its four funnels, was at first believed to be the flagship *Naka*, then supposed to be on patrol near the anchorage. After a second ship came in sight, the vessels were revealed as four-funneled enemy destroyers. Soon four enemy vessels closed in rapidly at a very high speed, passing at a very close range. Without attacking they disappeared."[7]

In fact, the U.S. ships did attack. The *John D. Ford* snapped off one quick torpedo that missed astern. The *Pope* could not train her tubes in time, but the *Parrott* fired five, launching two unintentionally and practically denuding her starboard batteries. Finally, at 0257 the *Paul Jones* contributed another. The eager destroyers squandered seven torpedoes against an insignificant target on a retiring course.

At 0300 Talbot saw he was passing the Japanese concentration and ordered a starboard turn for another try. As the *John D. Ford* tacked, the *Parrott*, tracking a target to port, launched three torpedoes. Two minutes later a blinding blast and then a concussion wave that left the Americans "gasping for breath" marked the end of the ammunition ship *Sumanoura Maru* (3,519 tons).[8] The *W16*, which was located north of the convoy, came about when she saw the huge pyre and glimpsed an enemy ship fleeing south. She hastened to the scene, but the *Sumanoura Maru* had vanished. Only nine members of her crew survived.

This marked the third attack the Japanese had experienced that night. Nishimura received *W15*'s alarm at 0310, but the *Naka* lay more than seven miles northeast of the anchorage still preoccupied by the submarine threat. "Making the situation worse," according to the official Japanese account, "he did not believe that more than one enemy destroyer could penetrate the port." As late as 0328 Nishimura was instructing his squadron to be "aggressively alert against enemy submarines and torpedo boat attacks."[9]

As the powerful Japanese force continued to patrol the channel, the Americans steadied on a southerly course. At 0303 the *John D. Ford* and *Pope* each fired one torpedo at the *P38* abeam to starboard. At 0306 the *Pope* spied a more promising target to starboard, a bunched group of ships signaling with blinkers. She sent five torpedoes boiling in their direction, and as they followed, the *Parrott* and *Paul Jones* added one torpedo each. An explosion marked a hit on the 7,064-ton *Tatsugami Maru*, and the Japanese ship sank a half hour later. At 0309 the *Pope* missed a chip shot at a "destroyer" passing abeam to port.

At 0314 the *John D. Ford* led her three consorts on a hard swing to starboard to penetrate the southern end of the Japanese line. The American flagship shot a torpedo at a "destroyer" to port, while at 0319 the *Pope* and *Parrott* heading west emptied their tubes, firing five and three torpedoes, respectively, at a "destroyer" less than 2,000 yards to port. Explosions and a towering column of smoke resulted as three of the Americans' eight "fish" clobbered the *P37*, two in the bow and one in the stern. The old Japanese patrol boat, which was a converted destroyer of the same generation as her foes, sank in shallow water, leaving thirty-five men dead or wounded. At 0322 the *Paul Jones* discharged one torpedo at the *Kuretake Maru* (5,175 tons), which was about a thousand yards off her port beam. This missed, but the *John D. Ford* led the American column around the *Kuretake Maru*, first south and then back east, and the *Paul Jones* scored with a second torpedo fired at 0325.

Circling the stricken *Kuretake Maru*, the *John D. Ford* led the American ships north. The *Pope* and *Parrott*, out of torpedoes, engaged the enemy with gunfire as targets flashed by to port. However, "due to maneuvers in column at high speed it was difficult for guns to remain directed very long upon any one target."[10]

MAP 2.2. BATTLE OF BALIKPAPAN, 24 JANUARY 1942

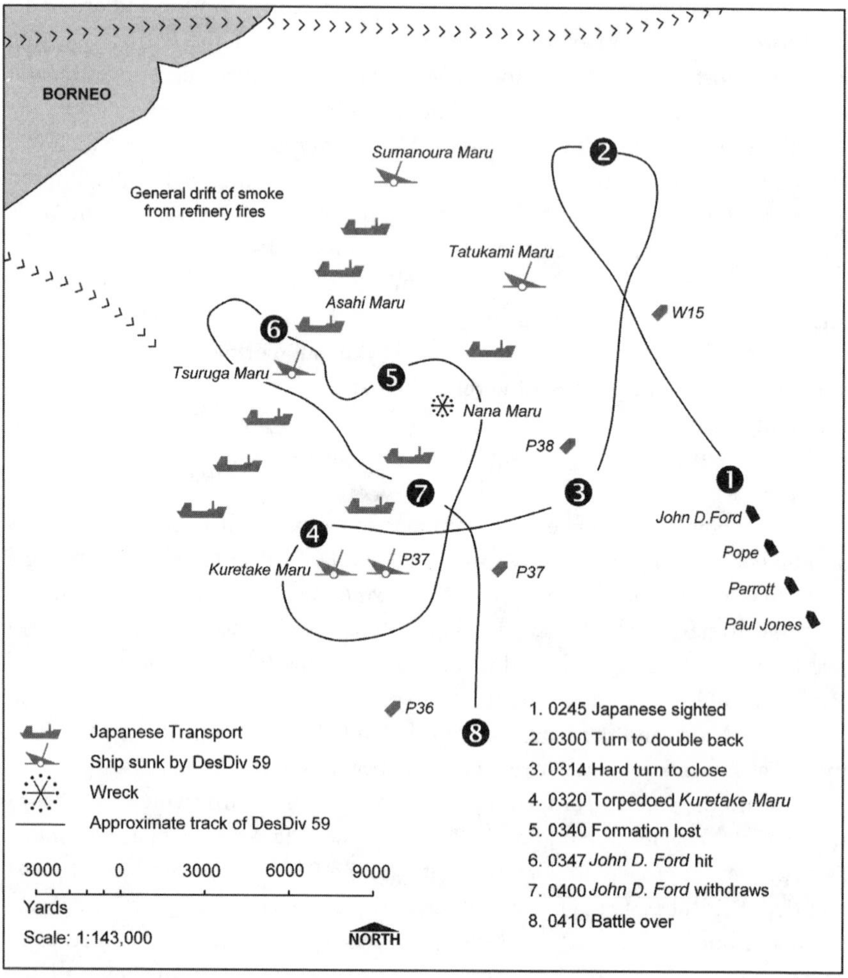

The *Parrott* even fired star shell at 0330. Although both the *Pope* and *Parrott* claimed multiple hits on "destroyers" and transports, the blinding flashes from their gun-fire made observation difficult.

The *Paul Jones* fired a single torpedo to port at this time. Despite high speed, intermitted visibility, and violent maneuvers, the American destroyers maintained formation, allowing their captains to safely target any vessel not in column.

At 0335 the *John D. Ford* turned northwest to penetrate the first line of Japanese transports once again. The America flagship passed "the smoking hulk of a merchant ship [the *Nana Maru*] standing on end with lifeboats nearby."[11] Then, at 0340 the *John D. Ford* sheered out of line to starboard, suddenly concerned that a minefield lay ahead. This forced the *Pope* to swerve to port to avoid a collision.[12] Then the *Parrott* and *Paul Jones* peeled off, circling south and out of the action, followed shortly after by the *Pope.*

The *John D. Ford* still had torpedoes. At 0346, under way once again, the American flagship discharged her last two to port at the *Tsuruga Maru*, which had been *K-XVIII*'s victim of four hours earlier. An explosion aboard the *Tsuruga Maru* shook the American destroyer, then one minute later, the *Asahi Maru* hit the *John D. Ford*'s aft deckhouse with a small-caliber shell, igniting a fire and wounding four men. The *John D. Ford* circled, her 4-inch guns shredding the Japanese transport and inflicting fifty casualties. Next, she hit the *Tamagawa Maru* ten times. The *John D. Ford*'s gunnery officer wrote, "I didn't use any of the complicated fire-control apparatus installed. . . . [A]s targets loomed out of the dark at ranges of 500 to 1,500 yards we trained on and let go a salvo or two, sights set at their lower limits."[13]

At 0400 Talbot turned south to find his division. Nishimura radioed the *P36* at 0408 to ask if she was mistaking Destroyer Division 2 for enemy cruisers. As late as 0420 Nishimura remained 7,000 yards east of the anchored convoy.

The ships of U.S. Destroyer Division 59 reunited by 0642, and at 0815 the welcome sight of the *Marblehead* and *Bulmer* hove into view. The Japanese remained confused. Admiral Ugaki Matome's diary entry for 25 January notes, "In Balikpapan a special transport, a tanker and a patrol boat were damaged. It must have been due to enemy submarines and planes which sneaked in there."[14] The *Naka*'s action record only mentioned her attack on the *K-XVIII*.

Although Talbot's old warships clearly won a tactical victory in the first surface engagement fought by the U.S. Navy since the Spanish-American War and the first victory achieved solely by warships against the Japanese, many historians consider his accomplishments inadequate. S.E. Morison wrote, "Three [sic] four-pipers had run amuck through an anchored and silhouetted convoy, choosing their own range and time to fire torpedoes; yet even the over-optimistic 'score' of the morning after was disappointing."[15]

Destroyer Division 59's "failure" is generally attributed to a lack of experience, a hasty approach, and defective torpedoes. But to what should Talbot's action be compared? During the First Battle of Narvik in April 1940, five British destroyers surprised a harbor crowded with twenty-three merchant ships and five enemy destroyers. Attacking targets one by one at slow speed, the British ships fired twenty-six reliable torpedoes and hit only two warships, which were their intended targets. The British, then, achieved a hit rate of just 7.7 percent at Narvik, compared with a hit rate of at least 12.5 percent for the Americans at Balikpapan.[16]

In fact, Talbot's division fought well. The Americans eluded a vastly superior force, sank a quarter of the enemy convoy with defective torpedoes, and escaped unharmed. More than a year of bitter and hard-fought defeats would pass before American destroyer torpedoes would again inflict damage.

Battle of Badung Strait, 19–20 February 1942

Balikpapan bruised one of Vice Admiral Kondo's three tentacles but did not deflect his offensive. Kendari fell on 24 January, and Ceram fell on 31 January.

Command problems bedeviled U.S. operations. Under Dutch pressure, Admiral Hart designated Rear Admiral Karel Doorman of the Netherlands Royal Navy to command a combined ABDA surface strike force. On 4 February Japanese bombers caught the Dutch admiral off Makassar and sharply rebuffed his first attempt to replicate the success at Balikpapan with four cruisers and eight destroyers. The *Houston* lost her aft turret and "only by masterful seamanship and Herculean effort did [the *Marblehead*] reach Tjilatjap, Java."[17]

Makassar fell on 8 February, and Banjermasin fell on 10 February. Four days later the politics of alliance warfare cost Hart his position, and Dutch Vice Admiral Conrad E.L. Helfrich became ABDAFLOAT. The same day, Helfrich ordered Doorman, leading a polyglot force of three Dutch cruisers, an Australian cruiser, a British cruiser, four Dutch destroyers, and six American destroyers to attack an invasion convoy off Sumatra. In the so-called Battle of Gaspar Strait, a Dutch destroyer ran aground while Japanese bombers damaged the USS *Bulmer* and *Barker*, forcing their withdrawal to Australia.

As Japanese forces approached Java, the pace of operations accelerated. On 18 February two transports, carrying a battalion of the 48th Infantry Division and escorted by the *Nagara*, flagship of Rear Admiral Kubo Kyuji, and eight destroyers of Divisions 8 and 21 departed Makassar bound for Bali. Being so close to Allied bases, the Japanese knew they had to conduct their landings quickly.

They arrived at Sanur Roads off southeastern Bali shortly before midnight, and the battalion scattered light Dutch resistance. But, recalled one Japanese participant, "just about when we thought this landing would culminate in success, all of a sudden B-17s flew over and bombed the convoy. Repeated bombing by enemy airplanes delayed our landing operation."[18]

Kubo and Division 21 departed for Makassar during the day, but aircraft had damaged both transports and unloading dragged on until 1600 hours on 19 February. At this point the *Sagami Maru* got under way on just one engine, accompanied by the *Arashio* and *Michishio*.

TABLE 2.2. FORCES ENGAGED AT THE BATTLE OF BADUNG STRAIT

	Type of Ship	Year Launched	Displacement, Full Load (tons)	Max. Speed (knots)	Guns (number by inch/caliber)	Torpedoes (number of tubes by diameter in inches)	Damage
Allied First Strike Group (Rear Admiral Karel Doorman)							
De Ruyter (DU) (F)	CL	1935	7,548	32	7 x 5.9/50		
Java (DU)	CL	1921	7,050	31	10 x 5.9/50		D1
Piet Hein (DU)	DD	1927	1,640	36	4 x 4.7/50 & 2 x 3/76.2	6 x 21	Sunk
Pope	DD	1920	1,308	30	4 x 4/51 & 1 x 3/76.2	12 x 21	
John D. Ford	DD	1920	1,308	30	4 x 4/51 & 1 x 3/76.2	12 x 21	
Allied Second Strike Group (Captain J.B. de Meester)							
Tromp (DU) (F)	CL	1937	4,800	33	6 x 5.9/50		D3
Allied Destroyer Division 58 (Cdr. T.H. Binford)							
Stewart (F)	DD	1919	1,308	30	4 x 4/51 & 1 x 3/76.2	12 x 21	D2
Parrott	DD	1919	1,308	30	4 x 4/51 & 1 x 3/76.2	12 x 21	D1
John D. Edwards	DD	1919	1,308	30	4 x 4/51 & 1 x 3/76.2	12 x 21	
Pillsbury	DD	1920	1,308	30	4 x 4/51 & 1 x 3/76.2	12 x 21	
Japanese Destroyer Division 8 (Captain Abe Toshio)							
Oshio (F)	DD	1937	2,450	35	6 x 5/50	8 x 24	D2
Asashio	DD	1936	2,450	35	6 x 5/50	8 x 24	D1

Japanese Division 8, Section 2							
Arashio	DD	1937	2,450	35	6 x 5/50	8 x 24	
Michishio	DD	1937	2,450	35	6 x 5/50	8 x 24	D4

CL—light cruiser, D1—light or superficial damage (including splinter damage), D2—moderate damage (combat ability not significantly impaired), D3—significant damage (combat or maneuvering ability somewhat impaired), D4—major damage (combat and maneuvering ability significantly impaired or eliminated), DD—destroyer, DU—Dutch, F—flagship

Time: 2225–0300
Weather: Cloudy, light breeze from east northeast
Visibility: Limited, new moon
Sea state: Calm with light swells
Surprise: Allies
Mission: Allies—beachhead attack; Japanese—amphibious attack

Luck did not bless Admiral Doorman's endeavors. While the Japanese assault on Bali, next door to ABDA's main base at Surabaja in eastern Java, demanded an immediate response, damage and other duties had scattered Doorman's powerful strike force. The British cruisers escorted troopships through Sunda Strait, the *Houston* sailed inbound from Port Darwin, and four American destroyers lay refueling at Ratai Bay, Sumatra.

Need and lack of time forced the Dutch admiral to strike in three waves. The first would sail from Tjilatjap. Doorman's cruisers would attack the enemy concentration with gunfire and retire north, clearing the area for a destroyer torpedo strike. The second wave would follow from Surabaja several hours later. Nine Dutch motor torpedo boats (MTBs) from Surabaja formed the third wave, which would dispatch the Japanese cripples. Such was the plan, but things began badly when the first wave's *Kortenaer* ran aground while threading Tjilatjap's narrow channel. According to one account, the port was "a rat trap. It had a long twisting entrance, very narrow, [and] there was no turning room inside the harbor worth mentioning."[19] At least, operating at night and close to base, Doorman was spared a rain of Japanese bombs during his approach.

The *Sasago Maru*, escorted by the *Asashio* and *Oshio* weighed anchor after dark. At 1900 the Army transport commander requested the *Sasago Maru*'s eight landing barges, so she returned an hour later. The *Asashio* stood by as the barges were unloaded, and the *Oshio* patrolled 3,000 yards offshore to the northwest.

By 2215 Doorman's first wave was steaming into Badung Strait at twenty-seven knots under a new moon and a thick overcast that obscured the stars. The cruisers advanced 5,500 yards ahead of HNLMS *Piet Hein*. Uncertain what to expect HNLMS *De Ruyter* had her guns trained to starboard, while HNLMS *Java*'s batteries aimed to port. At 0225 the *Java* sighted the *Asashio*, and the Dutch cruiser waited for Doorman's order to open fire as the range swiftly closed.

At 2230 the *Asashio's* searchlight snapped on, and the *Java* responded with star shell. As pyrotechnics and tracers shattered the darkness, the Japanese destroyer emerged from the anchorage, although "hampered by being just about to leave the port, [she] could not increase speed quickly enough to catch up."[20] The *Java's* 40-mm AA weapons rattled above the boom of her 5.9-inch guns shooting at a range of 2,200 yards. The Dutch cruiser's fire hit the *Sasago Maru*, but a 5-inch shell struck the *Java* astern. A Dutch round snuffed the *Asashio's* searchlight, killing four and wounding eleven men, but high speed hampered marksmanship, and the cruisers rushed past breaking contact. The action ended even before the *De Ruyter's* main battery could fire or the *Oshio* could engage.[21] The *Asashio* continued into the strait and then headed southeast assuming the enemy would return for another try (see Map 2.3).

The *Piet Hein* arrived on scene to find the Japanese destroyers athwart her course. The *Oshio* spotted the Dutch destroyer 6,000 yards away at 2235 and rushed southeast to attack. The Dutch ship turned sharply to starboard and began spewing a thick trail of black and white smoke.[22] Three torpedoes jumped from the *Piet Hein's* tubes aimed toward the transport, followed by a 4.7-inch broadside. The smoke blocked the view of the American destroyers following. The Americans consequently increased speed to twenty-eight knots and broke into the open, whereupon the *John D. Ford* spotted the *Sasago Maru* silhouetted against the shore and the *Oshio* off her port bow. Four-inch guns barked, and the *Pope's* spotters reported "two dull red flashes . . . at waterline of transport."[23] The *John D. Ford* fired three torpedoes, and the *Pope* launched two more at the *Sasago Maru*, again claiming hits. It was all wishful thinking.

Racing south by southeast, the *Asashio* opened fire at 2240, just 1,600 yards off the *Piet Hein's* port bow. By this time the *John D. Ford*, commanded by Lt. Cdr. E.N. Parker, had closed to nearly a thousand yards of the *Piet Hein* and had to swing hard left to avoid a collision. The American ships, under gunfire from the east, circled west. The *Pope* discharged a pair of torpedoes at a "cruiser"—either the transport or a false contact—2,000 yards to port.

The Dutch destroyer, now on her own, launched two more torpedoes, and then a 5-inch shell slammed into her aft boiler room. More shells followed and, burning fiercely, the *Piet Hein* drifted to a stop. Damage control restored some power, but it was too late. At 2246 an *Asashio* Long Lance smashed into the *Piet Hein*, and she capsized to starboard and sunk quickly. Sixty-four men died.

After finishing off the Dutch destroyer, the *Asashio* spun to port in a tight loop and targeted the American destroyers to the northwest. "As we swung away it became apparent that we would not be able to proceed north through Badung Straits as planned," wrote one of the *Pope's* officers. "From the *John D. Ford* via TBS [telephone between ships] came the word that we would head for the shadow of the shore to the east of us."[24]

MAP 2.3. BATTLE OF BADUNG STRAIT, ATTACK OF THE FIRST WAVE

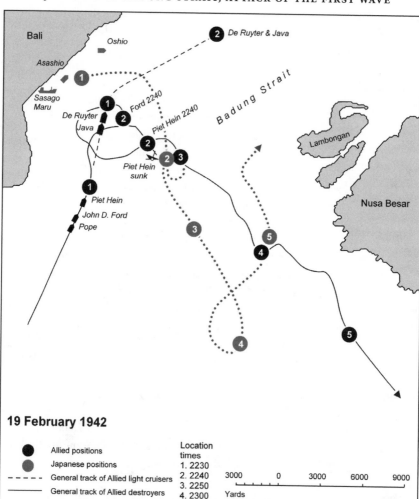

The *John D. Ford* laid smoke and bent her course to the southeast. The Japanese had become confused as to the number and location of their enemy. Assuming some Allied ships had escaped north heavily damaged, the Japanese began hunting southeast for more prey. At 2254 the *Asashio*'s lookout reported imaginary shapes to starboard. In fact, the *John D. Ford* and *Pope* were sailing on a parallel course off the Japanese destroyer's port quarter. As the *Asashio* began shooting to starboard, the *Pope* unleashed two more torpedoes to port. Both were shooting at phantoms. In just a few minutes later, however, Japanese lookouts spotted the Americans, and both destroyers immediately opened fire. This time they were right.

Japanese searchlights "well-controlled, of great size, very brilliant, and superbly focused" pierced the night.[25] Parker, concerned about the whereabouts of the Dutch cruisers, flicked his recognition lights for fifteen seconds. Japanese salvos splashed nearby in reply. "The *John D. Ford* disappeared from view, and everyone on the *Pope* . . . knew the *John D. Ford* was finished," a participant recalled.[26] In fact, Abe's ships missed.

At 2300 the *John D. Ford* sent torpedoes boiling toward the enemy. The *Pope* also fired five torpedoes, snapped off seven quick rounds, and made smoke. Japanese Division 8, mistaking the smoke for "heavy damage" to the enemy ships and "confirming that the Americans left northward," swung hard to starboard in hot pursuit.[27] In fact, the four-stackers raced in the other direction, and by 2310 had escaped southeast. Pressing north, the Japanese engaged more phantoms (possibly each other), and left one "sinking" and the other "engulfed in flames." At 0010 on 20 February, Abe proudly reported, "Two *Java* type cruisers retreated north through Lombok Channel. Two out of three destroyers sank and the last destroyer suffered huge damages. We did not receive any damage."[28] Admiral Kubo ordered the *Arashio* and *Michishio* to reinforce Abe while he hastened back with the *Nagara* and Destroyer Division 21.

Smoke from the first engagement still lingered overhead when the second Allied wave arrived. Sailing at twenty-five knots U.S. Destroyer Division 58, made up of the *Stewart, Parrott, John D. Edwards*, and *Pillsbury*, led the Dutch light cruiser *Tromp* by five miles. They expected to encounter "a large number of trans-ports and . . . a group of three or four cruisers and seven or eight destroyers."[29] At 0135 *Stewart* spotted a bright greenish light ahead. She held steady for a minute and then she and the *Parrot* emptied their portside tubes into the anchorage. The *Pillsbury* added three more torpedoes. The *Oshio* and *Asashio*, which were circling offshore as the *Sasago Maru* attended to damage suffered during the first strike, spotted what seemed to be two cruisers and a destroyer rushing the anchorage. As they steered into the strait, the *Stewart* saw them coming. She illuminated with her searchlight and engaged. The time was 0143.

As the *Stewart* crossed the *Oshio*'s bow, the Japanese warship returned fire. The skipper of the *John D. Edwards* described the exchange as intense, straddling both the *Stewart* and *Parrott*. "However, most of the Japanese salvos seemed to be 100 to 200 yards either over or short."[30] The *John D. Edwards* uncorked a pair of torpedoes, which proved as ineffective as the previous fifteen, while faulty prim-ers left two more jammed in their tubes.

At 0145 as Division 58 raced ahead, the Japanese destroyers likewise fired torpedoes at a range of 3,500 yards. Then, at 0146 a projectile ricocheted into the

Stewart, and another exploded in her steering engine room, flooding the machinery spaces. Although orders called for him to charge the anchorage, Commander Binford swung starboard to the east northeast. The *Arashio* and *Oshio* also turned starboard, which in their case was to the south.

The *Stewart*'s maneuver disrupted the American column, and the *Parrott* and *Pillsbury* nearly collided. The *John D. Edwards* veered south and assumed a parallel course, while the *Parrott* ended up off to the north. The *Asashio* and *Oshio* cut behind the *John D. Edwards* and then turned northeast to pursue. The shooting tapered off until about 0205 when the *Tromp*, uncertain what had become of the American destroyers, began flashing a bright blue searchlight. This caught the attention of Abe's destroyers following only 3,300 yards off the Dutch cruiser's starboard quarter.

A salvo of the *Oshio*'s Long Lances hit the water and, again, gunfire erupted. The *Asashio* landed eleven shells, hammering the *Tromp*'s fire directors, range finder, searchlights, and crew quarters. The *Tromp* gained a measure of revenge at 0216, hitting the *Oshio*'s aft bridge and killing seven men. Following this intense exchange, Abe's ships circled back and lost contact as the *Tromp* continued northeast.

By 0211 the *Steward* led the *John D. Edwards* on a northeast heading, as the *Parrott* hugged the northern shoreline steaming in the same direction. The *Tromp* trailed 8,000 yards off the *John D. Edwards*'s starboard quarter. The *Pillsbury* had ended up 3,000 yards off the *Tromp*'s starboard beam.

Meanwhile, hurrying toward the battle zone, the *Arashio* and *Michishio* saw searchlights flickering in the distance and heard the echoes of gunfire. At 0215 the *Michishio*'s lookout suddenly spotted white waves to starboard, much closer than expected. A searchlight sweep revealed two four-stack destroyers 5,000 yards away. The Japanese warships immediately engaged, but the *Steward* and *John D. Edwards* had a searchlight to aim at. One of the Japanese crewmen remembered, "Their rapid attack surprised us because we did not expect it so soon. We lost our mind momentarily."[31]

Then, the *Pillsbury*, off the port beam, pinned the *Michishio* in a crossfire. One of the American's thirty-three pound shells detonated in the large Japanese destroyer's number 2 mount, killing the crew. The *Michishio*, in the act of firing torpedoes, staggered to starboard with only one fish away, as the *John D. Edwards* hit her bridge and wounded the captain. Finally, the *Tromp*, advancing on the enemy's starboard bow, sent three more shells crashing into the wounded destroyer's engine room. Escaping steam hissed into the air as the *Michishio* wallowed dead in the water with sixty-four men killed, and the columns rushed past at high speed. During this brief action, the *Parrott* ran aground but quickly refloated.

Eight MTBs, *TM 4, 5, 8, 9, 10, 11, 13,* and *15* participated in the third strike, leaving their tender, HNLMS *Krakatau*, which was anchored at Pangpang Bay on the south coast of Java. The MTBs navigated the strait in two groups of four. The eastern group sighted ships, but couldn't maneuver into attack position. The western force saw nothing at all.[32]

The Japanese suffered light damage to the *Asashio* and moderate damage to *Oshio*, and the *Arashio* towed the *Michishio*, which had been "drifting, submerged to sea level from the middle to aft deck,"[33] back to Makassar for repairs that lasted until late October. The Japanese destroyer captains complained of ineffective searchlights and torpedoes exploding prematurely.[34] The *Oshio* and *Asashio* expended 217 and 310 five-inch shells, respectively, while the *Michishio* and *Arashio* fired 62 and 73 rounds. On the Allied side, the *Tromp* required repairs in Australia. The *Stewart* entered dry dock in Surabaja and ultimately suffered the ignominy of capture and service under the Japanese flag.

Collating the action reports, Doorman and his superiors believed they had fought a successful action. In truth, they missed their best chance to snatch a meaningless victory. On the Japanese side, "the success of the 8th Destroyer Division in this engagement against a numerically superior force raised the morale of the entire Japanese fleet [and it] gained great confidence in its ability to fight night engagements."[35] However, Japanese naval headquarters' unquestioning acceptance of Captain Abe's count of two cruisers and three destroyers sunk and two destroyers seriously damaged dangerously lowered its estimation of the ABDA forces available to confront the Java invasion fleet. These supposed battle results also prompted Japanese Combined Fleet Commander Admiral Yamamoto Isoroku to release Japan's carrier strike force and its fast battleships for an offensive cruise south of Java rather than using it to support the invasion fleets. This would be the first of many times exaggerated battle results influenced Imperial strategy. The battles of Badung Strait and Balikpapan also demonstrated how confusing it was to fight at night.

Interlude Before the End

By the last week of February 1942, only Java and scattered holdouts remained unconquered throughout the East Indies' vast expanse. The pace of Japanese operations had been breathtaking and, with the final prize in reach, Vice Admiral Kondo already had two invasion convoys at sea. On 19 February the Japanese Eastern Fleet, forty-one transports lifting the 48th Infantry Division, departed Jolo. Rear Admiral Takagi Takeo commanded the support group, *Sentai* 5 and Rear Admiral Tanaka Raizo's Destroyer Squadron 2, while Rear Admiral Nishimura led the escort, which included his Destroyer Squadron 4 and the base force of four minesweepers, six sub chasers, and a minelayer.

Preparing for the inevitable attack, Dutch Vice Admiral Helfrich marshaled his island's maritime defenses, on 21 February, creating strike forces at Batavia's port of Tandjong Priok in the west and at Surabaja in the east. The Western Force, commanded by the Australian Captain J.A. Collins, consisted of the cruisers HMS *Exeter*, HMAS *Hobart*, HMS *Dragon*, and HMS *Danae* and the destroyers HNLMS *Evertsen*, HMS *Electra*, HMS *Encounter*, HMS *Jupiter*, HMS *Scout*, and HMS *Tenedos*. The Australian light cruiser *Perth* joined the Western Force on 24 February. Doorman's Eastern Force included the *De Ruyter*, *Java*, *Houston*, HNLMS *Witte de With*, HNLMS *Banckert*, *Kortenaer*, *Paul Jones*, and *Alden*.

On 25 February a Dutch aircraft spotted the Eastern Fleet, and the *Exeter*, *Perth*, *Electra*, *Encounter*, and *Jupiter* rushed to reinforce Doorman. A *Perth* sailor remembered entering Surabaja: "It was a low gray day: smoke was rising thickly from two bombed-out ships, as well as from several warehouses ashore. . . . [I]t made a dismal and gloomy picture. Older members of the ship's company read the signs and remembered the fall of Greece and Crete."[36]

On 26 February the Allied captains met. Doorman seemed positive and aggressive, and indicated his hopes by advising that after successfully repelling the enemy's eastern thrust, he intended "to move promptly to the west and there to attack the main western invasion fleet."[37] The strike force sortied that evening, and navigating the channel, the *De Ruyter* inauspiciously rammed and sank a tug and water barge.

Japanese aircraft spotted the rump of the Allied Western Strike Force making a token probe on 26 February. Four cruisers and three destroyer divisions from the Western Invasion Fleet attempted to intercept, but the Allies withdrew before contact. The next day, Rear Admiral Arthur Palliser, the British navy's senior officer in Java, forced Helfrich's reluctant approval and ordered the British and Australian units to flee for Ceylon. They cleared Sunda Strait barely in time.

The Eastern Invasion Fleet, meanwhile, began passing Bawean Island at 1000 on 27 February in an unwieldy procession twenty miles long and angled toward its landing site at Kragan, west of Surabaja. Doorman was cruising outside Surabaja's minefield at the time. He had miscalculated the Japanese fleet's rate of advance and spent the night fruitlessly searching too far south.

At 0930, while fifty miles northeast of the convoy, portions of Rear Admiral Tanaka's Destroyer Squadron 2 left Rear Admiral Takagi's support force to join Nishimura. Takagi, believing that Allied airpower was neutralized and that most Allied ships were sunk or damaged, anticipated an untroubled voyage. Then, Nishimura reported an air attack, prompting Takagi to follow Tanaka with the rest of his force, *Sentai* 5, Destroyer Division 24, and Destroyer Division 7.

At 1100 Takagi received a troubling report that five enemy cruisers and six destroyers blocked his route. He increased speed and launched one of the *Nachi*'s floatplanes at 1137. Nishimura (who had the report forty minutes earlier) had already catapulted a plane, and he ordered the convoy to steer west away from the danger.

At 1235 the *Nachi*'s spotter confirmed an enemy force streaming due east. Minutes later, the same spotter radioed to report that the enemy was heading south.

At 1240 Doorman decided to return to Surabaja. The Dutch admiral had no aerial support and no idea of the enemy's position. His destroyers were running low on fuel, and his men were exhausted. The *Houston*'s crew, for example, had stood twelve-hour watches at battle stations for two nights running.

The Allies' maneuver left Takagi confused whether they intended to attack the Japanese convoy or had just been cruising offshore to avoid the daily air raids against Surabaja. Nevertheless, Takagi decided the landings could proceed. At 1340 Nishimura duly ordered the transports back to a southwesterly course.

Even as Takagi concluded there was nothing to worry about, the pilot of a Dutch Catalina finally fixed the convoy's position as fifty miles northwest of Surabaja. The *De Ruyter* had just cleared the swept channel through Surabaja's minefield when this intelligence reached Doorman accompanied by Helfrich's exhortations to engage. The time was 1427.

The *De Ruyter* reversed course almost immediately, signaling, "Am proceeding to intercept enemy unit, follow me, details later."[38] The convoy's proximity demanded haste, and, with a little luck, Doorman could have dealt Takagi a severe setback because the Japanese warships had begun dispersing toward their night landing positions.[39] But Dutch luck remained abominable.

The *Nachi*'s plane spotted Doorman's turnabout. Takagi increased speed and promptly recalled the two destroyer squadrons. Tanaka had intercepted the reports and was already hurrying west, but Nishimura "received the messages of the enemy's changing course late."[40] He detached the destroyers *Umikaze* and *Natsugumo*, which were in Division 24 under Captain Hirai Yasuji, to stay with the Japanese convoy and rushed south only at 1457. The convoy, greatly disorganized from its maneuvers, lurched west northwest once again.

Battle of the Java Sea, 27 February 1942

Doorman's force seemed well matched against Takagi's, but in fact the ABDA ships lacked maintenance and some operated damaged, like *Houston*, which fought with its number 3 turret disabled. Moreover, six weeks of coalition warfare had hardly solved the organizational problems that compounded the fleet's human and materiel strain. The strike force flew four flags and lacked mutually intelligible codes, much less common tactics. The American destroyers carried as few as six torpedoes.

However, the Dutch faced their final battle, and they knew it. During World War II, few admirals fought a major sea battle with the grim tenacity Doorman displayed at Java Sea.

TABLE 2.3. FORCES ENGAGED IN THE BATTLE OF THE JAVA SEA

	Type of Ship	Year Launched	Displacement, Full Load (tons)	Max. Speed (knots)	Guns (number by inch/caliber)	Torpedoes (number of tubes by diameter in inches)	Damage
Allied Strike Force (Rear Admiral Karel Doorman)							
Exeter (BR)	CA	1931	11,000	32	6 x 8/50 & 8 x 4/45	6 x 21	D3
Houston	CA	1930	11,420	32	6 x 8/55 & 8 x 5/25		D1
De Ruyter (DU) (F)	CL	1935	7,548	32	7 x 5.9/50		Sunk
Perth (AU)	CL	1936	9,150	32	8 x 6/50 & 4 x 4/45	8 x 21	
Java (DU)	CL	1925	7,205	31	10 x 5.9/50		Sunk
Witte de With (DU)	DD	1928	1,650	32	4 x 4.7/50 & 1 x 3/76.2	6 x 21	
Kortenaer (DU)	DD	1927	1,640	26	4 x 4.7/50 & 2 x 3/76.2	6 x 21	Sunk
John D. Edwards	DD	1919	1,308	30	4 x 4/51 & 1 x 3/76.2	12 x 21	
Alden	DD	1919	1,308	30	4 x 4/51 & 1 x 3/76.2	12 x 21	
John D. Ford	DD	1920	1,308	30	4 x 4/51 & 1 x 3/76.2	12 x 21	
Paul Jones	DD	1920	1,308	30	4 x 4/51 & 1 x 3/76.2	12 x 21	
Electra (BR)	DD	1934	2,025	36	4 x 4.7/45	8 x 21	Sunk
Jupiter (BR)	DD	1938	2,330	36	6 x 4.7/45 & 1 x 3/76.2	5 x 21	Sunk

Encounter (BR)	DD	1934	2,025	36	4 x 4.7/45	8 x 21	
Japanese Sentai 5 (Rear Admiral Takagi Takeo)							
Nachi (F)	CA	1929	14,980	33	10 x 8/50 & 8 x 5/40	8 x 24	
Haguro	CA	1928	14,980	33	10 x 8/50 & 8 x 5/.40	8 x 24	D1
Japanese Destroyer Squadron 2 (Rear Admiral Tanaka Raizo)							
Jintsu (F)	CL	1925	7,100	35	7 x 5.5/50 & 3 x 3.1/40	8 x 24	D1
Japanese Destroyer Division 16 (Captain Shibuya Shiro)							
Tokitsukaze	DD	1939	2,490	35	6 x 5/50	8 x 24	D1
Amatsukaze	DD	1939	2,490	35	6 x 5/50	8 x 24	
Yukikaze	DD	1939	2,490	35	6 x 5/50	8 x 24	
Hatsukaze	DD	1939	2,490	35	6 x 5/50	8 x 24	
Japanese Destroyer Division 24							
Yamakaze	DD	1936	1,980	34	5 x 5/50	8 x 24	
Kawakaze	DD	1936	1,980	34	5 x 5/50	8 x 24	
Japanese Destroyer Division 7 (Captain Konishi Kaname)							
Sazanami	DD	1931	2,427	34	6 x 5/50	9 x 24	
Ushio	DD	1930	2,427	34	6 x 5/50	9 x 24	
Japanese Destroyer Squadron 4 (Rear Admiral Nishimura Shoji)							
Naka (F)	CL	1925	7,100	35	7 x 5.5/50 & 3 x 3.1/40	8 x 24	D1
Japanese Destroyer Division 9 (Captain Sato Yasuo)							
Asagumo	DD	1937	2,370	35	6 x 5/50	8 x 24	D3
Minegumo	DD	1937	2,370	35	6 x 5/50	8 x 24	D1

Japanese Destroyer Division 2 (Captain Tachibana Masao)							
Murasame	DD	1935	1,980	34	5 x 5/50	8 x 24	
Samidare	DD	1935	1,980	34	5 x 5/50	8 x 24	
Yudachi	DD	1936	1,980	34	5 x 5/50	8 x 24	
Harusame	DD	1935	1,980	34	5 x 5/50	8 x 24	

AU—Australian, BR—British, CA—heavy cruiser, CL—light cruiser, D1—light or superficial damage (including splinter damage), D3—significant damage (combat or maneuvering ability somewhat impaired), DD—destroyer, DU—Dutch, F—flagship

Time: 1612–2355
Weather: Fair, high overcast, gentle east southeasterly breeze
Visibility: Good to poor
Sea state: Small to moderate swells
Surprise: None
Mission: Allies—interception based on specific intelligence; Japanese—escort and transit

As the Allies cleared the minefield, Doorman formed three parallel columns. The British destroyers led on the starboard bow of the cruisers *De Ruyter, Houston, Exeter, Perth,* and *Java.* The two Dutch and four American destroyers trailed on the port quarter. The *Kortenaer,* suffering from propulsion problems since her grounding before Badung Strait, could barely make twenty-six knots.

Tanaka sighted the *Nachi* at 1550. He took position 9,000 yards ahead of the cruisers and turned south to seek the enemy, while Takagi dispatched Destroyer Divisions 7 and 24 to form a second unit behind the *Jintsu.* Twenty minutes later the *Jintsu's* lookouts reported masts 30,000 yards to the south southeast. At the same time, Nishimura's squadron appeared 13,000 yards west of the heavy cruisers sighting the enemy at 1616.

In the Allied van, the *Electra* spotted the *Jintsu* at 1612. Shortly after, the Japanese cruiser steered southwest and opened fire from 18,000 yards, obtaining early straddles. At 1617 the *Nachi* joined the fray from 28,000 yards. The Japanese heavy cruiser's initial volleys fell 2,000 yards short. The *Houston* and *Exeter* replied at 1620, with the U.S. heavy cruiser using red dye to mark the fall of her shells. The immense blood-red geysers raised by the *Houston's* near misses startled some on the *Nachi's* bridge, as Takagi, a submarine specialist, experienced his first surface action. At 1621 Doorman steered 20 degrees to port, concerned the Japanese might cross his T. At the same time Tanaka veered starboard because enemy fire was falling too close (see Map 2.4).

At 1629 Doorman turned west southwest, still struggling to prevent the Japanese, with their seven-knot speed advantage, from crossing ahead. Unfortunately, this kept his 6-inch guns beyond range. The *Perth's* captain, Hector Waller, reported, "I found a long period of being 'Aunt Sally' very trying without being able to return the fire. (Range still over 26,000 yards.)"[41] The *Houston* claimed hits, but the Japanese scored first at 1631, when an eight-inch dud struck the *De Ruyter.*

MAP 2.4. BATTLE OF THE JAVA SEA, 27 FEBRUARY 1942

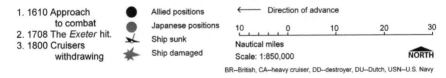

Relative Positions at Times Indicated - Locations of Ships Lost

1. 1610 Approach
   to combat
2. 1708 The *Exeter* hit.
3. 1800 Cruisers
   withdrawing

● Allied positions
● Japanese positions
✖ Ship sunk
✴ Ship damaged

← Direction of advance

Nautical miles
Scale: 1:850,000

NORTH

BR--British, CA--heavy cruiser, DD--destroyer, DU--Dutch, USN--U.S. Navy

Nishimura shared Waller's impatience with the long ranges. He had ordered a torpedo action within ten minutes of sighting the enemy and steered Squadron 4 south southwest, cutting ahead of the other Japanese columns. By 1630 Nishimura bore northwest of the enemy, and four minutes later the *Naka* launched four torpedoes from 15,000 yards. The *Jintsu* added four torpedoes at 1635 aimed to cross

Nishimura's stern. Then, between 1640 and 1645, Nishimura's six destroyers dispatched another twenty-three Type 93s toward the Allies from ranges as close as 13,000 yards, with the *Asagumo* firing three and all the others firing four.

As each destroyer attacked, it turned west northwest spewing smoke. The *Haguro* launched eight Long Lances at 1652 from 22,000 yards away and smacked the *De Ruyter* a minute later with another dud. The *Nachi* did not join in this initial salvo because an accident had bled the air pressure from her tubes. This barrage constituted the Imperial navy's first large-scale torpedo action of the war. It was, in other words, the first test of Japan's secret, war-winning weapon.

All the while, the gunnery duel raged. The *Houston* pumped broadsides from her forward turrets at the rate of five or six a minute. "Tight salvos lobbed around [the *Perth*], first 25 yards short, then 25 yards over." The streaking track of each shell became, for a split second, "a black image just before it struck the water."[42] Observers aboard the *Houston*, *Exeter*, and *Perth* all agreed that the *Haguro* suffered multiple hits, burst into flames, even sank. In fact, the Japanese ships escaped harm during the battle's first phase. Damage assessment under fire at great distances was a difficult art, and both Allied and Japanese observers too often saw what they wanted to see. Meanwhile, the Japanese noted multiple explosions amid the Allied formation. This caused some confusion with commanders claiming hits with their torpedoes while others worried about mines. In fact, the Type 93s were displaying an unsuspected propensity for detonating prematurely.

At 1704 the Japanese convoy reported an air attack by a flight of three A-24s escorted by ten P-40s, and Takagi realized the battle had drifted dangerously close to the transports. He originally intended to close and destroy what he believed was a superior enemy force with torpedoes after dark. Given the situation, however, he immediately ordered an all-out attack.

At this time Doorman turned slightly north. As the two forces closed, fortune favored the Japanese. First a dud hit the *Houston* and forced a temporary reduction in the heavy cruiser's speed. Then, at 1708, the *Nachi* delivered the battle's decisive blow: "An 8-inch shell hit [the *Exeter's*] after starboard 4-inch gun . . . [and] continued through a boiler-room ventilator, exploding in "B" boiler room with a terrifying roar, followed by the deafening noise of escaping superheated steam."[43]

Burning fiercely, the veteran of the famous River Plate battle against the German armored ship *Graf Spee* lurched out of formation to port with six of eight boilers knocked off line and losing headway rapidly. The three cruisers following her made 90-degree turns, assuming Doorman had ordered this maneuver, probably to comb the torpedoes suddenly appearing everywhere. The *De Ruyter* plunged ahead for several moments alone.

When the *Perth* realized the *Exeter's* plight, the smaller Australian ship circled and smothered the British cruiser in smoke. Random explosions punctuated the sea around the milling Allied ships. Ignorant of the Type 93's range, the Allies could not believe that vessels barely visible on the horizon fired the salvos that made the sea seem "alive with torpedoes running from all quarters."[44] Observers reported periscopes, even a submarine blowing up.

At 1713, a Long Lance packing a half ton of explosives hammered the *Kortenaer* amidships. The Dutch destroyer exploded and jackknifed. A witness on the *Witte de With* "saw both parts of the ship, covered with survivors, sink slowly."[45] In contrast, the *John D. Edwards's* captain timed the demise of the *Kortenaer* at one minute and fifty seconds.

Meanwhile, the *De Ruyter* finally turned to find her missing flotilla. The three Japanese columns likewise steered south at 1710 and then southeast in pursuit. In the hour of action up to 1720, the Japanese fired 1,271 eight-inch rounds, 141 5.5-inch rounds and thirty-nine torpedoes. They hit with five shells and one torpedo. Allied expenditures of ammunition were likewise heavy, but the projectiles failed to inflict damage on the Japanese.

It took Doorman nearly twenty minutes to establish control. The *Exeter*, screened by the *Witte de With*, and the British destroyers, limped south-southeast at five knots. The *De Ruyter* circled while signaling "Follow Me" and repositioned herself ahead of the other cruisers and the American destroyers. The Dutch cruiser led this reduced formation south by southeast until 1725, when Doorman turned northeast and cut across the *Exeter's* course. As the sun set, the *Exeter* burned, and artificial smoke swirled over the water.

At times the Japanese disappeared from sight, but spotter planes kept Takagi apprised of Doorman's position as twilight deepened. Realizing their enemy's distress, Tanaka and Nishimura concentrated off the *Exeter's* starboard quarter. At 1745 Doorman emerged from the smoke on a northerly heading to see this attack forming up. At the same time the Japanese heavy cruisers, 19,500 yards to the northwest, resumed fire.

The second mass torpedo attack on the Allies began at 1748. The *Nachi* and the *Haguro* each hurled eight Type 93s at the *Exeter* at 1754 at a range of 27,000 yards. Barreling down from the west northwest the *Naka* launched four torpedoes from 18,500 yards at 1750, and the *Jintsu* launched four more at 1754 from nearly 20,000 yards before turning away to starboard. Tanaka's squadron emptied their tubes next from 15,000 yards, one ship after the other, and then reversed course to port.

The *Electra* and *Encounter* circled to starboard to meet this threat. *Electra* skipper Commander C.W. May advised his men, "The Japanese are mounting a strong torpedo attack against the *Exeter*. So we are going through the smoke to counterattack."[46] The British destroyer emerged to see Tanaka's squadron bearing down on an opposite course, and her guns barked into action, landing a shell on the *Jintsu* that killed one man and wounded four. Meanwhile, Nishimura's Division 2 closed to 10,000 yards before launching torpedoes and turning away at 1804. Japanese Destroyer Division 9 continued independently. The *Asagumo* sent her fish swimming from 6,500 yards, but the *Minegumo*, forced to avoid friendly torpedoes launched earlier in the attack, missed the opportunity to fire.

The *Encounter*, skippered by Lieutenant Commander E. St. J. Morgan, broke through the smoke after the *Electra* and snapped off a few quick rounds at the *Jintsu*. Between 1800 and 1810 the *Encounter* traded volleys with the *Minegumo* as the destroyers looped northeast on parallel courses, with ranges dipping to 3,000 yards. In the encounter, the *Minegumo* suffered light damage, with four crewman being wounded.

For her part, the *Electra* took on the *Asagumo* and landed a shell in the Japanese destroyer's engine room from 5,000 yards, killing four men, wounding nineteen, and causing the Japanese ship to go dead in the water. The British destroyers also scored a hit on the *Tokitsukaze* during this period.

The *Asagumo*, however, dealt a deadly reply. First, a shell detonated beneath the *Electra*'s bridge. Then, as a crewman recalled, "a lucky shell hit us in number 2 boiler room, port side. This shattered the boiler . . . and in spite of the efforts of the engine room staff, steam was lost."[47]

The *Minegumo* then advanced and blasted the drifting British destroyer from close range. The *Electra* replied with a futile salvo of torpedoes as one by one her guns fell silent. The *Electra* sank at 1816. The USS *S38* rescued fifty-four of her crew the next morning.

The Japanese expended ninety-eight torpedoes from 1748 to 1810 without scoring a single hit. In addition to the loss of the Electra, the *Witte de With* suffered damage when a poorly secured depth charge rolled off during violent maneuvers and exploded alongside.

As the British destroyers pressed their attack, Doorman led the Allied cruisers in a full circle, and by 1750 resumed an east southeast heading parallel to the *Exeter* and her two escorts. The *Houston* aimed at the *Naka*, and at 1756 several U.S. broadsides straddled the Japanese ship, showering her deck with shrapnel and spray and severing an antenna. Observing the Allied ships, the *Amatsukaze*'s skipper, Commander Hara Tameichi, remembered, "Such tactics were not to be found in the Imperial Navy manual. I just stood and gaped."[48]

Commander H.E. Eccles aboard the *John D. Edwards* was also confused. "The crystal ball was our only method of anticipating the intention of Commander Combined Striking Force. Then came the orders 'Counter-attack', 'Cancel counter-attack', 'Make smoke', 'Cover my retirement.'"[49] The old four-stackers resolved the confusion at 1810 by charging Takagi.

At 1822 they fired their starboard torpedoes from 10,000 yards and then turned and emptied their port tubes as well, sending twenty-four torpedoes churning toward the *Nachi* and *Haguro*. Takagi easily sidestepped this attack, but with the Surabaja lighthouse in sight and worried about mines, he judged it best to re-form. As the sun disappeared, the Allies headed east while Takagi steered north. In the last hour Imperial forces had fired 302 eight-inch, 50 5.5-inch, and 515 five-inch rounds in addition to 98 torpedoes.

Doorman, however, was not ready to call it quits. Leaving the *Witte de With* to escort the *Exeter* to Surabaja, he signaled "Follow Me" and circled back at 1831. The *De Ruyter* led the *Houston*, *Perth*, and *Java*, while the *Jupiter* screened to port and the four American destroyers trailed off the starboard quarter.

At 1846 the *Jintsu's* plane reported Doorman's return. Takagi radioed his units to prepare for a night battle; however, his destroyers remained scattered. Division 7 only found the *Jintsu* at 1845, while Divisions 16 and 24 did not join the main Japanese force until 1907 because they had headed in opposite directions after their torpedo charges. Nishimura had completely lost Division 9. The heavily damaged *Asagumo* and the lightly damaged *Minegumo* had returned to the convoy. The *Jintsu's* plane reported that the Allies were heading directly for the convoy, so at 1904 Nishimura ordered the transports to immediately reverse course. This embarrassed Takagi because at 1857 Sentai 5 had stopped to recover its five floatplanes. At 1922, just as the last plane was being hoisted aboard, lookouts spotted Doorman's cruisers to the southeast.

Groping to make contact the Allies fired star shell. The *Naka* reported ten flares bearing 95 degrees at 1932, while Tanaka's force, which lay closer, unwittingly came between Doorman and Sentai 5 just as Takagi's ships were reversing course and preparing to engage. The *Perth* and *Houston* opened fire at 1933, and the *Jintsu* replied with four torpedoes from 21,000 yards. Observing the flashes, the *Perth* turned abruptly to starboard at 1936, and the other ships conformed. Tanaka increased speed, made smoke, and lost contact. Apparently, the Allies never sighted the stopped cruisers, although *Nachi* fired briefly at 1937.

Doorman decided to withdraw east and then head for the coast in an attempt to circle around the escorts. At 2100, now close inshore, the Dutch admiral swung back to the west. Commander Binford independently ordered his four destroyers, out of torpedoes and low on fuel, to return to Surabaja. Communications were such that he had to radio a message explaining his action to a shore station for forwarding to the commander. Then, at 2125, just as Doorman was turning back north, the *Jupiter* struck a Dutch mine. The British destroyer exploded, lost all her power, and sunk about four hours later.

The diminished Allied force steamed north and at 2200 sailed through the *Kortenaer's* drifting survivors. Doorman detached the *Encounter*, and she rescued 113 men. Throughout this period, the *Jintsu's* aircraft dogged the strike force, dropping magnesium flares and keeping Takagi advised of his enemy's moments. At 2120, however, the *Naka's* aircraft took over, and at 2200 Takagi lost communications with this plane, leaving the two commanders equally in the dark.

For another hour the four ABDA cruisers sailed north hoping to stumble into the Japanese convoy. At the same time Takagi steered south, nervous about the lack of information and ordering the two destroyer squadrons to rejoin him. At 2302 the *Nachi's* lookout sighted shadows south southeast about 16,000 yards away. It was Doorman.

The Japanese heavy cruisers swung to port on a parallel course. The Allied cruisers likewise spotted the foe and opened fire at 2310. Takagi did not reply until 2321, when he began firing intermittently in the moonlight. Both sides were exhausted and low on ammunition.

At 2322 the *Nachi* launched eight torpedoes, and the *Haguro* followed one minute later with a salvo of four fish at a range of 14,000 yards. At 2332 a huge column of fire lit the night. One of the *Haguro's* torpedoes struck the *De Ruyter* aft, detonating a magazine. Two minutes later a torpedo from the *Nachi's* spread smacked the *Java*. Her stern broke off, and she sank rapidly, taking 512 men with her.

On the Allied flagship power failed, and the fire spread out of control. The *De Ruyter* foundered after a struggle of several hours taking the admiral and 344 of his men. The *Houston* and *Perth* turned away to the southwest. The Japanese heavy cruisers expended just 46 eight-inch rounds during this brief action. Both Tanaka and Nishimura's squadrons spotted the explosions and attempted to engage. The *Jintsu's* report states, "[M]oved forward in an attempt to wage night battle, but the enemy laid down smoke and, taking advantage of high speed, appeared to have all fled to the southeast."[50] Nishimura imagined sighting ten ships at 0020 and prepared to engage this phantom fleet. In fact, the battle was over.

Rear Admiral Doorman fought the Battle of the Java Sea determined to obtain a decisive result. In this he succeeded, but it was not the result he desired. The long-range shooting on both sides was ineffective, despite the spotters the Japanese employed. Collectively, the Japanese heavy cruisers fired 1,619 eight-inch shells, two-thirds their total supply, to obtain five hits. The light cruisers added an additional 221 5.5-inch shells but scored no hits—save, perhaps, on the *Electra*—and the destroyers fired 515 five-inch rounds. The Allied cruisers likewise nearly emptied their magazines, but only the *Perth* connected with a six-inch round on the *Haguro's* catapult. Despite the Japanese emphasis on torpedo tactics and the impressive characteristics of their weapons, dozens of torpedoes prematurely exploded, and the Japanese obtained only 3 successes out of 153 torpedoes expended. Still, those three hits were enough to sink three Allied ships.

With the last threat to their safety eliminated, the Japanese convoy landed the 48th Division at Kragan the next day. The Allies had lost the naval campaign for Java and were about to reap the bitter fruits of defeat.

CHAPTER 3

Java Aftermath: The East Indies II

We had gotten the hell licked out of us.
　　　　　　　　　　—CDR. H.E. ECCLES, USS *JOHN D. EDWARDS*

The destruction of HNLMS *De Ruyter* signaled the final collapse of Allied sea power in the East Indies. From the deck of the *Perth* it seemed the Dutch cruiser "went up in an appalling explosion of flame and searing heat," and the Australian ship barely avoided ramming the stricken cruiser.[1] Similarly, the *Houston* only missed the *Perth* by steering hard to port.

Captain Waller, now senior officer, assessed the situation and ordered *Houston* to follow him to Tanjong Priok. The weary crews manned their battle stations all night, but contrary to expectations, the sun rose over an empty sea. The surviving Allied ships entered port around noon, threading between the wrecks protruding from the oily water. One of the *Perth*'s men remembered, "The place was strangely hushed and deserted. The exhausted ship's company were infinitely depressed by the lack of spirit there."[2]

The *Houston* "was a shambles. The shocks and concussions from the eight-inch guns had shaken loose everything that was not welded down and had even broken many things that had been secured."[3] Dockside, the *Perth* and *Houston* joined HNLMS *Evertsen*, which had failed to escape with the Allied Western Strike Force after becoming separated in a storm.

Both of the cruisers required ammunition and fuel. After mooring, however, they learned that only a thousand tons of fuel oil remained and this was reserved for Dutch requirements. The authorities finally permitted the *Perth* to take on 300 tons, bringing her to about 50 percent of capacity, and they permitted the *Houston* to take just enough to make Australia. The *Houston* retained 300 eight-inch shells, while the *Perth* had only 160 rounds left for her six-inch weapons. The Australian ship loaded some four-inch ordnance, but there were no main battery shells for either vessel.

It was a similarly grim day in Surabaja, where the other remnants of Doorman's force gathered. The *Pope* had missed the Java Sea battle due to engineering problems but had patched up in time to help shepherd the *Exeter* into port. The *Exeter* immediately commenced making repairs to her damaged boiler. The *Witte de With* docked and granted liberty to a portion of her crew. U.S. Destroyer

Division 58 arrived and refueled. The British destroyer *Encounter* made port last, carrying the *Kortenaer's* survivors.

The Japanese Imperial Navy had destroyed Allied sea power in the East Indies with the weakest and most exposed of its four fleets. It was a measure of his confidence that Admiral Yamamoto revised his original plan "with all the opportunism of the gambler that he was" and dispatched his strongest fleet into the Indian Ocean.[4] Yamamoto envisioned Japanese carriers and battleships harvesting Allied remnants fleeing the victories he expected his cruisers and destroyers to win. On 25 February Carrier Air Fleet 1, under the command of Vice Admiral Nagumo Chuichi, and the main force under Vice Admiral Kondo sailed from Kendari, steamed through Ombay Strait, and debouched into the Indian Ocean. Nagumo's force included the carriers *Akagi*, *Kaga*, *Hiryu*, and *Soryu*; the battleships *Hiei* and *Kirishima*; the heavy cruisers *Tone* and *Chikuma*; and Destroyer Squadron 1, which consisted of light cruiser *Abukuma* and eight destroyers. Kondo commanded the battleships *Haruna* and *Kongo*, the heavy cruisers *Atago*, *Maya*, and *Takeo*, and three destroyers.

The Western Invasion Fleet had left Cam Ranh Bay on 18 February. In testimony to the confidence and efficiency of Japanese planning, this was even before the capture of Bali. Unlike Takagi's Eastern force and its relatively small escort compared to cargo and mission, the Western force's fifty-six transports enjoyed generous protection. Rear Admiral Hara Kenzaburo commanded Protection Unit 3 aboard the light cruiser *Natori*. His 5th Destroyer Squadron also included thirteen destroyers of Divisions 5, 6, 11, 12, and 22, and the light cruiser *Yura*. Rear Admiral Kurita Takeo, commander *Sentai 7*, led the support force, flying his flag aboard the heavy cruiser *Kumano*, with heavy cruisers *Suzuya*, *Mikuma*, and *Mogami* and Destroyer Division 19. The light carrier *Ryujo*, escorted by a destroyer provided direct air support. Vice Admiral Takahashi Ibo, the commander of the 3rd Fleet and overall leader of the two invasion fleets, operated independently north of Java with the heavy cruisers *Ashigara* and *Myoko* and two destroyers.

Even after Doorman's defeat, the Dutch wanted desperately to believe Java could be held. Many soldiers and sailors, even high officers like Vice Admiral Helfrich, were East Indies natives. The army had hoarded its troops and could muster more than two divisions. Defeat seemed unimaginable. In this spirit Helfrich immediately ordered the *Houston*, *Perth*, and *Evertsen* to Tjilatjap, hoping to fight on from there.

The Netherlands' allies, however, felt differently about prospects for turning back the Japanese. With Singapore's fall on 15 February, the British concluded the Indies were doomed. The Allies dissolved ABDAFLOAT on 25 February, and Helfrich's authority over components of his force grew increasingly tenuous. On 1 March the senior British and American naval officers, Rear Admiral Palliser and Rear Admiral Glassford, asked Helfrich to revoke his orders to fight on from

MAP 3.1. JAVA AFTERMATH, MARCH 1942

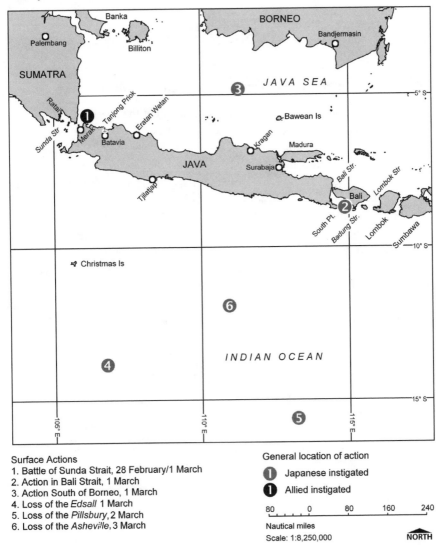

Surface Actions
1. Battle of Sunda Strait, 28 February/1 March
2. Action in Bali Strait, 1 March
3. Action South of Borneo, 1 March
4. Loss of the *Edsall* 1 March
5. Loss of the *Pillsbury*, 2 March
6. Loss of the *Asheville*, 3 March

General location of action

❶ Japanese instigated
❶ Allied instigated

80   0   80   160   240

Nautical miles
Scale: 1:8,250,000

NORTH

Tjilatjap. When Helfrich refused, the British admiral stated he would order all Royal Navy ships to Ceylon. When the Dutch commander in chief turned and asked Glassford what his intentions were, the American advised, "My instructions are to report to you for duty. Any order you give me will be obeyed at once." Glassford's response indicated that the "American Navy was going to honor its commitments to ABDACOM even if everyone but the Dutch pulled out."[5]

The USS *Langley*'s fate, bombed and sunk with her cargo of ready-to-fly P-40s by Japanese carrier aircraft south of Tjilatjap on 27 February—before Doorman's defeat—demonstrated both the sincerity of America's naval policy and the futility of its aims. Even as late as 1 March U.S. ships still ferried reinforcements to Java.

Battle of Sunda Strait, 28 February–1 March 1942

The *Perth* and *Houston* cast off at 1900 on 1 March but the *Evertsen*, not ready to steam and seeking confirmation of orders issued by Rear Admiral Glassford at Helfrich's direction, did not follow until 2045. Under way, the Allied ships steered west with subdued confidence. Aboard the *Houston* the general feeling was, "Thank God, we're going to get out of this Java Sea."[6] As late as 1500 hours on 28 February, aerial reconnaissance showed Hara's fleet standing ten hours north and the Sunda Strait clear. But there was one problem: The *Perth*'s Waller and the *Houston*'s Capt. Albert H. Rooks possessed bad intelligence. As Hara's invasion armada approached Java, seven transports escorted by the *Yura* and two destroyers split off for west central Java to land troops near Eratan Wetan. Allied flyers spotted this force, miscounted it as ten transports, two cruisers, and three destroyers and reported the Japanese ships as being about fifty miles northeast of Batavia, steering east. This misidentification explained why the two captains believed they could slip through the strait.

TABLE 3.1. FORCES ENGAGED AT THE BATTLE OF SUNDA STRAIT

	Type of Ship	Year Launched	Displacement, Full Load (tons)	Max. Speed (knots)	Guns (number by inch/caliber)	Torpedoes (number of tubes by diameter in inches)	Damage
Allied (Captain H. Waller)							
Perth (AU) (F)	CL	1936	9,150	32	8 x 6/50 & 8 x 4/45	8 x 21	Sunk
Houston	CA	1930	11,420	32	6 x 8/55 & 8 x 5/25		Sunk
Evertsen (DU)	DD	1926	1,640	36	4 x 4.7/50 & 3 x 3/55	6 x 21	Sunk
Japanese *Sentai* 7, Section 2 (Captain Sakiyama Shakao)							
Mikuma	CA	1934	13,668	34	10 x 8/50 & 8 x 5/40	12 x 24	D1

Mogami (F)	CA	1934	13,668	34	10 x 8/50 & 8 x 5/40	12 x 24	
Shikinami	DD	1929	2,389	35	6 x 5/50	9 x 24	D1
Japanese Destroyer Squadron 5 (Rear Admiral Hara Kenzaburo)							
Natori (F)	CL	1922	5,570	36	7 x 5.5/50 & 2 x 3.1/40	8 x 24	
Destroyer Division 11 (Captain Shoji Kiichiro)							
Shirayuki (F)	DD	1928	2,389	35	6 x 5/50	9 x 24	D1
Hatsuyuki	DD	1928	2,389	35	6 x 5/50	9 x 24	
Fubuki	DD	1927	2,389	35	6 x 5/50	9 x 24	
Japanese Destroyer Division 5 (Captain Nomaguchi Kanetomo)							
Harukaze (F)	DD	1922	1,747	37	4 x 4.7/50	6 x 21	D2
Hatakaze	DD	1924	1,747	37	4 x 4.7/50	6 x 21	
Asakaze	DD	1922	1,747	37	4 x 4.7/50	6 x 21	
Japanese Destroyer Division 12 (Captain Ogawa Nobuki)							
Shirakumo (F)	DD	1927	2,389	35	6 x 5/50	9 x 24	
Murakumo	DD	1927	2,389	35	6 x 5/50	9 x 24	

AU—Australian, CA—heavy cruiser, CL—light cruiser, D1—light or superficial damage (including splinter damage), D2—moderate damage (combat ability not significantly impaired), DD—destroyer, DU—Dutch, F—flagship

Time: 2306–0045
Weather: Clear
Visibility: Excellent, full moon
Sea state: Calm
Surprise: Allies
Mission: Allies—transit; Japanese—amphibious attack

In fact, Hara had already arrived off St. Nicholaas Point, the entrance to Sunda Strait. Six Japanese transports accompanied by Destroyer Division 12 and the *Satsuki, Minazuki, Nagatsuki,* and *Fumizuki* from Destroyer Division 22 continued into the strait, making for Merak. The main Japanese force anchored in Bantam Bay. The clear tropic night seemed very quiet, and the aide of General Imamura Hitoshi, commander of the 16th Army "heaved a sigh of disappointment to think that this landing operation was to be made without firing a single rifle or gun or without bloodshed."[7] Given that Japanese scout planes had observed Allied warships in Batavia that afternoon, the aide's complacency seemed premature. Nevertheless, it was widely shared.

Hara deployed the *Mikuma, Mogami,* and *Shikinami* twenty miles north of the bay. The *Natori,* with Divisions 11 and 5, patrolled around the landing zones. Admiral Kurita kept the *Ryujo,* the seaplane carrier *Chiyoda,* the heavy cruisers *Kumano* and *Suzuya,* and the destroyers *Isonami* and *Uranami* in the Java Sea. Four minesweepers stayed in the bay. Only the destroyer *Fubuki* patrolled east along the enemy's most likely avenue of approach.

At 2239 the *Fubuki* sighted a pair of strange ships 11,000 yards away, approaching from the east. The Japanese ship immediately reported this finding to Hara, who stood eight miles north of St. Nicholaas Point with the rest of Destroyer Division 11. At 2248 the *Natori* detected silhouettes 18,500 yards to the east southeast. Meanwhile the *Fubuki* slipped behind Babi Island and turned to trail the intruders.

At 2259 Hara decided the contacts were two enemy cruisers. Consequently, he ordered the heavy cruiser section to come south and Division 5 to join him. He then signaled his battle plan: "The enemy ships might flee if they see [the cruisers] and we will lose a good chance of sinking them. To take an advantage of this opportunity, we will use *Natori* as bait to lead the enemy to an open area away from the transports while avoiding mines. Then, after the enemy starts firing, we will counterattack with the second section of *Sentai* 7 and finish off the enemy."[8]

As the *Perth* passed 2,500 yards south of Babi, her navigator wrote, "The sea was calm, with little or no wind, a clear sky and a full moon, giving an extreme visibility of six or seven miles."[9] The *Houston's* log showed, "Speed about 22 knots. . . . Toppers Island Light plainly in view on starboard bow. Sighted ships, no identity, expected Dutch escort of patrol vessels."[10] Captain Waller shared this expectation, and when lookouts reported a shape about five miles ahead, he signaled a routine challenge. The unknown ship flashed back an unintelligible reply on a green lamp and turned away making smoke. Recognizing the silhouette of an enemy destroyer, Waller steered north and opened fire at 2315. This vessel was the *Harukaze,* which had reported sighting the *Perth* a few minutes earlier.

Trailing the *Houston* by 3,000 yards, the *Fubuki* reacted to the enemy's change of course. At 2314 the Japanese launched a salvo of nine Type 90 torpedoes and fired sixteen rounds while also turning north. She optimistically reported one torpedo hit.

Waller, not knowing Admiral Hara intended him to play hound to the *Natori's* hare, led the two cruisers in a loop to port. Imamura's aide jumped up to "the tremendous sound of guns" and saw "about 16 kilometers NNE of our anchorage . . . two battleships continuously firing their large guns."[11] On the Allied cruisers lookouts quickly reported more sightings of enemy ships covering the anchorage. These were probably the *Natori* and Destroyer Division 11 off St. Nicholaas

Point and certainly the *Hatakaze* and *Harukaze* and the minesweepers, which would have seemed to be destroyers in the dark and distance. The *Houston* probably spotted the *Fubuki* as well. However, it seems doubtful that the Allied captains realized they had stumbled upon the main Japanese invasion fleet. The *Perth's* report states, "I cannot attempt to estimate what force was opposing us. During the action a large number of destroyers engaged us from all directions; at least one and probably more cruisers were engaging us from the northward, and one officer on the bridge reported sighting a large number of vessels in close formation, probably transports."[12]

At 2315 Hara abandoned his plan and ordered Destroyer Divisions 5 and 11 to "rush" the enemy and Division 12 to return and help out. The *Harukaze* was already steaming northwest, trailing smoke from which the *Hatakaze* emerged barreling north. Waller steered to an easterly heading as the *Hatakaze* peppered the Allied cruisers with 4.7-inch rounds. At 2326 a light shell exploded on the *Perth's* forward funnel, carrying away a boat and damaging the port pom-pom and flag deck. Four minutes later the Allied cruisers, maneuvering tight and fast, turned south. At 2332 a second shell detonated near the *Perth's* flag deck. At 2338, with Pandjang Island looming near, Waller turned northeast.

After twenty-five minutes of action there had been much noise and light, but little harm inflicted by either side. The separate Japanese groups were finally converging, however. Division 5 regrouped as the *Hatakaze* retreated to join the *Harukaze* and *Asakaze* 11,000 yards north northeast of St. Nicholaas Point. Division 12 approached from the west, and the *Mikuma* and *Mogami*, followed by the *Shikinami*, arrived northeast of the point and turned east, spotting targets and calculating ranges, waiting for the destroyers to complete their attacks. Shortly before 2340 the *Hatsuyuki* and *Shirayuki* led the first attack, charging southwest under heavy Allied fire. A 6-inch shell blasted *Shirayuki's* bridge, killing one man and wounding eleven. At 2340 each Japanese destroyer fired nine Type 90 torpedoes south at a range of 4,000 yards and turned away spewing smoke.

The *Houston* and *Perth* then maneuvered east of St. Nicholaas Point just a few thousand yards northeast of the transports. The Australian fired four torpedoes of her own, although the senior surviving officer did not know their target. The *Houston's* log describes this portion of the battle with a single sentence: "Fight developed into a melee—*Houston* guns engaged on all sides, range never greater than 5000 yards."[13] It is clear from Japanese accounts, however, that Waller and Rooks directed most their firepower against the warships, not the transports.

Japanese Destroyer Division 5 followed Division 11, planning another torpedo attack. Several shells jolted the *Harukaze*, however, damaging her bridge, engine room, and rudder and killing three men and wounding fifteen. As she fell out of line, the *Asakaze* swung north northwest and at 2343 discharged six torpedoes

MAP 3.2. BATTLE OF SUNDA STRAIT, 28 FEBRUARY–1 MARCH 1942

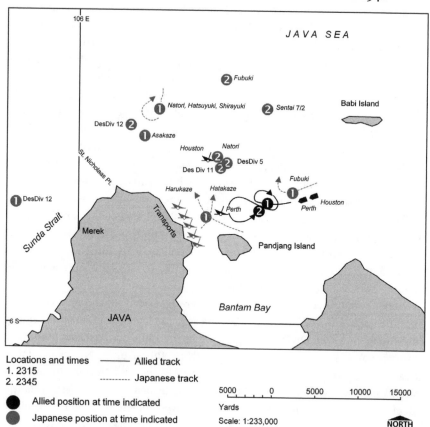

southeast from roughly the same range as the eighteen already speeding toward the two Allied cruisers. The *Hatakaze* could not launch because a forest of geysers from near misses "blocked her operation."[14] Finally, at 2344, the *Natori* discharged twenty-nine rounds at the *Perth* and contributed four torpedoes. Hara then turned north at 2346, making smoke, and ordered his squadron to concentrate on the *Natori* and reload tubes.[15]

Meanwhile, the Allied cruisers heeled in a hard loop back to the west at 2348 as the Japanese torpedoes began to arrive. The *Perth*'s four turrets fired independently; her four-inch guns spat star shells. An Australian participant recalled, "It was hard for them to tell what they were shooting at." From the *Houston*'s dim shape poured "stream after stream of red and blue and amber tracers."[16] Aboard the *Mikuma*, which was standing to the north, the view appeared much the same: "The enemy ships fired red tracers and machine guns. Those bullets drew red lines in the smoke screen which was lit by flares."[17]

By 2346 Hara's destroyers had cleared the way, permitting the heavy cruisers to engage the enemy ships. The *Mikuma* launched a spotter, and her skipper, Captain Sakiyama, "celebrating that we could finally fire" ordered a torpedo attack. One fish got away, but then "we couldn't fire the second and third torpedoes because the third torpedo had slipped down and landed on the second torpedo."[18] Three minutes after this mishap, however, both cruisers launched full salvos of six torpedoes at a range of 12,000 yards. The *Perth* and *Houston*, much to Sakiyama's annoyance began to target his ships, but most of the Allies' shells fell ahead.

The Japanese cruisers had paravanes deployed, and because this caused a large bow wave, Sakiyama believed Allied spotters overestimated his speed. Then, nearing Babi Island, Sakiyama reversed course to port so as to avoid getting too close to the enemy. A minute later, a shell struck the *Perth* in the ordinary seaman's mess. At 2352 as the Japanese cruisers steadied on their new course, they attacked with their main batteries, using searchlights to direct fire. The *Houston's* gunners latched onto this point of aim and at 2355 hit the *Mikuma*, killing six and wounding eleven men. Shortly thereafter, an electric circuit tripped disabling *Mikuma's* searchlights and silencing her guns.

At this time Waller steered toward St. Nicholaas Point. The *Perth* was down to practice shells, while aboard the *Houston*, a chain of sailors manhandled 260-pound eight-inch shells from the aft magazine forward. As the Allied fire slackened, the *Harukaze* and *Hatakaze* closed, anxious to deliver the torpedo attacks frustrated earlier. At 2356 the *Harukaze* discharged five 21-inch torpedoes, and the *Hatakaze* fired six more two minutes later, bearing southeast at a range of 4,200 yards. The Japanese ships became separated, with the *Harukaze* turning north and the *Hatakaze* turning west. Then, the *Mogami* launched six Long Lances at 2357 from 10,000 yards northeast of the Allied warships. At midnight, the *Mikuma* restored power, and she reported herself ready to attack and sink the enemy.

The Japanese cruisers commenced a heavy bombardment from 10,000 yards. Division 12, meanwhile, had been maneuvering off St. Nicholaas Point, trying to obtain an attack position. At midnight the *Shirakumo* and *Murakumo* each fired nine Type 90 torpedoes set to their maximum speed to the south southeast from only 5,000 yards. The *Natori*, heading north to reload her tubes, caught sight of the *Houston* and engaged from 9,000 yards. Aboard the transports, the second wave of troops began scrambling into boats, anxious to land. A shell slashed by the *Shikinami*, damaging her propeller and reducing her speed to twenty-four knots.

Despite being the target of forty-nine torpedoes, the Allied cruisers remained essentially undamaged after nearly an hour of intense combat. Now, another thirty-five, all launched within four minutes, streaked toward them. Captain Waller, perhaps sensing this danger, decided to force the strait and ordered full speed for Toppers Island beyond St. Nicholaas Point. The *Houston* followed.

At 0005 on 1 March five of the six Long Lances launched by the *Mogami* eight minutes earlier sped past their intended targets at forty-eight knots and boiled into Bantam Bay. A series of simultaneous explosions followed as the fish detonated against the army transports *Sakura Maru* (7,149 gross registered tons [GRT]), *Horai Maru* (9,162 GRT), and *Tatsuno Maru* (6,960 GRT), and the special vessel *Ryujo Maru* (8,160 GRT), which was carrying the headquarters staff of the 16th Army. All sank in shallow water. A fifth Long Lance clobbered the *W2*, and she broke in two. The explosions flung hundred of Japanese troops and sailors into the water to swim for their lives, including General Imamura and his aide.

Even as the explosions ripped the transports, however, a torpedo, possibly from the *Harukaze*, slammed into the *Perth*'s forward engine room, killing all but one of the black gang and reducing the ship's speed. Waller held on, but two minutes later, a second torpedo also struck on the starboard side under the bridge. Two more torpedoes, probably from the *Shirakumo* and *Murakumo*, followed shortly after. These hit the forward magazine and beneath X turret, respectively. The destroyers closed in and swept the now helpless Australian ship with gunfire, slaughtering topside personnel.

The *Perth* rolled to port and plunged to the bottom, bow first, at 0012. Waller and 351 members of his 686 man crew perished that night. Of the survivors, another 103 expired in Japanese hands.

As the *Perth* was being destroyed, Captain Rooks saw that the Japanese had the passage west firmly blocked. He turned back toward the transports and at 0010 his ship suffered her first damage. The *Houston*'s log reads, "First hit . . . was a salvo in Aft Engine Room which burst steam lines, believed killing all personnel within." In the span of just a few minutes the damage quickly accumulated: "Hit on forecastle steel deck and paint locker on fire which continued to burn. Received salvo completely thru wardroom. Turret II hit by dud in face plate just as powder was exposed for loading 28th salvo. . . . Received two torpedo hits to starboard and one to port. . . . First Abandon Ship passed but machine gun nests and some 5-inch crews continued to fire until all ammunition expended."[19]

From the *Mikuma*'s bridge the scene appeared thus: "At 0020, we opened fire. Two shells hit the enemy from 6,500 meters. We kept firing, hitting the target. But after three minutes we had to reverse the course because we were getting close to the shore. After completing a reverse turn, we resumed firing. Her bridge exploded. A huge flame shot out. Everyone on ship was excited to watch the victorious scene."[20]

Rooks ordered his crew to abandon ship at 0025. Five minutes later splinters from a bursting shell cut him down. At 0029 the *Shikinami* fired a final torpedo to finish off the *Houston*. Five minutes later the U.S. cruiser's stern rose into the air, and she slid into the deep. Several witnesses remarked on her colors waving in the glare of Japanese searchlights. Only 368 of Houston's 1,061 men survived.

Speeding north along Sumatra's west coast, the Australian cruiser *Hobart* intercepted a radio message suggesting the *Perth*'s plight, but other than that, both ships simply vanished as far as the Allies were concerned. Of the battle, Admiral Hara made several interesting observations: "It is very difficult in night warfare to judge how the battle situation is, where the main battery shells hit and what damages the torpedoes create due to heavy firing, the water columns by shell, torpedoes hits and enemy firings. Our reports tend to prematurely judge the effectiveness of firing and torpedo hits. They help to encourage our fighting spirit, but at the same time they influence the commander's judgments." He also noted that his destroyers experienced quite a few near misses from the torpedoes fired by Kurita's cruisers, remarking, "We felt very much in danger."[21]

Trailing the ill-fated *Perth* and *Houston*, the *Evertsen*, commanded by Lieutenant Commander W.M. de Vries, cleared Tanjong Priok at 2045 hours. Several hours later the Dutch destroyer saw flashes lighting the sky ahead. De Vries, concluding the cruisers had run into trouble, detoured north, hugging the Sumatran shore. *Evertsen* made it past the narrows, but at 0130 encountered the Japanese destroyers *Murakumo* and *Shirakumo* returning to their patrol area at high speed. One of the destroyers illuminated and fired a broadside to which the *Evertsen* responded by rapidly changing course. The Dutch broke contact briefly, but Japanese shells eventually ignited a large fire. De Vries' ship closed Sumatra as the blaze spread forward, and the Dutch skipper eventually beached the *Evertsen* on a reef near Sebuku Besar. The ship burned until her aft magazine exploded. After several days stranded on the island, the crew passed into captivity.[22]

Action in Bali Strait, 1 March 1942

Even as the *Houston* and *Perth* lay at Batavia before the Battle of Sunda Strait, the flotilla of Java Sea survivors at Surabaja were considering their options. The Bali Strait between Bali and Java lay closest to Surabaja, but Rear Admiral Palliser considered it too shallow for the *Exeter* to traverse. Lombok Strait between Bali and Lombok presented another possibility, but the Japanese held both shores and the *Exeter* could not clear the vicinity before daylight because her previous battle damage reduced her speed. For this reason, Palliser ordered the cruiser to flee via Sunda Strait escorted by the *Encounter*, the *Pope*, which still had twelve torpedoes, and the *Witte de With*.

Palliser reasoned that the cruiser could better avoid detection and an air attack by unexpectedly retreating toward the enemy. Commander Binford, on the other hand, wrangled with Rear Admiral Glassford during the course of 28 February, going so far as to take a taxi into town to use a telephone and ask for permission to lead his composite division in an escape attempt via the Bali Strait. This permission arrived that afternoon, and at 1700 hours on 28 February, after a day punctuated by air attacks and against a backdrop of black smoke, the four Asiatic Fleet veterans filed down Surabaja's winding channel for the last time.

Steaming in column at twenty knots, the Americans slipped into Bali Strait at 0200 on 1 March. "It was rather nerve wracking work entering that narrow one-mile

TABLE 3.2. FORCES ENGAGED IN THE ACTION IN THE BALI STRAIT

	Type of Ship	Year Launched	Displacement, Full Load (tons)	Max. Speed (knots)	Guns (number by inch/caliber)	Torpedoes (number of tubes by diameter in inches)	Damage
U.S. Destroyer Division 58 (Cdr. T.H. Binford)							
John D. Ford (F)	DD	1920	1,308	30	4 x 4/51 & 1 x 3/76.2	12 x 21	
Paul Jones	DD	1920	1,308	30	4 x 4/51 & 1 x 3/76.2	12 x 21	
John D. Edwards	DD	1919	1,308	30	4 x 4/51 & 1 x 3/76.2	12 x 21	
Alden	DD	1919	1,308	30	4 x 4/51 & 1 x 3/76.2	12 x 21	
Japanese Destroyer Division 21 (Captain Shimizu Toshio)							
Hatsuharu (F)	DD	1933	1,802	36	5 x 5/50	9 x 24	
Nenohi	DD	1932	1,802	36	5 x 5/50	9 x 24	
Wakaba	DD	1934	1,802	36	5 x 5/50	9 x 24	
Hatsushimo	DD	1933	1,802	36	5 x 5/50	9 x 24	

DD—destroyer, F—flagship
Time: 0220–0250
Weather: Clear
Visibility: Good, full moon
Sea state: Calm
Surprise: None
Mission: Americans—transit; Japanese—offensive and sea superiority patrol

wide strait as we expected the Japanese would be in it," recalled one officer.[23] Binford hugged the Javanese shore to avoid being silhouetted in the bright moonlight and increased speed to twenty-five knots once his ships emerged from the narrows.

A half hour later, the *John D. Edwards's* lookout reported a ship 8,000 yards off the port bow. The stranger assumed a parallel course and more ships joined her. This group was Japanese Destroyer Division 21, which was patrolling the strait.

After several minutes the Japanese flashed a challenge. When Binford failed to reply, the Japanese engaged from 6,000 yards. This signal Binford did answer, and a brief but intense exchange ensued. The *John D. Edward's* captain recalled, "I guess the Japanese were just as tired as we were because the shooting on both sides was poor."[24]

The ships of U.S. Destroyer Division 58 fled south, breakers on one side, broadsides on the other. At 0233 they ceased fire and made smoke. In just seven minutes the *John D. Edwards* had expended 240 rounds.

Captain Shimizu's guns fell silent a few minutes later. However, the Japanese continued to follow and at 0250 began shooting blindly hoping to provoke a response. The Americans failed to oblige and, as they rounded Java's South Point into the broad waters of the Indian Ocean, the Imperial warships turned back. Destroyer Division 58 made Fremantle, Australia, on 4 March.

Action South of Borneo, 1 March 1942

The *Exeter, Encounter,* and *Pope* weighted anchor two hours after Binford's division did. Emergency repairs had increased the *Exeter's* top speed to sixteen knots. In another example of inter-Allied miscommunication, the *Witte de With's* captain could not collect his crew or get his orders confirmed in time to join the escape attempt. Consequently, the Dutch ship remained at Surabaja to be bombed and scuttled the next day. Other major Dutch vessels lost at Surabaja included the destroyer *Banckert*; the submarines *K-X, K-XIII,* and *K-XVIII*; the minelayers *Soemenep, Bangkalen,* and *Rigel*; and the training ship *Soerabaja*.

A Japanese pilot observed the *Exeter's* departure and alerted Rear Admiral Takagi, whose ships were covering the transports then approaching Kragan. Vice Admiral Takahashi, commanding the with heavy cruisers *Ashigara* and *Myoko* and the destroyers *Akebono* and *Ikazuchi,* also got the word and circled north, thus casting a net across the *Exeter's* every exit.

Through the night the *Exeter* steamed north. At 2300 the British cruiser intercepted a radio message that a "severe sea battle was in progress off entrance to Sunda Strait."[25] Unfortunately, this news did not cause Captain O.L. Gordon of the *Exeter* to reconsider his orders. The morning of 1 March dawned calm and brilliant. The Allied fugitives approached 110 degrees east longitude sixty miles south of Borneo. The empty sea encouraged guarded optimism. But at 0750 the lookout in the crow's nest reported masts to the southwest, which belonged, in fact, to the *Exeter*'s old adversaries, the *Nachi* and *Haguro*.

TABLE 3.3. FORCES ENGAGED IN THE ACTION SOUTH OF BORNEO

	Type of Ship	Year Launched	Displacement, Full Load (tons)	Max. Speed (knots)	Guns (number by inch/caliber)	Torpedoes (number of tubes by diameter in inches)	Damage
Allies (Captain O.L. Gordon)							
Exeter (BR)	CA	1929	11,000	23	6 x 8/50 & 8 x 4/45	6 x 21	Sunk
Encounter (BR)	DD	1934	2,025	36	4 x 4.7/45	8 x 21	Sunk
Pope	DD	1920	1,308	30	4 x 4/51 & 1 x 3/76.2	12 x 21	Sunk
Japanese Support Force 3rd Fleet (Vice Admiral Takahashi Ibo)							
Ashigara (F)	CA	1928	14,743	35	10 x 8/50 & 8 x 5/40	16 x 24	
Myoko	CA	1927	14,743	35	10 x 8/50 & 8 x 5/40	16 x 24	
Akebono	DD	1930	2,389	35	6 x 5/50	9 x 24	
Ikazuchi	DD	1931	2,264	34	6 x 5/50	9 x 24	
Sentai 5 (Rear Admiral Takagi Takeo)							
Nachi (F)	CA	1927	14,743	35	10 x 8/50 & 8 x 5/40	16 x 24	
Haguro	CA	1928	14,743	35	10 x 8/50 & 8 x 5/40	16 x 24	
Destroyer Division 24							
Kawakaze	DD	1936	2,042	34	5 x 5/50	8 x 24	
Yamakaze	DD	1936	2,042	34	5 x 5/50	8 x 24	

BR—British, CA—heavy cruiser, DD—destroyer, F—flagship
  Time: 1010–1435
  Weather: Initially clear and sunny, light SW airs, then scattered squalls
  Visibility: Excellent
  Sea state: Light swell
  Surprise: None
  Mission: Allies—transit; Japanese—offensive and sea superiority patrol

The *Exeter* turned away, hoping that having the advantage of the light meant the enemy had not seen her. The British cruiser was to have no such luck, however. But because his cruisers had expended so much ammunition during the Java Sea battle, Takagi remained over the horizon for the time being. Gordon, his options horribly limited, made a loop to starboard before settling on a westerly course.

Both the seas before her and the *Exeter*'s radar scope remained empty for more than an hour. Then, at 0935 the lookouts again telephoned down bad news: topmasts to the northwest—Takahashi's cruisers and destroyers. Gordon altered course to the north, and Takahashi followed.

The Japanese destroyers closed, and at 1010 the *Encounter* and *Pope* initiated combat against the *Akebono* and *Ikazuchi* with their forward guns. The *Exeter*'s secondary battery joined in, but this combined effort "did no more than raise some splashes near the destroyer. The enemy reversed course and returned our fire with her after guns."[26] Simultaneously, Tanaki's cruisers reappeared to the southwest. The Japanese admirals had boxed Gordon in.

The *Exeter* came hard to starboard and fled east, with her destroyer escorts conforming. The engineering department's strenuous efforts had improved the British cruiser's speed to twenty-three knots on four boilers, but this was ten knots slower than her pursuers.

At 1020 Takahashi's cruisers opened fire from 25,000 yards as an aircraft circled overhead spotting salvos. The *Exeter* replied immediately. However, a mechanism in her fire control table failed, and the *Exeter*'s initial broadsides fell well out for line. In the action that developed the *Ashigara* and *Myoko* followed on the *Exeter*'s port quarter firing freely, while the *Nachi* and *Haguro* paced the British cruiser on her starboard beam conserving ammunition. Both groups of Japanese cruisers maintained a distance of roughly 18,000 yards.

The *Akebono* and *Ikazuchi* ducked behind the Allied ships and followed on a parallel course. The *Yamakaze* and *Kawakaze* edged north of the *Nachi* on the same heading but stayed south of the *Akebono* and *Ikazuchi*. Thus, the Japanese pursued in four two-ship columns, one of heavy cruisers to the north and the others south of their quarry.

The *Encounter* and *Pope* kept station off the British cruiser's port quarter. After a few minutes, when he saw that the Japanese gunners were getting the range, the *Pope*'s Lt. Cdr. W.C. Blinn made smoke. The *Encounter*'s Lieutenant Commander Morgan immediately followed suit, and the enemy bombardment slackened. The *Pope* then sped to a position off the *Exeter*'s port bow, avoiding salvos from the Japanese ships. The *Encounter* followed 3,000 yards off the cruiser's port quarter. All the Allied ships wove to confuse the enemy's aim.

Up to this point, neither side had suffered any damage, but with the Japanese gradually pinching the slower Allied column, this situation could not continue.

The *Exeter* began with her magazines only 20 percent full. The *Encounter* had no torpedoes, and Gordon could only hope for a lucky blow to reduce the odds against him. Accordingly, at 1100 when the *Ashigara* presented a long-range torpedo target, he emptied his port side tubes at her. He ordered Blinn to do the same and the destroyer flung two torpedoes at a range of 7,000 yards. Then the sight of rain squalls ahead offered a fugitive hope of cover. Fighting conservatively Takahashi evaded the torpedoes by making a tight 360-degree circle, while at 1115 the *Nachi* and *Haguro* finally opened fire from 17,000 yards.

Maneuvering through hanging smoke and splashes from Japanese shells, the *Pope* launched four more torpedoes at the *Ashigara*, cut ahead of the *Exeter*, and then emptied five tubes at the *Nachi*. Blinn remembered, "During this critical stage, all enemy ships closed determinedly and each vessel came under severe fire from several enemy ships. *Exeter* zigzagged right and left, firing alternately at both formations, only partly obscured by smoke."[27]

Then, the *Akebono* and *Ikazuchi* closed, and the Allied destroyers engaged them, supported by the *Exeter*'s four-inch guns. The battle was nearing a climax. At 1119 the *Kawakaze* fired two torpedoes. The *Nachi* and *Haguro* followed these with four each at 1120 and 1122, respectively, and the *Yamakaze* contributed four more at 1121. All these torpedoes proved academic, however, because at 1120 an eight-inch shell finally struck the *Exeter*. Like the blow two days before, it exploded in a boiler room, but with even graver results. A crewman painted the scene this way: "The main steam line was again penetrated and from it gushed the superheated contents. Fires broke out in the ship. We felt way come off . . . as the engines slowed and one by one the electric breakers 'fell off the board.'"[28]

Guns askew and emitting a column of gray smoke, the veteran British cruiser gradually slowed to four knots as eight-inch shells continued to rain down. Gordon ordered the destroyers to run for it. Closest to the enemy, the *Encounter* attracted the most fire. At 1135 a splinter fractured a suction pipe on the British destroyer and disabled the forced lubrication system. Bearings overheated, and the ventilation system sucked smoke into the engine room, forcing its evacuation. His ship thus immobilized, Lieutenant Commander Morgan ordered the *Encounter* scuttled and the crew over the side.

While the *Myoko*, *Ashigara*, and *Ikazuchi* continued to pump torpedoes at the stricken British ships, the *Pope* raced for the weather dead ahead. At about 1200, making smoke and chasing salvos, Blinn ducked into a rainsquall. Up to this point the U.S. destroyer had expended 345 four-inch shells and eleven torpedoes.

The *Nachi* and *Haguro* ceased fire at 1145 after shooting off 170 and 118 eight-inch rounds, respectively. With the *Exeter* slowly heeling and still under heavy fire, Gordon decided to speed the inevitable and ordered the flood valves opened. The crew was abandoning ship when the *Ikazuchi* finally scored with a Type 90 torpedo—the only one of twenty-five launched during the battle that hit. The *Exeter* capsized at 1200, and the *Encounter* followed her to the bottom five minutes later. Takahashi's ships rescued 651 men from the *Exeter* and 149 from the *Encounter*. In an hour and forty-five minutes of combat, the *Myoko* and *Ashigara* expended 1,171 eight-inch rounds.

The squall the *Pope* had steamed into had rain "so heavy that it was impossible to see more than fifty yards."[29] Her crew used the respite to lug ammunition to the forward magazines and secure damage from a collapsed firewall. A shell had partially carried away the main antenna, but *Pope* remained otherwise unharmed.

The U.S. destroyer emerged from a second squall at around 1230. Times were uncertain because "all chronometers were greatly in error as a result of shock of continuous gunfire."[30] Blinn resolved to head for Borneo and then swing south and enter Lombok Strait after dark. However, dusk remained six hours off, and, as the *Pope* steered northeast under skies now pitilessly clear, a Type 0, or "Pete," spotter plane from the *Chitose* droned into view. Eventually, ten Petes congregated, and at 1300 they attacked, one after the other, with 132-pound bombs.

The *Pope* fought back with her three-inch high-angle gun until it jammed after firing seventy-five rounds, leaving her just her four World War I–era Lewis guns for self-defense. Bomb fragments from a near miss damaged the range finder and wounded two men. On the last attack another near miss holed the destroyer and knocked her port propeller shaft out of line.

Then, six of the *Ruyko*'s Type 97 bombers—"Kates"—arrived. Beginning at 1335 the bombers dropped six 550-pound and twenty-four 132-pound bombs. Sluggish to the helm, settling aft, and running on only one propeller, the *Pope* still avoided every bomb. However, Blinn's ship was clearly doomed, and the captain ordered two scuttling charges set as the crew took to the destroyer's whaleboat and rafts.

Shortly after, the charges exploded, and as the boat and rafts were pulling away, the *Myoko* and *Ashigara* arrived to seal the valiant destroyer's doom with a few eight-inch broadsides. The *Pope* sank at 1420—the last Allied warship in the Java Sea. All but one of her 151 men survived to be rescued two days later by a Japanese destroyer. The ship's gunnery officer, a prewar language student in Tokyo, knew the destroyer's captain.[31] The Japanese sailors treated the *Pope*'s men well, but twenty-seven died later in captivity.

To sink the three Allied fugitives off of Borneo, the Japanese expended 2,650 shells and twenty-five torpedoes. But even if Captain Gordon's squadron had escaped into the Indian Ocean, it is unlikely they would have found refuge.

The *Edsall* versus Battleships, 1 March 1942

The U.S. destroyers *Edsall* and *Whipple* rescued *Langley*'s survivors on the afternoon of 27 February. They transferred these men to the navy oiler *Pecos* south of Christmas Island, itself about 260 miles southeast of Tjilatjap, on the morning of 1 March. Symbolic of the Navy's confused priorities, Rear Admiral Glassford ordered the *Edsall* to embark the thirty-two army pilots and mechanics and deliver them to Tjilatjap.[32] At 0830 hours on the morning of 1 March, the *Edsall* duly headed north northeast for Java while the *Whipple* steered toward the Cocos Islands to the west and the *Pecos* turned south for Australia, crammed with more than seven hundred men.

TABLE 3.4. FORCES ENGAGED WHEN THE *EDSALL* ENCOUNTERED BATTLESHIPS

	Type of Ship	Year Launched	Displacement, Full Load (tons)	Max. Speed (knots)	Guns (number by inch/caliber)	Torpedoes (number of tubes by diameter in inches)	Damage
Edsall (Lt. Joshua Nix)	DD	1920	1,308	30	4 x 4/51 & 1 x 3/76.2	12 x 21	Sunk
Japanese Sentai 3 (Vice Admiral Mikawa Gunichi)							
Hiei	BB	1912	36,600	30	8 x 14/45 & 14 x6/50		
Kirishima	BB	1913	36,600	30	8 x 14/45 & 14x 6/50		
Sentai 8 (Rear Admiral Abe Hiroaki)							
Chikuma	CA	1938	15,200	35	8 x 8/50 & 8 x 5/40	12 x 24	
Tone	CA	1937	15,200	35	8 x 8/50 & 8 x 5/40	12 x 24	

BB—battleship, CA—heavy cruiser, DD—destroyer
   1600–1730
   Weather: Clear, some mist, light southeasterly breeze
   Visibility: Extreme
   Sea state: Rough
   Surprise: Japanese
   Mission: Americans—transit; Japanese—offensive and sea superiority patrol

Aircraft from Vice Admiral Nagumo's carrier force, steaming only eighty miles to the east, spotted the oiler just a few hours later. Four squadrons of Type 99, or "Val," dive bombers attacked the *Pecos* over a period of five hours and finally sank her at 1546 about 240 miles south of Christmas Island. Only 233 men survived to eventually be rescued by the *Whipple*.

Meanwhile, the *Edsall*, commanded by Lt. Joshua Nix, had turned away from Java, probably responding to the distressed oiler's SOS. Nix's route led him some thirty miles astern of Nagumo's carriers and even closer to *Sentai* 3. Inevitably, a Japanese aircraft spotted the destroyer.

At 1558 Nagumo ordered Vice Admiral Mikawa to attack the "*Marblehead*-type" light cruiser just reported astern of his force. The *Hiei* sighted the *Edsall* immediately after and reversed course as Nix hauled off north by northeast, spreading smoke along his track. The *Chikuma* opened fire at 1602 from 23,000 yards.

At 1617 the *Hiei* and *Kirishima* joined the action after launching three floatplanes for spotting. The battleships flung their fourteen-inch shells from nearly 30,000 yards, but "the enemy ship took evasive tactics, every other minute, and skillfully created a smoke screen so a strike could not be achieved."[33]

At 1626 the *Edsall* charged the *Chikuma*, shot several salvos from her four-inch guns, and then ducked away into her own smoke. A rainsquall forced a lull, but when it passed, all four Japanese ships resumed their bombardment, with the *Tone* engaging at 1645 from 25,000 yards.

Nix continued to vary his speed and maneuver radically; nonetheless, the *Hiei* finally claimed a hit at 1654, and the *Tone* scored another at 1705. Moreover, seventeen Vals attacked beginning at 1657. They landed several bombs on the U.S. destroyer, sparking a large fire and damaging the *Edsall*'s machinery. As the destroyer slowed, the four Japanese warships closed and pounded her with their secondary batteries. The *Edsall* capsized at 1731, eighty-four minutes into the one-sided combat. The battleships fired 297 fourteen-inch and 132 six-inch shells while the cruisers expended 844 eight-inch and 62 five-inch rounds—totals worthy of a major sea battle. The Japanese rescued about forty *Edsall* crewmembers, most of whom were apparently beheaded at Kendari shortly after being brought ashore.[34] No one from the *Edsall*'s brave crew survived the war.

Pillsbury versus Cruisers, 2 March 1942

By the morning of 1 March Vice Admiral Helfrich finally conceded that Tjilatjap could not serve as a rallying point for continued naval resistance and issued permission for a general evacuation. The resulting exodus included the USS *Pillsbury*, USS *Asheville*, USS *Tulsa*, and the American armed yacht *Isabel*. However, Helfrich's painful decision did most of these ships little good.

Scouring the sea lanes south of Tjilatjap, Vice Admiral Kondo's surface strike force sank the Dutch motorship *Toradja* (981 tons) and the British auxiliary minesweeper *Scott Harley* (620 tons) and captured the Dutch steamship *Bintoehan* (1,020 tons). Then, on 2 March Japanese flyers reported bigger game 300 miles south of Bali. The *Maya, Arashi,* and *Nowaki* set off in pursuit and overhauled the British destroyer *Stronghold* at 1743 hours. After expending 635 eight-inch rounds and 290 and 345 five-inch rounds, respectively, the *Maya, Arashi,* and *Nowaki* sank the old British warship.

TABLE 3.5. FORCES ENGAGED WHEN THE *PILLSBURY* WAS SURPRISED AT SEA

	Type of Ship	Year Launched	Displacement, Full Load (tons)	Max. Speed (knots)	Guns (number by inch/caliber)	Torpedoes (number of tubes by diameter in inches)	Damage
Pillsbury (Lt. Cdr. H.C. Pound)	DD	1920	1,308	30	4 x 4/51 & 1 x 3	12 x 21	Sunk
Sentai 4 (Vice Admiral Kondo Nobutake)							
Atago (F)	CA	1938	15,738	34	8 x 8/50 & 4 x 4.7/45	8 x 24	
Takao	CA	1937	15,738	34	8 x 8/50 & 4 x 4.7/45	8 x 24	

CA—heavy cruiser, DD—destroyer, F— flagship
  Time: 2036–2055
  Weather: Unknown
  Visibility: Unknown
  Sea state: Unknown
  Surprise: Japanese
  Mission: Americans—transit; Japanese—interception based on specific intelligence

The *Atago* and *Takeo*, acting on the same report and expecting to find a *Marblehead*-type cruiser, hurried southeast at twenty-six knots and at 2036 spotted a silhouette 20,000 yards away, approaching them from the northeast. The *Pillsbury* maintained course, while the Japanese cruisers swung east and crossed in front of her. When the *Pillsbury* became aware of her danger, she turned west, but it was too late.

The *Atago* opened fire at 2055, just 6,000 yards south of her target using star shells to illuminate. The U.S. destroyer replied with her aft mounts, but "the shells hit nowhere near."[35] In just seven minutes of swift execution, the *Atago* and *Takeo* scored fatal hits, respectively expending 54 and 112 eight-inch rounds in the process.

The *Pillsbury* sank without survivors some five hundred-fifty miles southeast of Tjilatjap.

Asheville versus Destroyers, 3 March 1942

The exodus from Tjilatjap included the *Asheville*, an old gunboat that showed the U.S. flag in China for many years. Friendly ships passed the *Asheville* on 2 March. The next news of her came on the morning of 3 March, when the minesweeper USS *Whippoorwill* and the *Isabel* picked up a distress call that the gunboat was under attack.

At 0906 hours while sailing west 160 miles southwest of Bali, the Japanese destroyers *Arashi* and *Nowaki* encountered the gunboat, opened fire from 9,200 yards, and sank her in slightly over a half hour. The Japanese rescued one American crewman, but he did not survive the war.

TABLE 3.6. FORCES ENGAGED WHEN THE *ASHEVILLE* WAS ATTACKED

	Type of Ship	Year Launched	Displacement, Full Load (tons)	Max. Speed (knots)	Guns (number by inch/caliber)	Torpedoes (number of tubes by diameter in inches)	Damage
Asheville (Lt. Jacob W. Britt)	GB	1918	1,760	12	3 x 4/51		Sunk
Japanese Destroyer Division 4 (Captain Aruga Kosaku)							
Arashi	DD	1940	2,490	35	6 x 5/50	8 x 24	
Nowaki	DD	1940	2,490	35	6 x 5/50	8 x 24	

DD—destroyer, GB—gunboat
  Time: 0906–0936
  Weather: Unknown
  Visibility: Unknown
  Sea state: Unknown
  Surprise: Unknown
  Mission: Americans—transit; Japanese—offensive and sea superiority patrol

On the morning of 4 March 280 miles south southeast of Tjilatjap, Kondo's reunited force of the *Atago, Takao, Maya, Arashi*, and *Nowaki* eliminated an entire convoy escorted by the Australian sloop *Yarra*. In total, Nagumo and Kondo sank twenty ships at sea and another seventeen off of Tjilatjap. Thirteen vessels successfully escaped Java: the U.S. Navy's *Whipple, Parrott, Tulsa,* and *Isabel,* the Australian sloop *Warrego,* six Australian corvettes, a Dutch merchant ship, and the American *Sea Witch.*

By 4 March 1942 it seemed the fortunes of the U.S. Navy had reached their nadir. Committed to a losing campaign and honor bound to see it through, the Navy had experienced a stinging series of apparently one-sided defeats unequaled by any in its history. Despite the ease of these Japanese victories, however, signs existed that not all was right with the Imperial war machine and not all was wrong with the American one.

First, the Japanese accepted unnecessary risks. The Eastern Invasion Fleet advanced exposed to interception by a powerful force while Nagumo's carriers sailed far to the south to reap the fruits of a victory yet to happen. The Japanese surface forces exhibited poor marksmanship at the Battle of the Java Sea and against the *Exeter, Edsall,* and *Stronghold.* The results achieved by torpedoes, the chosen "decisive weapon," were disappointing considering numbers fired and prewar expectations. At Sunda Strait, fighting in the type of action that was supposed to be a Japanese specialty, Allied warships maneuvered mostly undamaged for more than an hour, dodging several major torpedo attacks. Obviously, realistic training was one thing, but battle execution was quite another.

The U.S. Navy, meanwhile, demonstrated it would fight regardless of the odds, regardless of the hope for victory, regardless of whether its battles would ever be known. These qualities would be needed in the months to come.

CHAPTER 4

Faltering Counteroffensive: Guadalcanal, August–October 1942

Victory rides with the first effective salvo.
—REAR ADM. ARTHUR J. HEPBURN

The futile campaign to defend Java ended on 9 March 1942. Five months passed before surface units of the U.S. and Japanese navies fought again. In the interim Imperial carriers ravaged the Indian Ocean in April, sinking a British flattop, a pair of heavy cruisers, five other warships, and twenty-three merchant vessels, all at the cost of just seventeen aircraft. In May, however, opposing carriers fought to a stalemate in the Battle of the Coral Sea, and in June the U.S. Navy won a great victory at Midway, sinking four large Japanese carriers while losing one.

On several occasions between April and June, the two sides nearly came to blows on the surface as well. During the Coral Sea battle a combined American and Australian cruiser force sortied to intercept the enemy convoy bound for Port Moresby, New Guinea. The Allied ships survived four strikes by Japanese Nell (G3M) and Betty (G4M2-J) bombers, and one by friendly B-26s, without sustaining damage only to find the invasion force had turned back. At Midway, Admiral Yamamoto considered a night surface action, but elected to withdraw instead.

The U.S. Navy's victory at Midway did not put an end to Japan's offensive plans, however. Imperial forces occupied Tulagi in May and Guadalcanal in June 1942 to protect the flank of their advance against Port Moresby and their bastion at Rabaul. On 23 June Admiral King, wishing to exploit Midway before the Japanese regained momentum, ordered Admiral Nimitz to seize Tulagi. The men on the spot, Vice Adm. Robert L. Ghormley, commander South Pacific Area, and Gen. Douglas MacArthur, Southwest Area commander, sought to postpone this thrust due to lack of strength and insufficient logistics. Also, Ghormley had only been on the job for six days. These objections merely provoked King's ire, and the operation was ordered to move forward.

As the Americans struggled to improvise an offensive, 2,000 Japanese construction troops roughly finished an airfield on Guadalcanal. The 8th Fleet at Rabaul wanted to base land attack planes there immediately, but the 11th Air Fleet begged off claiming inadequate strength.

On the morning of 7 August 1942 the matter became academic when an Allied fleet appeared in Savo Sound and began landing elements of the 1st Marine Division on the islands of Guadalcanal, Tulagi, and Gavutu-Tanambogo. Ghormley remained at his headquarters in Nouméa, New Caledonia, delegating command of the Allied attack force to Vice Adm. Frank Jack Fletcher, the victor of Coral Sea and Midway. Fletcher's air support force was commanded by Rear Adm. Leigh Noyes and included three carriers, a fast battleship, five heavy cruisers, a light cruiser, and sixteen destroyers. Rear Adm. Richmond Kelly Turner commanded the amphibious force, which consisted of nineteen transports, four destroyer transports (APDs), and five destroyer minesweepers (DMSs). Turner's screen, commanded by British Rear Admiral Victor Crutchley, included six heavy cruisers, four light cruisers, and fifteen destroyers.

When King assigned him the job of amphibious commander for the South Pacific, Turner protested he knew nothing about amphibious warfare. To this, King replied, "You will learn."[1] When it came to this type of operation, everyone was an amateur, and the commanders naturally focused on what they knew best.

As the Marines landed the Japanese construction troops, leavened with a few companies of naval infantry, fled for the hills. The 350 naval troops on tiny Tulagi enjoyed no such option and fought to the death—a two-day process that delayed U.S. unloading operations.

During the single planning session held by the top commanders, Turner optimistically estimated he could empty the transports within 3 days, or D plus 3, of the landing. Fletcher, who flew his flag aboard the *Saratoga*, was concerned that covering a landing operation put the Pacific Fleet's three heavy carriers in jeopardy, and he advised that it was his intention to withdraw the carriers prior to this day. In the event, Fletcher sought Ghormley's permission to withdraw at 1807 on D plus 1 because the carrier air groups had lost twenty fighters, fuel for the task force was becoming a concern, and the presence of enemy planes seemed threatening although the Japanese had, as yet, failed to spot the flattops.

If Turner was learning how to be an amphibious commander, Fletcher knew how to be a carrier commander. In concentrating on this aspect of his responsibilities, he demonstrated insufficient concern for the landing operation's progress. Communications between the two admirals were poor, and Fletcher did not know how far behind schedule Turner had fallen. But Fletcher's responsibilities included the entire operation, not just the covering force. Fletcher, or even better Ghormley, could have led the operation more effectively on the spot than from a distant flattop maintaining radio silence. A shortage of experienced carrier commanders in the South Pacific may have dictated Fletcher's presence aboard the *Saratoga*, and, if so, Ghormley expected Fletcher to wear too many hats.

MAP 4.1. GUADALCANAL, AUGUST–OCTOBER 1942

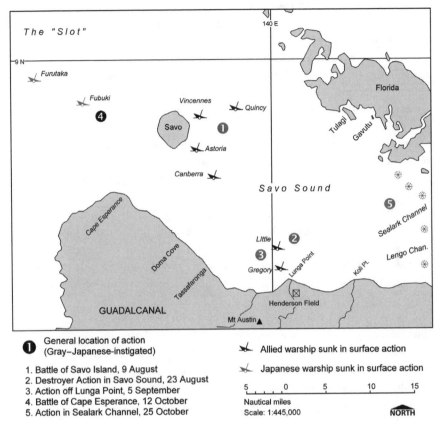

1. General location of action (Gray–Japanese-instigated)

1. Battle of Savo Island, 9 August
2. Destroyer Action in Savo Sound, 23 August
3. Action off Lunga Point, 5 September
4. Battle of Cape Esperance, 12 October
5. Action in Sealark Channel, 25 October

Allied warship sunk in surface action
Japanese warship sunk in surface action

5   0   5   10   15
Nautical miles
Scale: 1:445,000   NORTH

As the carriers headed south, a stunned Turner, left to the protection of Crutchley's cruisers and destroyers, continued unloading while calling a conference to consider the new situation (see Map 4.1).[2]

At Rabaul the first report of invasion—"Tulagi being heavily bombarded from air and sea"—electrified Japanese headquarters when it arrived at 0630. Just ninety-five minutes later an ominous final message stated, "The enemy force is overwhelming. We will defend our position to the death."[3] Although ignorant of American intentions and strength, the Southeast Area command reacted swiftly. A strong air strike winged south at 0930, and by 1000 Vice Admiral Mikawa Gumichi, the new 8th Fleet commander, decided to mount a surface attack. He ordered his flagship, the *Chokai*, and the four heavy cruisers of *Sentai* 6 at Kavieng to weigh anchor along with *Sentai* 18's two light cruisers at Rabaul. The destroyer-transport *Yunagi* tagged along. When leaving Rabaul's Simpson Harbor aboard the *Chokai*, Captain Ohmae Toshikazu, an 8th Fleet staff officer, recalled, "It was a fine clear day, the sea like a mirror. Our confidence of success in the coming night battle was manifest in the cheerful atmosphere on the bridge."[4]

Crutchley's amphibious support group spent much of the first forty-eight hours of the Guadalcanal invasion at action stations, conducting anti-submarine patrols and repelling several air attacks, one of which damaged the American destroyer *Jarvis* and transport *George F. Elliott*. Meanwhile, Mikawa steamed south. Although Allied pilots spotted the Japanese ships several times, a sorry litany of circumstances involving divided command, misinterpretations, inaccurate and delayed sighting reports, miscommunications, and faulty assumptions left the Allied commanders confident they would not face any opposition during their second night off the island.[5]

Crutchley, a British officer assigned to the Australian navy, a World War I Victoria Cross winner, and skipper of HMS *Warspite* at the Second Battle of Narvik, was Turner's second in command. The hurried nature of the operation precluded the development of a common doctrine and left time for only one landing exercise. In deploying his warships Crutchley calculated that he needed to guard two transport groups that were open to three avenues of approach and subject to threats from submarines, coastal craft, surface warships, and aircraft. He thus established seven semiautonomous groups. The destroyers *Henley* and *Ellet* screened the five Tulagi transports, accompanied by the APDs *Colhoun*, *Little*, and *McKean*. The destroyers *Selfridge*, *Mugford*, and *Dewey* and five DMSs—the *Trever*, *Hopkins*, *Zane*, *Southard*, and *Hovey*—guarded thirteen transports anchored off Lunga Point. Rear Adm. Norman Scott covered the eastern channels with the light cruisers *San Juan* and HMAS *Hobart* and the destroyers *Monssen* and *Buchanan*. The heavy cruisers *Vincennes*, *Quincy*, and *Astoria*, screened by the destroyers *Helm* and *Wilson*, patrolled the channel north of Savo, while Crutchley kept the heavy cruisers HMAS *Australia*, HMAS *Canberra*, and *Chicago* and the destroyers *Bagley* and *Patterson* astride the south channel. Two detached destroyers, the *Blue* and the *Ralph Talbot*, acted as nautical trip wires west and northwest of Savo. This arrangement seemed to work fine through the long, but quiet night of 7–8 August.

On the evening of 8 August Turner learned of Fletcher's request to withdraw the carriers, and at 2037 Turner called a conference with Crutchley and the U.S. Marine commander Maj. Gen. Alexander A. Vandegrift aboard his flagship, the transport *McCawley*, to discuss the situation. Rather than take a barge, Crutchley hauled the *Australia* out of line, leaving Capt. Howard Bode of the *Chicago* in tactical command of the southern group. Crutchley did not inform Capt. Frederick Riefkohl of the *Vincennes*, who was commander of the northern group, nor Admiral Scott of his whereabouts.

When he boarded the *McCawley* Vandegrift observed that "while he felt exhausted, the two sailors looked ready to pass out."[6] Turner had decided, much to Vandegrift's distress, to withdraw the transports at 0600 the next morning. The leaders also discussed an ambiguous and fragmentary sighting report received two hours before of three cruisers, three destroyers, and two seaplane tenders or gunboats heading north northeast 300 miles north of their position. Both Turner and Crutchley inferred that the Japanese intended to establish a seaplane base well north of their position. As Turner wrote, "I didn't think 3 Jap cruisers and 3 destroyers would come to Guadalcanal and attack our 7 cruisers and 25 destroyers and I didn't think any seaplane tenders would be sticking their nose up close to our carriers."[7]

As the Allied leaders conferred, Mikawa steamed south at high speed. His ships jettisoned all flammables and hoisted long white banners to assist identification. Beginning at 2300 they catapulted three planes to scout the target area. The Japanese captains had several hours to digest their simple battle plan: "We will penetrate south of Savo Island and torpedo the enemy main force at Guadalcanal. Thence we will move toward the forward area at Tulagi and strike with torpedoes and gunfire, after which we will withdraw to the north of Savo Island."[8]

Battle of Savo Island, 9 August 1942

It was 0115 when Crutchley boarded the *Australia* after the conference. Rather than return to station, he decided to patrol northeast of Lunga Point. Again, he did not communicate this decision to Turner or his subordinates. The Japanese, proceeding in a column consisting of the *Chokai* followed by the *Aoba*, *Kako*, *Kinugasa*, *Furutaka*, *Tenryu*, *Yubari*, and *Yunagi*, sighted Savo Island at 0040. Four minutes later an outlook shouted, "Ship approaching, thirty degrees starboard."[9] This was the *Blue*, one of the Allied picket destroyers. Dozens of Japanese guns trained around, and then, unexpectedly, the *Blue* reversed course and proceeded away at twelve knots. The Americans believed nothing could slip past their SC radar, but they obviously remained unpracticed in its use and limitations.

Mikawa altered course to port, intending to pass north of Savo instead of south as originally planned. But, as Captain Ohmae recalled, "in almost the same instant, and before we could fully appreciate our good fortune, another lookout reported: 'Ship sighted, twenty degrees port.'"[10] This was either the second Allied lookout destroyer, the *Ralph Talbot*, steaming away from the Japanese column or a schooner the Americans had previously reported in the area. In any case Mikawa came to starboard, and his long column filed between the two contacts.

The failure of the picket destroyers to sight the approaching Japanese ships was just one in a series of lapses. Around midnight Japanese floatplanes began buzzing Savo Sound. Many Allied ships noticed them, and the *Ralph Talbot* even broadcast an alarm. When Turner did not confirm the alert, however, individual ships assumed the planes must be friendly. One even showed running lights. This general lack of curiosity reflected a state of exhaustion. As one participant wrote three days later, "The prolonged periods spent at action stations, day and night, with very little rest coupled with mental strain … waiting for enemy air attacks and submarine and surface ship attacks, were calculated at times to produce a feeling of lassitude, both mental and physical."[11]

TABLE 4.1. FORCES ENGAGED IN THE BATTLE OF SAVO ISLAND

	Type of Ship	Year Launched	Displacement, Full Load (tons)	Max. Speed (knots)	Guns (number by inch/caliber)	Torpedoes (number of tubes by diameter in inches)	Damage
Allied Southern group (Capt. H. Bode)							
Chicago (F)	CA	1930	11,420	32	9 x 8/55 & 8 x 5/25		D2
Canberra (AU)	CA	1927	14,190	31	8 x 8/50 & 4 x 4/45	8 x 21	Sunk
Patterson	DD	1937	2,245	38	4 x 5/38	16 x 21	
Bagley	DD	1937	2,245	38	4 x 5/38	16 x 21	
Allied Northern group (Capt. F. Riefkohl)							
Vincennes (F)	CA	1936	12,463	32	9 x 8/55 & 8 x 5/25		Sunk
Astoria	CA	1933	12,463	32	9 x 8/55 & 8 x 5/25		Sunk
Quincy	CA	1935	12,463	32	9 x 8/55 & 8 x 5/25		Sunk
Helm	DD	1937	2,245	38	4 x 5/38	16 x 21	
Wilson	DD	1937	2,245	38	4 x 5/38	16 x 21	
Picket ships							
Blue	DD	1937	2,245	38	4 x 5/38	16 x 21	

Ralph Talbot	DD	1936	2,245	38	4 x 5/38	16 x 21	D3
Japanese 8th Fleet (Vice Admiral Mikawa Gumichi)							
Chokai (F)	CA	1931	14,604	34	10 x 8/50 & 8 x 5/40	16 x 24	D2
Japanese Sentai 6 (Rear Admiral Goto Aritomo)							
Aoba (F)	CA	1926	10,651	33	6 x 8/50 & 4 x 4.7/45	8 x 24	D1
Kinugasa	CA	1926	10,651	33	6 x 8/50 & 4 x 4.7/45	8 x 24	D1
Furutaka	CA	1925	10,341	33	6 x 8/50 & 4 x 4.7/45	8 x 24	
Kako	CA	1925	10,341	33	6 x 8/50 & 4 x 4.7/45	8 x 24	
Japanese Sentai 18 (Rear Admiral Matsuyama Mitsuhara)							
Tenryu	CL	1918	4,350	33	4 x 5.5/50 & 1 x 3.1/40	6 x 21	D1
Yubari	CL	1923	4,400	34	6 x 5.5/50 & 1 x 3.1/40	4 x 24	D1
Yunagi (attached)	APD	1924	1,553	35	3 x 4.7/50	4 x 21	

APD—destroyer transport, AU—Australian, CA—heavy cruiser, CL—light cruiser, D1—light or superficial damage (including splinter damage), D2—moderate damage (combat ability not significantly impaired), D3—significant damage (combat and/or maneuvering ability somewhat impaired), DD—destroyer, F—flagship

Time: 0125–0223
Weather: Overcast, light northeasterly airs, intermitted rain squalls
Visibility: Variable, generally fair
Sea state: Smooth
Surprise: Japanese
Mission: Allies—amphibious attack; Japanese—beachhead attack

At 0133 the *Chokai* passed southwest of Savo Island and emerged from a heavy cloud bank, a shadow against the island's dark mass (see Map 4.2). One minute later the Japanese heavy cruiser passed the previously damaged American destroyer *Jarvis* bound for an Australian dockyard. It seemed incredible to Mikawa and his staff that the enemy, within "easy gun and torpedo range" failed to respond. Some of the Japanese officers suspected the Americans were luring them into an ambush.[12] Despite the urgings of his officers, Mikawa held fire, although the *Furutaka* could not resist sneaking four torpedoes toward the *Jarvis*, all of which missed.

MAP 4.2. BATTLE OF SAVO ISLAND, 9 AUGUST 1942

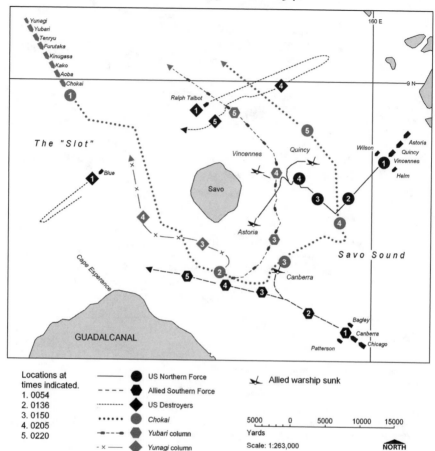

At 0136 the *Chokai's* lookouts reported more silhouettes against the clear horizon off the starboard bow at a range of 12,500 yards. These belonged to the *Patterson* and *Bagley*, which were leading the *Canberra* and *Chicago*. Then, at 0138 the *Chokai* launched four down-the-throat torpedoes at the *Canberra*, perhaps expecting the enemy would turn to unmask batteries and thus present a broadside target. Meanwhile, the *Yunagi* left formation to attack the *Jarvis*, which was passing the Japanese column 3,000 yards to port.[13]

Mikawa continued to hold fire. The trailing cruisers also waited. This was Japanese night attack doctrine being applied offensively for the first time: "At the command ("all forces attack"), the night combat forces would work together in an all-out assault, guided by aircraft reports of enemy movement, parachute flares above the enemy capital ships, and floating flares dropped ahead of the enemy course. Within a few moments of this order, the mass of torpedoes fired earlier would . . . begin to explode against the hulls of the enemy."[14]

As torpedoes smacked the water, the *Chokai*'s farseeing lookouts reported more shapes 18,000 yards to the northeast. This was the *Vincennes* group. At 0140 the *Chokai* swung 30 degrees to port, straight for the transports, crossing the *Canberra*'s bow.

At 0143 the scales fell from the eyes of the *Patterson*'s lookouts, revealing the enemy just a few thousand yards ahead. The American destroyer immediately broadcast, "Warning—Warning: Strange Ships Entering Harbor!"[15] Simultaneously, the Japanese floatplanes dropped intensely brilliant, blue-white flares, silhouetting the Allied cruisers.

The *Canberra*'s first intimation of danger was a distant explosion, probably one of the *Furutaka*'s torpedoes detonating prematurely. As the Japanese ship emerged from the mist to the north, Captain F.E. Getting and other officers hurried to the bridge. They saw torpedoes tracks streaking toward them fine on the port bow, and Getting ordered "hard a'starboard full ahead!" Orange-red flashes signified an enemy salvo. The sound arrived almost simultaneously, and the shells, fired from just 4,500 yards, followed within seconds. Explosions rocked the *Canberra*'s bridge and engine spaces. "Steam pressure to all units and in both engine rooms, failed; and simultaneously all lights dimmed and died," recalled the cruiser's engineer commander.[16] Getting fell, mortally wounded.

Following up the *Chokai*'s salvo, the *Furutaka* opened fire from 9,000 yards within a half minute and launched four torpedoes. At 0144 the *Aoba*'s guns rang in from 5,500 yards, and she contributed three more torpedoes. The *Kako* joined the slaughter at 0146. By 0150 twenty-four 8-inch shells had ripped the Australian cruiser, and she listed dead in the water, ablaze from stem to stern.[17]

As the night erupted in thunder and fire, the *Patterson* rang up full speed, turned to port, and fired star shells. She had a good torpedo setup against the *Furutaka*. Cdr. Frank R. Walker, the *Patterson*'s skipper, ordered torpedoes away, but nothing happened. Either the din drowned out his orders, or the torpedo officer arrived on station late. The American destroyer's five-inch guns began thumping shells, but almost immediately an enemy round exploded astern, igniting a large fire and disabling mounts 3 and 4.

At 0150 the Americans scored a hit on the *Yubari*. The shell penetrated from frame 70 but failed to explode.[18] The *Patterson* looped around to the southeast and started heading northeast, keeping between the enemy and the Allied transports. Walker was one of the few Allied captains to respond appropriately that night. The *Bagley*'s commander, Lt. Cdr. George A. Sinclair, on the other hand, swung sharply to port and attempted a torpedo salvo, but the ship lost position before she could fire. The *Bagley* continued to circle and finally discharged her portside tubes at 0149, but her targets had sailed beyond range. After this brief engagement, the *Bagley* crossed the enemy's wake and headed northeast. She never raised an alarm.

At 0144 Mikawa swung the *Chokai* to the northeast, electing to attack the northern cruisers that had been sighted some minutes earlier rather than the Allied transports. "By this decision," a Naval War College analysis concluded, Mikawa "lost an opportunity to convert a tactical success into a strategical victory which could have been of enormous consequence to the Japanese cause."[19]

As the rest of the Japanese ships followed, trying to maintain station at high speed in poor visibility, the formation, unsurprisingly, became disrupted. The *Furutaka* lost contact with the *Kinugasa*. The *Tenryu* turned inside the radius of the other ships, and the *Yubari* cut the mark even tighter and ended up on the *Tenryu*'s port beam. Eventually, the *Furutaka* dropped all the way back to the *Tenryu*'s starboard quarter. This proved a fortunate mistake for Mikawa, as his ships advanced on both flanks of the northern group, which was still serenely maintaining station.

The Japanese column's concentration on the *Canberra* granted the *Chicago* a respite. Captain Bode reached the bridge of the U.S. heavy cruiser and tried to understand what was happening as precious minutes passed. Then, at 0147 lookouts reported a torpedo track to starboard. As Bode ordered a turn to starboard, more tracks appeared to port, and Bode countermanded his order. Then, perceiving a threat to the southwest, he swung his ship further to port away from the enemy and the transports under his protection.

Despite the maneuvering, a torpedo from the *Kako* clipped the *Chicago*'s bow, making the whole ship jump and casting a water column higher than the foretop. Another torpedo struck abreast the *Chicago*'s starboard engine room but did not explode. Then a shell glanced off the base of the *Chicago*'s foremast.

Despite these blows, the American cruiser remained capable of twenty-five knots. But, as the Japanese battle line sailed past, Bode fixed on the *Patterson*'s battle with the *Tenryu* and *Yubari*. The *Chicago* engaged the *Tenryu* with her secondary battery and scored one hit, but the Japanese target vanished by 0150. As the *Patterson* looped back toward the transports, the *Chicago* continued west. The *Chicago*'s report complains that of forty-four star shells fired (both to port and starboard) during this encounter, thirty-eight malfunctioned.

At 0155 the *Yunagi* and *Jarvis* began trading broadsides. Bode headed to investigate these gun flashes 14,000 yards northwest of his position, missing the pyrotechnics from the much larger battle to the northeast. In fairness, a heavy cloud bank lay to the *Chicago*'s northeast. For nearly a half hour, then, the *Chicago* silently probed far to the west of the action. During this period Bode did not communicate with his superiors or the ships under his command and left the transports exposed to enemy attack.[20]

As the *Chicago* headed west conditions to the east of Savo Island were dark and overcast with occasional mists and rain. A light breeze blew from the southeast over a smooth sea, and visibility hovered at 10,000 yards. Capt. Riefkohl emerged from his emergency cabin to see star shells on the *Vincennes's* port beam and gunfire to the southeast. He later wrote, "I thought this contact probably a destroyer and a ruse to draw off my group while the main attack force passed through my sector to attack the transports. If enemy heavy ships had been sighted I expected the *Australia* group would illuminate and engage them, and the situation would soon be clarified. . . . I signaled speed 15 knots and decided to hold my course."[21]

At 0150 Japanese searchlights suddenly snapped on. With synchronized efficiency the *Chokai* illuminated the *Astoria* from 7,700 yards, the *Aoba* spotlighted the *Quincy* from 9,200 yards, and the *Kako* fixed on the *Vincennes* from 10,500 yards. Within minutes broadsides erupted from all three Japanese ships. These salvos fell short, but with ranges dropping rapidly and targets maintaining a steady course and speed, Japanese gunners quickly found the mark. The *Aoba* and *Kako* hit with their third volleys, and the *Chokai* scored with her fifth. On the *Chokai's* bridge it seemed an incredible spectacle: "Every other salvo caused another enemy ship to burst into flames. For incredible minutes the turrets of enemy ships remained in their trained-in positions, and we stood amazed. . . . Strings of machine-gun tracers wafted back and forth between the enemy and ourselves, but such minor countereffects merely made a colorful spectacle."[22]

When the Japanese attacked, each American cruiser had half its crew at battle stations and every captain slept. Each ship's reactions varied, but in no case did they pace the swift unfolding of events. The *Quincy's* skipper, Capt. Samuel Moore, ordered his fighting lights turned on. Riefkohl sent out a broadcast on TBS and radio, ordering the searchlights to stop illuminating. The *Astoria* did better, opening fire on the initiative of her gunnery officer after he watched two Japanese salvos splash progressively closer to his ship. But when Capt. William Greenman arrived on the *Astoria's* bridge, his first words were, "Who sounded the general alarm? Who gave the order to commence firing? I think we are firing on our own ships. Let's not get excited and act too hasty. Cease firing."[23]

At 0153 the *Aoba* set the *Quincy's* seaplane ablaze and then hit the American's bridge. Moore ordered his gunners to fire on the searchlights, but, with personnel still scrambling to battle stations, his main battery remained silent. The *Vincennes* fired a broadside at 0153 and an eight-inch round from her second salvo struck the *Kinugasa*, failing to explode but damaging the Japanese heavy cruiser's steering. Then a volley from the *Kako* slammed the *Vincennes* amidships and ignited her floatplane.

At 0154, just as Captain Greenman decided to resume shooting, the *Chokai*'s fifth and sixth broadsides destroyed the *Astoria*'s number 1 turret, disabled its number 3 turret, and torched its seaplane. At 0155 the *Furutaka* and *Tenryu* illuminated the *Quincy* and added their firepower to the assault from the other beam. At the same time two torpedoes launched by the *Chokai* seven minutes earlier detonated against the *Vincennes* just as Riefkohl swung his ship toward the enemy.

By 0157, before she had fired a single shot, the *Quincy* sat in the crosshairs of three enemy cruisers and was heavily ablaze. Finally, at 0158, the beleaguered cruiser lashed out at the enemy with "a full 9-gun salvo to port . . . and now the targets had passed astern. Turrets I and II could no longer bear. . . . Control was quickly shifted aft to Director II so Turret III could fire, but it was too late. Turret III had already been hit and jammed in train."[24] Moore steered the *Quincy* to port to avoid a collision with the *Vincennes* and headed almost straight toward the *Chokai*.

The *Chokai*'s column passed four miles astern of the *Astoria* and then up her starboard side as the *Yubari* led the other Japanese column up the *Astoria*'s port side. Searchlights became redundant as the American cruisers burned. Then, at 0200 the *Chokai* altered course 40 degrees to starboard. Admiral Goto in the *Aoba*, having Mikawa's authorization to operate independently, did not follow the Japanese flagship and turned north instead, continuing the attack. The *Chokai* came back around, but the flagship's strange maneuver left her operating separately on *Sentai* 6's starboard quarter. At this time the *Kako* fired four torpedoes at the *Astoria*, and the *Kinugasa* winged three toward the transports.

At 0203 a torpedo from the *Yubari* hit the *Vincennes*. The *Astoria*, under fire from the *Aoba*, *Kinugasa*, and *Kako* suffered a crippling blow to a kerosene fuel tank that forced the abandonment of her after engine room and reduced her speed to eight knots. A minute later two of the *Tenryu*'s torpedoes blasted the *Quincy*. A minute after that the *Quincy*, firing on the *Kako*, overshot her mark and landed two shells on the *Chokai*, hitting the Japanese flagship's chart room and missing Mikawa and his staff by five yards.

By this time the *Quincy* seemed to be heading straight for the Japanese eastern column, and some Japanese observers believed the Americans intended to ram. Captain Moore's last communication declaimed, "We're going down between them—give them hell!"[25]

At 0210 an enemy round devastated the *Quincy*'s bridge and mortally wounded Moore. At 0215 the *Quincy* lay dead in the water, and a minute later a torpedo from the *Aoba* sealed the American cruiser's fate. The *Astoria*'s final shot penetrated the *Chokai*'s number 1 turret at 0216 and exited without exploding. By this time the Japanese cruisers had ceased fire.

The *Vincennes* shot thirty-three rounds in five salvos. She sank at 0250, destroyed by three torpedoes and as many as seventy-four shells. The *Quincy* sank by the bow, hit by fifty-four shells and three torpedoes. She expended twenty-one rounds in three broadsides. The *Astoria* fired 53 eight-inch rounds in thirteen salvos. She escaped the torpedoes, but at least thirty-four (and perhaps up to sixty-three) eight-inch shells penetrated her superstructure and hull. The *Vincennes* lost 332 men, the *Quincy* 370, and the *Astoria* 216.

The Japanese ignored the *Wilson*. The *Helm* never spotted any enemy ships. One writer described the participation of these two destroyers as "a hellish scramble of blindman's buff."[26]

By 0216 the *Yubari*'s column had passed north of Savo Island, and the *Chokai* group had streamed northeast. At 0217 the *Tenryu* spotted and illuminated *Ralph Talbot*, which was still patrolling her zone, and hurled a 5.5-inch salvo down the beam of light. As one shell detonated against the American destroyer's torpedo tubes, Lt. Cdr. Joseph W. Callahan, flashed recognition signals. This gave the *Tenryu* pause, but the *Yubari* came up and clobbered the *Ralph Talbot* four more times.

Because of difficulties with the tube mounts the American ship was able to reply at 0223 with only a single torpedo aimed at the *Yubari*'s searchlight. However, the Japanese light cruiser doused its light, leaving Callahan without a point of aim. A later analysis noted that "visibility was much reduced in this area because of the proximity of rain squalls." Although the *Yubari* passed just 2,000 yards abeam, the *Ralph Talbot* escaped by ducking into a providential rain squall. Listing heavily and with fourteen dead and twenty-three wounded, the American destroyer sheltered in the lee of Savo Island and limped back to Tulagi the next day.[27]

At this point Mikawa considered his options. He figured he needed several hours to re-form before attacking the transports. By then dawn would be breaking, and, unaware the American carriers had streamed beyond range, he feared being caught by their aircraft. He had expended half his torpedoes and a third of his ammunition and had plainly smashed the enemy's surface forces (see Table 4.2). He considered this accomplishment sufficient and set course for Rabaul.

Mikawa's force exacted a horrible toll: 1,023 Allied sailors dead and 709 wounded. Three 8-inch shells had struck the *Chokai*, killing 34 and wounding 32. One shell hit the *Aoba*'s port torpedo tube mount. A fire broke out on the heavy cruiser, but she had fired most of her torpedoes when this happened and damage was minimal. The *Kinugasa* suffered four killed and slight damage from an eight-inch and a five-inch shell. The *Tenryu* absorbed a five-inch round from the *Chicago* and had two men wounded. A five-inch dud struck *Yubari* inflicting slight damage.[28]

Mikawa applied a doctrine; his men followed their training. Torpedoes hit the water before the enemy perceived a threat. Planes, permitted to loiter over the enemy at will, dropped their effective pyrotechnics at the right time and in the right place. Ships that had never operated together before coordinated their actions effectively. The ability of three cruisers to illuminate different targets nearly simultaneously, to open fire within minutes of each other, and to hit every target within three minutes—all while rushing at twenty-six knots through a dark and squally night—was an outstanding accomplishment. Following by minutes the neutralization of two other cruisers—indeed, while the end of the column was still engaging the first target—it seemed an incredible achievement. The Japanese captains even turned their failure to maintain formation into an advantage, attacking the northern cruisers from both sides. As Admiral Ugaki gleefully wrote, "Those conceited British and Americans who regard the battles of the Coral Sea and Midway as supreme victories cannot say anything now."[29]

TABLE 4.2. AMMUNITION EXPENDITURE DURING THE BATTLE OF SAVO ISLAND

Ship	Main battery shells fired	Secondary battery shells fired	Torpedoes fired
Chokai	308	120	8
Aoba	182	85	13
Kako	192	130	8
Kinugasa	185	224	8
Furutaka	153	94	8
Yubari	96	0	6
Tenryu	80	23	6
Canberra	0	3[a]	0
Chicago	0	25	n/a
Vincennes	33	20[a]	n/a
Quincy	21	0	n/a
Astoria	53	59	n/a
Patterson	33[a]	n/a	0
Ralph Talbot	12[a]	n/a	1
Wilson	212	n/a	0
Bagley	0	n/a	8

Sources: Lacroix and Wells. *Japanese Cruisers of the Pacific War*, 306; Bates, *Battle of Savo Island*, 356–7.
a. These numbers are estimates.

However, Allied failures facilitated Mikawa's victory. Allied commanders did not communicate with subordinates or subordinates with commanders, assumptions satisfied curiosity, hesitation replaced decision. Some historians point to the tropical heat and the men's exhaustion as contributing factors, but the problem went deeper than that. The Allied captains lacked situational awareness and proved insufficiently aggressive. Faced with a crisis, they did not apply a common doctrine. Instead, each captain had his own individual response. But Savo Island sounded a wake-up call. As Admiral King said upon hearing the news of the battle, "That, as far as I am concerned, was the blackest day of the war."[30]

Nevertheless, in the end, despite the brilliance of the Japanese attack, despite Allied mistakes, despite suffering its greatest defeat ever, the U.S. Navy fulfilled its mission, and the Japanese failed in theirs. Mikawa ignored the transports and missed Japan's best opportunity to win a truly important victory. Admiral Turner demonstrated resolution and a deft strategic sense when he exploited Mikawa's mistake by continuing to unload throughout the day following the Battle of Savo Island. Still, the Marines received barely enough supplies to sustain their position. Then, on 10 August the real battle, the battle of attrition, began when *S44* became the first U.S. submarine to sink a large Japanese warship. She smacked the *Kako* with three torpedoes from a spread of four as the cruiser returned to Kavieng. After being hit, the *Kako* capsized and sank in five minutes, taking seventy-four men with her.

The Imperial Japanese Navy believed victory in a great sea battle automatically bestowed sea control. Thus, it failed to actively exploit Mikawa's deed and granted the Marines nearly two weeks to solidify their position. In fact, four U.S. APDs crammed with supplies reached Guadalcanal on 15 August, the day before the first Japanese reinforcements—a mere 113 naval troops—were put ashore by the destroyer *Oite*. Although American strength remained unknown 17th Army headquarters in Rabaul hopefully concluded that a thrust by the troops readily available at Rabaul, one battalion of the 28th Regiment, could expel the enemy. The unit's commander, Colonel Ichiki Kiyonao, illustrated the attitude of "unbounded optimism" at headquarters "by asking if he could also occupy Tulagi."[31] Ichiki's battalion arrived on 18 August aboard six destroyers, constituting the first of many deployments the Japanese called "Rat Operations" and the Americans dubbed "Tokyo Expresses."

Destroyer Action in Savo Sound, 22 August 1942

With Ichiki's arrival, the pace of naval operations accelerated. By 20 August small Japanese and American convoys streamed for Guadalcanal, while the Combined Fleet and three American carrier groups shadowboxed in the distance, ready to lunge.

On 21 August Japanese flyers spotted the American convoy of the transports *Fomalhaut* and *Alhena* escorted by the destroyers *Blue*, *Henley*, and *Helm*. The Japanese also spied Vice Admiral Fletcher's carriers lurking southeast of Guadalcanal.

The Japanese convoy bearing the balance of Ichiki's regiment, which had since been slaughtered applying "bamboo spear" tactics against impressed but unintimidated Marines, escorted by Rear Admiral Tanaka's Destroyer Squadron 2, retired north to let the situation develop. Then, Vice Admiral Tsukahara Nishizo, commander of the Southeast Area Fleet, ordered Tanaka to send a destroyer to meet the 8th Fleet's *Yunagi*, which was steaming down from Rekata Bay. Tsukahara wanted these ships to sweep the sound and annihilate any Allied transports they encountered. Tanaka dispatched the *Kawakaze* on this mission. Meanwhile, Admiral Turner sent the destroyers *Blue* and *Henley* ahead to counter a suspected enemy landing and ensure a safe environment for the transports.

TABLE 4.3. FORCES ENGAGED IN THE DESTROYER ACTION IN SAVO SOUND

	Type of Ship	Year Launched	Displacement, Full Load (tons)	Max. Speed (knots)	Guns (number by inch/caliber)	Torpedoes (number of tubes by diameter in inches)	Damage
U.S. Destroyer Division 7 (Cdr. R.H. Smith)							
Blue (F)	DD	1937	2,245	38	4 x 5/38	16 x 21	D4
Henley	DD	1937	2,245	38	4 x 5/38	16 x 21	
Japanese (Commander Wakabayashi Kazuo)							
Kawakaze	DD	1933	1,802	36	5 x 5/50	9 x 24	

D4—major damage (combat and maneuvering ability significantly impaired or eliminated), DD—destroyer, F—flagship
Time: 0345–0400
Weather: Light southeasterly breeze, 30 percent overcast
Visibility: Poor, no moon
Sea state: Calm
Surprise: Japanese
Mission: Americans—offensive and sea superiority patrol; Japanese—interception based upon general intelligence

A weather front swept the Solomons the night of 21 August, and the *Yunagi*, running foul of the rain and rough waters, radioed that she could not make the rendezvous. The *Kawakaze* plowed on undaunted, however.

The Americans entered Lengo Channel at 0140 and sighted four vessels heading out. The destroyers' men scrambled to general quarters and trained guns. The *Blue* flashed a challenge, which the contacts ignored. As tension mounted the *Blue* repeated her challenge and again received no response. The division commander, Cdr. Robert Hall Smith, was about to order "Open Fire" when someone recognized the distinctive flush deck profiles as belonging to friendly APDs.

After this excitement the *Blue* and *Henley* arrived in Savo Sound at 0235 hours, where they found conditions moonless, murky, and black. Proceeding at ten knots with the *Blue* leading by 400 yards, the destroyers began their patrol with crews mindful of the danger of misidentification. Meanwhile, the *Kawakaze* passed Savo Island, cruising slowly to avoid leaving a telltale wake.

At 0324 a signal flashed on the *Blue*'s radar and crossed her bow, closing from 4,500 to 2,900 yards before disappearing at 0335. The division commander, Smith, assessed the contact as a "small 20-knot surface craft, assumed to be friendly patrol boat."[32] Meanwhile, as the *Kawakaze* headed southeast the Japanese ship's lookouts spotted a slight disturbance in the darkness ahead. Commander Wakabayashi Kazuo distinguished two shapes approaching on a reciprocal course 4,000 yards to port. They passed before he could train his torpedo tubes, and the *Kawakaze* came about trying to reestablish contact.

Then, at 0353 after casting about in the darkness for nearly twenty minutes, the *Kawakaze*'s lookouts again reported the inky outlines of enemy vessels off the starboard bow on an opposite course. This time Wakabayashi did not hesitate. Accepting a poor torpedo solution, he snapped out the orders, and six Long Lances whooshed into the water one after the other. The *Kawakaze* came to starboard and, working up to full speed, crossed the wake of the American column headed back for Savo Island, her guns silent.

The *Blue*'s radar operator reported a high-speed contact 5,000 yards on the starboard beam. Guns and torpedoes trained in that direction, but there was nothing to see. The *Blue* notified the *Henley* that the contact had passed astern, and as that contact seemed to be the "friendly" patrol boat detected just minutes before, the *Blue* continued on course. Then, at 0359 American lookouts spotted the wakes of at least two torpedoes. Ten seconds later a tremendous explosion "sliced off several feet of the *Blue*'s stern, immobilized the propeller shafts, [and] tossed men and gear as much as 50 feet in the air."[33] Nine men died and twenty-one fell wounded. The *Henley* stood by her stricken sister as the *Kawakaze* withdrew. After an attempt to tow the wreck to safety failed, the *Blue*'s crew scuttled their ship the next evening off Tulagi harbor, anticipating the arrival of another Tokyo Express.

This minor engagement marked America's first test of the nocturnal conditions off Guadalcanal since Savo Island and confirmed its precedent. The Japanese navy ruled the night.[34]

As the *Kawakaze* ran north, the Americans established a precedent of their own. The first Marine fighters and bombers had landed at Henderson Field the day before. At 0800 a pair of American warplanes jumped the *Kawakaze*, strafing her and wounding one man. The Americans would dominate the waters around Guadalcanal during the day as long as they possessed the airfield.

On Monday 24 August Japanese and U.S. carriers finally clashed in the Battle of the Eastern Solomons. The Japanese lost the light carrier *Ryujo*, and the large American flattop *Enterprise* suffered damage. The Japanese reinforcement convoy then advanced as the carriers withdrew. On 25 August a combination of Navy, Marine, and Army Air Force planes harassed Tanaka's force and eventually forced the Japanese to retire after sinking one destroyer and two transports and damaging a light cruiser.

That same day Japanese forces landed on Rabi Island, on Nauru in the Gilberts, and on Goodenough Island, indicating that Imperial headquarters remained enmeshed in its own offensive plans and still did not fully comprehend the significance of the growing struggle for Guadalcanal. In fact, for a brief moment at the end of August, the Guadalcanal campaign nearly ended by default. On the evening of 28 August eleven U.S. dive bombers (SBDs) jumped Japanese Destroyer Division 20, which was rushing an infantry battalion to Guadalcanal sinking the *Asagiri* and heavily damaging the *Shirakumo*. Learning of Division 20's fate, Japanese Destroyer Division 24, at sea on the same task, aborted its mission without orders and sulked back to base.

The 17th Army considered writing off Guadalcanal but Mikawa urged another try. On 29 August six destroyers of Divisions 24 and 11 landed 550 men at Taivu Point. A Japanese historian commented that "through the success of this landing, a tangible method for reinforcing Guadalcanal was established, and, therefore, 'Rat' landings became the standard method of landing troops on Guadalcanal."[35]

Thereafter, the tempo of Japanese reinforcements to Guadalcanal accelerated. On three consecutive nights beginning 31 August, Rat operations brought nearly 2,000 men of the Kawaguchi detachment to the island. On 4 September the light cruiser *Sendai*, leading eleven destroyers—six acting as transports and five as the screen— deposited almost a thousand men at Taivu Point. Following this successful mission, Japanese Destroyer Division 11 continued on to bombard Henderson Field.

Destroyer Action off Lunga Point, 5 September 1942

Operating out of Tulagi the *Little* and *Gregory* ferried a Marine raider force to Savo Island on the morning of 4 September and returned it to Guadalcanal that evening. The force commander, Cdr. Hugh W. Hadley, decided to patrol off Lunga rather than risk a return to Tulagi after dark. Captain Sugino Shuichi's division passed Hadley's force unseen to seaward. The Americans had just made a 180-degree turn to the northwest when at 0055 hours lookouts reported gun flashes to the east as the Japanese commenced their bombardment.

Hadley interpreted these flashes as a submarine conducting a nuisance attack, but at 0102 radar revealed multiple contacts 4,000 yards astern. While Hadley

TABLE 4.4. FORCES ENGAGED IN THE ACTION OFF LUNGA POINT

	Type of Ship	Year Launched	Displacement, Full Load (tons)	Max. Speed (knots)	Guns (number by inch/caliber)	Torpedoes (number of tubes by diameter in inches)	Damage
			Americans (Cdr. Hugh W. Hadley)				
Little	APD	1917	1,793	22	2 x 4/51		Sunk
Gregory	APD	1918	1,793	22	2 x 4/51		Sunk
			Japanese Destroyer Division 11 (Captain Sugino Shuichi)				
Hatsuyuki	DD	1928	2,057	38	6 x 5/50	9 x 24	
Murakumo	DD	1928	2,057	38	6 x 5/50	9 x 24	
Yudachi	DD	1936	1,950	34	5 x 5/50	8 x 24	

APD—destroyer transport, DD—destroyer
Time: 0100–0135
Weather: Squalls
Visibility: Poor, no moon
Sea state: n/a
Surprise: Americans
Mission: Americans—offensive and sea superiority patrol; Japanese—shore bombardment

debated running or attempting a surprise attack, a patrolling American seaplane, unaware any U.S. ships were nearby, dropped five flares hoping to illuminate the enemy for Marine gunners ashore. Unfortunately, the flares floated down only 1,000 yards ahead of the ex-destroyers, silhouetting them nicely for the surprised Japanese. The *Yudachi* swung a searchlight around, and gunfire quickly followed.

Both American APDs fought back with their stern mounts, but the *Gregory* had only discharged five rounds when the *Yudachi's* broadside penetrated the *Gregory's* boiler room stopping the engines and igniting a large fire. Another shell toppled the minesweeper's second stack, and a third cut through the *Gregory's* bridge. Then, as a witness aboard the *Gregory* recalled, "a flare burst about a thousand yards off the port bow. . . . A searchlight about 2,000 yards off the starboard quarter illuminated the USS *Little*, then on our starboard bow, turning right. Three salvos were fired; the *Little* burst into flames."[36] Shells exploded in the *Little's* steering-engine room and fuel tanks and destroyed the aft gun. By 0115 both crews streamed into boats or jumped overboard as the Japanese warships sliced between them and pulverized the APDs, expending nearly 500 rounds in the process. The *Gregory* sank at 0140, and the *Little* followed at 0330. The next morning boats from Guadalcanal rescued 238 men. Eleven of the *Gregory's* complement and twenty-two of the *Little's* crew perished in Savo Sound.[37]

The first Japanese buildup climaxed on 7 September, when the last of the Kawaguchi and Ichiki detachments debouched on the coconut-fringed beaches of Tassafaronga Point, ten miles east of the American perimeter. The 17th Army command scheduled the airfield's recapture for 12 September. In total, Rat landings had transported 4,500 troops to Guadalcanal since 28 August, and another 700 had arrived by barge. The U.S. Navy, three times defeated in night combat, tolerated these nocturnal excursions.

Meanwhile, Admiral Yamamoto mustered the Combined Fleet and sortied from Truk, poised to smash any desperate Americans sallies: "Everyone in this large fleet was optimistic as the ships sped on their way."[38] Kawaguchi attacked south of the airfield along high ground soon to be named Bloody Ridge. A Japanese account dryly records, "Enemy resistance was unexpectedly strong, and the main body suffered heavy losses.... Thus the first general ground attack on Guadalcanal ended in failure, and there was no course open but to pour in ground troops and reattempt the attack."[39]

The second Japanese buildup began before the bitter taste of the first attack's failure was a day old. On 15 September seven destroyers landed a thousand troops. More men and provisions followed on 17, 18, 20, 21, and 24 September. On 18 September an Allied convoy landed Guadalcanal's first substantive reinforcement, the 7th Marine Regiment. Many nights, Japanese warships stood offshore and lofted shells into the American perimeter. Even worse, the U.S. Navy lost the equivalence of a major carrier battle when, first, a submarine torpedoed the *Saratoga* on 31 August and another sank the *Wasp* on 15 September.

After a weeklong pause for the full moon, the Japanese resumed nightly Rat landings on 1 October, with several hundred to a thousand men pouring ashore per trip. Vice Admiral Ghormley husbanded his heavy forces to the south, not daring to test the Imperial Japanese Navy's nighttime mastery of Savo Sound. Henderson Field remained in operation, however, and continued to enforce its daylight authority over waters within 200 miles, but the Marines weakened as a lack of supplies, isolation, and attrition exacted a growing toll. Meanwhile, "on board Japanese ships and around their campfires there was an even stronger feeling of 'On to Victory!'"[40]

In fact, as the summer of 1942 ended, the Allies seemed to be losing the war. German troops stood on the Volga River and the frontiers of Asia. Axis armies threatened Suez. The despised Italian navy dominated the central Mediterranean. Wolfpacks seemed poised to close the North Atlantic, and the Arctic route had become a death trap for the Allies. China's armies had disintegrated. Civil unrest paralyzed India. In this situation the U.S. Joint Chiefs of Staff faced some hard decisions regarding what forces the United States would commit—what sacrifices it would make—to retain Guadalcanal. Given the focus on the upcoming North

African operation, the South Pacific seemed an ugly stepsister low in the chain of priorities. Nonetheless, the Navy elected to hang on. This meant, first of all, accepting greater risk and putting a mousetrap in the path of the Rat operations.

On 7 October Ghormley dispatched Task Force 64, which had been formed as a surface strike force on 20 September, under Rear Admiral Scott and scheduled the 164th Infantry Regiment to reinforce the Marines on 13 October. Scott's task force cruised near Rennel Island waiting to intercept the next enemy foray towards Guadalcanal. Two months after suffering its greatest defeat, the U.S. Navy's surface force was finally climbing back into the ring.

The American convoy departed Nouméa on 9 October. Meanwhile, the 17th Army relocated to Guadalcanal and readied its next "final" offensive. It scheduled an important high-speed convoy carrying the 2nd Division's heavy weapons for 15 October. The problem of Henderson Field, however, continued to vex. Bad weather frustrated what was "by far the strongest bomber strike sent against Guadalcanal" on 11 October, as well as an attempt to catch the Americans on the ground with a follow-up attack.[41]

The failure of Japanese airpower to suppress Henderson required the 8th Fleet to plan a heavy bombardment of the airfield. On the night of 11–12 October the seaplane carriers *Nisshin*, *Chitose*, and six destroyers would conduct the Rat operation while Rear Admiral Goto's *Sentai 6*, victors of Savo Island, smashed the airfield two hours after their arrival. The Americans had never disputed a transport mission, and neither Mikawa nor Goto had reason to think 11 October would be different.

Scott had experienced the defeat at Savo Island, if from a distance, and he began to forge a night combat doctrine based on his observations of that battle. While Task Force 64 remained an improvised unit—Ghormley tacked on the *Helena*, *Duncan*, and *McCalla* just before Scott sailed—at least Scott had a few weeks to drill most of his ships and conduct nocturnal gunnery exercises. In many respects, Scott's battle plan mimicked his understanding of Mikawa's tactics. The American ships would operate in line ahead formation, and the cruisers would deploy floatplanes to spot and illuminate when appropriate. Destroyers would illuminate potential targets as soon as possible after radar contact, and if illuminated themselves, the U.S. ships would counter-illuminate immediately and open fire. Scott emphasized "maintaining formation to facilitate identification."[42]

On 9 and 10 October Task Force 64 marked time patrolling beyond enemy air range and waiting for news of the Japanese convoy. On 11 October a B-17 reported sighting two cruisers and six destroyers in New Georgia Sound, which combatants often called "the Slot," heading south with an expected time of arrival of 2300 on 11 October. At 1600 Scott set course for Savo Island, aiming to give the enemy an unexpected welcome.

Battle of Cape Esperance, 11–12 October 1942

TABLE 4.5. FORCES ENGAGED IN THE BATTLE OF CAPE ESPERANCE

Type of Ship	Year Launched	Displacement, Full Load (tons)	Max. Speed (knots)	Guns (number by inch/caliber)	Torpedoes (number of tubes by diameter in inches)	Damage
American Task Force 64 (Rear Adm. Norman Scott)						
San Francisco (F)	CA	1931	12,463	32	9 x 8/55 & 8 x 5/25	
Salt Lake City	CA	1927	11,512	32	10 x 8/55 & 8 x 5/25	D2
Boise	CL	1936	12,207	32	15 x 6/47 & 8 x 5/25	D3
Helena	CL	1938	12,207	32	15 x 6/47 & 8 x 5/38	
American Destroyer Squadron 12 (Capt. Robert G. Tobin)						
Farenholt (F)	DD	1941	2,395	35	5 x 5/38	10 x 21	D3
Buchanan	DD	1941	2,395	35	5 x 5/38	10 x 21	
Laffey	DD	1941	2,395	35	5 x 5/38	10 x 21	
Duncan	DD	1941	2,395	35	5 x 5/38	10 x 21	Sunk
McCalla	DD	1941	2,395	35	5 x 5/38	10 x 21	
Japanese Sentai 6 (Rear Admiral Goto Aritomo)						
Aoba (F)	CA	1926	10,651	33	6 x 8/50 & 4 x 4.7/45	8 x 24	D3
Kinugasa	CA	1926	10,651	33	6 x 8/50 & 4 x 4.7/45	8 x 24	D1
Furutaka	CA	1925	10,341	33	6 x 8/50 & 4 x 4.7/45	8 x 24	Sunk
Japanese Destroyer Division 11 (Captain Sugino Shuichi)						
Hatsuyuki	DD	1927	2,057	38	6 x 5/50	9 x 24	D1
Fubuki	DD	1927	2,057	38	6 x 5/50	9 x 24	Sunk

CA—heavy cruiser, CL—light cruiser, D1—light or superficial damage (including splinter damage), D2—moderate damage (combat ability not significantly impaired), D3—significant damage (combat or maneuvering ability somewhat impaired), DD—destroyer, F—flagship

    Time: 2345–0033
    Weather: Fair, light southeasterly breeze
    Visibility: Mixed, no moon, light haze, low, broken clouds
    Sea state: Moderate swells
    Surprise: Americans
    Mission: Americans—interception based on general intelligence; Japanese—shore bombardment

Although spotters reported the seaplane carriers and destroyers of the Japanese transport group, they missed Goto's division following some distance behind. As a result Scott had no intimation of Goto's presence. At 2200 Scott ordered each of his cruisers to launch a floatplane. However, the *Helena* missed the command and the *Salt Lake City*'s plane crashed on takeoff, burning for three minutes before it sank. The Americans worried this would disclose their presence, and the *Aoba*'s lookouts did report a distant flare, but Goto assumed it signified some type of friendly signal. Then, at 2250 the *San Francisco*'s spotter reported one large and two small vessels off Guadalcanal north of the Marine perimeter. This report confused more than it enlightened because it contradicted Scott's preconceived picture based on the partial (and incorrect) intelligence he possessed.

By this time the American column patrolled a line northwest of Cape Esperance in a northeasterly to southwesterly direction. Radar had failed miserably at Savo Island; at Cape Esperance it played a larger, although still imperfect, role. The *San Francisco*, the American flagship, carried SC radar, which indicated contacts individually, and temporarily as it passed over them, as a disturbance within a field of bouncing green lines. The light cruisers in the U.S. force possessed the newer SG radar, which displayed contacts continuously as dots, or "pips," with the receiving vessel in the center of the scope. Captains fought their ships from the bridge and relied on telephone talkers to describe the radar picture, using nonstandardized vocabulary and procedures.

At 2325 the *Helena*'s SG picked up a surface contact bearing northwest at 27,700 yards, but the *Helena*'s skipper, Capt. Gilbert C. Hoover, did not forward this information to Scott. At 2332, about six miles west of Savo Island, Scott ordered his column to reverse course to the southwest. At this point, the *Farenholt, Duncan,* and *Laffey* led, followed by the *San Francisco, Boise, Salt Lake City,* and *Helena.* The *Buchanan* and *McCalla* brought up the rear. The course change required each ship to tack one after the other in the same position, as if they were rounding a buoy. However, the *San Francisco*'s skipper, Capt. Charles H. McMorris, immediately swung hard to port, putting the three van destroyers on his starboard side. Next in column, the *Boise*'s Capt. Edward J. Moran faced a choice of whether to maneuver as ordered or to follow the flagship. Not surprisingly, Moran followed the flag, thereby cutting the three destroyers from the formation.

Meanwhile, *Sentai* 6 bore in at thirty knots, heading straight toward Lunga Point in a T formation: the *Aoba* followed by the *Furutaka* and *Kinugasa* in column, with the *Fubuki* 3,300 yards off the *Aoba*'s port beam and the *Hatsuyuki* occupying the same position to starboard. The Japanese cruisers carried special HE shells designed to fragment on impact, perfect for savaging soft land targets. The Japanese crews had been training for a bombardment mission since September. Goto's orders required him to fling a thousand shells into an area of half an acre. He believed American PT boats might intervene, but his biggest concern was to do his job and be 150 miles away by dawn.

At 2220 the *Nisshin* signaled the Japanese transportation group's arrival, and ten minutes later Guadalcanal's garrison commander reported good weather. When the *Nisshin* heard aircraft overhead thirty-five minutes later, she did not report it. Thus, all seemed routine.

At 2343 Goto reduced speed to twenty-six knots. Then lookouts reported three ships 10,000 meters fine off the port bow. Goto held course, confident the contacts must be friendly. When lookouts shouted "Enemy Ships" and the *Aoba*'s crew began running to their battle stations, Goto still hesitated. He ordered a course change to port and began flashing a query.

At 2342, as the American column steadied on its new course steaming directly across Goto's bow, the *Helena* and *Boise* broadcast an enemy alert. Scott worried that the radars were pinging the three destroyers presumably racing up his starboard side to resume position ahead of the *San Francisco*. Moreover, ambiguous language further confused the situation; the *Boise*, for example, reported five "bogies," a word usually reserved for aircraft.

Then the *Duncan*, her gunnery radar indicating targets only four miles northwest, abandoned formation to charge in that direction at thirty knots without advising Tobin, the destroyer commander, or Scott. The *Laffey*, trailing the *Duncan*, declined to participate in this excursion and closed on the *Farenholt*. On the *San Francisco* Scott finally obtained radar contact only 5,000 yards to starboard, but he still hesitated.

Meanwhile, the *Helena*'s Captain Hoover, was growing frantic. He had been tracking a clearly identifiable and rapidly closing enemy force for twenty minutes (see Map 4.3). In fact, it threatened to cross astern at point-blank range. Then a crewman reported, "Ships visible to the naked eye!" An officer asked, "What are we going to do—board them?"[43] At 2345 Hoover radioed for permission to engage. Radar showed a range of only 3,600 yards, with the Japanese closing at a thousand yards a minute. Scott acknowledged with "roger," which meant message received but which Hoover chose to interpret as permission. At 2346 15 six-inch guns roared into action. The *Boise* followed within seconds, and then the *Salt Lake City*. Finally, the *San Francisco* joined in.

The *Aoba*, the nearest and biggest target, attracted fire from the *Boise, Salt Lake City, Farenholt,* and *Laffey*. The *Helena* targeted two ships abeam, probably the *Hatsuyuki* and the *Duncan,* which was mistaken as an enemy due to the American destroyer's position. Admiral Goto's chief of staff, Captain Kijima Kikunori, wrote that the sudden eruption of gunfire across their line of advance stunned the admiral. The 6-inch/.47 guns carried by the American light cruisers could spit a 130-pound AP projectile 26,000 yards at a rate of nine rounds a minute. This equated to nearly nine tons of metal a minute.

As her bow slowly swung to starboard, the Japanese cruiser briefly paralleled Scott's ships before heading away. One of the first broadsides ripped the *Aoba*'s flag bridge. The rounds failed to detonate, but they did cut communications, scythed through the crew, and mortally wounded Goto. Kijima carried him below decks and then returned to command *Sentai* 6. Direct hits disabled the *Aoba*'s main fire control and both forward turrets before they could be fired.

The sudden gunfire also stunned Admiral Scott. He had issued no orders, but the whole task force blazed away, excluding him from his own party. He quickly ordered a cease-fire over the TBS. Nothing happened. He repeated his order, and the *Salt Lake City* complied at 2348. Finally, at 2350 Scott climbed to the navigation bridge and personally ordered McMorris to desist. The *Helena* and *Boise,* however, continued to bang away.

Just before the gun flashes lit the night, the *Duncan* found herself alone. The pointer on the destroyer's number 2 mount remembered, "One moment I saw nothing but darkness and the faint sheen of starlight on calm seas. The next moment, ghostly forms took shape. Ships seemed to suddenly leap out of the darkness. . . . I called out: 'Enemy ships—visible to the naked eye!'"[44] Brushing elbows with the *Aoba,* which was just a thousand yards off her port bow, the *Duncan* spun away as the Japanese ship veered to starboard.

The *Duncan* missed her first torpedo setup and turned back, guns firing on the *Furutaka*. "The target was so near that tracers hardly arced," an American sailor later wrote. "Shells trailing red flame streaked straight across the water and ate at the enemy vessel."[45] One of the *Duncan*'s torpedoes hit the water as well. But, positioned in the middle, the American destroyer caught it from all sides.

A shell toppled the *Duncan*'s funnel, and then another smashed into the pilot house and ammunition handling room, igniting an intense fire. The beleaguered American destroyer launched another torpedo under local control and circled away, badly damaged. Eventually, the blaze forced the crew to abandon their still moving ship. The *Duncan* sank the next day, but not before inspection revealed that American six-inch shells inflicted much of the ship's damage.

The commencement of action also found the *Farenholt* and *Laffey* between battle lines. On the first destroyer's bridge the captain saw "dozens of low-flying meteors

MAP 4.3. BATTLE OF CAPE ESPERANCE, 11–12 OCTOBER 1942

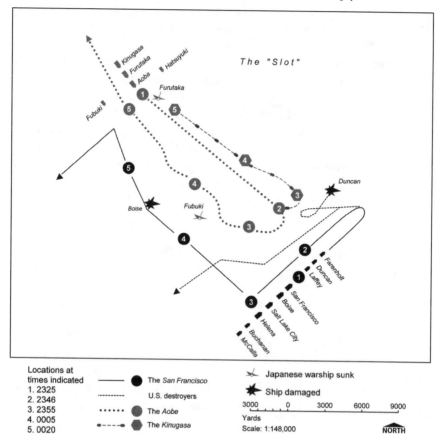

Locations at times indicated
1. 2325
2. 2346
3. 2355
4. 0005
5. 0020

———— The *San Francisco*

--------- U.S. destroyers

• • • • • • The *Aobe*

•– – –• The *Kinugasa*

⚓ Japanese warship sunk

✦ Ship damaged

3000   0   3000   6000   9000

Yards

Scale: 1:148,000   NORTH

crossing ahead, astern, and overhead . . . converging at points out in the dark near eye level."[46] The *Farenholt* tried to accelerate past the crossfire but took a hit at 2348. The *Laffey*, on the other hand, came about and headed for a safer position at the rear of the American column, five-inch guns hammering the *Aoba* along the way. Meanwhile, Scott queried his destroyers regarding their status and had them flash recognition lights. Finally satisfied, he gave permission to reopen fire at 2351.

The *Aoba* continued turning to starboard and rang up full speed. The Japanese flagship's aft turret managed to fire only seven rounds over open sights during this period. The *Furutaka*, following 1,640 yards behind the *Aoba*, counted more than a dozen ships in action. The *Furutaka's* skipper, Captain Tsutau Araki considered the situation "not good" and ordered a turn to port to open his starboard arcs. But then, seeing the *Aoba* in trouble, Tsutau steered to the flagship's aid.

The *Furutaka*'s secondary battery snapped off one salvo at 2148, but then American shells began pouring aboard. At 2349 a hit wrecked the Japanese heavy cruiser's number 3 turret. At 2351, as the *Furutaka* advanced to make her turn in the *Aoba*'s wake, a round detonated on the port torpedo tubes and sparked a large blaze that attracted enemy attention. At about the same time the *Aoba* made smoke, causing American observers to think the Japanese flagship had sunk and rendering the *Furutaka*'s plight all the worse.

The *Kinugasa* and *Hatsuyuk*i had disregarded Goto's orders and turned to port, away from the American advance, and thus avoided the worst of the bombardment. The *Fubuki* swung parallel to the American cruisers on the same heading however, and came under concentrated fire. The *Fubuki* exploded and sank at 2353. The Americans believed they had deluged the Japanese destroyer with shells, but the Japanese counted only four hits.[47]

The *Farenholt*, which was in the same general vicinity as the *Fubuki*, absorbed two American six-inch rounds at 2355 and 2357. Heavily damaged, she crossed ahead of the *San Francisco* and fell out of the American line on the disengaged side. The *Furutaka* continued to take a beating, however, and shells penetrated two engine rooms. She discharged about 30 eight-inch rounds in reply, and at 2354 one of these sparked a fire in the *Boise*'s captain's cabin. The *Buchanan* aimed five torpedoes at a cruiser at 2353. At 2355 an enemy short sprayed the *Salt Lake City* with fragments, wounding several men and inflicting minor damage.

At 2353 Scott began bending his disordered column west northwest to parallel the Japanese. American action reports wax enthusiastic when describing the effects of their gunfire: Between 2355 and 2400 the *Boise*, *Salt Lake City*, *Helena*, *McCalla*, and *Buchanan*, separately reported sinking a cruiser, two destroyers, and an auxiliary ship.[48] Fires raged aboard the *Aoba*, *Furutaka*, *Farenholt*, and *Duncan* during this period, and gunners continued to register hits. But the carnage fell short of what the American observers imagined. It resembled the blind men and the elephant, a fact Scott obviously appreciated because at midnight he again ordered all ships to cease fire and flash recognition lights.

Off in the dark, 8,000 yards north of the *San Francisco* and screened by her burning division mates, the *Kinugasa*'s gunners aimed and landed a tight salvo in the American flagship's wake. A few minutes later the *Boise* barely dodged a pair of torpedoes from the *Kinugasa*. The Americans reengaged with the *San Francisco*, shooting at the *Aoba*. At 0005 a shell exploded in the *Furutaka*'s other forward engine room, and fragments sliced the main steam line in her last undamaged engine room, cutting power.

At 0009 the *Boise*'s searchlight snapped on to probe for a radar contact just abaft her starboard beam. The *Kinugasa*'s guns trained on this target, and at 0010 an eight-inch shell struck the *Boise*'s forward barbette. Just a minute later a second shell pierced the American light cruiser's hull below the waterline and detonated in the main magazine between turrets 1 and 2. A fire erupted, and a magazine explosion would have followed if massive flooding had not immediately doused the conflagration.

As the *Boise* lurched out of line, the *Salt Lake City* drew abreast and the *Kinugasa*'s accurate broadsides fell upon her. A shell penetrated the armor belt at 0014, causing minor flooding. Two minutes later another sparked an oil fire that burned for five hours and caused a steering failure. However, as the Japanese ships continued north, this proved to be the battle's final blow. The *Salt Lake City*'s observers claimed they sank their target, and she may have dealt one or more of the four hits the *Kinugasa* suffered. At 0028 Scott, concerned the *San Francisco* might pull too far ahead and become an American target, terminated the pursuit.

The *Furutaka* slowly flooded and sank at 0248, losing 258 men. Between 2346 and 0010, 24 eight-inch and six-inch shells ravaged the *Aoba* and killed eighty-one men. However, the stoutly built Japanese ship made Shortland Island under her own steam and returned to action in February 1943. Two shells inflicted minor damage on the *Hatsuyuki*. The *Fubuki* lost seventy-eight men killed, and the Americans rescued 111.

The *Salt Lake City* fired 296 eight-inch AP rounds, 125 five-inch star shells, and 50 rounds of five-inch common. Five of her crewmen were killed, and her damage required six months to repair. The *Farenholt*, which was hit three times, lost three killed. The *Boise* had 107 dead and was lucky to survive. Forty-eight of the *Duncan*'s men went down with their ship.[49]

Cape Esperance represented the U.S. Navy's first attempt at applying a night combat doctrine based on the experience of previous defeats. The Americans sank fifteen ships according to the accumulated claims of their reports. In light of post-battle assessments, Scott lowered this to two heavy cruisers, one light cruiser, one auxiliary ship, and five destroyers. Captain Kijima comforted Goto before he died with the good news that he sank two heavy cruisers. Ugaki tallied the score the next day as two American cruisers sunk, one seriously damaged, and one destroyer sunk. The Americans believed they won a lopsided victory, the Japanese claimed a close victory.

Cape Esperance boosted American confidence and encouraged the unfounded belief that Scott had devised a winning formula. The lesson missed was that one commander could not control a night surface action involving several divisions. The battle reaffirmed the importance of alertness. The curious mental lassitude that so afflicted American captains at Savo Island blanketed Japanese bridges at Cape Esperance. That mattered more than Scott's hesitations and reluctance to trust his captains. In fact, Captain Hoover's willingness to act independently proved the true key to victory. Strategically, the Japanese accomplished their reinforcement mission and failed in their bombardment mission, while the Americans failed to do what they had set sail to accomplish—prevent the landing of Japanese reinforcements. The Navy first informed the public about the results of Savo Island on 12 October and followed that somber news the next day with a much happier account of Cape Esperance.

However, self-proclaimed victories do not win campaigns. In fact, Scott's "victory" enervated American surface forces while the Imperial navy's strength remained undiminished. On 13 October the U.S. Army's 164th Regiment arrived at Guadalcanal. But the Japanese had bigger plans afoot—another final offensive scheduled for late October.

The Southeast Area command planned a major convoy and more bombardments to suppress Henderson Field. On 14 October Vice Admiral Kurita, with the battleships *Haruna* and *Kongo* supported by a destroyer squadron, turned the air base into a "sea of flames" with 918 fourteen-inch shells, destroying forty-eight of ninety planes and brushing off an attempt by newly arrived PT boats to interfere.[50]

The next night Mikawa churned down the Slot with the *Chokai* and *Kinugasa* and a pair of destroyers and piled on 752 eight-inch shells. A Japanese convoy of six transports arrived that same night and discharged 4,000 men, guns, tanks, and supplies. The official U.S. account bleakly describes the consequences this way: "Dawn of the 15th revealed . . . in full view enemy transports lying-to off Tassafaronga, unloading troops and supplies with as much ease as if they had been in Tokyo Bay."[51] Then, on 16 October Rear Admiral Omori Sentaro with the heavy cruisers *Maya* and *Myoko* plowed Henderson Field with another 1,500 eight-inch shells. Meanwhile, the Japanese carriers hovered offstage to the north; their planes damaged several cargo ships, sank the destroyer *Meredith*, and turned back a sorely needed convoy.

On 17 October three Japanese cruisers and eight destroyers landed more men and provisions at Tassafaronga, and five destroyers put reinforcements ashore at Cape Esperance while destroyers shelled the airfield. The Imperial Japanese Navy had nearly blasted the Cactus Air Force out of existence. American fortunes had reached their nadir. Ghormley radioed Nimitz that if the enemy made a determined effort, he could not hold on. This was not the spirit U.S. Navy headquarters desired, and, already concerned about Ghormley's health, Nimitz decided to switch commanders. On 18 October Vice Admiral Halsey relieved Ghormley.

With reinforcements completed, the Japanese launched their next "final" offensive. However, the Imperial army squandered the navy's splendid effort and did not come as close to success as in September. In the end, the Japanese soldiers could not overcome unrealistic planning, a long jungle approach, abominable coordination, and the resilience of the American troops facing them. Blindly confident of victory, however, the 17th Army signaled on 24 October that its troops occupied Henderson Field. In response, Yamamoto launched the intricate naval movements designed to seal victory. The 8th and 2nd Fleets headed for positions northwest and northeast of Guadalcanal, and Mikawa ordered Destroyer Squadron 4 to make a high-speed dash to Savo Sound to provide fire support for the victorious troops as he followed with the rest of the 8th Fleet.

Skirmish in Sealark Channel, 25 October 1944

At 0530 hours on 25 October, at the very height of the crisis, two converted destroyer minesweepers, the *Trever* and *Zane*, arrived at Tulagi loaded with ammunition and drums of gasoline and towing four PT boats. They discharged their dangerous cargo by 0650 and remained in the harbor expecting orders to conduct a fire support mission that afternoon. Air raid alerts brought the crews to general quarters, and then at 0955 worse news followed. Three Japanese warships were standing down the passage between Savo and Florida Islands. They belonged to

TABLE 4.6. FORCES ENGAGED IN THE ACTION IN SEALARK CHANNEL

	Type of Ship	Year Launched	Displacement, Full Load (tons)	Max. Speed (knots)	Guns (number by inch/caliber)	Torpedoes (number of tubes by diameter in inches)	Damage
Americans (Lt. Cdr. D.M. Agnew)							
Trever (F)	DMS	1920	1,090	29	3 x 3/76.2		
Zane	DMS	1919	1,090	29	3 x 3/76.2		D2
Japanese Destroyer Division 6 (Commander Yamada Yusuke)							
Akatsuki (F)	DD	1932	1,950	38	6 x 5/50	9 x 24	D1
Ikazuchi	DD	1931	1,950	38	6 x 5/50	9 x 24	
Shiratsuyu	DD	1935	1,950	34	6 x 5/50	8 x 24	

D1—light or superficial damage (including splinter damage), D2—moderate damage (combat ability not significantly impaired), DD—destroyer, DMS—destroyer minesweeper, F—flagship

    Time: 1010–1104
    Weather: Calm, sunny
    Visibility: Excellent
    Sea state: Smooth
    Surprise: None
    Mission: Americans—self-defense; Japanese—shore bombardment

Destroyer Division 6, which was preceding Rear Admiral Takama Tamotsu's attack unit of the light cruiser *Yura* and five more destroyers of Squadron 4.

Lieutenant Commander Agnew declined to take shelter up the Maliala River along with the camouflaged PT tender *Jamestown* and the damaged seaplane tender *McFarland* and risk being "trapped like rats."[52] Poorly charted reefs and coral heads made a run straight east impossible, so he elected to head south southeast, hoping to escape via Sealark Channel.

At 1014 the converted destroyers cleared the channel with the *Zane* in the lead. Then lookouts reported masts 21,000 yards distant. The Americans thus found themselves: "outnumbered, outgunned, outrun and because of the navigational situation out maneuvered."[53] Commander Yamada Yusuke's ships had the angle and a five-knot advantage in speed. At 1030 with the range to *Trever* down to 11,000 yards, the Japanese opened fire.

The first Japanese salvo fell several hundred yards over, and the second was an equal distant short. Seeing he was already straddled, Agnew ordered the *Trever* to steer for the splashes of the second salvo. Running at their top speed, both American ships sheared "as wildly as possible consistent with adjacent shoals."[54] They fired back with three-inch weapons aimed over open sights, the only fire control system available, at the rate of fifteen rounds a minute. At first this was merely for show, as these guns only ranged 9,900 yards, but the Japanese quickly crossed this threshold. By 1034 with the enemy only 8,000 yards back, Agnew concluded he would never reach Sealark Channel and ordered his force hard left, preferring to risk the shoals.

Japanese fire grew increasingly accurate, and many near misses churned the waters around the fleeing American ships. The *Zane*'s gunnery officer remembered, "Splashes mounted up alongside and spilled onto the decks. I felt the pressure wave and heat from several rounds which literally submerged us in spray."[55] At 1038 a five-inch projectile smacked *Zane*, killing three men and disabling the forward three-inch mount. "Other shells cut away rigging, antennae and every halyard except the one to the gaff," according to the ship's history.[56]

Then, at 1040 American aircraft appeared overhead. Japanese reports of Henderson Field's capture had been wishful thinking. Yamada turned south to fulfill his mission and engage two more targets. The *Trever* and *Zane*—the crewmen watching in "stunned and silent disbelief at our deliverance"—made their escape.[57] The *Zane* suffered considerable splinter damage in addition to the one hit, and lost three men killed and four wounded. Action reports indicate that the *Zane* expended 120 rounds during the Sealark Channel run and that the Japanese fired an estimated 450 shells in reply.

Deliverance for the DMSs represented death for two slower auxiliaries. Unlike Agnew, Yamada had no reason to risk the shoal-strewn waters and, besides, lookouts had spotted the American tug *Seminole* (1,500 tons, 16 knots, and a single three-inch gun) and the small patrol craft *YP-284* unloading supplies about three and a half miles east of Lunga Point. The Japanese destroyers demolished *YP-284* at 1050. The *Seminole* was carrying gasoline, and when the first Japanese shell struck her, a tremendous column of black smoke rose into the air. She "disappeared in a puddle of fire" at 1120.[58]

The Japanese destroyers then commenced their bombardment mission. However, Marine shore batteries fought back and hit the *Akatsuki*'s number 3 mount at 1055, killing four men. With American ships in the sound, American shore batteries returning fire, American aircraft bombing and strafing, conditions were not what the Japanese destroyers expected or were prepared to endure. They made smoke and retired. Aircraft jumped Takama's squadron in Indispensable Strait that afternoon and sank his flagship, the *Yura*.

This episode disgusted Combined Fleet headquarters. However, news that the American carriers had at long last been sighted restored optimism. "A great sea and air battle is thus to be unfolded in the area east of the Solomons and north of the Santa Cruz Islands," wrote Admiral Ugaki.[59] In fact, the USS *Enterprise*, her damage suffered in August repaired to the point where she could operate, joined the USS *Hornet*. Thrown into action by Halsey with little reason, they clashed with Combined Fleet's strike force based around the heavy carriers *Shokaku* and *Zuikaku* and the light carriers *Junyo* and *Zuiho*. In the war's penultimate carrier battle, the Japanese defeated the U.S. Navy's carrier force, disabling the *Hornet* and damaging the *Enterprise* while suffering damage to the *Zuiho* and *Zuikaku*. Japanese destroyers sank *Hornet*'s burning hulk that night after American destroyers failed to do so with repeated barrages of defective torpedoes.[60]

This defeat at sea canceled the U.S. Marine victory on Guadalcanal. An intact force of American carriers might have been able to reestablish control over the waters surrounding Guadalcanal, instead the Marines merely obtained a respite as the Japanese built up their forces once again for another decisive battle. As Lt. Cdr. E.B. Hooper of the *Washington* remarked of this time, "One wondered when the Japanese tide would be stemmed—Midway notwithstanding."[61]

CHAPTER 5

The Turn of the Tide: Guadalcanal, November 1942

It looks like the enemy is finally about to make an all-out effort against CACTUS. . . . I fear we can't turn back this time and still have the chance to go in later.

— REAR ADM. RICHMOND K. TURNER TO
REAR ADM. DANIEL J. CALLAGHAN, 10 NOVEMBER 1942

The October fiasco left Japan's 17th Army more resolved than ever. It redrew its plans based on lessons learned and decided to eschew jungle end runs in favor of a methodical, frontal offensive against Henderson Field. But there was a problem, according to a Japanese assessment: "To achieve such an Army operation, 30,000 troops, 300 artillery pieces and 30,000 tons of military supplies would have to be transported. If transports were used, 150 vessels would be needed, whereas if destroyers were used, more than 800 would be necessary."[1] Even as its carriers withdrew north to repair damage or replenish air groups, the Imperial Japanese Navy measured its oil reserves and squared its shoulders for another supreme effort.

Between 23 October and 11 November Rat operations delivered 8,000 fresh troops of the 38th Division. This fell far short of requirements, so the navy arranged a special effort for the night of 14–15 November, when eleven fast transports would deliver the rest of the division and its heavy weapons. To ensure the convoy's arrival Combined Fleet command scheduled another series of airfield bombardments of the kind that proved so successful in October.

The Japanese convoy departed Shortland Island on the afternoon of 12 November, escorted by a dozen destroyers of Tanaka's Destroyer Squadron 2. The 8th Fleet, consisting of four heavy cruisers, one light cruiser, and six destroyers, provided indirect support. The Combined Fleet's one fleet carrier, four battleships, three heavy cruisers, three light cruisers, and twenty-one destroyers under Vice Admiral Kondo sallied from Truk in a number of groups to smash the airfield and provide extra support (see Map 5.1).

Vice Admiral Halsey, meanwhile, scrambled to reinforce Guadalcanal. Some matériel arrived on 6 November, but Rear Admiral Turner commanded the real effort: two convoys crammed with supplies and nearly 6,000 soldiers in seven transports.

MAP 5.1. GUADALCANAL, NOVEMBER 1942

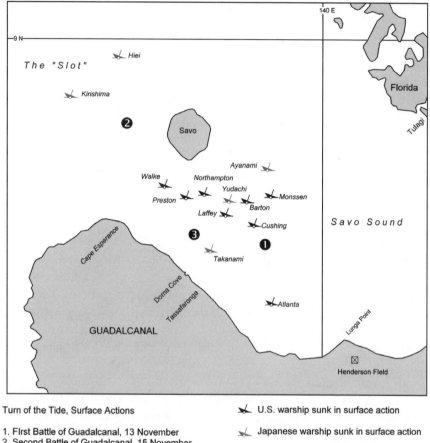

Turn of the Tide, Surface Actions

1. First Battle of Guadalcanal, 13 November
2. Second Battle of Guadalcanal, 15 November
3. Battle of Tassafaronga, 30 November

● General location of action
  Black–U.S. instigated

✕ U.S. warship sunk in surface action

✕ Japanese warship sunk in surface action

5 ___ 0 ___ 5 ___ 10 ___ 15
Nautical miles
Scale: 1:445,000   ◤ NORTH

The first arrived on 11 November, and the second anchored off Lunga Point the next day. Turner knew the Japanese planned a truly massive offensive thanks to intelligence from a number of sources, including radio intercepts, the decrypting of Yamamoto's plan, coast watchers (who reported the intimidating count of thirty-nine major warships at Shortland on 10 November), and aerial reconnaissance. In Washington, according to one historian, "the 'atmosphere of tense expectation' had reached a level that would only be matched on the eve of the Normandy invasion."[2] Similarly, the mood in Admiral Yamamoto's Combined Fleet headquarters "was grim and tense."[3] Both the Americans and the Japanese sensed they were coming to a fork in the road.

Despite being outnumbered, Halsey could not allow the Imperial navy to oblit-erate Henderson Field with its big guns and freely run transports to the island. His most powerful force, Rear Admiral Kinkaid's *Enterprise*, operating despite damage suffered during the Battle of Santa Cruz Islands and accompanied by two battleships, one heavy cruiser, one anti-aircraft cruiser, and eight destroy-ers, departed Nouméa late and lost more time in flight operations on the way north. This left Turner to forestall the crisis. He had Rear Admiral Scott, the vic-tor of Cape Esperance, leading the first convoy's escort and Rear Adm. Daniel J. Callaghan's support group. Callaghan had been Vice Admiral Ghormley's chief of staff, but when Halsey relieved Ghormley, he naturally replaced Ghormley's staff. Turner gave Callaghan a seagoing command, and the rear admiral hoisted his flag aboard the USS *San Francisco*, which he had skippered from May 1941 to May 1942. Enjoying fifteen days' seniority over Scott, Callaghan commanded the joint force at Guadalcanal, according to naval practice, despite Scott's battle experience.

Callaghan enjoyed a quiet night sweeping Savo Sound on 11–12 November. The next day air reconnaissance and traffic analysis alerted Turner to enemy movements. In fact, a formidable armada steamed south. Vice Admiral Abe Hiroaki was leading a bombardment and screening group consisting of two battleships and Destroyer Squadrons 4 and 10. In addition Destroyer Division 27, the *Shigure*, *Yugure*, and *Shiratsuyu*, screened the western approaches to the Russell Islands. Turner did not know if the enemy battleships were after his transports or the airfield, but he cor-rectly guessed the later and ordered Callaghan to stop the bombardment.

First Battle of Guadalcanal, 13 November 1942

Ashore, a Japanese naval observer, Lieutenant Commander Mitsui Kenji, reported American ships off Guadalcanal, which Combined Fleet command assumed would depart by dark. Nonetheless, Abe intended to avoid unpleasant surprises of the type that killed his friend Rear Admiral Goto.

At 1530 hours, while still 200 miles north of his destination, Abe deployed into an open order, with Takama's squadron scouting 8,750 yards ahead. The main body followed with the *Nagara* leading the two battleships, each ship 2,200 yards apart. The other destroyers proceeded in line of bearing, three on either side of the light cruiser like a giant arrow with a large head and a short tail aimed southeast. Around 2200 an intense thunderstorm enveloped the Japanese fleet. Abe rode the storm south thankful for its concealment, but his captains, struggling to keep sta-tion, did not share his contentment. The wakes of the nearest escorts broke barely visible from the *Hiei's* bridge. Commander Hara complained, "I never experienced such a rain. It was completely enervating."[4]

TABLE 5.1. FORCES ENGAGED IN THE FIRST BATTLE OF GUADALCANAL

	Type of Ship	Year Launched	Displacement, Full Load	Max. Speed (knots)	Guns (number by inch/caliber)	Torpedoes (number of tubes by diameter in inches)	Damage
Americans Task Group 67.4 (Rear Adm. D. Callaghan)							
San Francisco (F)	CA	1931	12,463	32	9 x 8/55 & 8 x 5/25		D4
Portland	CA	1932	12,755	32	9 x 8/56 & 8 x 5/25		D3
Helena	CL	1938	12,207	32	15 x 6/47 & 8 x 5/38		D2
Juneau	CLA	1941	8,340	32	16 x 5/38	8 x 21	D4
American Destroyer Division 10 (Cdr. T.M. Stokes)							
Cushing (F)	DD	1935	2,103	36	4 x 5/38	12 x 21	Sunk
Sterett	DD	1938	2,250	38	4 x 5/38	8 x 21	D3
Laffey	DD	1942	2,395	35	4 x 5/38	5 x 21	Sunk
O'Bannon	DD	1942	2,924	38	5 x 5/38	10 x 21	D1
American Task Group 62.4 (Rear Adm. N. Scott)							
Atlanta (F)	CLA	1941	8,340	32	16 x 5/38	8 x 21	Sunk
Destroyer Division 12 (Capt. R.G. Tobin)							
Aaron Ward (F)	DD	1942	2,395	35	4 x 5/38	5 x 21	D3
Monssen	DD	1942	2,395	35	4 x 5/38	5 x 21	Sunk
Barton	DD	1942	2,395	35	4 x 5/38	5 x 21	Sunk
Fletcher	DD	1942	2,924	38	5 x 5/38	10 x 21	

Japanese Sentai 11 (Vice Admiral Abe Hiroaki)							
Hiei (F)	BB	1913	36,400	30	8 x 14/45 & 14 x 6/50		D3
Kirishima	BB	1913	36,400	30	8 x 14/45 & 14 x 6/50		
Japanese Destroyer Squadron 10 (Rear Admiral Kimura Susumu)							
Nagara (F)	CL	1921	5,570	36	7 x 5.5/50 & 2 x 3.1/40	8 x 24	
Japanese Destroyer Division 6 (Captain Yamada Yusuke)							
Akatsuki (F)	DD	1932	1,950	38	6 x 5/50	9 x 24	Sunk
Inazuma	DD	1932	1,950	38	6 x 5/50	9 x 24	
Ikazuchi	DD	1932	1,950	38	6 x 5/50	9 x 24	D3
Japanese Destroyer Division 16 (Captain Shoji Kiichiro)							
Amatsukaze (F)	DD	1939	2,450	35	6 x 5/50	8 x 24	D3
Yukikaze	DD	1939	2,450	35	6 x 5/50	8 x 24	
Japanese Destroyer Division 61 (Captain Norimatsu Sanji)							
Teruzuki	DD	1941	3,430	33	8 x 3.9/65	4 x 24	
Destroyer Squadron 4 (Rear Admiral Takama Tamotsu)							
Asagumo (F)	DD	1937	2,330	35	6 x 5/50	8 x 24	
Japanese Destroyer Division 2 (Captain Tachibana Masao)							
Harusame (F)	DD	1936	1,950	34	5 x 5/50	8 x 24	
Yudachi	DD	1936	1,950	34	5 x 5/50	8 x 24	Sunk
Samidare	DD	1936	1,950	34	5 x 5/50	8 x 24	D1
Murasame	DD	1936	1,950	34	5 x 5/50	8 x 24	D1

BB—battleship, CA—heavy cruiser, CL—light cruiser, CLA—anti-aircraft light cruiser, D1—light or superficial damage (including splinter damage), D2—moderate damage (combat ability not significantly impaired), D3—significant damage (combat or maneuvering ability somewhat impaired), D4—major damage (combat and maneuvering ability significantly impaired or eliminated), DD—destroyer, F—flagship

Time: 0148–0226
Weather: Squalls, light southwesterly breeze
Visibility: New moon, very dark
Sea state: Smooth
Surprise: Americans
Mission: Americans—interception based upon specific intelligence; Japanese—shore bombardment

Storm or no storm, Callaghan expected the enemy. He and Capt. Cassin Young, who had assumed command of the *San Francisco* on 10 November, discussed the situation on the evening of 12 November. A witness remembered Cassin "in an understandably agitated state, sometimes waving his arms, as he remarked: 'But this is suicide.' Admiral Dan Callaghan replied. 'Yes I know, but we have to do it.' He was calm, unemotional, resolute, and perhaps resigned to his fate."[5]

The American transports cleared Savo Sound at 1815 hours. Callaghan preceded them into Indispensable Strait and returned at midnight via Lengo Channel. He deployed his ships in line-ahead formation, as Scott had done at Cape Esperance. Destroyer Division 10 led, followed by the *Atlanta, San Francisco, Portland, Helena, Juneau,* and Destroyer Division 12. The destroyers maintained intervals of 500 yards, the cruisers 700 yards, and the divisions 800 yards. Mitsui reported the expected sailing of the transports, but missed Callaghan's return. The moon had set in an overcast sky, and murky darkness shrouded the sound. Ashore, Japanese troops lit two bonfires to assist Abe's navigation, and on Mt. Austin Mitsui settled down, binoculars at hand, to spot the fall of shot.

At 2350 Abe's force approached Savo Island but "extremely poor visibility" rendered "the bombardment impossible," so at 0005 on 13 November he ordered a simultaneous 180-degree turn to clear the storm.[6] Not surprisingly, the wild run south had disrupted the Japanese formation. Feeling the loom of land, Squadron 4 had come about even before the admiral gave the order to do so and veered north while the main body steamed northeast. At 0038, after hearing the weather had cleared over Henderson Field, Abe ordered another 180-degree turn. By this time Squadron 4's *Asagumo, Murasame,* and *Samidare,* rather than being 9,000 yards ahead of the main body, had ended up behind the battleships and the squadron's other two ships, the *Yudachi* and *Harusame,* preceded the *Nagara* by only a few thousand yards. The left wing of Squadron 10—the *Yukikaze, Amatsukaze,* and *Teruzuki*—straggled off the *Hiei's* port beam, and the right wing, which consisted of Division 6, proceeded on a line of bearing behind the *Nagara's* starboard quarter.

At 0046 Abe ordered Squadron 4 to probe Savo Sound. As the battleships swept past Savo Island at twenty-three knots, the admiral received word from shore that the area appeared clear. Minutes later at 0130 Abe, unaware that most of Squadron 4's ships trailed him and with that group of destroyers remaining silent, decided to start the bombardment at 0138. The battleships had finished loading their Type 3 bombardment shells, a fourteen-inch HE round packed with incendiary cylinders. Visibility was good with a slight haze at sea level.

American radar detected Abe completing his preparations. The *Helena*'s SG radar caught the *Yudachi* at 0124 from 27,000 yards and the main body at 32,000 yards, bearing 310 degrees true. At 0128 Callaghan turned his column northwest, straight toward the Japanese. Reports began flooding into the *San Francisco*'s flag bridge from the *O'Bannon*, *Aaron Ward*, and *Helena*. The *San Francisco* mounted inferior SC radar, and Callaghan struggled to grasp the rapidly evolving tactical situation. An officer standing watch on the flagship's bridge recalled, "Reports from those ships [with better radars] were eagerly awaited in Flag Plot. . . . [But] this information was sometimes slow in coming, sometimes contradictory, and frequently incomplete."[7] As Callaghan sought clarification via the crowded TBS net, the fleets barreled toward each other at 1,350 yards a minute.

Callaghan intended to turn to starboard and cross the Japanese T, but he waited too long. At 0137 he ordered the lead ship, the *Cushing*, to turn 50 degrees starboard to due north. The first few destroyers made the turn. Then, at 0141 the *Cushing* suddenly spotted shapes crossing her bow 3,000 yards ahead. Her skipper, Lt. Cdr. Edward Parker, a Balikpapan and Badung Strait veteran, maneuvered left to unmask his ship's torpedo batteries as the division commander, Cdr. Thomas M. Stokes, sought permission to fire. The *Yudachi*'s captain, Commander Kikkawa Kiyoshi, who had also been at Badung Strait, remembered, "I was flabbergasted to see an enemy destroyer suddenly emerging from the darkness and bearing down to strike us amidships."[8] Kikkawa immediately steered to avoid and broadcast an alarm. This electrified Abe, but where was the *Yudachi*? The *Hiei*'s lookouts then spotted four objects 10,000 yards ahead. By this time Callaghan had radioed permission for the *Cushing* to engage, but the opportunity had long vanished.

At 0145 the American admiral alerted all ships to stand by to open fire. For his part, Abe ordered *Sentai* 11 to steer east by northeast and switch to surface targets. Meanwhile, the American column disintegrated into disarray as captains were forced to account for the *Cushing*'s unexpected maneuver and changed course to avoid collisions rather than focusing on the enemy.

At 0147 Callaghan insisted he wanted the task force on a course of 000 degrees but the *Atlanta* came sharply to port to miss the *O'Bannon*, which was steering to avoid ramming the *Sterett*. As the *San Francisco* did the same, Callaghan radioed, "What are you doing?" The *Atlanta* replied, "Avoiding our own destroyers."[9]

At 0148 American intentions became irrelevant. A Japanese history notes, "Visibility allowed shelling without use of searchlight, but Abe ordered *Hiei* to use her searchlight so the whole fleet would know enemy targets and to screen the Japanese fleet."[10] The *Akatsuki* and *Nagara* also illuminated. After sweeping the American line the *Hiei*'s powerful lights settled on the *Atlanta*'s tall superstructure.

One sailor recalled, "You could just about feel the heat it was throwing off."[11] The *Atlanta*'s skipper, Capt. Samuel P. Jenkins, opened fire before Callaghan's orders—even before Abe's gunners let loose. A flurry of *Atlanta*'s five-inch shells hurled back up the tunnel of light from a range of 1,600 yards. By then, the *Nagara, Hiei, Inazuma, Ikazuchi,* and (perhaps) *Akatsuki* had fixed the *Atlanta* in their crosshairs (see Map 5.2).

MAP 5.2. FIRST BATTLE OF GUADALCANAL, SITUATION AT 0150

At this point Callaghan finally unleashed his gunners with the order, "Odd ships fire to starboard, even to port."[12] Moving down the American column, the *Cushing* targeted the *Yukikaze* (or maybe the *Yudachi*) 2,000 yards off her starboard bow while nervously eyeing the much larger *Hiei* just a thousand yards to port and closing. The *Laffey*, although tracking targets to starboard, picked out the *Akatsuki* on her port side. The *Sterett's* guns, already aimed to port, swung to starboard at a shape—probably the *Nagara*—4,000 yards distant.

The eruption of gunfire caught the *O'Bannon* "making many rudder and engine changes to avoid collision with ship ahead."[13] She had been tracking a target to starboard but switched to a searchlight on her port bow. The *Atlanta's* guns lashed out at the *Hiei* and *Akatsuki*. The *San Francisco* engaged the *Yudachi* 4,000 yards to starboard. The *Portland* shot at a target 6,200 yards to starboard, again the *Yudachi*. The *Helena* commenced firing rapidly to port at the *Akatsuki*. The *Juneau* also went to port against either the *Akatsuki* or *Hiei*. The *Aaron Ward* gauged her target, probably the *Hiei*, as being 7,000 yards off her port bow. The *Barton* and *Monssen* waited, but at the column's rear the *Fletcher* sniped at the *Inazuma* to port.

The *Nagara* crossed the American T from west to east, illuminating and firing on a "*Portland*-class heavy cruiser."[14] The *Hiei* and *Kirishima*, still following the *Nagara*, engaged using Type 3 rounds. They screened the *Yukikaze*, *Amatsukaze*, and *Teruzuki* sailing on *Hiei's* port side. The *Yudachi* and *Harusame* maneuvered to starboard of the American formation. Led by the *Asagumo* the rest of Squadron 4 swung behind the main body and steamed to catch up from the *Teruzuki's* port quarter. The *Akatsuki* and *Yudachi* attracted most of the enemy attention as the *Inazuma* and *Ikazuchi* bore down, preparing a torpedo attack.

Captain Jenkins recalled that the *Atlanta's* gunnery action against the Japanese only lasted one or two minutes, but in that space the unarmored American cruiser absorbed thirty-two shells.[15] This barrage may have killed Admiral Scott. The only survivor from his staff recalled being hit by a splinter, glancing at the admiral standing outside the charthouse, and seeing Scott collapse to the deck as he stepped forward.[16] Then things deteriorated for the *Atlanta*.

The *Inazuma* and *Ikazuchi* launched six torpedoes each from a thousand yards, and at 0153 a Long Lance clobbered the *Atlanta* in her port side forward engine room. All power failed, her guns fell silent, and *Atlanta's* bow began to swing to port as she lost way. The opening exchange inflicted less damage on the other American ships. The *Hiei* landed a shell on the *Portland's* hanger, and three 5-inch shells struck the *Helena*, one of which stopped her clock at 0148.

The Americans still used smokeless power that ignited with a bright orange flash, while the Japanese flashless powder provided a poor point of aim. This made the *Akatsuki's* Captain Yamada Yusuke's decision to illuminate one he barely lived long enough to regret, as the *Atlanta's* first shells smashed the Japanese destroyer's bridge and slaughtered the personnel there. Flames erupted on the *Akatsuki*, drawing the attention of at least five American ships. After slicing through the American column ahead of the *Atlanta*, the *Akatsuki* drifted to a stop. The *Inazuma* and *Ikazuchi* sheered away to the northwest and mingled in the American line.

The *Ikazuchi* absorbed perhaps three 8-inch shells from the *Portland* and maybe the *San Francisco* and three 5-inch rounds from the *San Francisco*. This barrage killed twenty-one men aboard the *Ikazuchi* and wounded twenty-eight. Her number 1 mount disabled, a blaze raging in her gun's handling room, and her ammunition cooking off, the *Ikazuchi's* captain, fearing a magazine explosion, ordered his men to stand by to abandon ship. However, the crew managed to douse the flames and save their ship.

The *Hiei* towered over the other combatants. A Japanese history relates, "At the same time she deployed her searchlight enemy small shell and machine guns concentrated on *Hiei*, and swept everything above the upper deck. The foremast immediately flamed up and all the light antiaircraft guns were destroyed, electricity to the main guns was cut, the fire director for the secondary guns was also destroyed and she lost for some time fire directors and her ability to communicate with both wireless and signals."[17]

The four American destroyers that unintentionally swarmed the *Hiei* also suffered greatly. The *Cushing*, obeying Callaghan's instructions, had to content herself with hosing the giant vessel's superstructure with 20-mm bullets. She launched one torpedo, but the Japanese battleship's secondary batteries lashed back, and a six-inch shell massacred the destroyer's torpedo crew. Then, as she passed just 500 yards to port, the *Cushing* saw the *Yukikaze* to the north. Hit at least ten times, with some of the shells coming from friendly ships, the *Cushing* suffered a disabled gun and feed pump that caused a gradual loss of power.

The *Laffey*, meanwhile, pumped a hundred 5-inch rounds at the *Akatsuki*. When she saw the *Hiei* looming to port, the *Laffey* swung every gun against this target. Her centerline torpedo mount, trained to starboard, took a minute to rotate and discharge five fish. Two failed to run the 450 yards required to arm and bounced off the *Hiei's* hull. Then, the *Laffey* squeezed under the *Hiei's* bow with just yards to spare. The Japanese battleship could not depress her guns enough to shoot back. An officer, stationed high on the *Hiei's* towering mast lamented, "We missed the antiquated rams very badly."[18] The *Laffey's* fifty-five–pound shells shattered against the battleship's armor, but they shredded the *Hiei's* superstructure and slaughtered exposed crewmen. Abe and Captain Nishida Masao fell wounded. Abe's chief of staff, Commander Suzuki Masakane, was killed.

Flames raged up and down the *Hiei's* bridge structure, and the survivors eventually scrambled down a rope nearly a hundred feet to the deck. Meanwhile, either the *Inazuma* or *Ikazuchi* shelled the *Sterett*, sparking explosions and disabling her steering gear. The *O'Bannon*, dueling the *Akatsuki*, nearly collided with the *Sterett* in passing. Falling in behind the *Laffey*, the *O'Bannon* also engaged the *Hiei*.

The two destroyers in the Japanese van, the *Yudachi* and *Harusame*, had bounced northeast. When he saw the battle erupt behind him, the *Yudachi's*

Commander Kikkawa looped southwest toward the thick of the action. The *Harusame* lost sight of the *Yudachi* in a forest of shell splashes and headed northwest. After cutting through the American column the *Nagara* turned northwest as well. Although her larger silhouette drew fire from all along the line the light cruiser escaped harm. After battling the *Cushing*, the *Yukikaze* picked up the *Nagara* and thereafter stuck by her side.

The *Amatsukaze*, which was abeam of the *Hiei* when the action began, accelerated to escape enemy shells dropping around her. Commander Hara described it as a "spectacle so dazzling that for many moments I stood blinded on the bridge." Then he saw "numerous American ships moving like wraiths in the darkness along the coast of Guadalcanal to the right."[19] The *Amatsukaze* dashed to the south southeast and turned at 0154, hurling a spread of torpedoes toward the rear American destroyers.[20] The *Teruzuki* initially engaged the *Atlanta*, *Cushing*, and *Sterett*. She closed on the *Yukikaze* after that.

The *San Francisco*, steering due north, targeted the *Harusame*, but the crippled *Atlanta* drifted into the *San Francisco*'s line of fire. The American heavy cruiser's gunners proved devastatingly accurate, hitting the *Atlanta* seven times with a nine-gun broadside that blasted through the *Atlanta*'s bridge in an area six by eight yards without exploding and which might have killed Scott. Six shells from another *San Francisco* salvo destroyed the *Atlanta*'s 4 and 5 turrets. Six more scattered hits damaged turrets 3 and 6 and compromised the light cruiser's watertight integrity.

The *San Francisco* then switched targets and had flung two salvos toward the *Hiei* when a blaze beyond the *Atlanta*—probably the *Akatsuki*'s death throes—revealed to Callaghan the *Atlanta*'s plight and his ship's horrible mistake. He grabbed the TBS and shouted, "Cease fire own ships" at 0153. The *San Francisco*, *O'Bannon*, *Helena*, and *Fletcher* complied, as did the *Portland* after Capt. Laurence T. DuBose asked Callaghan if this is what he really intended.

The *Akatsuki*'s burning hulk also illuminated new targets lurching down from the north. Callaghan broadcasted his final orders: "Give 'em hell" and "We want the big ones! Get the big ones first!"

As the American and Japanese flagships passed on opposite courses, the range dropped to 500 yards. The *San Francisco*'s gun crews loaded and fired, knowing their lives depended on it, while the *Laffey* and *O'Bannon* harassed the *Hiei* from the other beam. The Japanese battleship's first two broadsides fell short. The range was so close, the incoming shells appeared as "black dots surrounded by orange glows."[21] The third volley scored three solid hits with Type 3 rounds. They sparked many small blazes, but the *San Francisco*'s five-inch turret armor defeated the fourteen-inch shell that struck turret 2. Attracted by the continuous flash of gunnery, the *Nagara* and *Kirishima* targeted the *San Francisco* as well. Caught in a crossfire, the flagship's men, including Admiral Callaghan and Captain Young, were scythed down.

Lt. Cdr. Bruce McCandless, climbed to the navigation bridge and found "a weird place ... in the intermittent light of gunfire. . . . Bodies, helmeted and lifejacketed, limbs and gear littered the deck. The siren was moaning and water was raining down through holes in the deck above."[22] As damage accrued, the *San Francisco* veered south, but McCandless brought her back to a westerly course lest the battle line think the flagship had abandoned the struggle. He did not know the battle line no longer existed.

Captain Kikkawa's *Yudachi* bore much of the responsibility for breaking the American line. After spinning in her tracks, the *Yudachi* headed southwest to starboard of the American column. At 0155 she launched eight torpedoes west northwest, targeting an enemy heavy cruiser. She then sliced between the *Aaron Ward* and *Juneau*. The American ships nearly collided. Some time between 0158 and 0201 one of the torpedoes the *Yudachi* had launched walloped the *Portland* aft on her starboard side. The impact ripped open forty-five feet of hull and jammed the after eight-inch turret. Worse, blast damage twisted the ship, creating "the same effect as if she were using right full rudder."[23] For the rest of the battle the *Portland* sailed in circles.

Aboard the *Hiei*, meanwhile, riddled by between 28 and 38 eight-inch shells and between seventy and seventy-four 5-inch shells (nearly a third of which were duds), all guns operated under local control and external and internal communications had been blasted into nonexistence. The most critical blow to the *Hiei* came from an eight-inch dud that struck beneath the waterline, penetrated the hull, and ruptured a ventilation duct. This flooded the steering room and caused an eventual loss of steering control.

The *Kirishima* stalked in her flagship's shadow until 0155, when Abe ordered her to withdraw. The *Kirishima* suffered only a single eight-inch hit and some casualties from machine gun fire. She expended 59 fourteen-inch shells (22 of which were Type 3 bombardment rounds) and 313 six-inch rounds.

After the first flow of battle swept past the *Cushing*, she enjoyed five minutes to attend to her damage. Then the *Hiei* appeared on her starboard quarter. The *Cushing*'s torpedo crew rushed to fire six tubes from 1,200 yards. All weapons missed, malfunctioned, or ran deep. Then the *Nagara* and *Yukikaze* bombarded the drifting, burning American ship as they passed heading west and registered at least seven more hits. These doomed the *Cushing*. Although she managed to launch three more torpedoes at around 0201 at what was taken to be a transport, she had no power for firefighting. Parker reluctantly ordered his crew to abandon ship at 0220. In all, the *Cushing* lost fifty-nine men and had fifty-six wounded.

After being nearly rammed by the *Hiei*, the *Laffey* experienced calm until Rear Admiral Takama's *Asagumo*, *Murasame*, and *Samidare* swept past. The *Asagumo* loosed a volley of eight Long Lances, and the division bashed the *Laffey* with at least 3 five-inch shells. Flames erupted, catching the *Kirishima*'s notice; a fourteen-inch round destroyed the *Laffey*'s after boiler room. At 0202 one of the *Asagumo*'s torpedoes smashed the tortured American destroyer and obliterated her stern. Lt. Cdr. William E. Hank ordered his men overboard, and shortly thereafter the *Laffey* exploded with heavy casualties.

Takama's force continued and reached a position northwest of the American cruisers just before 0200, at which time the *Asagumo* engaged the *Helena* to starboard. The *Murasame*, trailing by 2,200 yards, illuminated the *Monssen* also to starboard at 0202. The *Murasame*'s five-inch guns barked and eight torpedoes splashed into the water on an 1,100-yard run. In return, a shell struck the Japanese ship's forward fireroom wounding three men. The *Murasame* doused her searchlights and spun in a circle to escape. Boiler damage reduced the Japanese destroyer's speed to 27.5 knots.

Two minutes later one of the *Murasame*'s torpedoes blasted the *Juneau*, which had been trailing the *Helena*. Observing this, the *Samidare*—hit by one shell that sparked a small fire—canceled the torpedo salvo she had been about to unleash.

The *Juneau*'s activities in the First Battle of Guadalcanal passed largely undocumented.[24] Her action report merely notes that she crossed the *San Francisco*'s bow from port to starboard and was then torpedoed. It credited her with firing approximately 25 five-inch rounds, but this seems conservative. When the *Yudachi* cut astern of the *Juneau* at 0159, the two ships swapped salvos. The *Juneau* hit the Japanese destroyer's bridge, forcing Kikkawa to make smoke. Then the American light cruiser actually lifted out of the water as one of the *Murasame*'s Long Lances destroyed her forward fireroom and fractured her keel. Listing to port and unable to work her guns, the *Juneau* exited the scene of battle, nearly colliding with the *Helena* on the way.

At 0155, after a point-blank exchange of volleys and a near collision with the *Yudachi*, the *Aaron Ward* observed two torpedoes pass underneath. The *Barton*, immediately behind, was not so fortunate. She had slung about seventy rounds and five torpedoes to port at 0154 and then rang up emergency stop to avoid plowing into the *Aaron Ward*. At that moment the *Amatsukaze*'s torpedo salvo churned past. At 0159 a Long Lance bashed the *Barton*'s forward fireroom and another smashed into the forward engine room seconds later. A massive sheet of flame erupted from the *Barton*'s number two stack, and the ship broke in half. The stern sank immediately, but the bow floated stem up like a temporary grave marker for ten minutes. Only forty-two of the *Barton*'s men survived.

A snapshot of the situation at 0200 would show the Japanese in two groups and the rear ships in the long American column beginning to pile between them. Flashes, explosions, flames, and the tumultuous racket of gunfire ranging from the nervous burst of machine guns to the deadly, deep-throated roar of 1,500-pound battleship projectiles assailed the senses. The clouds glowed from the harsh light of drifting pyrotechnics; orange and red reflections shot over the water and disappeared. The bitter smell of high explosives, smoke, fuel oil, and death lashed the air. No frame of reference existed to comprehend the bedlam of this, the most intense and confused night melee ever fought.

At 0159 the *Aaron Ward* continued north at eighteen knots, attracting friendly eight-inch shellfire. At 0207 she barely avoided another collision, this time with the *Sterett*. Then, at 0210 the *Aaron Ward* pumped twenty-five salvos at the *Yudachi*, which had reappeared off her starboard bow. One shell landed in the Japanese destroyer's forward fireroom and another scorched her forecastle. The *Sterett* chimed in with two torpedoes. The *Yudachi* wandered off to the west to reload her tubes and then doubled back.

At 0220 or thereabouts, the *Yudachi* tangled with the *Sterett* once again. Kikkawa, thinking a friendly ship was attacking him, was flashing recognition signals even as American shells hit the *Yudachi*'s bow and number 1 boiler room. The *Yudachi* shot back, but more projectiles struck her fire director, bridge, and forward engine room. Then, the *Teruzuki* appeared off the *Sterett*'s port side. The rapid-shooting Japanese anti-aircraft destroyer registered two effective hits, disabling the American's fire control and her two aft mounts. The *Sterett* fled northeast but then lost steering control, and by 0235 she lay burning, dead in the water with her forward engine room flooded. Twenty-eight of the *Sterett*'s men died, and four leapt overboard to escape the flames. The encounter left the *Yudachi* drifting without power, twenty-six of her men dead and thirty-five wounded.

The *Monssen* gained a temporary reprieve when a torpedo from the same salvo that undid the *Barton* passed beneath her. The *Monssen* headed north partially blind because a Japanese air attack that afternoon had disabled her fire control radar. Then she encountered the *Hiei* 4,000 yards off her starboard bow. Five of the *Monssen*'s torpedoes hit the water, but the entire volley missed. Next, she aimed five torpedoes from her forward mount one at a time at a target several thousand yards to starboard, which may have been the *Nagara*. These also missed.

Then the *Monssen* found trouble. A ship to port lit her with a star shell. Thinking it was an American round, the *Monssen* flashed recognition lights. The *Nagara*, *Yukikaze*, and *Teruzuki* lurked off her starboard beam, and these lights attracted a pair of searchlights followed by a storm of shells and four torpedoes. The *Monssen* barely avoided two torpedoes, and two others ran deep. The American ship fought back and landed one shell on *Nagara* that damaged the cruiser's number 7 mount, killing six men and wounding seven. In return thirty-seven rounds fatally perforated the *Monssen*'s hull and superstructure. The 110 survivors abandoned ship at 0220, and the wreck burned until the next afternoon before finally sinking. The *Nagara* fired a total of 136 rounds during the entire action.

The *Helena*, like the *O'Bannon* and *Fletcher*, benefited from the improved view her SG radar provided and Captain Hoover's trust in it. The rapid-firing light cruiser blasted the *Akatsuki* and engaged another target with her secondary battery, expending 175 six-inch and 20 five-inch rounds in the process. Hoover then paused at about 0154 to assess the situation, and Callaghan's cease-fire order kept the *Helena*'s guns silent.

The *Helena* passed the *Portland* when the torpedoed heavy cruiser swung out of line and maneuvered, trying to sort friend from foe. At 0204 the *Helena* came upon the *Amatsukaze* pummeling *San Francisco*. The American flagship was in a bad way by this time. Hara described the *San Francisco* as "a phantom ship . . . spewing fire and smoke throughout [her] length."[25] He claimed he launched four torpedoes, but it was too close for them to arm. The *Helena*'s gunners unleashed their six-inch weapons and hosed the surprised destroyer with 130-pound shells for ninety seconds. Hits ignited fires along the length of Hara's ship and destroyed the *Amatsukaze*'s hydraulics, so the Japanese destroyer could not train her turrets or steer. Forty-three of *Amatsukaze*'s men died. The *Helena* ceased firing only when another ship fouled her range.

Heading north, the *Helena* passed the *Kirishima* and peppered the battleship's bridge with 40-mm rounds, to which the battleship replied with a salvo of fourteen-inch shells. One of the giant Japanese shells exploded on the face of the *Helena*'s number 4 turret and did minimal damage. With that, the 40-mm guns prudently fell silent. The *Helena* engaged two other targets in the next few minutes, one of which was more than 16,000 yards away, before turning to follow the *San Francisco* south and out of the fight.

The *Fletcher*, skippered by Cdr. William M. Cole, enjoyed the rear position, modern radar, and a prototype combat information center. At 0200, having observed the *Barton*'s demise, the *Fletcher*'s position seemed equally dangerous. The *Fletcher*'s action report records, "[O]ne torpedo was seen to broach and porpoise about 50 yards ahead, two were seen to pass under the ship . . . and one passed astern. Medium caliber shells were splashing on both sides of us." The *Fletcher* tore north at thirty-five knots while her "[o]wn five-inch guns continued to fire all during the preceding events with unknown results."[26]

At 0205 the *Fletcher* hauled around to the south. She stalked the *Helena* for ten minutes, and at 0222 sent ten torpedoes streaking toward the American cruiser. She observed "two or three low horizontal flashes. . . . [A] series of increasingly large explosions took place . . . followed by continuous burning." Finally, the target "blew up and completely disintegrated."[27] Fortunately, however, all of the *Fletcher*'s torpedoes missed. The *Fletcher* emerged from the battle completely unscathed.

At 0200 Abe ordered his fleet to withdraw east of Savo Island. By 0220 the *Yukikaze* and *Teruzuki* had begun steering north; the *Inazuma* had preceded them.

The *Harusame*'s report describes her heading north until she encountered an enemy cruiser to starboard at 0215. This, she illuminated and shelled, causing a great fire. The *Harusame* then launched three torpedoes and finished off her target. It is uncertain which ship the *Harusame* engaged, probably the *Monssen* but it may have been the *Yudachi*. The crippled Japanese ships *Amatsukaze* and *Ikazuchi* limped north independently, with the *Amatsukaze* making twenty knots and being steered manually. Hara noted that the *Amatsukaze* "moved like a drunken man, skidding wildly from side to side."[28] Later, the Japanese destroyer's crew counted thirty-three holes bigger than an inch ventilating the vessel.

The *Samidare* stayed south to assist the *Yudachi*. After rescuing the *Yudachi*'s crew, the *Samidare* attempted to sink the hulk with three torpedoes, but two ran deep and one failed to explode or missed. The *Hiei*, meanwhile, wobbled slowly up the strait west of Savo. Admiral Kimura aboard the *Nagara* swung back to assist Abe. The *Kirishima*, steaming at high speed, had already escaped into the Slot.[29]

At 0226 the *Helena*'s Captain Hoover determined that he was senior surviving American officer. He led the *San Francisco, Juneau, O'Bannon, Fletcher,* and *Sterett* south toward Sealark Channel. Five U.S. and two Japanese ships remained on the scene. The *Aaron Ward* had no power, and the *Portland* continued to circle while the *Atlanta*'s crew fought fires and flooding. The *Cushing, Monssen,* and *Yudachi* all burned. At 0630 the *Portland* hurled six six-gun salvos at the *Yudachi* from a range of 12,500 yards. The *Portland* tallied hits and the valiant Japanese destroyer finally sank.

At 0635 the *Hiei* got back into the act and winged four two-gun volleys toward the *Aaron Ward* from a range of 26,000 yards. The *Hiei*'s shells straddled the *Aaron Ward*, but then American aircraft found the Japanese battleship. After that, the *Hiei* was too busy to bother cripples. The *Portland* and *Aaron Ward* finally made Tulagi, but the *Atlanta* foundered off Lunga Point. She lost 172 men killed and 79 injured.

The *Hiei*'s engine spaces remained intact, but flooding in the steering engine room shorted the steering motor and forced her to keep the rudder centered manually and to conn by engines alone. Progressive flooding finally forced the engine room's abandonment, and the rudder jammed full right. This left the *Hiei*, much like the *Portland*, sailing in a wide circle north of Savo with the *Shigure, Shiratsuyu, Yugure, Yukikaze,* and *Teruzuki* attending. The sight of such a fat, helpless target bewitched the Americans. U.S. dive-bombers and torpedo bombers from Henderson Field and the *Enterprise* and B-17s conducted seventy sorties and scored three bomb hits and at least four torpedo hits. However, none of these sank the battleship. In fact, the *Hiei*'s loss seemed more a matter of nerves. Abe, who transferred to the *Yukikaze*, ordered the *Hiei* abandoned at 1020 and 1235. Captain Nishida, much against his wishes, finally complied at 1535, and the battleship foundered unseen during the night.

Admiral Callaghan tried to manage this confusing and unique battle, but conditions rendered his efforts futile, even counterproductive. (The same can be said of Scott at Cape Esperance.) Callaghan's failure to cross the Japanese T resulted from the *Yudachi* and *Harusame*'s advance position, which left him unable to form a coherent picture of the Japanese force. The Japanese force had no coherence. But perhaps Callaghan's charge into the heart of Abe's formation best met the situation. If, for example, Callaghan had managed to cross the T of the two lead destroyers and the American line had opened fire, presumably concentrating on the near targets, it is easy to imagine a scenario in which Abe's flank destroyers counterattacked with torpedoes while the Japanese battleships stood off and bombarded the burning American wrecks.

Ultimately, a commander's actions must be judged by their results. A more elegant or economic solution was doubtlessly possible. Nonetheless, Callaghan saved Henderson Field from a devastating, perhaps decisive, blow, if the results of the October battleship bombardment provided any measure. Callaghan's sacrifice also fatally delayed Tanaka's grand convoy. These two outcomes preserved the American position on Guadalcanal.

Abe ordered a withdrawal at the very moment when the battle hung in the balance. Except for the *Hiei* and three destroyers, his force remained intact, and most of the Japanese destroyers still retained their torpedo reloads. However, Abe lost the ability to visualize the situation. A battleship was apparently very much superior to a destroyer, but battleships were not designed to fight destroyers—even ones lacking functional torpedoes—at close range and the *Hiei*'s fate showed why.

The performance of the infamous Japanese Type 93 Long Lance torpedoes likewise merits comment. The Japanese launched as many as seventy-two of these fearsome weapons. Six of the Type 93s struck five targets, accounting for all but one of the U.S. ships sunk, including the *Juneau*, but given the very short ranges and reports of torpedoes running deep, it could have been far worse. The fact that the battleships had to fight the battle's most critical minutes with bombardment rounds undoubtedly saved the Americans from some harm. The *Portland* reported afterwards, "Examination[of] two fourteen-inch hits . . . clearly indicates Japanese battleships were loaded with bombardment shell instantaneous[ly] fused. Practically no penetration and little damage."[30]

Abe and Callaghan's wild melee, for all its blood and sacrifice, merely postponed a decision. Although Admiral Yamamoto possessed the resources to neutralize Henderson Field, he proved reluctant to risk his "important striking force" because it "could hardly be supplemented afterwards."[31] Yamamoto, considering his dwindling fuel reserves, was being thrifty as well. The U.S. Navy demonstrated more determination at this critical juncture. Admiral Halsey was willing to risk almost everything, although it helped that Admiral Nimitz and Admiral

King could look over their shoulders at shipyards bulging with new construction. In the end, this made the difference.

The Battle in the Balance

Representative of Combined Fleet's state of mind, Yamamoto ordered Admiral Kondo to bombard Henderson Field, but, according to Admiral Ugaki, "The rest of the day [13 November] was spent in long, involved discussions on how to deal with the *Hiei*."[32] The battleship's fate received more attention than the real problem facing the Imperial command: How to guarantee the convoy's arrival. Abe failed, but at least, he cleared the way for Vice Admiral Mikawa to conduct the previously scheduled cruiser bombardment. On the American side, Halsey pondered his staff's arguments against sending his last major surface assets, the fast battleships *Washington* and *South Dakota*, to Savo Sound. He then ordered them to form a task force and head north. These American ships lay 360 miles away, however. Even steaming hard, they could only reach Lunga Point by 0800 hours on 14 November, too late to confront Mikawa.

Mikawa arrived on schedule and undetected—a reconnaissance failure facilitated by the American preoccupation with the *Hiei*. The Japanese 8th Fleet commander, however, cautiously retained his two heavy cruisers, the *Chokai* and *Kinugasa*, and one light cruiser, the *Isuzu*, northwest of Savo Island while Rear Admiral Nishimura took the heavy cruisers *Suzuya* and *Maya*, the light cruiser *Tenryu*, and the destroyers *Yugumo*, *Makigumo*, *Kazagumo*, and *Arashio* into Savo Sound. At 0130 on 14 November the *Maya* commenced flinging what amounted to 485 eight-inch shells, and the *Suzuya* added 504 rounds.[33]

The only resistance to the Japanese bombardment of Henderson Field came from a pair of overmatched PT boats. Nonetheless, Nishimura's ships missed their main target, instead cratering dirt around the auxiliary airstrip, Fighter One, and destroying three aircraft and damaging fifteen. These results fell far short of what Japan required. At a minimum Mikawa could have used his other cruisers to augment the bombardment. However, this indication that the Japanese admirals had learned caution was the signal that their nighttime dominance of Savo Sound had come to an end, even in the absence of American warships. This was another fruit of Callaghan's and Scott's sacrifices.

As Mikawa's cruisers hustled north knowing they had failed to knock out American airpower, Rear Admiral Tanaka's convoy sailed south, cheerfully expecting Henderson Field to have been neutralized. The first American search planes began winging north at 0600 hours on 14 November, and Mikawa's purgatory started at 0930, when a dive bomber attack left the *Kinugasa* with a 10-degree list to port. Later, one of the American airplanes crashed into the *Maya* and inflicted damage that killed thirty-seven men and forced the cruiser to return to Japan for repairs. Bombs near missed the *Chokai* and *Isuzu*.

After roughing up the Japanese cruisers, the American flyers scourged the advancing convoy. Aware of the implications of the arrival of the Japanese force, "the American airfield complex bustled with fevered activities," one historian has written.[34] Men hustled to rearm and refuel returning aircraft for yet another strike. These shuttle attacks sank six transports outright and sent one limping back to Shortland Island heavily damaged. The need to evade attacks and rescue survivors cost Tanaka precious hours. He considered retreating to wait for a more propitious time, but Combined Fleet command ordered him to press forward regardless of losses.

Although air attacks had already eviscerated the Japanese convoy, Vice Admiral Kondo steamed south to bombard Henderson anyway. Abe claimed he had sunk or damaged nine cruisers and nine destroyers, but Japanese flyers reported two more cruisers and four destroyers barreling north to contest Savo Sound. Combined Fleet tasked Kondo with the twin missions of "bombard[ing] the airfield while preparing for the enemy's counterattack on our convoy."[35] The Japanese admirals seemed trapped in a labyrinth, hedged in by their belief in the invincibility of Japanese fighting spirit, their need to fulfill agreements with the army, their own faulty intelligence, and a sense the campaign did not really merit their complete effort. There was no feeling that the Empire's fate could be decided in Savo Sound.

Rear Adm. Willis A. Lee, pacing the *Washington*'s high bridge, possessed a keener sense of the moment's urgency. He was breaking all the rules. He was leading new, nonexpendable capital ships—the last significant U.S. surface assets in the South Pacific—to offer a night battle in restricted waters against the best the Japanese had to offer. Moreover, a lack of preparation and compelling need forced him to repeat all of Scott and Callaghan's mistakes, as well as to make some new ones of his own. The destroyers under Lee's command came from four different divisions, chosen only because they had the most fuel—two lacked fire control radar. He placed his only modern, radar-equipped destroyer last in line and assigned her the task of firing star shell. He did not designate an overall destroyer commander. The *Washington*'s and *South Dakota*'s experience operating in division formation consisted of their thirty-hour run up to the battle zone. The *Washington* had conducted just one night battle practice eleven months earlier. He didn't even possess radio call signs to communicate with Guadalcanal. Under way, Lee improvised a battle plan and signaled it to his captains on the fly. He deployed the U.S. ships in a column formation.

However, one vital factor helped mitigate this dismal list: The *Washington* was the world's finest, most powerful surface warship in commission, and, except for two damaged guns in turret 2, the *South Dakota* was nearly her equal.

Lee knew Kondo's ships were coming. Although the Japanese force had escaped the attention of the otherwise-occupied Cactus Air Force, an American submarine spotted the Imperial flotilla that afternoon. By the evening of 14 November Lee's scraped-together task force loitered west of Guadalcanal ready to penetrate Savo Sound as darkness fell. For his part, Kondo expected a sea fight and arranged his powerful force accordingly. The latest information from his floatplanes was that "two cruisers and eight destroyers were heading at high speed to the island, [leading] to the conclusion that enemy battleships were withdrawing southward as usual."[36]

Kondo intended to brush the U.S. ships aside using his destroyer squadrons and then bombard the airfield before supporting the unloading of the transports. He instructed Tanaka to delay landing until he had accomplished tasks one and two. At 2300 hours he sent the so-called Sweeping Unit consisting of Destroyer Squadron 3 some 16,000 yards ahead to spring any enemy traps. The Screening Unit, Destroyer Squadron 10, would thrash the opposition thus revealed. Finally, Kondo himself would lead the Bombardment Unit down the western passage into Savo Sound and plaster the airfield.

Second Battle of Guadalcanal, 15 November 1942

Lee steamed north by northeast between Guadalcanal and the Russell Islands. The *Walke, Benham, Preston,* and *Gwin* preceded the *Washington* by 5,000 yards, while the *South Dakota* followed 1,500 yards behind the flag. Reaching a point twenty-one miles north northwest of Cape Esperance, Lee turned due east at 2210 and arrived ten miles north of Savo Island at 2249. From there he cruised south southeast at seventeen knots into Savo Sound.

Lee's journey did not go unnoticed. At 2313, as Rear Admiral Hashimoto Shintaro led his squadron away from the main Japanese force, the *Shikinami's* lookouts, peering through their special light-gathering binoculars, saw shapes moving into Savo Sound along the same course. Hashimoto pondered this unexpected development and then sent the *Ayanami* down the western shore of Savo Island to scout that passage. The *Sendai, Shikinami,* and *Uranami* investigated the eastern channel. Meanwhile, Kondo, dealing with reports of contact to the west, dispatched the *Asagumo* and *Teruzuki* in that direction.

As the American column coursed past Savo Island, the ships' magnetic compasses spun wildly as they passed over the graves of the American cruisers sunk three months before. Lee tried to contact Guadalcanal Island for the latest intelligence, and at 2332 the *Washington* picked up PT boats reporting, "There go two big ones, but I don't know whose they are!" Lee strode to the TBS, broadcasting in plain language, "Refer your big boss about Ching Lee; Chinese, catchee? Call off your boys."[37]

TABLE 5.2. FORCES ENGAGED IN THE SECOND BATTLE OF GUADALCANAL

	Type of Ship	Year Launched	Displacement, Full Load	Max. Speed (knots)	Guns (number by inch/caliber)	Torpedoes (number of tubes by diameter in inches)	Damage
American Task Force 64 (Rear Adm. W.A. Lee)							
Washington (F)	BB	1940	44,377	28	9 x 16/45 & 20 x 5/38		
South Dakota	BB	1941	44,519	27	7 x 16/45 & 16 x 5/38		D3
Walke	DD	1939	2,313	35	5 x 5/38	8 x 21	Sunk
Benham	DD	1938	2,250	38	4 x 5/38	16 x 21	D4
Preston	DD	1936	2,103	36	4 x 5/38	12 x 21	Sunk
Gwin	DD	1940	2,395	35	4 x 5/38	5 x 21	D3
Japanese Bombardment Unit: *Sentai* 11 and 4 (Vice Admiral Kondo)							
Kirishima	BB	1913	36,400	30	8 x 14/45 & 14 x 6/50		Sunk
Atago (F)	CA	1927	14,604	34	10 x 8/50 & 8 x 5/40	16 x 24	D1
Takao	CA	1927	14,604	34	10 x 8/50 & 8 x 5/40	16 x 24	
Japanese Sweeping Unit: Destroyer Squadron 3 (Rear Admiral Hashimoto Shintaro)							
Sendai (F)	CL	1922	7,100	35	7 x 5.5/50 & 2 x 3.1/40	8 x 24	
Destroyer Division 19 (Captain Ooe Ranji)							
Ayanami	DD	1929	2,057	38	6 x 5/50	9 x 24	Sunk
Uranami	DD	1929	2,057	38	6 x 5/50	9 x 24	
Shikinami	DD	1929	2,057	38	6 x 5/50	9 x 24	

Japanese Screening Unit: Destroyer Squadron 10 (Rear Admiral Kimura Susumu)							
Nagara (F)	CL	1922	7,100	35	7 x 5.5/50 & 2 x 3.1/40	8 x 24	
Samidare	DD	1936	1,950	34	5 x 5/50	8 x 24	
Teruzuki	DD	1941	3,430	33	8 x 3.9/65	4 x 24	
Inazuma	DD	1931	1,950	38	6 x 5/50	9 x 24	
Asagumo	DD	1937	2,330	35	6 x 5/50	8 x 24	
Shirayuki	DD	1928	2,090	38	6 x 5/50	9 x 24	
Hatsuyuki	DD	1928	2,057	38	6 x 5/50	9 x 24	
Japanese Destroyer Division 15 (Captain Sato Torajiro)							
Kagero	DD	1938	2,450	35	6 x 5/50	8 x 24	
Oyashio	DD	1938	2,450	35	6 x 5/50	8 x 24	

BB—battleship, CA—heavy cruiser, CL—light cruiser, D1—light or superficial damage (including splinter damage), D3—significant damage (combat or maneuvering ability somewhat impaired), D4—major damage (combat and maneuvering ability significantly impaired or eliminated), DD—destroyer, F—flagship

Time: 0000–0210
Weather: Clouds, light south-southeasterly airs
Visibility: Quarter moon setting at midnight, clear and good
Sea state: Calm
Surprise: None
Mission: Americans—interception based on specific intelligence; Japanese—shore bombardment

At 2352, with everyone's identity established, Lee arrived at a point 13.5 miles southeast of Savo Island's southern tip, and from there he began steering due west. The American flagship was settling on course when at 0001 on 15 November, long after the Japanese had established visual contact, a PT reported sighting three ships northeast of Savo. At the same time the *Washington*'s radar scoped the *Sendai* 18,000 yards to the north northwest. Meanwhile, Hashimoto radioed Kondo that the enemy—misidentified as two cruisers and four destroyers—had turned west. If Kondo continued on his planned course a Callaghan-esque head-on confrontation would follow, so at 0015 the Japanese commander dispatched Rear Admiral Kimura Susumu's squadron down the western passage about ten miles behind the *Ayanami*. Very concerned to avoid mixing his units, Kondo turned northeast to give his subordinates time to defeat the enemy.

Admiral Lee tracked the *Sendai*, while his main battery director, confused by the proximity of land, fluttered between targets. Visual contact came at 0012.

MAP 5.3. SECOND BATTLE OF GUADALCANAL, 14–15 NOVEMBER 1942

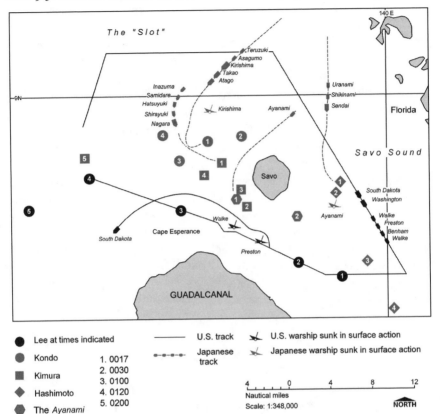

At 0014, having decided the enemy was Kondo's bombardment force, Lee gave his captains, Capt. Glenn B. Davis of the *Washington* and Capt. T.L. Gatch of the *South Dakota*, permission to engage. At 0017 at a range of 18,500 yards, an enormous flash lit the *Washington* signifying the Pacific Fleet's first combat use of the Navy's heaviest—and favorite—weapon, the sixteen-inch rifle. The *South Dakota* main battery rumbled to life thirty seconds later, at a calculated range of 15,700 yards (see Map 5.3). The roar of the monstrous guns echoed across Savo Sound's confined waters. Hashimoto watched giant geysers erupt in his wake. When the next set spouted in his path, Hashimoto immediately came about, covering his tracks with a dense blanket of smoke.

At 0019 Lee ordered twenty-three knots as he veered slightly starboard. The *Gwin*, dutifully but—due to the range and smokescreen—ineffectively, flung star shells in support of the battleships. A minute later the *Washington* lost the target and ceased fire after expending 42 sixteen-inch rounds and about 100 five-inch rounds in three minutes. The *South Dakota* continued shooting at gradually increasing ranges, discharging a total of eight salvos. She reported her target sunk, and her lookouts credited the *Washington* with setting an enemy battleship "ablaze from stem to stern." The *Washington's* lookouts more soberly reported "heavy black smoke from [main battery] target . . . possibly a smoke screen."[38] In fact, Hashimoto's three ships escaped unharmed when the admiral prudently decided he had accomplished his job of springing the American trap. He later explained that by this withdrawal he had "diverted enemy in order to decoy enemy to our main strength."[39]

As the echoes from the first exchange faded, the *Walke's* radar picked up a contact to starboard. This was the *Ayanami*, whose skipper, Commander Sakuma Eiji, was pugnaciously tackling the American battle line single-handedly. Meanwhile, about 10,000 yards behind, the *Nagara* led her flock of destroyers around Savo Island. At 0022 the *Walke's* forward mounts began spitting shells at the *Ayanami* from a range of 15,000 yards and closing rapidly. The *Benham* joined in. The *Preston* had problems acquiring a target because the *Ayanami's* flashless powder provided a poor point of aim. When the *Washington's* secondary battery roared to life, eventually flinging a total of 133 five-inch shells toward the Japanese destroyer, the Americans began tallying hits.

At 0027 in the moon's dim light, the *Preston's* lookouts spied silhouettes separating from Savo Island's dark mass. This was Kimura's improvised destroyer squadron entering the action. The *Preston's* gunners focused on this new threat, estimating the range to be 9,000 yards. The *Walke* and *Gwin* followed suit. American observers excitedly imagined flames erupting on their targets, but shells began roaring back from the other direction almost immediately.

The *Nagara* may have been old and under-gunned in comparison with American light cruisers, but she was an experienced and well-handled ship. At 0028 a flurry of eighty-four–pound shells ripped into the *Preston*. According to the U.S. Office of Naval Intelligence's account, "One landed between the two firerooms, killing all personnel. Several fires broke out, including one in the TNT of warheads cracked open by the shock. The second stack fell onto the searchlight."[40] More Japanese shells followed, slaughtering the *Preston's* crew and transforming the ship's aft section into a flaming mess. American rounds merely splashed around the Japanese cruiser and destroyers. The island backdrop blurred enemy silhouettes and confused American radar.

About 7,000 yards ahead of the *Nagara*, the *Ayanami* unleashed a volley of eight Long Lance torpedoes at 0030. Quickly after, the *Ayanami* lost steering and power. At 0032 a large explosion rocked the *Preston*, as her own torpedoes cooked off in the conflagration. The American destroyer began settling, and her skipper, Cdr. Max C. Stormes, ordered his men to abandon ship just nine minutes after sighting the enemy.

The *Gwin* swerved hard right to avoid the *Preston's* burning wreck as a shell smashed though the *Gwin's* engine room and exploded near the control station. The torpedo safety links failed, and three torpedoes tumbled over the side. As the *Gwin* straightened back on course, another shell jolted open two depth charges. One of the *Ayanami's* torpedoes missed astern by thirty yards. Then, American observers reported the enemy was turning away. They were. From 0035 Kimura's ships had also been launching a torpedo strike at what they reported to Kondo were one cruiser and three destroyers.[41]

Between 0030 and 0033 the *South Dakota* lobbed five salvos toward the *Sendai* off to the north. Unable to observe results, the American battleship checked her fire. However, gunfire shock sparked a short circuit that led to an overload and tripped a circuit breaker. This was possible because "her electrical circuits were, counter to damage control procedures, all connected. . . . Once a circuit was shorted by a hit, there was a loss of electrical power throughout the entire ship."[42] The electrical problems silenced the battleship's radio, blinded her radars, and paralyzed her gun mounts for three long minutes. In the South Dakota's action report, Captain Gatch described the reaction: "The trust and faith in the search radar equipment is amazing. After this ship lost both SG and SC equipment, the psychological effect on the officers and crew was most depressing. The absence of this gear gave all hands a feeling of being blindfolded."[43]

Meanwhile, Lee's flagship, her guns quiet since 0034, began to overrun her devastated screen. Lee ordered twenty-six knots as the *Washington* conned to port of the sinking *Preston*, dropping rafts to the shouting men in the water. Ahead, the *Benham* finally engaged, aiming at gun flashes off her starboard bow. The *Gwin* targeted flashes as well. As the *Washington* steadied on a west-by-northwest course, a very large pip appeared on her SG radar to the northwest.

At 0036 the *South Dakota* restored power, except to mounts 6 and 8, although intermittent outages continued to plague her. Citing gun flashes and poor visibility, Gatch failed to maintain station behind the *Washington*, and when confronted with the *Preston's* burning wreck, Gatch steered starboard. This outlined his ship against the flames for Japanese inspection.

Baffled by the Japanese turn away, the *Gwin* had ceased firing. Meanwhile, Kimura's torpedoes churned south. A Long Lance bashed the *Benham's* bow at 0037 and blew it away. The force of the blast caused the destroyer to heel to port and then rock 30 degrees back to starboard. A wave of water swept one man overboard as her speed plummeted from twenty-seven to five knots. Nearby, the *Preston's* wreck exploded, and a series of 5.5-inch shells wracked the *Walke*. The *Walke* turned to port preparing to launch torpedoes when a Type 93 walloped her, detonating beneath mount 2. The blast ignited the five-inch ready ammunition and sprayed burning oil topside. The destroyer's bow broke off and the rest of the ship literally sailed underwater.

By 0040 the *Washington* had plotted fire solutions for the *Kirishima*, but Lee, uncertain of the *South Dakota*'s whereabouts, restrained his eager gunners. Kondo, pondering reports of unidentified warships to the west, ordered the bombardment force to steer in that direction. Kimura's squadron withdrew northwest to reload tubes while Hashimoto looped southeast and, after detaching the *Uranami* to stand by the *Ayanami*, continued sweeping toward Lunga Point.

At 0041 the *Washington* passed the *Walke*'s wreckage, and the *South Dakota* flung another volley toward Hashimoto's *Sendai* off her starboard quarter. The blast of her own guns ignited two of the three floatplanes sitting on the *South Dakota*'s stern catapults. The aircraft flared up like beacons until the next American salvo blew them overboard. After a few more rounds the *South Dakota* sheered to starboard to pass the *Walke*'s wreckage.

Lee, chain-smoking Chesterfields on the *Washington*'s bridge, ordered the *Benham* and *Gwin* to retire. Kondo, correctly concluding that the reports of ships to his west pertained to Tanaka's convoy, turned the bombardment force due north at 0050, still concerned to keep his divisions separated. Meanwhile, the *Washington* passed Cape Esperance, steaming about 14,000 yards southeast of Kondo's position. Lee remained doubtful of the *South Dakota*'s location because Gatch's ship trailed off the *Washington*'s starboard quarter in the 60-degree radar blind spot caused by the array's placement on the flagship's foremast structure. Lee continued, however, to track Kondo. Then the *South Dakota*'s SG radar went on the fritz again for five minutes. During this relative lull Kondo evaluated an optimistic report from the *Ayanami* and concluded that the Sweeping and Screening Units had done their job and the Americans' force lay sunk or crippled, meaning the bombardment could proceed.

At 0054 Kondo turned his force southeast and steered straight for Lunga Point. The *Asagumo* and *Teruzuki* sprinted ahead to lead the column. Then Kimura injected doubt into Kondo's rosy appraisal of the situation when he radioed that two "new-type" American battleships were stalking north of Cape Esperance.[44] The Japanese commander dismissed this as an exaggeration. One minute later, as the quarter moon set behind Guadalcanal's mountains, lookouts aboard the *Atago* picked out the *South Dakota*'s towering superstructure, and the torpedo men on Kondo's cruisers sprang into action. By 0059 the *Atago* had a school of eight Long Lances swimming toward the unsuspecting battleship; there was no time to increase the depth setting from three meters.

At about this time, the *South Dakota*'s radar glowed back to life, and Captain Gatch suddenly perceived four ships off his starboard bow only 5,800 yards away. Earlier indications of this force had been overlooked in the excitement of directing fire against the *Sendai*. Then the *Atago*'s searchlights blinked open, painting the American battleship in harsh light. The main batteries, secondary batteries, and machine guns on all five ships of the bombardment force erupted into life. The time was 0100.

Kondo's heavy cruisers shot well; red glows marked round after round slamming into the American battleship's superstructure. The *South Dakota*'s main battery director continued to malfunction, and she discharged only five inaccurate sixteen-inch salvos. The Japanese assumed they had destroyed the main guns due to their lack of activity but noted that the *South Dakota*'s secondary batteries fired back "very fiercely."[45] The *Kirishima* reported, "[O]pened fire on a *North Carolina*–class BB and scored a hit with the first main battery salvo, blowing up the fire-control station and all structure above it. Subsequently scored many direct hits with both main and secondary batteries, making sinking of ship imminent."[46]

Lee observed these proceedings from the *Washington*'s bridge. With the *South Dakota*'s position finally fixed, Lee ordered his gunners to commence firing a few seconds past 0100. Two 5-inch mounts targeted the *Atago*, another pair fired upon the *Kirishima*, and one spat star shells. The 3 sixteen-inch turrets trained on the *Kirishima*. The range was 8,400 yards—"body punching range for guns that could reach five times that distance."[47] In two and a half minutes the *Washington* hurled thirty-nine 2,700-pound projectiles on an eleven-second trajectory toward the *Kirishima*. Several hit, knocking out two turrets and leading sky control to excitedly report that the *Kirishima* had been sunk.

At 0102:30 Lee ordered a cease fire to assess the situation. The *Kirishima*, despite the claims in her report, had not shot very effectively at the *South Dakota*, scoring only one hit. The Japanese dreadnought used the pause in the *Washington*'s assault to direct her surviving guns against the *Washington*. Meanwhile, the *Asagumo* launched four torpedoes. The Type 93s dispatched several minutes before were due to arrive. The *Atago*'s lookouts noted explosions in the right place at approximately the right time and claimed three to five hits. Despite the short range and good angle, however, every one of the Japanese torpedoes missed or, suffering from oversensitive detonators, exploded prematurely in the *South Dakota*'s massive wake.

As the *Washington* held fire, the Japanese continued to pelt the *South Dakota*. By 0104 the *South Dakota* had absorbed 18 eight-inch rounds, 6 six-inch rounds, 2 rounds of lesser caliber, and a single fourteen-inch shell that exploded against turret 3's barbette and blew a thirty square foot hole in the main deck before being stopped by the armored deck beneath. These strikes never endangered the *South Dakota*'s buoyancy, but, as Lee noted in his action report, "A few minutes intense fire, at short range, from secondary battery guns can, and did, render one of our new battleships deaf, dumb, blind and impotent through destruction of radar, radio and fire control circuits."[48]

When the *Washington* resumed firing, her first broadside missed the *Kirishima*. The second American salvo, however, resulted in several hits, and spurts of flame rose from the Japanese battleship. The *Kirishima* fought back, but the nearest shell the *Washington*'s observers reported splashed 200 yards off the port quarter.

At 0105 Kondo sheered right to bring more torpedoes into action and create some separation from the enemy. The *Kirishima*, however, had circled out of line heavily ablaze. By the time the *Washington* ceased firing at 0107, she had shot 75 sixteen-inch shells and 107 five-inch shells at the *Kirishima*, 120 five-inch rounds at the Japanese cruisers at ranges of 7,400 and 9,500 yards, and 62 star shells. As many as 9 of the sixteen-inch shells and 40 of the five-inch shells pulverized the *Kirishima*. Japanese reports counted "at least six or more hits."[49] The *Kirishima* lost two turrets, had a jammed rudder, and experienced massive flooding due to holes punched into her hull below the waterline.

Lee again ordered a cease-fire, frustrating his subordinates, because he had again lost track of the *South Dakota*. An officer later wrote, "Subsequently while attempting to ascertain the source of uncertainty on the part of the admiral and captain, I checked silhouettes of models of *Kirishima* and *South Dakota*. They were essentially identical when viewed from the quarter, which had been the angle of the Japanese battleship at the time of the cease fire."[50] Lee continued northwest intent on flushing Tanaka's convoy. Meanwhile, Kondo came due west.

At 0110 the *South Dakota*'s Captain Gatch decided to retire. The battleship's action report gives these reasons: "The location of the *Washington* was not known. Radio communication had failed. Radar plot had been demolished. Three fire control radars had been damaged by shells, and number 4 secondary was inoperative due to electrical troubles. Many dead and wounded had been reported."[51] Lacking radio, Gatch could not advise Lee of his action.

In all, the *South Dakota* suffered thirty-nine men killed and fifty-nine wounded. Nearly two dozen minor fires scorched her superstructure. It could have been worse. The *South Dakota*'s report notes that "[f]ragmentation of projectiles was chiefly due to impact rather than explosion. The damage caused by enemy hits was very small compared with what we would expect from high order explosives."[52] It seemed that many of the shells used by the *Kirishima* and the cruisers were bombardment types, not AP. Although Gatch boasted that "every enemy ship brought under our fire was hit," in fact all of the 115 sixteen-inch shells and 305 five-inch shells the *South Dakota* expended missed, with the possible exception of a hit on the *Ayanami*.[53] The *Atago* suffered insignificant damage from the *Washington*'s five-inch battery, and the *Takao* escaped unharmed.

Kondo continued more cautiously, with searchlights doused and guns silent. At 0113 the *Atago* and *Takao* each fired eight torpedoes at the *Washington* from 4,000 yards and at a depth of twenty-two feet. At the same time, the Japanese ships altered course 30 degrees to starboard to parallel the American battleship. Kondo also ordered the convoy to turn away as the battle was drifting in its direction. Japanese lookouts observed explosions at 0118 and claimed hits. At the same time the *Washington* noted "firing" on the starboard quarter, which probably signified torpedoes detonating in her wake.[54]

At 0120, still attempting to pinpoint the Japanese convoy, Lee altered course to north by northwest, provoking three more torpedoes from the *Atago*. Despite the pleas of his subordinates, who reported perfect fire control solutions for Kondo's ships, Lee continued to hold fire, reasoning that gun flashes would reveal his position and unaware that the *Washington* was already a target.

Hashimoto arrived off Lunga Point, and he radioed Kondo at 0123 that all was clear and the bombardment could proceed. Kondo did not know the whereabouts of Kimura's squadron, and he ordered all units to attack enemy battleships north of Cape Esperance at 0125. Kimura, sailing a few thousand yards west of Savo Island and still reloading his tubes—a task he completed by 0130—sailed to comply. Tanaka, meanwhile, had already dispatched the *Oyashio* and *Kagero* from the convoy's escort to counter the approaching American threat. At 0128 Kondo increased speed to thirty knots, turned to parallel Lee, and ordered his ships to make smoke. Kondo had developed a fearful respect for the *Washington*'s guns and preferred silent torpedo strikes to a gunnery duel. The *Washington* fixed her radar eye on three separate groups of enemy ships bearing northeast, southeast, and northwest. A complicated and dangerous picture emerged.

At 0132 Kondo canceled the bombardment, and a minute later Lee noted the *Kagero* and *Oyashio* laying a smoke screen off to starboard. In response he turned the *Washington* sharply to starboard, correctly anticipating a torpedo ambush. Lookouts aboard the *Washington* observed a heavy explosion off her port quarter five minutes later; this was probably another prematurely detonating torpedo.

Lee wisely decided he had delayed the transports long enough and circled around on a southwesterly heading. Tanaka's two destroyers followed off the *Washington*'s starboard quarter while Kimura pursued to port. Kimura's flagship, the *Nagara*, fired torpedoes at "a new type battleship which appeared to have rudder trouble" and heard three of her fish explode.[55] At 0139 the *Oyashio* sent six torpedoes up the *Washington*'s wake, and six minutes later the *Samidare* did the same. The American battleship's lookouts reported multiple threats during this period, including torpedo tracks on the port quarter, a ship signaling, gunfire from dead astern, dull flashes ahead, and MTBs to all sides. As the *Washington* commenced evasive maneuvers, Kondo lost contact. He released the *Asagumo* and *Teruzuki* to join the chase while he remained northwest of Savo Island for nearly another hour to protect the depleted convoy, which the Japanese fought through to Guadalcanal at such sacrifice. The *Atago* and *Takao* did not start north until 0230. The *Kagero* and *Nagara* hustled the *Washington* away from the island until finally breaking contact at 0240.

At 0400 Tanaka, who had anxiously monitored the battle from a distance, ordered the four surviving transports beached to unload their cargoes. Mikawa jumped in to object, but Combined Fleet command endorsed Tanaka's decision.

The *Kirishima*, meanwhile, proved a lost cause. Her steering gear room was flooded completely, "the engine rooms became intolerable because of the increased heat, and most of the engineers were killed."[56] When flames threatened the *Kirishima's* fore and aft magazines, these were flooded and that doomed the ship. At 0425, seacocks open, the *Kirishima* sank eleven miles west of Savo Island. By 0530 the *Asagumo*, *Teruzuki*, and *Samidare*, loaded with 1,128 survivors, began the voyage north. The *Ayanami* foundered at 0306, losing forty men.

With the dawn American aircraft and the destroyer *Meade*, in her combat debut, bombarded the beached transports and left them wrecks "blazing with many internal explosions."[57] The supplies the Japanese had brought to shore at such cost were destroyed as they sat in hastily assembled dumps near the beach. The *Meade* also rescued 266 of the *Walke's* and the *Preston's* men floating in the sound. The *Benham's* crew abandoned the struggle to save their ship the next day, and the *Gwin*, the only American destroyer to survive, scuttled the *Benham* with shellfire after missing with three torpedoes and having another explode prematurely.

In Japanese eyes, Kondo had utterly defeated a powerful American force in the Second Battle of Guadalcanal, sinking one battleship, two heavy cruisers, and two destroyers and damaging two other battleships and two cruisers. The Americans also exaggerated their accomplishments, but on 15 November, sitting on a hill and surveying the beached hulks and burning supplies up the beach, General Vandegrift wrote Admiral Nimitz, "It was indeed a glorious sight."[58]

The results would have been different if a few of the many torpedoes the Japanese fired at the American battleships had struck. In contrast, Lee's destroyers failed to get even one torpedo into the water. He lost his screen, lost his other battleship, maintained a steady course while Japanese warships launched repeated torpedo broadsides at close range, and somehow emerged unharmed and victorious. As Halsey noted, "the use we made of [the battleships] defied all conventions, narrow waters, submarine menace, and destroyers at night. Despite that, the books, and the learned and ponderous words of the highbrows it worked."[59] Kondo remarked: "Above all, it was my great regret that not a few torpedoes fired by our fleet exploded on their unfinished way."[60]

In the one encounter in which they both saw action, the American "super" weapon, the sixteen-inch rifle, outdid the Japanese "super" weapon, the Type 93 torpedo. Never again would the Japanese dominate the nighttime waters of Savo Sound, nor would Henderson Field be so threatened. From 15 November to 30 November the Cactus Air Force grew from 85 to 188 aircraft while Japanese observers jealously lamented: "an average of two [U.S.] transports were being anchored daily at Lunga."[61]

Emergency Measures

Despite ammunition shortages and a starvation diet, the Japanese held their line on Guadalcanal, repelling an American offensive in late November. As the 17th Army urgently demanded supplies, the 8th Fleet faced a similar crisis at Buna, New Guinea, the loss of which Combined Fleet command deemed a greater threat to the Empire's security. Thus, November saw the Japanese navy committing most of its resources to Buna and trying to develop less dangerous ways to provision Guadalcanal. A submarine could carry twenty to thirty tons of rice and grain, which was theoretically enough for a day's rations. The first attempt at submarine transport came on 24 November, but American PT boats foiled the Japanese that night. With practice, however, the subs gradually improved their technique and success rate. Another method the Japanese employed to get supplies to Guadalcanal involved lashing watertight drums packed with 330 pounds of provisions to a destroyer's afterdeck and casting them off close to shore, where, theoretically, small boats could tow them ashore.

On the American side during November, Admiral Halsey cobbled together another surface strike force, Task Force 67, by joining the newly arrived cruisers *Honolulu* and *New Orleans* to the *Helena*, *Minneapolis*, *Northampton*, and *Pensacola*, the last three of which had been freshly released from screening duty. On 24 November Halsey assigned Rear Admiral Kinkaid to command the new task force, even though a week earlier Halsey had recommended relieving Kinkaid for a "rest."[62] Trying to apply lessons from Guadalcanal's four major night actions, Kinkaid devised detailed operating procedures that included putting an SG radar-equipped ship in each tactical unit, an unambiguous code, strict radio procedures, instructions for specific situations, and a new battle formation in which a picket unit operated 10,000 yards ahead of the flagship. On 28 November Rear Adm. Carleton H. Wright, who had commanded a cruiser division throughout the Guadalcanal campaign, did relieve Kinkaid and, perforce, had inherited these procedures when he sailed the next day to intercept a reported Japanese force of eight destroyers and six transports that was expected to arrive off Guadalcanal the night of 30 November.

The first of five scheduled "drum" runs departed Buin, Bougainville, the night of 29 November. Rear Admiral Tanaka commanded six transport and two escort destroyers. His Destroyer Squadron 2 has been described as a seasoned unit with eighteen months' operational experience. This was not true.[63] Of Tanaka's three divisions—15, 24, and 31—the last two had been attached to the squadron on 14 July and 31 August 1942, respectively. The new ships of Division 31 had seen just a few months of service. For this mission, Tanaka's flagship, the *Naganami*, and the *Takanami* provided escort, and the other six ships each carried 200–240 supply drums, along with just one torpedo per tube. The *Makinami* was attached to Division 15 for this operation.

Battle of Tassafaronga, 30 November 1942

Hoping to avoid aerial spotters, Tanaka approached Guadalcanal using an indirect route that took him north of the island. Allied aircraft spotted the Japanese force anyway, leading Tanaka to expect an alert enemy. After a trip bedeviled by heavy rain squalls, Destroyer Squadron 2 arrived off Cape Esperance forty-five minutes before midnight and cautiously steered for the landing zones. The moon was not due to rise for another hour, and a thick overcast obscured the stars. Lookouts spotted aircraft over Savo Island, heightening the expectation of contact. However, as the Allied planes droned on in the distance and did not drop flares, Tanaka judged it safe to continue. *Takanami* proceeded independently, scouting ten miles ahead. The *Oyashio*, skippered by Captain Sato Torajiro, came next, leading the *Kuroshio, Kagero, Makinami, Naganami*, Captain Nakahara Giichiro's *Kawakaze*, and *Suzukaze*. As the *Naganami* neared Doma Cove, Tanaka took his ship and Nakahara's division out of line. The other four ships continued toward the second disembarkation point five miles down the coast off Tassafaronga.

Wright's force sped north to keep its rendezvous with the enemy, emerging from Lengo Channel at 2225. On the way, the Americans passed a group of three U.S. transports and five destroyers clearing the area. Halsey had ordered Destroyer Division 9 to join Wright. The newly mustered ships did not know Wright's plan, nor even the recognition signal. Nevertheless, Wright instructed them to fall in behind the *Northampton* and rely on "good sense and tactical signals," to guide their participation.[64]

As the Americans entered Savo Sound, the *Fletcher* led, followed by the *Perkins, Maury*, and *Drayton*. Four thousand yards back, the cruisers and Division 9 sailed in a quarter line of bearing, with the *Minneapolis* leading the *New Orleans, Pensacola, Honolulu, Northampton, Lardner*, and *Lamson*. Wright expected to encounter Japanese transports along the shore being screened by destroyers in the sound. He did not have to wait long for this expectation to be at least partially fulfilled. At 2306 the *Minneapolis*'s SG display sprouted a contact bearing nearly due west at a range of 23,000 yards. Wright digested this information and at 2310 ordered his cruisers into a column formation on a northwest heading.

At 2312, as Wright maneuvered, the *Takanami* reported sighting shapes on a bearing 100 degrees. She then elaborated: "Seven enemy destroyers sighted."[65] At 2316 Tanaka suspended the supply operation. This order came at a bad time for the *Suzukaze* and *Kawakaze* because they had already lowered boats and were preparing to pitch drums overboard. At the same time the *Fletcher* had Sato's four southerly coursing ships and the *Takanami* firmly fixed on its plan position indicator (PPI). Cdr. W.M. Cole brought the destroyers of Task Group 67.2.4 to the west northwest. As the target angle approached 270 degrees, he requested permission to fire torpedoes. The time was 2316. Wright queried his own radar operators, decided the range remained excessive, and advised Cole of this. Cole, watching

TABLE 5.3. FORCES ENGAGED IN THE BATTLE OF TASSAFARONGA

	Type of Ship	Year Launched	Displacement, Full Load	Max. Speed (knots)	Guns (number by inch/caliber)	Torpedoes (number of tubes by diameter in inches)	Damage
American Task Force 67.2.2 (Rear Adm. C.H. Wright)							
Minneapolis (F)	CA	1931	12,463	32	9 x 8/55 & 8 x 5/25		D4
New Orleans	CA	1931	12,463	32	9 x 8/55 & 8 x 5/25		D4
Pensacola	CA	1927	11,512	32	10 x 8/55 & 8 x 5/25		D4
AmericanTask Group 67.2.3 (Rear Adm. M.S. Tisdale)							
Honolulu (F)	CL	1937	12,207	32	15 x 6/47 & 8 x 5/25		
Northampton	CA	1929	11,420	32	9 x 8/55 & 8 x 5/25		Sunk
American Task Group 67.2.4 (Cdr. W.M. Cole)							
Fletcher (F)	DD	1942	2,924	38	5 x 5/38	10 x 21	
Drayton	DD	1936	2,103	36	5 x 5/38	10 x 21	
Perkins	DD	1936	2,103	36	5 x 5/38	10 x 21	
Maury	DD	1938	2,219	38	4 x 5/38	16 x 21	
American Destroyer Division 9 (Cdr. L.A. Abercrombie)							
Lamson	DD	1936	2,103	36	5 x 5/38	10 x 21	
Lardner	DD	1942	2,395	35	5 x 5/38	10 x 21	
Japanese Destroyer Squadron 2 (Rear Admiral Tanaka Raizo)							
Naganami (F)	DD	1942	2,480	35	6 x 5/50	8 x 24	D1

Japanese Destroyer Division 31 (Captain Shimizu Toshio)							
Takanami (F)	DD	1942	2,480	35	6 x 5/50	8 x 24	Sunk
Makinami	DD	1941	2,480	35	6 x 5/50	8 x 24	
Japanese Destroyer Division 15 (Captain Sato Torajiro)							
Kagero	DD	1938	2,450	35	6 x 5/50	8 x 24	
Kuroshio	DD	1938	2,450	35	6 x 5/50	8 x 24	
Oyashio	DD	1938	2,450	35	6 x 5/50	8 x 24	
Japanese Destroyer Division 24 (Captain Nakahara Giichiro)							
Kawakaze	DD	1936	1,950	34	5 x 5/50	8 x 24	
Suzukaze	DD	1936	1,950	34	5 x 5/50	8 x 24	

CA—heavy cruiser, CL—light cruiser, D1—light or superficial damage (including splinter damage), D4—major damage (combat and maneuvering ability significantly impaired or eliminated), DD—destroyer, F—flagship

Time: 2306–2348
Weather: Overcast, light east-northeasterly breeze
Visibility: Fair, last quarter moon
Sea state: Slight swells
Surprise: None
Mission: Americans—interception based upon specific intelligence; Japanese—transport

his torpedo setup deteriorate as the Japanese passed, replied the range was okay. At 2320 Wright finally radioed, "Go ahead and fire torpedoes."[66]

The *Fletcher* reset her weapons for a long-range, slow-speed swim at a retiring target and fired her first half-salvo. The *Perkins* discharged eight torpedoes, but the *Maury*, lacking SG radar and unable to see the enemy, held back. The *Drayton*, also unsure of her target, launched only two torpedoes. This episode demonstrated one reason the Americans remained inferior to the Japanese in night combat. Japanese doctrine expected destroyer commanders to attack, not seek permission. But given that the Americans were shooting defective torpedoes, Wright's hesitation—bad as it was—probably did not affect the battle's outcome.

At 2320:30 the TBS cracked to life with Wright ordering, "Roger, [open fire], and I do mean Roger."[67] At 2321 all nine of the *Minneapolis's* eight-inch guns thundered into life. As one witness described it, "The flash was dazzling, lighting up the ocean for hundreds of yards. Anyone caught with his eyes open could see nothing except the brilliant orange blob the flash had etched into the retina."[68] A minute later the *New Orleans* and *Northampton* joined in. The destroyers in the van and the secondary batteries on the first two cruisers pumped out star shells and followed with service rounds (see Map 5.4).

MAP 5.4. BATTLE OF TASSAFARONGA, 30 NOVEMBER 1943

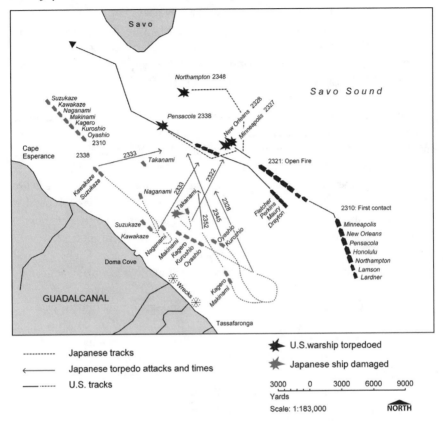

Tanaka ordered his units to close and attack, but, he later reported, "numerous illuminating shells and parachute flares suddenly set off by the enemy brightened our vicinity so that it was extremely difficult to make out the formation of the enemy fleet."[69] The *Naganami* immediately reversed course to starboard, and Nakahara's Division 24 abandoned their boats and got underway. At 2322 the *Takanami*, already tracking the enemy, launched eight Type 93s. Sato's Division 15 continued heading southeast at twelve knots, unobserved against the dark shore.

By 2324 the *Pensacola* had a target, and the *Honolulu*'s quick-firing six-inch guns opened up a minute later. Unfortunately for the Americans, this storm of steel proved neither effective nor well distributed. The *Takanami* was the target of more than 180 five-inch shells from the *Perkins*, *Maury*, *Minneapolis*, and *New Orleans*; 155 eight-inch rounds from all four heavy cruisers, and 90 six-inch rounds from the *Honolulu*. In large part, this occurred because a few early hits ignited fires making her the most visible target.

Aboard the American van destroyers the glare of star shells and a "wall of splashes" confounded both eye and radar, and by 2325 they had steamed past their targets.[70] When a salvo bracketed his ship, Cole immediately steered north by northwest and accelerated to thirty knots, clearing the battle zone up the west side of Savo Island. Except for the *Drayton*, the U.S. destroyers played no further part in the battle. At 2338 the *Drayton* aimed a Parthian torpedo salvo toward the *Naganami* from a range of 11,000 yards.

For seven minutes following their destroyers' departure, the American cruisers held steady, their big guns blazing away and their lookouts reporting targets burning, breaking in half, disappearing, and sinking. The *New Orleans* even targeted the beached wrecks from Tanaka's 15 November convoy. As Admiral Wright later wrote, "The gunnery performance of our cruisers was excellent. The volume of fire was very impressive and great havoc was raised with the enemy ships. I doubt that any of the groups taken under fire escaped, with the exception of two cruisers."[71] Be that as it may, the *Takanami*'s torpedo salvo proved far more effective. At 2327 a giant explosion shook the *Minneapolis* as a Long Lance mangled her bow. A wall of water surged masthead high and rained down as another explosion amidships stunned all those aboard the cruiser. As the *Minneapolis* staggered out of formation, the *New Orleans* steered to avoid a collision and sailed right into the path of a third torpedo. This detonated deep beneath turret 1 and set off the contents of the small arms and bomb and mine magazine, which contained, among other things, forty-nine 100-pound bombs.[72] A column of flame shot twice as high as the *New Orleans*'s foremast. The forward part of the cruiser as far back as turret 2 broke off and bumped its way down the crippled ship's port side.

Thus, the turning point of the battle came not from unified and trained response on the part of Tanaka's veterans, nor from a deliberate and massive salvo of Long Lance torpedoes. It came from one ship's dying sting, because by the time *Takanami*'s torpedoes struck, she was dead in the war and burning fiercely.

The *Pensacola*, suddenly confronted by two flaming cruisers in her path, swung out of line to port. Eager Japanese eyes fastened on the silhouetted cruiser and exaggerated the *Pensacola*'s prominent mainmast and her balanced profile of two turrets fore and aft into that of a *Texas*-class battleship. As she swung back to the original west northwest heading four enemy destroyers lined their tubes on this attractive target.

By 2330 Nakahara's division had completed its sharp turn to port and was proceeding west northwest up the coast, working up to twenty-four knots. The *Suzukaze* loosed a couple of broadsides at the enemy, but the *Kawakaze*'s men eyed the *Pensacola* nearly 10,000 yards off their starboard quarter. By 2333 the *Kawakaze* had eight torpedoes speeding toward the *Pensacola*. The *Naganami* had also turned and was traveling at a speed of thirty-five knots on a northwest course. At 2332 eight torpedoes from the *Naganami* whooshed into the water toward *Pensacola* 8,500 yards off the flagship's starboard bow.

Sato's four ships had been steaming east southeast, largely unnoticed. When the *Pensacola* leapt into view the *Kuroshio* and *Oyashio*, respectively, aimed two and eight Type 93s in the American cruiser's direction. Twenty-six torpedoes launched from widely separated locations surged toward the same target of opportunity. Then Sato turned his column to port and began steaming back up the coast. The *Makinami* and *Kagero* ran ahead and closer to the American line.

Meanwhile, the *Honolulu* and *Northampton* both steered to starboard, keeping the burning ships between them and the enemy. The *Lamson* also went to starboard while *Lardner* fell out to port. The *Honolulu* targeted Tanaka's flagship, and he remembered her gunnery: "The *Naganami* was showered by fragments from near misses but, miraculously, sustained no direct hits. I have always felt that our good luck was accountable to the high speed [thirty-five knots] at which the *Naganami* was traveling, and that enemy shells missed us because of deflection error."[73] In fact Tanaka's "good luck" had more to do with inexperience. The Americans shot too many star shells and the glare, smoke, and flash of their own weapons impaired the gunners' night vision. This forced the gunners to depend on radar for judging both range and train. The operator of the *Honolulu*'s fire control radar averaged the return range from the columns of water thrown up by the cruiser's initial salvos and, in effect, chased the ship's own fall of shot. This led to the deflection errors.[74] Moreover, although *Honolulu*'s prodigious output caused the gunnery specialists to enthuse about her effectiveness, it also disabled her SG radar. She shot her last six-inch round at 2331 and her final star shell five minutes later.

The *Pensacola*, meanwhile, returned to the base course and cast about for targets. She hurled seven salvos at the fast-moving *Naganami* and then another three to port. Next, she illuminated the *Honolulu* off to starboard, prompting the light cruiser to flash her recognition lights. At 2338 the *Pensacola*'s battle ended. A Long Lance clobbered her amidship near the base of the mainmast. The damage was horrendous. Flames erupted throughout the ship, and she listed 13 degrees to port.

The *Northampton* made a large loop to port of the stricken cruisers. Over the next ten minutes she tossed nine salvos at the *Takanami*. Then, with Savo Island looming ahead, she swung west to clear the island and find more targets. Also at 2339 the vengeful *New Orleans* opened fire on the *Lardner* with her 40-mm and port five-inch battery. The American destroyer immediately hauled out for safer waters to the east. The *Lamson* suffered a similar experience and did the same.

On her way north the *Kuroshio* launched four torpedoes at 2345, probably at the *Northampton*. By this time Japanese Destroyer Division 24, joined by the *Naganami*, had reached Cape Esperance, chased on their way by the *Northampton*'s broadsides. Observing the *Pensacola* exploding, the *Makinami* and *Kagero* edged to the northeast with the intention of finishing off the American cruiser, and the *Kuroshio* and *Oyashio* continued about two miles ahead and closer inshore. The *Makinami*, however, couldn't clear the cargo drums blocking her torpedo mounts and turned left to work on this problem, leaving the *Kagero* to continue alone. At 2352 the *Kagero* launched four torpedoes toward the *Pensacola*. After this, Japanese Destroyer Division 15 continued northwest and cleared the area, rendezvousing with Tanaka northwest of Cape Esperance.

The battle was essentially over by 2348, when a final disaster struck the Americans. The *Honolulu* was already cutting around Savo Island when a gigantic explosion, far larger than any other, ripped the night behind her. Two Type 93s churning through the sound that had presumably been aimed at the *Pensacola* at least fifteen minutes before caught the *Northampton*. If this was the case, it must be considered the final crowning of a cursed night for the U.S. Navy. The cruiser, stricken by an uncontrollable conflagration and massive flooding, capsized at 0304.

After Tanaka gathered his destroyers, he noted the *Takanami*'s absence and sent the *Oyashio* and *Kuroshio* to find her. On the way they spotted the *New Orleans* retiring toward Tulagi, and the *Kuroshio* discharged her last two torpedoes at this target at 0040. At 0115 the returning Japanese destroyers found the *Takanami* smoldering but still afloat. The *Kuroshio* maneuvered to attempt a rescue, but the sight of an enemy vessel and the knowledge that they were out of torpedoes caused both the *Kuroshio* and *Oyashio* to abandon the rescue attempt. Of the *Takanami*'s crew, 211 men died. The Americans rescued twenty-six, and thirty-three made it ashore.

The *Minneapolis* lost thirty-seven men. She painfully navigated the eighteen miles to Tulagi at three knots and missed ten months of action; the *Pensacola*, which suffered 125 dead, got to Tulagi in only three hours, still burning when she arrived. She did not return to action for a year. The *New Orleans* lost 120 feet of her bow and 183 men. A jury-rigged cofferdam made of palm logs got her to Sydney. Although the most severely damaged, she completed repairs in only nine months.[75]

Rear Admiral Wright reported engaging seventeen enemy ships and sinking nine of them; Nimitz eventually reduced this to four destroyers sunk and two damaged out of eight engaged. After all the loss and carnage suffered in five major night actions, Nimitz thought the remedy was training, but the U.S. Navy still did not appreciate the skill and capabilities of Japanese lookouts or the lethal range and striking power of Japanese torpedoes. Tassafaronga proved to be the most deadly Japanese torpedo action of the war, not counting the *Mogami*'s blow against friendly transports at Sunda Strait. It stands much in contrast with the effort against Lee's battleships at the Second Battle of Guadalcanal.

The Battle of Tassafaronga was the last time the U.S. Navy used large surface warships to dispute Japanese supply operations to Guadalcanal. This conventional strategy was too costly and, as events proved, unnecessary.

Tanaka returned three nights after the Battle of Tassafaronga and conducted what from a naval point of view was a successful mission that set 1,500 drums adrift off the shore of Guadalcanal. Most of the tethers on the drums broke, however. The next morning Marine flyers from Henderson Field found 1,200 floating targets for strafing practice. On 7 December, a force of eight PT boats repulsed a drum run led by Captain Sato without loss to either side. Following the torpedoing of a supply submarine by American PT boats on 9 December, Combined Fleet command advised the army they would not have enough ships left to fight the decisive battle if supply runs continued with these results.

This decision was confirmed when, on 11 December, Tanaka set 1,200 drums adrift, but a PT torpedoed his flagship, the *Teruzuki*, marking the first success for a surface-launched American torpedo against a Japanese warship since the Battle of Balikpapan nearly a year earlier. The Imperial army recovered only 220 drums from the 11 December run, and the cancellation of this method of supply soon followed.

By the second week of December, the American blockade of Guadalcanal was nearly complete. The United States finally replaced the battered but victorious 1st Marine Division with Army troops. Admiral Ugaki wrote, "How to rescue twenty-five thousand men at Guadalcanal has turned out to be the most urgent matter."[76] But Combined Fleet did not issue the evacuation orders until January, and then the Imperial navy, in a virtuoso performance, completely outfoxed the U.S. Navy and American intelligence by evacuating the survivors in operations on 1 February (4,935 men), 4 February (3,921 men) and 7 February (1,796 men). American PT boats disputed the first operation at great cost to themselves, but the second and third met no resistance.[77]

Thus, at the very end of the Guadalcanal campaign, the Americans failed to exploit their hard-won sea superiority and let their trapped enemy escape. The scale of the evacuation runs, which were carried out by twenty, twenty, and eighteen destroyers, respectively, makes one wonder why the Japanese navy did not put similar force into their reinforcement operations.

CHAPTER 6

Africa: Casablanca, November 1942

If you attack us, or if you come without being called, we will shoot.
—MARSHAL HENRI PHILIPPE PETAIN TO U.S. AMBASSADOR
TO VICHY FRANCE WILLIAM D. LEAHY, JANUARY 1942

In the autumn of 1942, despite the heavy slaughter of men and ships and the very thin margin by which Allied forces maintained their precarious positions in the Pacific, America marshaled its major military effort in Africa against the erstwhile Allied, and now theoretically neutral, possessions of France.

Allied grand strategy originally called for a cross-channel attack on France in the summer of 1942 to gain a lodgment and then a full-blown invasion in 1943. However, fearing a bloody repulse, British leaders lobbied for a delay or a strike elsewhere. A vigorous debate led to deadlock between the Allies. Finally, greatly against the wishes of Admiral King and Gen. George Marshall, President Roosevelt, driven by the political need to see American troops fighting German soldiers somewhere before the end of 1942, broke the impasse by designating French North Africa as the place to strike. Roosevelt even believed "the French authorities themselves might be induced to welcome it."[1]

The plan called for landings in Morocco, at Oran, and at Algiers, which are all far from the Allies' critical objective of Tunisia. The choice of invasion sites reflected the Americans' desire to maintain a line of communications with the United States and their fears of being trapped in the Mediterranean by a sudden Axis descent on Gibraltar. Great Britain and France were already engaged in a bitter, undeclared war precipitated by a British attack against the French fleet at Mers-El-Kébir on 2 July 1940, and significant naval battles had taken place at Dakar in September 1940 and off Syria in June 1941.[2] Anglo-French animosity, therefore, required the North Africa operation to masquerade as an American affair, but the U.S. Navy conducted only the Moroccan assaults. The British navy, with Dutch, Canadian, and Polish contingents, supplied the overall command and handled the Mediterranean operations.

By 1942 the Moroccan city of Casablanca was France's principal Atlantic port and, next to Toulon, its largest naval facility. The French battleship *Jean Bart* docked there, uncompleted and unable to leave her berth. The 4 fifteen-inch guns in her forward turret worked fine, however. The French force at Casablanca also contained a light cruiser, three "super" destroyers, seven fleet destroyers, three sloops, and eleven submarines all under the command of Vice Admiral Fritz Michelier. Four major shore batteries ringed the harbor, and a total of 55,000 troops and 170 aircraft garrisoned Morocco. A U.S. Army assessment noted that "the great port and city of Casablanca was so strongly defended that direct frontal assault would have been extremely costly. The objective had to be attacked from the rear by forces landing near enough to reach it."[3] This caution prompted the decision to make three separate landings along 220 miles of coast.

U.S. Task Force 34, consisting of one carrier, four escort carriers, three battleships, seven cruisers, and thirty-eight destroyers and commanded by Rear Adm. H. Kent Hewitt, sailed from the United States on 23 October. Hewitt's armada materialized off the Moroccan coast on 8 November, catching the French by surprise. Needing to cover three widely dispersed landings, Hewitt divided his fleet accordingly, and four groups of U.S. ships conducted the Casablanca operation: Hewitt assigned Task Group 34.1 to contain the French fleet in Casablanca, neutralize the *Jean Bart*, and watch out for a sortie by the other modern French battleship, the *Richelieu*, which was based at Dakar. Task Group 34.9, under Hewitt's direct command, was to provide fire support for the landings at Fédala, which is fifteen miles north of Casablanca. Six U.S. destroyers were set to screen the transports, and a light cruiser and five destroyers were assigned to escort the carriers *Ranger* and *Suwannee*. Hewitt dispatched the other components of his force to support landings at Safi, which is 140 miles south of Casablanca, and at Mehdla, which is ninety-five miles north of the city.

Battle of Casablanca, 8 November 1942

Hewitt commenced landings at Fédala without a conducting preliminary, bombardment hoping the French would not resist (see Map 6.1). Dawn broke shortly after 0630, and the sea was calm. The wind blew four knots from the southwest, and a low, thick haze lay along the coast. Shortly after dawn, U.S. aircraft began to report flak, and the El Hank shore battery loosed a long-range salvo at Task Group 34.1 at 0701. As green gouts of water straddled the *Massachusetts* the Americans realized their hopes of an unopposed landing were naïve, and three minutes later the *Massachusetts* and *Tuscaloosa* engaged the *Jean Bart*, initially from 24,400 yards. The *Wichita* answered El Hank from 21,800 yards.

At 0708 the *Jean Bart* entered the fray.[4] Her initial salvos—marked by yellow dye—fell about 600 yards off the *Massachusetts*'s starboard bow. Bracketing shots then splashed close to port. However, while the French spotters could barely see their targets, the Americans had the *Jean Bart*'s location precisely calculated. A 2,700-pound sixteen-inch shell bashed the French battleship aft over the admiral's cabin at 0713. The American projectile ripped through two of the French ship's

TABLE 6.1. FORCES ENGAGED IN THE BATTLE OF CASABLANCA

	Type of Ship	Year Launched	Displacement, Full Load (tons)	Max. Speed (knots)	Guns (number by inch/ caliber)	Torpedoes (number of tubes by diameter in inches)	Damage
American Task Force 34 (Rear Adm. H.K. Hewitt) and Task Group 34.1 (Rear Adm. R. Giffen)							
Massachusetts (F)	BB	1941	44,519	27	9 x 16/45 & 20 x 5/38		D1 (SB)
Tuscaloosa	CA	1933	12,463	32	9 x 8/55 & 8 x 5/25		
Wichita	CA	1937	13,015	33	9 x 8/55 & 8 x 5/38		D1 (SB)
American Destroyer Squadron 8 (Capt. D.P. Moon)							
Wainwright (F)	DD	1939	2,313	35	4 x 5/38	8 x 21	
Rhind	DD	1938	2,250	38	4 x 5/38	8 x 21	
Mayrant	DD	1938	2,250	38	4 x 5/38	8 x 21	
Jenkins	DD	1942	2,924	38	5 x 5/38	10 x 21	
AmericanTask Group 34.9 (Hewitt)							
Augusta (F)	CA	1930	11,420	32	9 x 8/55 & 8 x 5/25		
Brooklyn	CL	1936	12,207	32	15 x 6/47 & 8 x 5/25		D1
American Destroyer Division 26 (Cdr. E.R. Durgin)							
Wilkes (F)	DD	1940	2,395	35	4 x 5/38	10 x 21	
Swanson	DD	1940	2,395	35	4 x 5/38	10 x 21	
Ludlow	DD	1940	2,395	35	4 x 5/38	10 x 21	D2
Murphy	DD	1940	2,395	35	4 x 5/38	10 x 21	D1 (SB)
French (Vice Admiral Fritz Michelier)							
Jean Bart	BB	1940	47,548	0	4 x 15/45		D3

French Light Squadron 2 (Rear Admiral Gervais de Lafond)							
Primauguet	CL	1924	9,350	33	8 x 6.1/55 & 4 x 3/60	12 x 21.7	D4
French Destroyer Division 11							
Milan (F)	DD	1930	3,410	36	5 x 5.45/40	7 x 21.7	D4
Albatros	DD	1930	3,410	36	5 x 5.45/40	6 x 21.7	D4
French Torpedo Division 2							
Alcyon	DD	1926	2,000	33	4 x 5.1/40	6 x 21.7	D1
Fougueux	DD	1928	2,000	33	4 x 5.1/40	6 x 21.7	Sunk
Frondeur	DD	1929	2,000	33	4 x 5.1/40	6 x 21.7	Sunk
French Torpedo Division 5							
Boulonnais	DD	1927	2,000	33	4 x 5.1/40	6 x 21.7	Sunk
Brestois	DD	1927	2,000	33	4 x 5.1/40	6 x 21.7	Sunk
French Torpedo Division 6							
Tempête	DD	1925	1,900	33	4 x 5.1/40	6 x 21.7	
Simoun	DD	1924	1,900	33	4 x 5.1/40	6 x 21.7	
French Patrol Division 6							
La Grandière	PS	1939	2,600	15	3 x 5.45/40		
La Gracieuse	PS	1939	895	20	2 x 3.9/45		
Commandant Delage	PS	1939	895	20	2 x 3.9/45		
Shore Batteries							
El Hank					4 x 7.64/50 & 4 x 5.45/40		
Sherki					4 x 5.45/40		
Cape Fédala					3 x 3.9/45 & 3 x 3/50		
Table d'Oukasha					3 x 3.9/45		

BB—battleship, CA—heavy cruiser, CL—light cruiser, D1—light or superficial damage (including splinter damage), D2—moderate damage (combatability not significantly impaired), D3—significant damage (combat or maneuvering ability somewhat impaired), D4—major damage (combat and maneuvering ability significantly impaired or eliminated), DD—destroyer, F—flagship, PS—sloop, SB—damage cause by fire from shore batteries

Time: 0815–1505
Weather: Fair, light westerly breeze
Visibility: Coastal haze, good to seaward
Sea state: Slight swells
Surprise: Americans
Mission: Americans—amphibious attack; French—self-defense

armored decks before exploding in the aftermost six-inch magazine, which, fortunately, was empty. At 0725 a second sixteen-inch round penetrated three decks into the after control station but failed to explode.

The *Tuscaloosa* then switched targets from the *Jean Bart* to the submarine berthing area, and the *Wichita* pounded the docks. The French fought back. As one historian and participant described the scene, "Throughout this action, heavy stuff was whizzing over *Massachusetts* and splashing in the water close aboard."[5] But the Americans kept hitting. At 0735 and 0736 sixteen-inch projectiles splashed near the *Jean Bart* and tore holes in the plating around her waterline. At 0737 a heavy round struck the French battleship's main funnel and pierced two light decks and a bulkhead before passing out through the hull just above the 150-mm armored deck.

The *Massachusetts* checked her fire at 0740 after discharging thirteen three- to six-gun salvos. The *Jean Bart* had been quiet for five minutes, and the American spotters could not gauge her damage because of flames on the mole and in the port. At 0748, after receiving reports that the French ship remained operational, the *Massachusetts* resumed firing. At 0806 a ricocheting dud jammed the *Jean Bart's* active turret. Another shell from the same salvo bounced off the number 2 turret's barbette, likewise failing to explode. Four minutes later a projectile smashed the quarterdeck forward of the *Jean Bart's* starboard catapult. After penetrating a 100-mm armored deck, it exploded in a ballast tank and wrecked the after control station. Fragments exited through the bottom of the ship.

The batteries at El Hank and Table d'Oukasha remained fully operational despite periodic attention from all three American warships. The *Wichita*, for example, fired 225 rounds at El Hank, 91 at Table d'Oukasha, and 278 eight-inch rounds into the port. Visibility deteriorated as dense smoke shrouded the harbor.

As Task Group 34.1 and the French swapped salvos, planes from the aircraft carrier *Ranger* dive-bombed the harbor. One historian has described the carnage in the following manner: "Alongside the breakwater, three submarines [the *Amphitrite*, *Oréade*, and *La-Psyché*] went down at their mooring, their officers and men cut to pieces by flying stones. Others, cutting their wires, made for the harbour entrance, zigzagging through the barrage of shells."[6] A French officer

MAP 6.1. BATTLE OF CASABLANCA, 8 NOVEMBER 1942

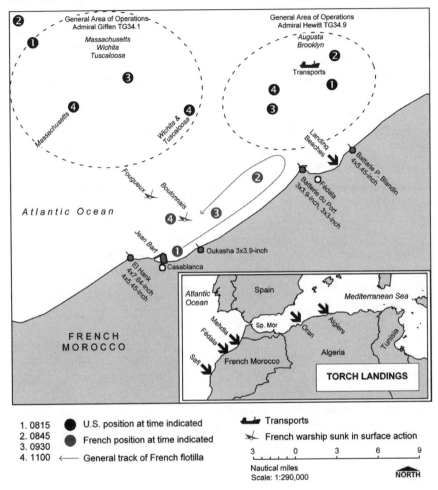

recalled, "In the commercial harbor, it was a massacre: 10 freighters or passenger ships were sunk, with a loss of 40 dead and 60 wounded among their crews."[7] Then, Rear Admiral Giffen received a telephone message: "This is from Army—you are killing townspeople, no opposition ashore."[8] Giffen ordered a cease-fire at 0835. Many concluded the French were defeated.

By this time Task Group 34.1 had run sixteen miles northwest of the entrance to the harbor at Casablanca and twenty-five miles from Fédala. This made it impossible for Giffen to fulfill his principal mission of containing the French warships, and at 0815, under billowing clouds of black smoke, the *Milan, Albatros,*

Brestois, Boulonnais, Fougueux, Frondeur, and *Alcyon* began filing out the harbor channel at eighteen knots. The *Primauguet, Tempête,* and *Simoun* remained in port, hastily repairing minor damage; the *Malin* was laid up and unable to sail. Rear Admiral Gervais de Lafond, who had defeated a British destroyer flotilla off Syria in June 1941, planned to lead the French ships out of Casablanca, proceed northeast along the coast with the rising sun behind his warships, and attack the U.S. transports off Fédala. So much for welcoming the Americans!

The *Ranger's* Wildcats reported the enemy column at 0818 and proceeded to strafe it "so savagely that the French ships glittered from all the bullets ricocheting off their superstructures."[9] The .50-caliber rain wounded de Lafond and many others. Nonetheless, he pressed up the coast, and the *Milan* began shelling the helpless landing boats at 0828, sinking one and striking others. Rear Admiral Hewitt, caught off guard by the French foray, alerted the *Augusta* and *Brooklyn,* which had been on the far side of the landing zone conducting fire support. Only the American destroyers *Wilkes, Swanson,* and *Ludlow,* which had been engaging the Cape Fédala battery, stood between the enemy and the transports. However, when de Lafond's force targeted the Americans, they mistook his "super" destroyers for cruisers. Moreover, the U.S. ships suffered a shortage of ammunition. The *Ludlow,* for instance, had already expended 1,238 rounds against the shore batteries.

The *Wilkes* and *Swanson* retreated at flank speed in a northerly direction, while the *Ludlow,* zigzagging to confuse the enemy gunners, fled west. Pink, green, blue, and plain shell splashes surrounded the *Ludlow,* and a few splinters rattled aboard. At 0834 a round detonated on her forecastle deck and sparked several large fires. When the *Ludlow* finally escaped she retired to the convoy area to carry out repairs.

At 0840, just 7,000 yards short of the nearest transports, de Lafond observed the *Augusta* and *Brooklyn* threading through the landing zone. He turned his force 180 degrees to the southwest, hoping to lure the Americans within range of El Hank. The *Fougueux* missed this order, however, and became separated from the column. Visibility remained poor, as dark clouds from burning on-shore oil tanks blew to sea to mix with white and black funnel smoke pouring from the French destroyers.

At around 0845 (reports of the time disagree) the American cruisers opened fire as the *Wilkes* and *Swanson* reversed course and assumed screening positions. The *Augusta* snapped off six nine-gun salvos to starboard within three and a half minutes, as the range to the French column fell from 19,000 to 16,700 yards. Red splashes from the *Milan* began to fall very close to the American ships—good shooting near the maximum effective range of the French 5.45-inch gun. At 0850 the *Augusta* turned northwest, and at 0857, now a comfortable 26,700 yards from the enemy, the *Augusta* came about to a southwesterly course. She then turned southeast at 0905, always maintaining ranges above twenty thousand yards. Smoke periodically forced the American cruisers to resort to indirect fire.

At 0915 de Lafond, still paralleling the coast, reversed back toward the landing zone. Recalled by Hewitt, Giffen's ships had been closing at twenty-seven knots since 0855. The *Massachusetts* finally engaged at 0918 from 19,400 yards north northwest of the French column. The *Wichita* and *Tuscaloosa* joined shortly after.

Having passed the baton, the *Augusta* and *Brooklyn* resumed their screening and fire support mission. Moreover, Admiral Hewitt had the army commander, Gen. George Patton, impatiently pacing the decks of his flagship. The sooner Patton was safely ashore, the better.

The French ships returned Task Group 34.1's fire. Viewed from the *Massachusetts*, the French "turned to starboard and began a series of evasive tacts [*sic*] by making many large changes of course and speed. Each time a ship emerged from the Smoke [*sic*] she was immediately taken under fire."[10] Meanwhile, the light cruiser *Primauguet*, finally got under way at 0900. Along with El Hank, she engaged the *Massachusetts* at 0935. At the same moment Giffen reversed course to east by northeast and closed to within 11,400 yards of the French column. The *Milan*, again nearing Cape Fédala, came about to the southwest. Almost immediately, a round from the *Massachusetts* struck the *Fougueux*, which was operating independently 11,000 yards northeast of Casablanca. Shortly after, a *Tuscaloosa* broadside also jolted the unfortunate French destroyer. Near the same time, the *Frondeur* and *Alcyon* both suffered light damage. However, the French fire, particularly from El Hank, remained intense, as the following chronology from *Massachusetts*'s log shows:

0943: Enemy shells were falling within fifty yards of the ship on both sides.

0945: Shell fragments were falling close aboard.

0951: Fall of enemy shells becoming heavy.[11]

Despite this, the *Massachusetts*'s gunners did not ignore the port. At 0955 a dud sixteen-inch shell stuck the *Malin*, which was moored in the inner harbor. The *Fougueux*, still under fire, blew up and sank five minutes later. At 1000 the *Massachusetts* was sailing west of El Hank when "a shower of wooden splinters so stunned [her] executive officer . . . that it took him a few seconds to realize the ship had been hit."[12] A 7.64-inch projectile had struck the *Massachusetts* opposite of No. 2 turret on the port side, penetrated a deck and detonated in a second deck compartment, inflicting minor damage. Three minutes after being hit, the *Massachusetts* narrowly maneuvered between a spread of four torpedoes launched by one of the eight French submarines that had made it to sea. The closest torpedo passed just yards from the starboard side of the American battleship.

With the *Massachusetts* out of sight and his ships shrouded in cloaks of smoke, de Lafond took the opportunity to again rush the transports. The Americans were playing a curious game. With Task Group 34.1 heading west and the French column again threatening the transports, Hewitt was forced to order the *Augusta*, *Brooklyn*, *Swanson*, *Wilkes*, and *Bristol* back into the fight. Led by the *Swanson* the three destroyers formed a column and dashed for Cape Fédala. However, the cruisers had once again migrated to the far side of the transport park. The *Augusta* was refueling a plane and preparing to put Patton ashore.

The *Brooklyn* managed to interpose herself between the French and their targets just in time after dodging a spread of five torpedoes launched by the French submarine *Amazone* along the way. At 1009 shells from the *Alcyon* straddled the American light cruiser, and one minute later the *Brestois* and *Boulonnais* launched torpedoes at the *Brooklyn* from 13,000 yards. But at 1012 the *Brooklyn's* rapid-firing six-inch guns walloped the *Boulonnais* with a crippling broadside. Meanwhile, the Cape Fédala battery opened up, forcing the Americans, particularly the three destroyers, to divide their fire.

Far to the west, the French submarine *Méduse* attacked the *Tuscaloosa*. At 1021 a torpedo streaked past the American heavy cruiser, missing by 100 yards. At the same time the *Augusta* finally engaged the French squadron, forcing General Patton to witness more naval action. Patton recalled, "I could just see them and make out our splashes . . . all firing and going like hell in big zig-zags. You have to put cotton in your ears. Some of the people got white but it did not seem very dangerous to me—sort of impersonal."[13]

The *Jenkins* and *Wainwright* moved up to support the cruisers, and the *Edison* replaced the *Swanson*, which, suffering a jam in Mount 51, retired to the transport park.

At 1030 the *Massachusetts* swung back to the east and flung a broadside toward the French warships from 30,000 yards. At 1035 the *Massachusetts* commenced firing rapidly even though her gunners complained of the smoke and difficulty in acquiring targets. Moreover, one historian has noted, the American cruisers "steered radically evasive courses: ellipses, snake tracks, and figure eights—dodging shells every few seconds and footing so fast that their screening destroyers with difficulty kept out of their way."[14] This did not improve marksmanship. At 1046 a dud struck the *Brooklyn* on a five-inch mount and bounced over the side, wounding six men.

By 1103 after shooting twenty-three six- to nine-gun salvos in the previous half hour, the *Massachusetts* ceased fire. She had expended 60 percent of her sixteen-inch ammunition and wanted to conserve the remainder in case the *Richelieu* appeared. The *Tuscaloosa* and *Wichita*, screened by the *Rhind*, continued to press de Lafond, closing to 14,000 yards.

For two and a half hours the Americans had flung tremendous amounts of ordnance. Skillfully using smoke, the French flotilla had been hurt but remained very much in the fight and a continuing threat to the landing. All that changed in the quarter hour between 1100 and 1115. De Lafond's force was milling several thousand yards north of the harbor jetty when the *Augusta* and *Brooklyn*, firing from around 17,000 yards, hit the lightly armored *Primauguet* four times, blasting three holes below the French cruiser's waterline and blowing her number 3 turret overboard. Then the *Augusta* landed two shells on the *Milan*, and the *Brooklyn* followed those with two more. Next, at least six of the *Augusta*'s eight-inch projectiles battered the *Brestois*. The *Primauguet* retired toward the harbor and anchored off Roches Noires. The *Milan* and *Brestois* followed. The *Augusta* ceased firing at 1105 and returned to the transport area, leaving the *Tuscaloosa* and *Wichita* to finish off the enemy. Previously damaged, the *Boulonnais* rolled over and sank at 1112.

These losses reduced the French surface force to the *Frondeur, Alcyon,* and *Albatros*. At 1115 the French survivors formed up to deliver a torpedo attack against the American heavy cruisers while El Hank covered. The *Wichita* recorded the shore battery's fire as "very deliberate, resulting in many straddles on cruisers and destroyers of Task Group 34.1."[15] The cruisers broke up this attack at 1125 when an eight-inch round crippled the *Frondeur*. She limped back to port with flooded machinery spaces and capsized the following night. A retaliation round from El Hank passed diagonally through the *Wichita* from port to starboard at 1128 and detonated on impact with the starboard platting, wounding fourteen men and sparking fires. Two minutes later a pair of projectiles hammered the *Albatros*. With only three guns operational, the French destroyer continued the fight, but the *Ranger*'s aircraft swarming overhead landed two bombs, flooding an engine and fire room. Then another eight-inch shell knocked out the *Albatros*'s last engine, and she went dead in the water with twenty-five men dead and eighty more wounded. At 1138 the *Wichita*, in a close call, dodged three submarine-launched torpedoes.

At 1150 reports of the dreaded *Richelieu* prompted the *Tuscaloosa* and *Wichita* to sail west to investigate. But the Americans kept a careful eye on the collection of cripples stranded around the harbor entrance, and the *Ranger*'s aircraft continued to harass them.

An hour later, the large colonial sloop *La Grandière* and the smaller sloops *La Gracieuse* and *Commandant Delage* sortied to rescue survivors. The destroyers *Tempête* and *Simoun*, which missed the morning's engagement repairing damage suffered in a previous collision, also emerged staying just off the harbor channel, hoping the sight of fresh targets would lure the Americans into El Hank's range. For the third time the *Augusta* and *Brooklyn* rushed southwest to meet an enemy intrusion. The *Brooklyn* opened fire at 1315, and the *Augusta*, delayed because she launched a spotter at 1319, opened up ten minutes later from 18,000 yards. Once again, the French laid down a heavy smoke screen and confounded

American spotters. The *Ranger*'s ubiquitous bombers buzzed overhead, however, and at 1330 reported a direct hit on one French ship. In any case, aircraft damaged the *La Grandière* at some point during the afternoon.

The two American cruisers maneuvered continually, shooting at ranges that varied between 21,000 and 13,000 yards. The French returned fire sporadically. By 1356 the *Augusta*'s spotters reported the target ships were all smoking and apparently badly damaged. At 1400 Hewitt broke off and headed back for the transport area. Throughout all phases of the battle, the *Augusta* fired 794 rounds in 104 salvos, including twelve broadsides discharged during the initial shore bombardment.

Hewitt had wanted Giffen to contain the French ships clustered around the harbor entrance, but fear of the *Richelieu* had been a magnet constantly drawing Task Group 34.1 away from the action all day long. The *Massachusetts* did exchange salvos with El Hank from 1341 to 1351, but Hewitt ordered her to conserve her remaining ordinance. This gave the French warships a respite, during which a tug towed the *Albatros* back toward the port so she could beach herself near the *Primauguet* and *Milan*.

The *Wichita* and *Tuscaloosa*, their magazines down to 20 percent capacity, returned, and at 1444 the *Wichita* engaged the *Primauguet* from 17,000 yards. She fired sixty-three rounds through 1505, reporting that "excellent spotting coupled with improved visibility resulted in effective fire."[16] Nonetheless, the *Wichita* and *Tuscaloosa* failed to register any additional hits. With El Hank's guns straddling frequently, the cruisers decided it would be best to withdraw. For the French, the *Primauguet*, *Milan*, and *Albatros* were heavily damaged, the *Fougueux* and *Boulonnais* sank offshore, and the *Frondeur* and *Brestois* limped back to port where they capsized the next day. From de Lafond's original force, only the *Alcyon* remained nearly intact.

Casablanca was a confused, daylong action. The Americans had aircraft assisting their ships, while shore batteries and submarines served as potential equalizers for the outnumbered French. The American gunners relied on traditional fire control, generously supplemented by spotter aircraft to direct their weapons. Generally shooting at ranges in excess of 15,000 yards and hampered by their enemy's effective use of smoke, they turned in a creditable performance. The *Massachusetts* disabled the *Jean Bart*'s sole turret early in the action. Given that the *Jean Bart*'s guns ranged as far as the transport area, this proved an important contribution to American success. The *Massachusetts* also severely damaged the docked destroyer *Le Malin* and hit the *Primauguet*, *Milan*, and *Fougueux*—an effective performance for a new ship experiencing her first combat with 2,000 fresh recruits in her crew of 2,400 men. The *Augusta* also enjoyed a hot streak, hitting the *Primauguet*, *Milan*, and *Brestois* in the space of five minutes. On the other hand, American dispositions led to some dangerous moments. Giffen had too many jobs—suppress the *Jean Bart* and El Hank, watch for the *Richelieu*, and contain the French warships—to perform all effectively. The same held true for Task Group 34.9.

Second Action off Casablanca, 10 November 1942

Despite the destruction of the French surface fleet and the successful, if sloppy, landings by American troops on 8 November, Casablanca, against expectations, resisted for three more days. Certainly, the men of the French navy proved they did not lack courage when they ventured out to challenge the American Navy one more time.

Time: 1110–1150
Weather: n/a
Visibility: n/a
Sea state: n/a
Surprise: None
Mission: Americans—interception based upon specific intelligence; French—shore bombardment

Survivors from the four sunken French destroyers and a Senegalese battalion dug in east of the city. Late in the morning of 10 November the *La Gracieuse* and *Commandant Delage* sortied up the coast to support them by bombarding the American right flank with their 3.9-inch guns. The *Boyle* raised an alarm, and the *Augusta, Edison, Boyle, Tillman,* and *Rowan* headed southwest to intervene. At 1125 the *Edison* and *Tillman* opened fire. The *Edison* engaged the leading sloop and her target "seemed to disappear in a smother of splashes."[17] At 1139 the *Augusta* joined the fray from 18,000 yards.

Already lightly damaged and faced with the tall geysers thrown up by eight-inch shells, the French vessels made smoke and retreated toward port. However, the *Jean Bart*'s men, after working feverishly for nearly two days, had cleared the jammed turret, and the sight of a worthwhile target within range provoked a reaction. At 1146 the battleship's main battery sent a salvo arching 19,500 yards toward the *Augusta*. "Suddenly and mysteriously straddled by stalks of yellow water," according to one account, the *Augusta* immediately turned to sea to open the range.[18] The *Jean Bart* fired nine more two-gun salvos, chasing the *Augusta* out to 29,000 yards. The last three French volleys straddled the *Augusta* closely, and the final one drenched the bridge with yellow water. Then, the *Ranger*'s aircraft appeared. They dropped nine 1,000-pound bombs, and at least two struck and cratered the battleship's deck. This knocked the *Jean Bart* out of action for good.

Casablanca surrendered the next day. The French suffered severe losses in the naval battle because they fought a protracted action against a vastly superior foe, even after they realized that foe was American, not British. Many writers dismiss the first French sortie as a meaningless action undertaken only to uphold the navy's honor. This interpretation trivializes both French and American efforts.

During World War II major warships attacked nearly a dozen times to break up an amphibious landing. Indeed, the U.S. Navy found itself on the defensive in many such engagements—Savo Island, Empress Augusta Bay, and Leyte Gulf to list a few. However, Japanese warships never brought American landing craft under fire like the French did at Casablanca.

In light of the battle's final results it is easy to forget that a thin margin decided many actions. A hesitation in command, a shell falling a few yards one way or the other, a lapse in training or attention, and the naval engagement at Casablanca could have ended much differently. Sharp-eyed lookouts and adept maneuvering neutralized the French submarines, but they could have disabled the *Massachusetts* or one or more of the cruisers, perhaps leading to an unexpected result like the British defeat at Dakar. A repulse of the main American landing in Africa would have had serious short-term repercussions for the Allies, not least for the British who, at that point, regarded the Americans as their juniors in experience and ability.

An armistice between the Vichy French and Allies ended the fighting on one front, although German submarines were soon to exact a heavy toll on the American transports crowded off Casablanca. However, the important fact was that the template for future amphibious operations was being refined. Just as in the Solomons, success required a strong surface fleet, not just to bombard shore positions, but to prevent intervention by enemy warships. Aircraft carriers—at least in the numbers then available—could not do the job alone.

1. The battleship USS *South Dakota*, the repair ship USS *Prometheus*, and two *Mahan*-class destroyers, November 1942. *Photo courtesy U.S. Naval Institute Photo Archive*

2. The heavy cruiser USS *San Francisco* off Mare Island, December 1942. The white circles on the ship's starboard side mark the locations of enemy shell hits sustained during the 13 November action off Guadalcanal. *Photo courtesy Naval Historical Center 19-N-44715*

3. The light cruiser USS *Montpelier*, flagship of Cruiser Division 12 at Vila-Stanmore and Empress Augusta Bay, en route to the Saipan invasion, 11 June 1944. *Photo courtesy U.S. Naval Institute Photo Archive*

4. The destroyer USS *Fletcher*, first of her class and participant in the Battles of Guadalcanal, Tassafaronga, and Biak on 18 July 1942, just a few weeks after being commissioned. *Photo courtesy U.S. Naval Institute Photo Archive*

5. The heavy cruisers of *Sentai* 7—the *Kumano, Mikuma,* and *Suzuya*—in Ise Bay, Honshu, during the summer of 1938. *Photo courtesy U.S. Naval Institute Photo Archive*

6. The Japanese light cruiser *Jintsu*, flagship of Destroyer Squadron 2, which was sunk at Kolombangara, 12 July 1943. *Photo courtesy U.S. Naval Institute Photo Archive*

7. The *Fubuki*-class destroyer *Usugumo*. With six 5-inch guns and nine 24-inch torpedo tubes, this "Special Type" was an early realization of Japan's philosophy of building destroyers capable of sinking battleships. *Photo courtesy U.S. Naval Institute Photo Archive*

8. The USS *Houston* at Sunda Strait, pinned by searchlights from two directions and about to receive a torpedo attack from starboard. *Photo courtesy USS* Houston *(CA30) Survivors Association—The Next Generation*

9. A salvo from the El Hank shore battery splashing near the USS *Mayrant* during Battle of Casablanca. Note the tight pattern and the height of the geysers relative to the destroyer's length. *Photo courtesy Naval Historical Center 80-G-30422*

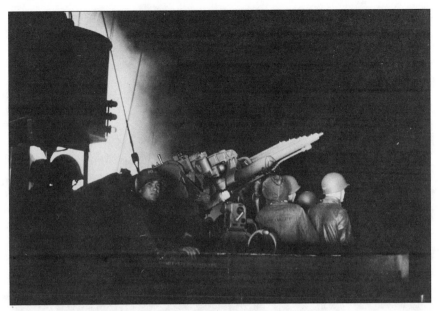

10. The problems of night combat. The flash from another ship's gunfire lights the faces of a cruiser's 1.1-inch crew during the Battle of Kula Gulf, 6 July 1943. *Photo courtesy U.S. Naval Institute Photo Archive*

11. The USS *Helena* fires her last salvo before being struck by torpedoes during the Battle of Kula Gulf, 6 July 1943. *Photo courtesy U.S. Naval Institute Photo Archive*

12. Splinter damage the USS *Boise* suffered at Cape Esperance, October 1942. *Photo courtesy Naval Historical Center 80-G-36296*

13. The USS *New Orleans* lost her bow to a Type 93 Long Lance torpedo at Tassafaronga, 30 November 1942. Here, she is back at Tulagi pumping out and preparing to place a temporary bow. *Photo courtesy Donald J. Klein Jr.*

14. The Japanese destroyer *Nagatsuki* ran aground during the Battle of Kula Gulf on 6 July 1943 and was then bombed into a wreck by U.S. aircraft that same day. *Photo courtesy U.S. Naval Institute Photo Archive*

15. The skippers of Destroyer Squadron 23 enjoy a beer at Cloob Des-Slot in Purvis Bay, Solomon Islands, on 24 May 1944. Pictured from left to right are Cdr. R.A. Gano, USS *Dyson*; Cdr. Luther K. Reynolds, USS *Charles Ausburne*; Squadron Commodore Capt. Arleigh A. Burke; Cdr. B.L. Austin, commander Destroyer Division 46; Cdr. D.C. Hamberger, USS *Converse*; Cdr. Herald Stout, USS *Claxton*; and Cdr. Henry J. Armstrong, USS *Spence*. *Photo courtesy U.S. Naval Institute Photo Archive*

16. Rear Adm. Walden Lee Ainsworth standing on the *Honolulu*'s bridge on 23 July 1943. As commander of Task Force 67 and Cruiser Division 9, Ainsworth fought three engagements in July 1943. *Photo courtesy U.S. Naval Institute Photo Archive*

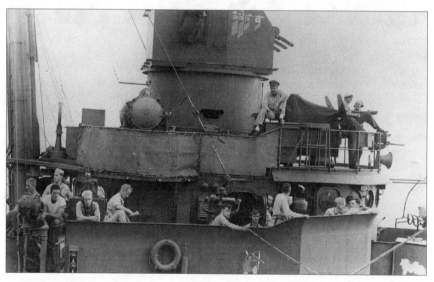

17. Capt. Arleigh Burke (fifth from left), commander of Destroyer Squadron 23, reads on the bridge wing of USS *Charles Ausburne*. Judging by the hash marks on the Mark 37 Director, this picture was taken after the Battle of Cape St. George. *Photo courtesy U.S. Naval Institute Photo Archive*

18. Change of command ceremonies between Capt. Francis X. McInerney and Capt. T.J. Ryan, who took over command of Destroyer Squadron 21 on board the USS *Nicholas* on 7 August 1943. McInerney is reading the orders turning over command to Capt. Ryan, who is standing to McInerney's right. Lt. Cdr. A.J. Hill, skipper of *Nicholas*, is on the left.
Photo courtesy Naval Historical Center 80-G-56083

19. The march of technology. Officers huddled around the USS *Albert W. Grant*'s combat information center plot, July 1945. *Photo courtesy U.S. Naval Institute Photo Archive*

20. The view of the pips. This shows the USS *Denver*'s SG radar plot during the Battle of Vila-Stanmore. The large splashes of light to the left and right are land masses. *Photo courtesy Naval Historical Center NH100387*

Chapter 7

Alaska: Komandorski, March 1943

Meteorological conditions become progressively worse as the western end of the island chain is approached. On Attu five or six days a week are likely to be rainy, and there are hardly more than eight or ten clear days a year. The rest of the time, even if rain is not falling, fog of varying density is the rule rather than the exception.

—OFFICE OF NAVAL INTELLIGENCE

In 1942 the territory of the Japanese Empire and the United States of America came closest in the north Pacific, where Alaska's Aleutian chain curved west beyond the 180th meridian to Attu Island. The last island in the Aleutian chain sits just 700 miles from Paramushiro in the Kuriles, which was Japan's northern bastion during World War II. On the atlas the Aleutians seem a natural route between North American and Japan, but horrific weather negated any geographic advantages the chain offered.

Nevertheless, Japan brought the war to Alaska on 3 June 1942. Aircraft from the carriers *Ryujo* and *Junyo* raided Dutch Harbor on Amaknak Island, and on 6 June 1942 Imperial navy troops occupied Kiska Island (see Map 7.1). Originally, the Japanese planned to hold Kiska as the northern anchor of a forward defensive line that included Midway Island. But after the U.S. Navy decimated Tokyo's fast carrier force at the Battle of Midway, Japan occupied Attu 200 miles west of Kiska and held these barren, snow-swept points independent of any larger defensive scheme.

Japan's occupation of North American territory contained more propaganda than military value. Gen. William "Billy" Mitchell asserted that "if Japan seizes Alaska, she can take New York,"[1] and a nervous American public demanded the reconquest of the Aleutians. The United States duly massed men, ships, and planes in the far north. Japan had originally intended to evacuate the Aleutians during the winter of 1942–43. The American buildup, however, led the Japanese to reinforce their Alaskan outposts to stave off an enemy attempt to leapfrog from the northwest.

In preparation for the assault, American engineers constructed a chain of island bases, and submarines and aircraft harassed Japanese shipping. Winter slowed operations; nonetheless, Captain Arichika Rokuji, Destroyer Squadron 1's chief of staff, recalled that efforts to supply Kiska "were exciting because in order to avoid detection by American planes, the ships had to run in during the night,

MAP 7.1. DUTCH HARBOR TO PARAMUSHIRO: THE ALEUTIAN THEATER

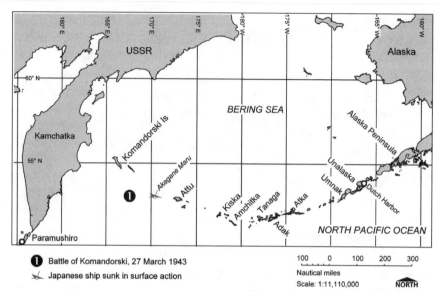

unload cargo and get clear before daylight.... We had to take advantage of storms and fogs."[2]

There were plenty of storms for the Japanese to use as cover, so in early February 1943 the theater's newly appointed American commander, Rear Admiral Kinkaid, upped the excitement by sending surface warships to patrol west of Attu. On 19 February the heavy cruiser *Indianapolis* and the destroyers *Coghlan* and *Gillespie* ran down the freighter *Akagane Maru* (3,100 tons) sixty miles southwest of Attu. The American warships engaged at 2316, and within ten minutes fires raged along the freighter's length and secondary explosions punctuated the night. The heavy cruiser expended 107 eight-inch shells in the brief engagement. Then, nervous the flames might attract an enemy submarine, the *Indianapolis* left the destroyers to complete the job.

Over the course of an hour the *Coghlan* and *Gillespie* launched six torpedoes. One passed under, two missed astern, two detonated short, and one malfunctioned. It required several five-inch broadsides to send the *Akagane Maru* to the bottom at 0124 on 20 February. The patrol boat *Kanjiri* cruising fifteen miles to the east heard the gunfire, but escaped notice.

This event caused Vice Admiral Hosogaya Boshiro, the commander of Japan's 5th Fleet and the officer responsible for the northern theater, to collect a high-speed convoy and escort it to Attu's Holtz Bay on 9 March. The matter had become urgent because the Japanese needed to complete construction of an all-weather airstrip if they were to hold their positions in the Aleutians. Six months of work had seen scant progress, and the effort required more men and material.

On 23 March under scudding clouds and high winds the entire 5th Fleet weighed anchor in Paramushiro once again to join two large and fast merchant ships, the *Asaka Maru* (7,399 GRT, 17 knots, four 5.5-inch guns) and *Sakito Maru* (7,158 GRT, 18 knots) already at sea. The slow transport *Sanko Maru* (5,491 GRT) and her escorting destroyer, the *Usugumo*, had set out even earlier. Hosogaya planned to unite these groups south of the Russian Komandorski Islands and proceed in force to Attu.

Kinkaid knew something was up. The intelligence summary out of Pearl Harbor for 18 March warned, "There is growing suspicion the enemy may be planning a move in this area."[3] However, the Pacific Fleet's Combat Intelligence Unit underestimated the 5th Fleet's strength. The Americans believed it consisted of only one heavy cruiser, one light cruiser, and four destroyers. On 22 March Kinkaid sent Task Group 16.6 under the newly promoted Rear Adm. Charles H. McMorris, formerly the *San Francisco*'s skipper, to intercept the enemy with a force matched to his estimated maximum strength. After Task Group 16.6 had fruitlessly maintained station in the stormy waters west of Attu for four days, Pearl Harbor transmitted portions of an intercepted radio message indicating the expected transports had sailed. It did not mention the escort, or that two cruisers had recently reinforced Hosogaya.[4]

Battle of Komandorski Islands, 27 March 1943

The hour before dawn on 27 March found the American task force sweeping north by east on the far side of the International Date Line, 180 miles west of Attu and a hundred miles south of Russia's Komandorski Islands. Six miles separated each ship, with the *Coghlan* leading. McMorris' flagship, the old light cruiser *Richmond,* followed. Completing the line were the *Bailey,* the *Dale,* the *Salt Lake City*—her battle damage from Cape Esperance repaired and half her crew raw recruits—and the *Monaghan.*

After weathering a violent storm, Hosogaya's main body met the fast transports at 1400 hours on 26 March, and they waited together for the *Sanko Maru.* The *Nachi,* veteran of Java Sea and Hosogaya's flagship since April 1942, led the Japanese column, followed by the *Maya,* which had arrived on 27 February 1943. Then came the *Tama,* another 5th Fleet veteran, the destroyers *Wakaba* and *Hatsushimo,* the other new cruiser the *Abukuma,* the destroyer *Ikazuchi,* the transports *Asaka Maru* and *Sakito Maru,* and, last, the destroyer *Inazuma.* At 0400 on 27 March the Japanese began executing a 180-degree turn to the north. Lookouts maintained a sharp watch. The *Inazuma,* still heading south waiting her turn to come about, spotted

TABLE 7.1. FORCES ENGAGED IN THE BATTLE OF KOMANDORSKI ISLANDS

Type of Ship	Year Launched	Displacement, Full Load (tons)	Max. Speed (knots)	Guns (number by inch/ caliber)	Torpedoes (number of tubes by diameter in inches)	Damage
American Task Group 16.1 (Rear Adm. C.H. McMorris)						
Salt Lake City	CA	1927	11,512	32	10 x 8/55 & 8 x 5/25		D3
Richmond (F)	CL	1921	9,508	34	10 x 6/53 & 2 x 3/50	6 x 21	
American Destroyer Squadron 14 (Capt. R.S. Riggs)						
Bailey (F)	DD	1941	2,395	35	5 x 5/38	10 x 21	D3
Coghlan	DD	1942	2,395	35	5 x 5/38	10 x 21	D1
Dale	DD	1935	2,064	36	5 x 5/38	8 x 21	
Monaghan	DD	1935	2,064	36	5 x 5/38	8 x 21	
Japanese Sentai 21 (Vice Admiral Hosogaya Boshiro)						
Nachi (F)	CA	1924	14,743	35	10 x 8/50 & 8 x 5/40	8 x 24	D2
Maya	CA	1928	14,604	35	10 x 8/50 & 8 x 5/40	8 x 24	
Tama	CL	1921	5,832	36	7 x 5.5/50 & 2 x 3.1/40	8 x 24	D1
Japanese Destroyer Squadron 1 (Rear Admiral Mori Tomokazu)						
Abukuma	CL	1925	5,570	36	7 x 5.5/50 & 2 x 3.1/40	8 x 24	
Japanese Destroyer Division 21 (Captain Amano Shigetaka)						
Wakaba	DD	1934	1,802	36	5 x 5/50	8 x 24	
Hatsushimo	DD	1934	1,802	36	5 x 5/50	8 x 24	
Ikazuchi	DD	1932	1,980	38	6 x 5/50	9 x 24	

CA—heavy cruiser, CL—light cruiser, D1—light or superficial damage (including splinter damage), D2—moderate damage (combat ability not significantly impaired), D3—significant damage (combat or maneuvering ability somewhat impaired), DD—destroyer, F—flagship

Time: 0542–0912 (Z+12)[5]
Weather: Overcast, light southwesterly breeze
Visibility: Excellent
Sea state: Slight swells
Surprise: None
Mission: Americans—interception based on general intelligence; Japanese—escort and transit

a mast 27,000 thousand yards ahead and to port. Receiving the destroyer's contact report, Hosogaya assumed the *Sanko Maru* and her escort had arrived.

Meanwhile, spotters aboard the *Asaka Maru* counted two, then three, sets of masts. She sent a "red Morse urgent" signal to Rear Admiral Mori Tomokazu aboard the *Abukuma* that the enemy was in sight.[6] After fifteen minutes and several repetitions of the alarm, with the range between the Japanese column and the unknown vessels closing rapidly, the *Abukuma* finally acknowledged. By 0515 Hosogaya realized he had stumbled upon the enemy, and at 0530 Squadron 1 followed by *Sentai* 21 turned starboard to the southeast. The two transports, escorted by the *Inazuma*, withdrew north northwest.

The day dawned under a light overcast, with remarkable visibility, a glassy sea, and a seven-knot breeze from the southeast. The water temperature was 28°F, and the air was a few degrees warmer.

The *Richmond* and *Coghlan* independently scoped ships to the north at 0430, a half hour after the *Inazuma's* initial sighting of the Americans. McMorris ordered his dispersed fleet to concentrate on the *Richmond*, "secure in the knowledge that his force was equal to any covering force the convoy might have."[7] Closing on the American formation took some time, as the *Monaghan*, the hindmost ship, trailed the lead vessel by twenty-four miles. Meanwhile, the masts of first one and then two heavy Japanese cruisers hove into sight, and eager anticipation melted into worry for the Americans. As the *Salt Lake City* steamed hard to catch up, the American admiral realized this was no lightly escorted convoy he had happened upon. He continued, however, hoping "judicious maneuvers . . . might bring the merchantmen within gun range before the Japanese combatant ships could intervene."[8]

By 0539 the *Richmond* led the *Salt Lake City* by a thousand yards. The *Bailey* and *Coghlan* cruised off the flagship's port bow, and the *Dale* and *Monaghan* were off the *Salt Lake City's* starboard quarter. One minute later the *Nachi*, and then the *Maya*, sent shells arcing 20,000 yards toward the American column (see Map 7.2). The blast from this opening salvo wrecked the Zero on the *Nachi's* starboard catapult, but the plane on the port catapult managed to take off shortly thereafter. Moreover, the *Nachi* immediately suffered an electrical failure because engineers shifted generator steam supply to a boiler just raising steam. This froze her main guns at their maximum elevation.

The *Maya's* second broadside straddled the *Richmond*. A shell sliced between stacks 3 and 4 of the American light cruiser and severed a guy. The *Salt Lake City*

MAP 7.2. BATTLE OF KOMANDORSKI ISLANDS, 27 MARCH 1943

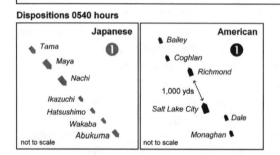

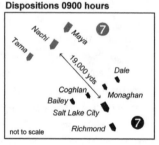

and *Richmond* returned fire within two minutes. Mistaking the *Nachi*'s burning floatplane for shell impacts, the *Salt Lake City* claimed hits on the *Nachi* with her third and fourth salvos. At 0544 with the range still closing, the *Maya* shifted fire to the *Salt Lake City*, and the *Nachi* launched eight torpedoes. The *Richmond*'s lookouts claimed that one passed beneath her bow and another porpoised near the *Bailey*'s starboard quarter.

At 0545, with the *Maya*'s tight broadsides falling close by, the two enemy columns converging, and the Japanese transports fleeing, McMorris admitted he had bit off more than he could chew. He ordered a turn to port and rang up twenty-eight knots. The *Salt Lake City*'s aft turrets continued pumping out shells as the

Americans fled to the southwest, and the heavy cruiser's sixteenth salvo drew blood at 0550 from 16,000 yards. An eight-inch shell struck the *Nachi*'s compass bridge, killing eleven men, wounding twenty-one, and damaging the gunnery control electrical circuit. Aboard the *Nachi*, one officer remembered, "[T]he Admiral was standing at the forward center of the flag bridge with his two principal staff officers on either side and slightly behind him. The other staff officers were standing in a single rank to the rear. Miraculously, all shell fragments missed the officers, but killed three communication personnel whose station was further aft, and set fire to the after end of the bridge."[9] A second American round damaged a mainmast strut. Two minutes later a third struck the *Nachi*'s aft aircraft deck, killing two and wounding five in the torpedo room below.[10]

The *Nachi*, although jolted by these blows, continued to chase the Americans from their port quarter. Rear Admiral Mori and his destroyers also followed on the American's starboard quarter, ready to intervene should the Americans swing north toward the convoy. The *Nachi* steered to avoid fouling the *Maya*'s aim while the *Maya* zigzagged to fire full broadsides because only 4 of her 10 eight-inch guns could bear forward. These maneuvers negated Hosogaya's speed advantage, and the range gradually opened. Also, at 0607 the *Maya* fired four torpedoes. Although these missed, her accurate gunnery forced Capt. Bertram J. Rodgers, the *Salt Lake City*'s skipper, to chase salvos. Even worse, the direction of the pursuit gradually put the 5th Fleet astride McMorris' line of retreat to Alaska.

At 0610 an eight-inch projectile struck the *Salt Lake City*'s starboard floatplane, killing two men. Damage control quickly extinguished the fire and dumped the aircraft overboard.[11] Near misses shook the cruiser at 0621, causing Rodgers to think she had been hit again. At this time, McMorris began gradually steering west. He believed the *Salt Lake City* had dealt the *Nachi* a hard blow, causing the pursuit to falter, and that it might still be possible to take a crack at the transports. Hosogaya encouraged this belief by having his ships hold fire from 0621 to 0630, when the *Nachi*, her electrical problems resolved, could reenter the fray.

When the Japanese bombardment resumed, McMorris finally gave up on the transports. The chase continued in a west-northwesterly direction, the opponents specks on the horizon and the scream of oncoming shells broken by massive waterspouts, some very near, that splashed men stationed as high as the bridge. By 0645 the *Tama*, sailing north and slightly ahead of the Japanese heavy cruisers, had advanced to within 18,000 yards of the *Salt Lake City*'s starboard quarter. Rodgers sheered out of line and blasted eight ten-gun broadsides at the *Tama*, forcing her to maneuver away radically. Mori's destroyers continued to trail east of the Americans, maintaining position to protect the convoy.

At 0652 the *Salt Lake City* lost steering control due to repeated concussions from both near misses and her own salvos. At this time the *Richmond*, steaming at thirty knots, led the heavy cruiser by a thousand yards. The *Coghlan* and *Bailey* stood 1,000 and 1,500 yards off the *Salt Lake City*'s starboard bow, and the *Dale* and *Monaghan* kept similar station off her starboard quarter. As the *Salt Lake City*'s engineers patched her steering, McMorris maneuvered northwest to confront the *Abukuma*, which was finally pulling into range. Mori looped away when the *Richmond* opened fire.

At 0702 the *Salt Lake City* lost her rudder stops, and she momentarily fell out of line to starboard in the direction of the Japanese. Damage control shifted to steering aft a minute later, but this casualty restricted her to course changes of no more than 10 degrees, severely limiting her ability to chase salvos.

Hosogaya chose this point to order all units to attack. Destroyer Squadron 1's turn away had taken the smaller Japanese ships out of position, but the *Tama* complied, putting four torpedoes into the water at 0707. At 0710 an eight-inch projectile struck the *Salt Lake City* from a range greater than 20,000 yards; the shell passed through her main deck and out her hull three feet below the waterline, causing flooding in several compartments. At 0718, with the *Salt Lake City* taking on water and having trouble steering, McMorris ordered his destroyers to make smoke. The cold, still air favored this tactic, and dense clouds of white chemical and black funnel smoke soon hung thick behind the Americans. Frustrated by this development Hosogaya ordered Mori's squadron to cross astern to a position south of the flagship, expecting the Americans would flee in that direction. However, Mori, who missed Hosogaya's earlier signal to increase speed, had dropped further back. When Hosogaya ordered a torpedo attack, the cruisers were steaming at thirty-three knots while the destroyers, suffering from postponed maintenance, had difficulty making twenty-eight. "Although they 'cut corners' trying to catch up, they could not execute their mission," recalled one Japanese participant.[12]

The *Salt Lake City* steered west seeking maximum cover from the smoke as the destroyers screened her engaged side. McMorris reduced speed to twenty-five knots to keep his ships relatively concentrated. With enemy cruisers between him and base and his most powerful ship damaged, he faced a grim situation. Possessing the advantages of speed, guns, and the weather gauge, Hosogaya had the ability to force a decision. Instead he continued zigzagging to fire full broadsides and did not close range, as McMorris feared he would. At 0737 the *Richmond* came to the west northwest and increased speed to twenty-eight knots, hoping to open range. Then the *Tama* reappeared on the north end of the smoke screen only 16,000 yards away. The Americans concentrated to drive her off. At 0746 the *Bailey* reported being straddled, and she lost her gyro a few minutes later from the shock of near misses. By 0750 smoke again descended between the combatants.

Between 0718 and 0800 the *Nachi* and *Maya* periodically engaged but found it difficult to gauge their gunfire. Although the *Nachi*'s spotter plane flew overhead, "the reports were meager because of the smoke screen, and . . . jeopardized by the inability of the observers."[13] From the American perspective, however, it seemed that "from the expeditious and accurate manner in which the Japanese heavies shifted their fire during this phase . . . one of those ships possessed fire control radar."[14]

At 0755 the *Richmond* turned west southwest, and at 0802 McMorris signaled a further 30-degree turn to southwest by south. At 0803, just as the *Salt Lake City* was turning, a 5.5-inch shell from the *Abukuma* struck aft, glanced off the hull, and exploded alongside. The impact compounded the flooding from the previous blow, and oil began spurting into the *Salt Lake City*'s after gyro room. The American cruiser took on a 5-degree list but continued at full speed. Hosogaya, meanwhile, due to smoke and distance, missed the American turn south. He continued west as McMorris gradually circled around him.

At 0805 the *Maya* fired four torpedoes. The *Nachi* followed these with eight of her own at 0807, and the *Abukuma* launched four at 0815 at a range of 17,500 yards. These sixteen torpedoes passed behind the Americans, and although the *Maya* fired steadily during this period, the Japanese heavy cruisers did not turn hard south until 0824. Flooding shut down the *Salt Lake City*'s after engine room at 0825, reducing her speed to twenty knots. At this point the *Richmond* stood 6,000 yards ahead. The destroyers slowed to maintain position between Rodger's ship and the Japanese. From the *Dale*, the range to the *Nachi* dropped to 18,000 yards. McMorris ordered his destroyers to attack, but he changed his mind at 0838 as the *Salt Lake City*'s speed worked back up. Hosogaya closed by about 3,000 yards during this period, and the battle's tempo accelerated with the drop in range. By 0840 the *Nachi*, *Maya*, and *Abukuma* were shooting steadily, joined a few minutes later by the *Tama*—by far the greatest concentration of fire the Americans had faced.

Despite the intensified Japanese effort, the Americans struck first when, at 0848, a five-inch shell clipped the *Nachi*'s number 1 turret's starboard gun tube, killing one man and wounding another. The shell failed to detonate, but it rendered the turret unusable, halving the cruiser's critical forward firepower. A minute later, the Japanese destroyers finally engaged. The *Wakaba* launched six Long Lances at 0849, and the *Hatsushimo* loosed five more at 0854. As their fish sped toward the American destroyers, the battle reached its crisis. Engineers, counterflooding to correct the *Salt Lake City*'s list, accidentally contaminated the fuel oil with water and extinguished her burners. A war correspondent aboard the heavy cruiser recalled, "Above decks the terrible warning signal was a burst of white smoke from the two stacks—white smoke that was more steam than smoke . . . then the sick moment came when the vibrations of the engines, the pulses of the four propellers, died."[15] Hosogaya's cruisers bore down from 19,000 yards north northwest, and "8-inch shells came lobbing in a steady rain over *Salt Lake City*'s smoke screen."[16]

At 0855 Captain Rodgers hoisted the signal, "My speed zero." An enemy round emphasized his message, shooting the flag from the halyard. There seemed little hope of saving the cruiser. McMorris immediately ordered his destroyers to attack. At 0859 the *Bailey, Coghlan,* and *Monaghan* reversed course to close on Hosogaya's force while the *Dale* maintained the smoke screen. The *Richmond* dropped back to rescue the *Salt Lake City*'s crew. Rodgers, however, refused to give up his ship. After frantic exertions, damage control teams got the burners relit, and by 0900 the cruiser had headway.

As the American destroyers charged northwest, the *Coghlan*'s five-inch guns fired shells at the *Maya* at the rate of one every four seconds while the other two ships targeted the *Nachi*. Hosogaya trained his turrets on this threat, and the *Bailey* quickly suffered. At 0900 an eight-inch shell struck the American destroyer's starboard galley door "like a bullet going through cardboard", killing five men.[17] In the next two minutes Japanese shells smashed the *Bailey*'s forward fireroom and engine rooms, knocking out boilers 1 and 2. A Japanese officer recalled that he "did not know how a ship could live through the concentration of fire which was bought to bear on the leading destroyer" and expressed admiration for "the skill and daring of the attack and the volume of 13-cm fire which the destroyers delivered."[18]

A five-inch shell struck the *Nachi* on a signal platform to starboard. The *Bailey* then launched five torpedoes at 0903 from 10,000 yards and turned away. The punishing fire from the Japanese discouraged the other two American destroyers, and they reversed course, torpedoes still in tubes. Even as she retreated, flying shrapnel peppered the *Coghlan*, wounding four and disabling both her radars.

The *Salt Lake City* reengaged just before the *Bailey*'s torpedoes hit the water. With speed slowly building, McMorris steered his formation east. Hosogaya turned west at 0903. The Japanese ceased fire at 0904, and the Americans stopped firing at 0912. Then, both forces headed toward their respective bases.

Hosogaya's turnabout seemed miraculous to the Americans, but he had his reasons. According to a Japanese participant, Hosogaya based his decision to disengage on three factors: "First, the air attack was overdue and considered imminent. Second, by this time the ammunition remaining was below the minimum prescribed by doctrine. . . . Third, the fuel consumption was high and there would not be sufficient remaining to return to base from chase. Even the chance of sinking an American ship did not warrant continuing the action."[19] Obviously, Hosogaya did not know the gravity of the *Salt Lake City*'s problems, and his decision to turn away irritated his men. They "silently cursed the caution of their chief which deprived them of a victory already won."[20]

During this action the *Salt Lake City* expended 832 eight-inch shells, and the *Richmond* expended 271 six-inch rounds. Among the American destroyers, the *Coghlan* fired a high of 750 five-inch rounds, and the *Monaghan* fired a low of 235.

On the Japanese side, the *Maya* shot 904 eight-inch shells; the *Nachi* shot 707 eight-inch rounds. The *Tama* and *Abukuma* contributed 136 and 95 5.5-inch rounds, respectively. The Japanese fired forty-three torpedoes and the Americans only five.

Precious few of these thousands of shells hit their target, and every torpedo missed. The *Nachi*'s moderate damage required eight days to patch up before she returned to Japan for an overhaul. Two 5-inch hits on the *Tama*'s catapult inflicted minor harm. Both the *Salt Lake City* and *Bailey* retired stateside for repair.

McMorris' rash attempt to slip past a superior force let Hosogaya cut off the Americans from their base. The Japanese admiral then played the odds, but he failed to grasp his opportunity when it arrived. Although the Japanese inflicted more damage than they received, their transports returned to base without delivering the badly needed supplies they held. Imperial Japanese Navy headquarters relieved Hosogaya. Admiral Nimitz rewarded McMorris by making him his chief of staff.

After this battle, Japan abandoned future efforts to supply Attu using surface ships. Although submarines did deliver limited amounts of ammunition and matériel, the airfield the Japanese needed remained incomplete.

On 12 May 1943 American troops invaded Attu, and Imperial headquarters concentrated a major force in Tokyo Bay in mid-May, planning a relief sortie. After the Americans completely eliminated the 2,400-man garrison on 28 May, however, the Japanese canceled this operation and decided to evacuate Kiska instead. Japanese submarines extracted 800 men at the prohibitive cost of three boats sunk.

On 22 July 1943 the 5th Fleet sailed to Alaska for the last time. Two light cruisers and ten destroyers arrived at Kiska harbor in thick fog on 29 July and embarked 5,100 troops in just forty-five minutes. Thirty-four thousand American and Canadian soldiers invaded Kiska on 16 August, finding only a few abandoned dogs. The Aleutian campaign thus ended, decided by one naval battle, and a tactical defeat at that.[21]

Intermezzo. Sunday, 7 March 1943

On 7 March 1943 the war was fifteen months old. Basically, Japan still held all the territory that it had conquered except the southern Solomons and the tip of eastern New Guinea (see Map I.1). Anxious to apply lessons painfully learned at Guadalcanal, the Japanese army and navy planned to reinforce key points in the middle Solomons—the Empire's southeastern defensive boundary—prior to the anticipated Allied offensive. The Japanese would then "throw in our entire sea, land, and air strength at the first sign of an enemy landing to engage it in decisive combat."[1]

The U.S. military, meanwhile, stood at a crossroads. King had warned against "frontal operations such as are involved in expulsion of enemy from [Guadalcanal] which if followed in principle thorough Guadalcanal-Rabaul area will keep us busy for years."[2] However, King and Nimitz faced two limitations. First, President Roosevelt and the Combined Chiefs of Staff had made a strategic decision to defeat Germany before concentrating on the war in the Pacific. Second, a Central Pacific campaign, the road to victory the Navy had been studying since it first considered Japan a potential enemy, could not start until late 1943, when significant numbers of newly constructed warships became available.

Both MacArthur's Southwest Pacific Command and Halsey's South Pacific Command had limited resources. The imperative Nimitz and King faced was to keep these resources in the Pacific and in productive use. On Sunday, 7 March Nimitz met with staff officers from both commands to discuss future moves. He warned that possible losses in the Atlantic during the spring and summer of 1943 might require withdrawals from the Pacific.[3] He was holding intelligence assessments, and they were not favorable. While the U.S. Navy enjoyed slight advantages over the Japanese in carriers, including escort carriers, of 11 to 10 and in battleships of 13 to 12, the Japanese had 36 cruisers to the Americans' 15 and 104 destroyers to the Americans' 81.[4] These were not the odds desired by a commander considering new offensives in the Aleutians, in the Solomons, and in New Guinea.

From intercepted Japanese radio transmissions and radio traffic analysis, Nimitz had a good idea of how much harm the U.S. Navy had caused the Japanese, and this was considerably less than what his captains and admirals claimed. Through February 1943, counting only ships in the destroyer category and larger and excluding submarines, the Japanese had sunk forty-one major U.S. warships with a total tonnage of 363,000. They had sunk another thirty-six Australian, British, and

MAP I.1. THE GENERAL SITUATION IN THE PACIFIC, MARCH 1943

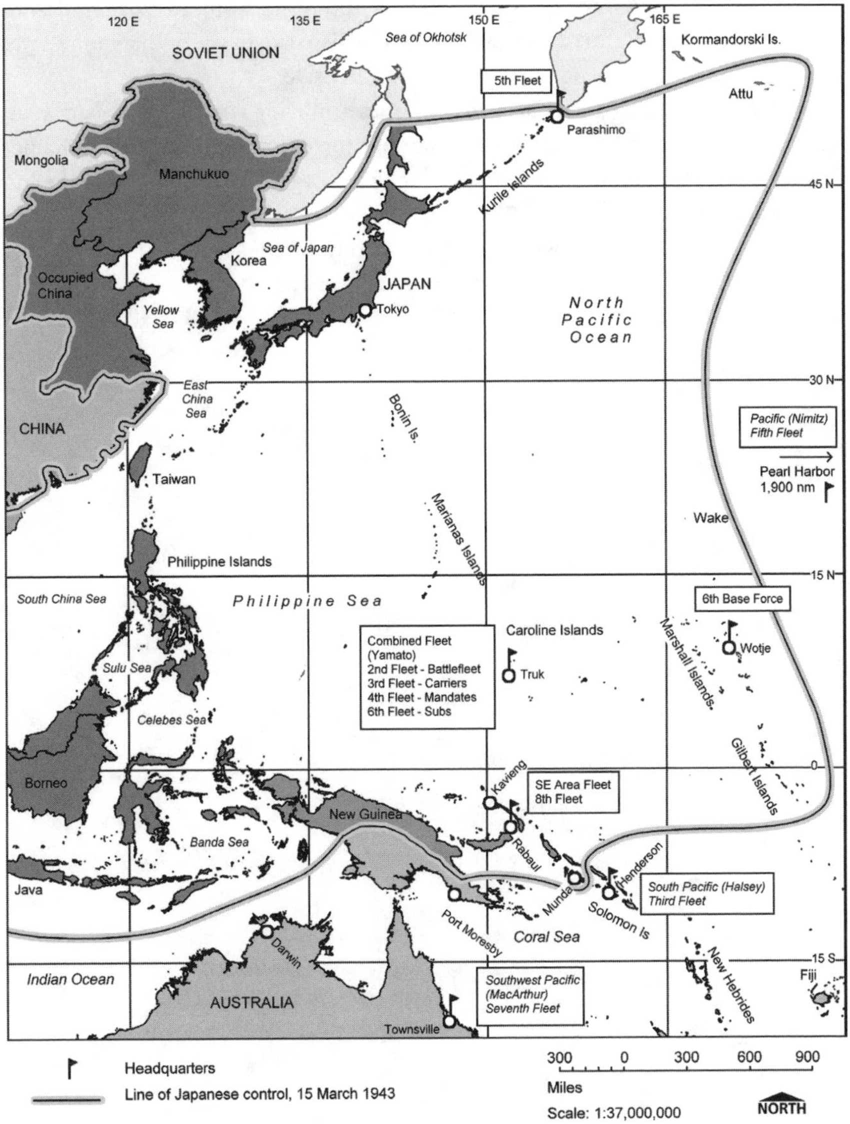

Dutch warships, adding up to 183,000 tons. Against this, engagements with Allied forces had cost the Japanese just forty-six major warships weighing a total of 305,000 tons. In surface combat, the ratios were even worse. The Japanese had destroyed thirty-seven major warships of 130,000 tons while, excluding the *Hiei*, the Allies had sunk only nine vessels of 55,000 tons. And even after winning the

Battle of Midway in June 1942 and forcing the evacuation of Guadalcanal in February 1943, the United States remained 3,000 miles from Tokyo. Yet, despite the inferior Allied performance to date and the disparity in strength, Nimitz acted on 7 March to recommend a new Solomons offensive.

As Nimitz reached this decision, Japanese military commanders had many reasons to be satisfied. So far the defensive perimeter had held, the fleet remained largely intact, the captured resources were being organized, and, despite the loss of Guadalcanal, the Japanese still had faith in their fighting superiority. The statistics confronting Nimitz would have justified this belief, but the numbers used by Imperial headquarters were vastly more optimistic.

CHAPTER 8

Advance up the Solomons, March–August 1943

The new officers fervently hoped we would run into the whole Japanese Navy; the older and more experienced quietly prayed that any engagement would be short, with a minimum of casualties to our forces.
— J.D. JEFFREY OF THE USS *STERETT*
BEFORE THE BATTLE OF VELLA GULF

At least one historian has lamented that "[h]istories of the Pacific war inevitably gloss over the events between the end of the Guadalcanal campaign and the landings in the Gilbert Islands. In this period 'nothing happened.'"[1] In fact, nothing could be further from the truth. After fighting the protracted attritional campaign the Japanese desired at Guadalcanal, the Americans developed a winning strategy in the Solomons that they proceeded to apply throughout the war. The Solomons campaign decided the Pacific War, and key to victory was the U.S. Navy's growing competence in, and then domination of, naval surface warfare (see Map 8.1).

On 15 March the U.S. Navy reorganized and assigned odd numbers to major units in the Pacific. Thus, Halsey's South Pacific Command became the Third Fleet. Halsey deployed two carrier forces, a fast battleship force, a mixed group of old battleships and escort carriers, and two light cruiser-plus-destroyers groups. He also received an infusion of fresh leadership. Scott and Callaghan were dead, and MacArthur kept Crutchley. Admirals Wright and Tisdale, who both commanded a task group during the Tassafaronga disaster, were beached and kicked upstairs, respectively. The cutting edge of Halsey's command consisted of Task Force 37 under Rear Adm. W.L. Ainsworth, who was a gunnery specialist and the former captain of the *Mississippi*, and Task Force 38 led by Rear Adm. Aaron S. Merrill, who had most recently skippered the *Indiana*. Each of these American task forces consisted of four light cruisers and eight destroyers.

In comparison, Vice Admiral Mikawa's 8th Fleet mustered the *Chokai* and Destroyer Squadron 3 under Rear Admiral Akiyama Teruo, which included the *Sendai*, and Destroyer Divisions 11, 22, and 30. Yamamoto's formidable Combined Fleet lurked at Truk husbanding its strength. The Battle of the Bismarck Sea in March, when U.S. Army aircraft destroyed an entire convoy of eight transports and half of Destroyer Squadron 3 trying to reach New Guinea, convinced the Japanese that the use of slow transports in disputed waters was not practicable

MAP 8.1. THE SOLOMON ISLANDS, MARCH–AUGUST 1943

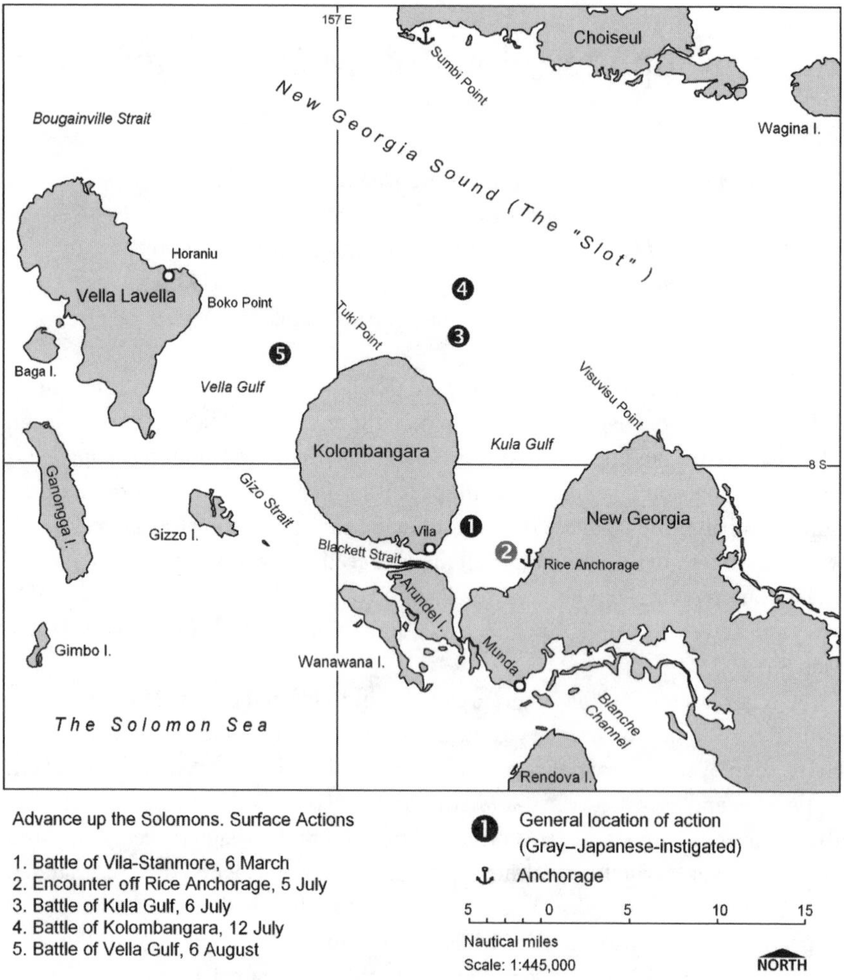

Advance up the Solomons. Surface Actions

1. Battle of Vila-Stanmore, 6 March
2. Encounter off Rice Anchorage, 5 July
3. Battle of Kula Gulf, 6 July
4. Battle of Kolombangara, 12 July
5. Battle of Vella Gulf, 6 August

❶ General location of action
(Gray–Japanese-instigated)

⚓ Anchorage

Nautical miles
Scale: 1:445,000

NORTH

"without neutralizing enemy aircraft at their bases or taking drastic measures [to strengthen] air defenses for convoys. Since these demands could not be met with the available air strength . . . the use of transport ships necessarily had to be abandoned."[2] This forced the Imperial Japanese Navy to use destroyers and small craft to supply garrisons in the middle Solomons.

Ainsworth's division bombarded the Munda airstrip on 5 January and Vila-Stanmore on neighboring Kolombangara on 24 January. On the basis of wildly overstated results—"Five thousand killed for the operation might be an overstatement, but not by much,"[3] reads a nearly contemporary account—Halsey dispatched Merrill for an encore. Merrill left Espirtu Santo at 1530 hours on 4 March and passed Guadalcanal the next afternoon. At 2000 hours the *Fletcher, O'Bannon, Radford*, and *Nicholas*, under Capt. Robert P. Briscoe, proceeded independently to shell Munda. Three cruisers and three Americans destroyers continued toward Kula Gulf. Merrill intended to sneak to the base of the gulf and then run north, bombarding Vila on the way out.

Battle of Vila-Stanmore, 6 March 1943

The *Murasame* and *Minegumo* departed Shortland Island on 5 March at 1910 hours on a "rice-and-bullet" run to Vila. En route, an Allied PBY Black Cat happened to overfly the Japanese destroyers at 700 feet and broadcast an alert at 2330. Not realizing they had been spotted, the Japanese ships arrived at Vila and quickly transferred their cargo onto barges. A half hour later Merrill led the ships of Task Force 38 around New Georgia's Visuvisu Point at twenty knots, making to enter Kula Gulf. The *Waller* scouted 4,000 yards ahead of the *Conway*. The *Montpelier, Cleveland*, and *Denver* followed 2,000 yards back at thousand-oyard intervals. The *Cony* trailed 2,000 yards off *Denver*'s port quarter.

At 0039 on 6 March Merrill turned south by southwest; Vila lay twenty-five miles ahead. The night was still and very dark, and the Black Cats working for Merrill could not even spot the wakes of the friendly cruisers, even though the ships were steaming at twenty knots. Meanwhile, Captain Tachibana Masao slowly eased into Kula Gulf, electing to return via the gulf rather than navigate narrow and dangerous Blackett Strait. At 0057 *Waller*'s SG radar got a contact eight miles off the starboard bow that she assumed was land until the pip bifurcated and began moving. As the contact closed, the American cruisers also began tracking it. At 0101 the TBS crackled with the message, "Stand by to commence firing."[4] A minute later, at a range of 7,000 yards from the enemy, the *Waller* loosed five torpedoes set to run at twenty-four knots. At 0103 Merrill ordered, "Commence firing," and the *Montpelier*'s 12 six-inch guns spat steel, smoke, and flame.[5] The *Cleveland*'s and *Denver*'s main batteries came to life shortly thereafter.

Aboard the *Murasame* lookouts spotted ominous twinkling lights off the starboard bow. They had just sixteen seconds to pass the word before the first thirty-six shells arrived in their vicinity; another seventy-two were already flying. An analysis of the action concluded, "Spotting [was] impossible due to the large number of splashes arising almost simultaneously around the closer target, which radar [showed] to be straddled, and to the naked eye [was] definitely exploding with flames."[6] From the *Cony* it seemed "like a complete bridge of fire, looking as though you could walk on it, and every one of the three branches ending right in that Jap ship."[7] After six salvos, flames engulfed the *Murasame*.

TABLE 8.1. FORCES ENGAGED IN THE BATTLE OF VILA-STANMORE

	Type of Ship	Year Launched	Displacement, Full Load (tons)	Max. Speed (knots)	Guns (number by inch/ caliber)	Torpedoes (number of tubes by diameter in inches)	Damage
American Cruiser Division 12 (Rear Adm. A.S. Merrill)							
Montpelier (F)	CL	1942	14,131	32	12 x 6/47 & 1 2x 5/38		
Cleveland	CL	1941	14,131	32	12 x 6/47 & 12 x 5/38		
Denver	CL	1942	14,131	32	12 x 6/47 & 12 x 5/38		
American Destroyer Division 43 (Cdr. A.A. Burke)							
Waller (F)	DD	1942	2,924	38	5 x 5/38	10 x 21	
Conway	DD	1942	2,924	38	5 x 5/38	10 x 21	
Cony	DD	1942	2,924	38	5 x 5/38	10 x 21	
Japanese Destroyer Division 2 (Captain Tachibana Masao)							
Murasame	DD	1935	1,950	34	5 x 5/50	8 x 24	Sunk
Minegumo	DD	1936	2,330	35	6 x 5/50	8 x 24	Sunk

CL—light cruiser, DD—destroyer, F—flagship
  Time: 0101–0130
  Weather: Clear, light breeze
  Visibility: No moon, very dark
  Sea state: Smooth
  Surprise: Americans
  Mission: Americans—shore bombardment; Japanese—transport

The *Minegumo* zigzagged east of the *Murasame*, aiming at the enemy gun flashes and silhouetting herself in the process. At 0106 the *Minegumo* became a target in turn. Her gunnery officer remembered, "We were hit so quickly that we were able to return only a few shots."[8] She began to burn and lost way by 0110. Two minutes earlier one of the *Waller*'s torpedoes had walloped the *Murasame* after a 6.4-minute run. Briscoe's destroyers, bombarding Munda twenty five miles away, heard the blast.

At 0114 Merrill ordered his ships to cease fire. The American cruisers had shot 1,101 six-inch shells and 234 five-inch shells, and the *Waller* and *Cony* added another 304 five-inch rounds. After drenching Blackett Strait with star shells to ensure no Japanese ships lurked there in ambush, Merrill led his force northeast and at 0125 began shelling the airbase. After eight minutes and the expenditure of an additional 1,635 six-inch and 1,123 five-inch rounds, the task force sped north at thirty knots. They rounded Visuvisu Point at 0228 and headed for home.

The *Denver* had suffered a steering casualty and fell 2,000 yards out of station. She also lost one man due to blast effects. The *Conway* did not open fire against the Japanese destroyers at all due to a mechanical failure in her target bearing designator. These were the only blemishes in an outstanding performance for the Americans at Vila-Stanmore.

The *Murasame* sank at 0115, loosing 128 men from her crew of 181. The *Minegumo* went under at 0130 with a loss of forty-six men. American spotters also enthused that the raid caused spectacular damage to the airbase, but the Japanese described the effects as "none in particular." The bombardment of Munda inflicted more harm. Briscoe's destroyers expended 1,700 five-inch shells and detonated an ammunition dump containing 1,000 three-inch rounds.[9]

This engagement, although brief and one-sided, marked several milestones on the road to Tokyo. It was the U.S. Navy's first surface action to involve only ships launched after America entered the war. The Americans made better use of radar and employed improved night-fighting techniques, and a destroyer finally scored the first torpedo success since Balikpapan in January 1942.

In April Yamamoto launched his I Operation, an aerial counteroffensive intended to erode American strength and buy more time for Imperial forces to dig in. In the largest air strikes since Pearl Harbor the Japanese attacked Guadalcanal on 7 April, Oro Bay on 11 April, Port Moresby on 12 April, and Milne Bay on 14 April. Typically exaggerated claims gave the Japanese a false sense of accomplishment. In addition to being a failure, I Operation also cost Yamamoto his life; U.S. army fighters intercepted his transport plane as he made a tour of forward bases to boost morale and shot him down.[10]

Ships under Ainsworth's and Merrill's command bombarded Vila and Munda on 8 and 13 May in conjunction with mine-laying operations. Several accidents, including a turret explosion in the *Nashville* that cost twenty lives, led Nimitz to question whether the results justified the dangers, but mining Blackett Strait paid a dividend when Japanese destroyers ran into the field on 8 May. The *Kuroshio* sank immediately, and the *Oyashio* and *Kagero* suffered damage. An Australian coast watcher on Kolombangara called up an air strike that finished off the *Oyashio* and *Kagero* later that day. After this blow the Imperial navy preferred the Kula Gulf route to Vila.[11]

The American offensive finally commenced with the invasion of Rendova and New Georgia on 30 June 1943. Japan's defensive strategy called for a naval counterattack wherever the enemy landed. In late June, when radio intelligence and other signs indicated that an American assault was forthcoming, a cruiser and four destroyers of the 2nd Fleet reinforced the 8th Fleet at Shortland Island. When enemy radio traffic diminished, however, the counterattack force disbursed for maintenance or transport duty. Thus, the 30 June invasion caught the Japanese completely off guard. Moreover, the Japanese found "the speedy disembarkation of the enemy [to be] absolutely miraculous."[12] The 8th Fleet scrambled to assemble a counterattack force while other units sailed for Rabaul.

On the night of 30 June five ships under Destroyer Division 11's Captain Yoshimura Matake sortied and reached Rendova at 2330 hours. Because of poor visibility and excessive caution, however, they could not locate the debarkation point and withdrew accomplishing nothing. The next Japanese attempt to duplicate the victory of Savo Island came when the *Yubari* and nine destroyers raided the American anchorage on 3 July. Three Japanese destroyers expended about a hundred rounds on Rendova Plantation between 0245 and 0305 with little results while the rest of the Japanese force stood guard. They tangled with PT boats in Balfour Channel on their way out.

Encounter off Rice Anchorage, 5 July 1943

The American's invasion of New Georgia consisted of several landings at widely scattered points around the large island, including an extemporized 4 July affair at Rice Anchorage opposite Vila. Ainsworth's cruisers and Destroyer Squadron 21 covered the operation. Seven APDs and two DMSs screened by the destroyers *Radford*, *Gwin*, *McCalla*, *Ralph Talbot*, and *Woodworth* carried the landing force of three Marine and two Army battalions. Meanwhile, having failed to blunt the American offensive with a surface strike, Japanese destroyers reverted to serving as transports. On the afternoon of 4 July Japanese Destroyer Division 22 departed Buin bound for Vila loaded with Imperial troops.

Ainsworth's ships entered Kula Gulf shortly before midnight with the *Nicholas* and *Strong* scouting ahead. Not far behind, Akiyama's force rounded Kolombangara's Tuki Point. The newly commissioned *Niizuki* carried prototype radar. This detected the enemy as the *Niizuki* nosed into Kula Gulf, and Akiyama prudently decided to abort his mission. Starting at 0015, however, the *Niizuki* and *Yunagi* put four torpedoes in the water while coming about, and *Nagatsuki* fired six more. Meanwhile, Ainsworth's scouts radioed the all clear, and he began shelling Vila at 0026 on 5 July. The American formation then turned east to strike the shore batteries protecting New Georgia's Bairoko Harbor south of Rice Anchorage. This bombardment began at 0037 and lasted for six minutes.

TABLE 8.2. FORCES ENGAGED IN THE ENCOUNTER OFF RICE ANCHORAGE

Type of Ship	Year Launched	Displacement, Full Load (tons)	Max. Speed (knots)	Guns (number by inch/caliber)	Torpedoes (number of tubes by diameter in inches)	Damage
American Cruiser Division 9 (Rear Adm. W.L. Ainsworth)						
Honolulu (F)	CL	1937	12,207	32	15 x 6/47 & 8 x 5/38		
Helena	CL	1938	12,207	32	15 x 6/47 & 8 x 5/38		
St. Louis	CL	1938	12,207	32	15 x 6/47 & 8 x 5/38		
American Destroyer Squadron 21 (Capt. F.X. McInerney)						
Nicholas (F)	DD	1942	2,924	38	5 x 5/38	10 x 21	
Strong	DD	1942	2,924	38	5 x 5/38	10 x 21	Sunk
O'Bannon	DD	1942	2,924	38	5 x 5/38	10 x 21	
Chevalier	DD	1942	2,924	38	5 x 5/.3	10 x 21	
Japanese Destroyer Squadron 3 (Rear Admiral Akiyama Teruo)						
Niizuki (F)	DD	1942	3,700	33	8 x 3.9/32	4 x 24	
Japanese Destroyer Division 22 (Captain Kanaoka Kunizo)						
Nagatsuki (F)	APD	1925	1,913	33	2 x 4.7/50	6 x 24	
Satsuki	APD	1925	1,913	33	2 x 4.7/50	6 x 24	
Yunagi	APD	1924	1,553	35	3 x 4.7/50	4 x 21	

APD—destroyer transport, CL—light cruiser, DD—destroyer, F—flagship
  Time: 0015–0050
  Weather: Occasional squalls, moderate breeze
  Visibility: No moon, very dark
  Sea state: Short chop
  Surprise: Japanese
  Mission: Americans—amphibious attack; Japanese—transport

At 0031 the *Ralph Talbot* got a radar contact, which by 0040 she interpreted to be ships fleeing Kula Gulf (see Map 8.2). Rear Admiral Ainsworth, four minutes into his run north, heard about this possible "skunk" at 0047. Then, a torpedo that seemed to come out of nowhere punched into the *Strong* at 0049. The *Strong*'s

MAP 8.2. ENCOUNTER OFF RICE ANCHORAGE, 5 JULY 1943

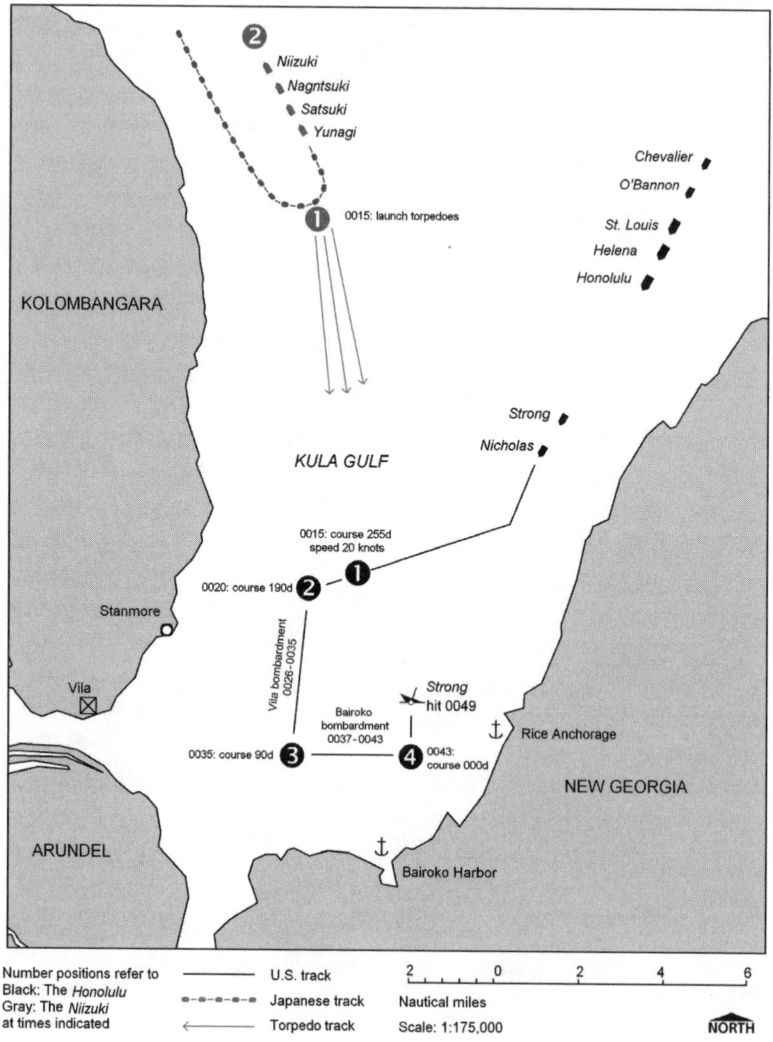

skipper, Cdr. Joseph Wellings, recalled, "The explosion completely destroyed number one fireroom and the adjacent number one engine room. . . . A large hole was torn in the portside of the ship and also in the main deck." Flooding immediately induced a 15-degree list to port, and Bairoko Harbor's batteries opened up and began peppering the stationary warship.

The *Chevalier* and *O'Bannon* dashed to assist. Wellings related, "I was horrified but still most thankful at [0113] to see the destroyer *Chevalier* appear out of the darkness steaming at about ten knots and crash into our port side. . . . I thought the *Strong* would roll over from the crash."[13] The *Chevalier* quickly loaded 241 survivors, then the *Strong* broke in two and sank at 0124; forty-six men died.

Ainsworth ordered the American ships home at 0230. He did not realize he had been involved in a surface engagement, which the Japanese dubbed the "4 July Night Battle of Kula Gulf," or that his ships had forestalled a Tokyo Express. Rather than a destroyer-launched torpedo, Ainsworth supposed the *Strong* had fallen victim to a midget submarine. At eleven miles Akiyama's salvo may have been the war's longest successful torpedo strike.

As Ainsworth retired south, a coast watcher spied enemy warships departing Shortland. Halsey ordered Cruiser Division 9 and the *O'Bannon* and *Nicholas* to reverse course, assuming the enemy intended to reinforce Vila. The *Radford* and *Jenkins*, refueling at Tulagi, hurried to join Ainsworth, replacing the sunken *Strong* and the *Chevalier*, which was crowded with the *Strong*'s survivors.

Battle of Kula Gulf, 6 July 1943

Task Force 37 had operated together since January, and Ainsworth had developed a specific battle doctrine. For Ainsworth's command, guns were the primary weapon, and the ideal range for a night action lay between 8,000 and 10,000 yards, which would place the Americans within effective gunnery range while keeping them safe—Ainsworth thought—from enemy torpedoes. Once in the prescribed range, cruisers should fire first, and destroyers should seek torpedo targets afterward—largely to dispatch cripples. This doctrine reflected an ignorance of Japanese torpedo capabilities and discounted the potential of American torpedoes, which was understandable given their lack of success.

The growing New Georgia crisis and Akiyama's failure to deliver his men on 5 July impelled the Japanese navy to mount a larger operation with three destroyer divisions, two of which were transporting troops while the third acted as an escort. Screened by inclement weather, the force, again led by Akiyama, arrived off Kula Gulf at midnight and dispatched the first transport division led by Captain Orita Tsuneo to Vila while Akiyama stood watch.

At the same time, the *Honolulu*, steaming at twenty-five knots, made radar contact with Visuvisu Point, which was twenty-eight miles off her port bow. An hour later Ainsworth began sweeping across the head of the gulf. Lacking definite intelligence and not guessing the Japanese possessed radar, Ainsworth chose to keep his ships in cruising formation. Capt. Francis X. McInerney's destroyers ringed the cruisers, with the *Nicholas* and *O'Bannon* 3,000 yards off the *Honolulu*'s starboard and port bow, respectively. The *Radford* followed 2,500 yards off the *Helena*'s starboard quarter, and the *Jenkins* sailed off the *St Louis*'s port quarter at the rear of the formation.

TABLE 8.3. FORCES ENGAGED IN THE BATTLE OF KULA GULF

	Type of Ship	Year Launched	Displacement, Full Load (tons)	Max. Speed (knots)	Guns (number by inch/caliber)	Torpedoes (number of tubes by diameter in inches)	Damage
American Cruiser Division 9 (Rear Adm. W.L. Ainsworth)							
Honolulu (F)	CL	1937	12,207	32	15 x 6/47 & 8 x 5/38		
Helena	CL	1938	12,207	32	15 x 6/47 & 8 x 5/38		Sunk
St. Louis	CL	1938	12,207	32	15 x 6/47 & 8 x 5/38		
American Destroyer Squadron 21 (Capt. F.X. McInerney)							
Nicholas (F)	DD	1942	2,924	38	5 x 5/38	10 x 21	
Radford	DD	1942	2,924	38	5 x 5/38	10 x 21	
O'Bannon	DD	1942	2,924	38	5 x 5/38	10 x 21	
Jenkins	DD	1942	2,924	38	5 x 5/38	10 x 21	
Japanese Destroyer Squadron 3 Support Group (Rear Admiral Akiyama Teruo)							
Niizuki (F)	DD	1942	3,700	33	8 x 3.9/32	4 x 24	Sunk
Suzukaze	DD	1937	1,950	34	5 x 5/50	8 x 24	D2
Tanikaze	DD	1940	2,450	35	6 x 5/50	8 x 24	D1
Japanese Destroyer Division 30-First Transport Group (Captain Orita Tsuneo)							
Mochizuki (F)	APD	1925	1,913	33	2 x 4.7/50	6 x 24	D2
Mikazuki	APD	1925	1,913	33	2 x 4.7/50	6 x 24	
Hamakaze	DD	1940	2,450	35	6 x 5/50	8 x 24	
Japanese Destroyer Division 11-Second Transport Group (Captain Yamashiro Katsumori)							
Amagiri (F)	DD	1930	2,057	38	6 x 5/50	9 x 24	D2
Hatsuyuki	DD	1930	2,057	38	6 x 5/50	9 x 24	D2
Nagatsuki	APD	1925	1,913	33	2 x 4.7/50	6 x 24	Sunk
Satsuki	APD	1925	1,913	33	2 x 4.7/50	6 x 24	

APD—destroyer transport, CL—light cruiser, D1—light or superficial damage (including splinter damage), D2—moderate damage (combat ability not significantly impaired), DD—destroyer, F—flagship

Time: 0157–0630

Weather: Squalls, overcast, fresh east-southeasterly breeze

Visibility: Poor, no moon

Sea state: Choppy southeasterly swells

Surprise: None

Mission: Americans—interception based on general intelligence; Japanese—transport

At 0106, while cruising south southeast into the gulf ahead of the Americans, the *Niizuki*'s radar picked up a contact. This was probably a false return, but Akiyama, retaining the second transport group, reversed course to investigate at 0118.[14]

At 0136 the *Honolulu*'s radar detected something 20,500 yards to the southwest and standing out of the gulf. This single pip resolved into three, and perhaps four, pips zigzagging north. At 0141 Ainsworth got on the TBS and ordered his ships to follow Battle Plan A: Cruisers engage at between 8,000 and 10,000 yards using radar to direct gunfire and maneuvering by simultaneous turns to maintain broadsides toward the enemy; destroyers close up in column. The *O'Bannon* immediately steered to fall in behind the *Nicholas*, but just three minutes later Ainsworth ordered a 60-degree simultaneous turn left to southwest by west. The *O'Bannon*'s captain recorded, "We were not astern of the *Nicholas* as yet and this turn sort of complicated matters somewhat due to inability to follow leader in the dark."[15]

At 0142 Akiyama, who had led his ships to sea to ferry troops rather than fight and unable to confirm his fleeting radar contact, ordered Captain Yamashiro Katsumori's division to head for Vila. This confused the American plots because the group of pips on their radar screens separated as the Japanese destroyers turned.

At 0150, after running southwest for eight minutes and pondering this strange reading, Ainsworth concluded the enemy consisted of two groups heading in opposite directions and ordered another simultaneous 60-degree turn right to northwest by west. This put the cruisers in column and opened their broadsides. But the American commander debated whether he should target the pips ahead or the pips astern. His indecision was reflected in the contradictory orders he rapped out over TBS.

First, Ainsworth bade his rear destroyers to take the stern group, but he changed his mind within a minute, and radioed, "[T]he big ships are the ones astern." He then ordered the lead destroyers to target the first group, adding the "cruisers will take the heavy ships."[16] The *O'Bannon*'s report notes that at 0153 Ainsworth ordered the destroyers to commence firing. This contradicted Battle Plan A, and McInerney asked, "Is that by gun fire?" Ainsworth replied at 0154, "[G]un fire first but hold everything for a minute. [The cruisers] will open on nearest target."[17] A minute later he clarified that the task force would deal with the forward group and then would reverse course and strike the second group on the way back. Ainsworth asked the cruisers individually if they were ready and waited another three minutes for the range to close before again ordering his ships to open fire.

As Ainsworth worked out his plan the *Niizuki*'s lookouts, peering through eight miles of darkness, spotted shadows bearing down at 0147. Akiyama ordered battle stations and radioed for Yamashiro to turn back and lend a hand. The *Niizuki* maneuvered to deliver a torpedo attack as the range dropped rapidly, but, at 0157, now just 7,000 yards away, the American cruisers—equipped for night action with a new flashless powder—finally opened fire. As the following gunnery report reflects, Ainsworth believed he won the battle in the first six minutes: "*Honolulu* opened radar controlled fire on nearest . . . target at 0157.3 range 6,650 yards bearing 198°20T. . . . After continuous straddling by radar observation and when target was observed optically to be in flames, checked fire at 0159 and shifted immediately to second target range 6,600 yards, bearing 192°T. Radar spotting indicated straddling; fires observed on target. At 0201.5 shifted fire to third target range 7,700 yards bearing 174°T with radar indicating straddling until 0203 at which time target signal disappeared from screen."[18]

The *Helena* and *St. Louis* similarly reported 100 percent hit rates. According to the *Helena*'s report, she fired at the nearest target and shifted when she saw it sink: "Both batteries fired in continuous fire in complete automatic and using radar train throughout the action. . . . Three targets on which the *Helena* was firing were definitely observed to have been sunk. Both of the remaining two targets on which the *Helena* was firing are believed to have been sunk."[19]

The *Nicholas* opened fire immediately, but the *O'Bannon*'s skipper, Lt. Cdr. Donald J. MacDonald, wrote, "Remembering so well the November 13th battle there was only one thought in my mind and that was to fire my torpedoes. . . . [T]he order to commence firing was held up until [I] finally decided we were not going to be in position for a torpedo attack for sometime."[20] The *Radford*, deep on *Jenkins*'s quarter and with her lines of fire blocked, did not participate in this phase of the action. The *Jenkins* was also quiet at this time, but for more obscure reasons. Eventually, the *Jenkins* made its first of only two contributions to the battle when it sent three low-speed torpedoes in a long, low-probability shot toward the retiring Japanese at 0201.

All three American cruisers targeted the *Niizuki*, inflicting damage that kept the Japanese flagship from launching torpedoes. The *Suzukaze* and *Tanikaze*, however, both emptied their tubes within a half minute of the first gun flashes. Ayikama's ships then made a 90-degree turn to port, belching a protective cloud of smoke as their turrets swung toward their starboard quarters and returned fire. The *Honolulu* assessed the Japanese gunnery as "relatively light and ineffectual. Numerous salvos were observed to fall short and astern, a few were reported to have landed over. A few shell fragments fell on deck."[21]

After a few minutes, the *Niizuki*, heavily ablaze, dropped out of line. Four American shells slammed the *Suzukaze*, jamming her forward mount and damaging her searchlight and hull. A solitary dud thumped the *Tanikaze*. These destroyers continued north northwest out of the battle to reload torpedoes, which was normally a twenty- to thirty-minute procedure.

At 0203 Ainsworth, satisfied he had eliminated the first enemy group, ordered a 180-degree turn to the south southwest to get the second group. A minute later, a Long Lance clobbered the *Helena*, causing a large flash and sending up a towering column of water that drenched personnel as high as the forward main battery director. The blow sheared off the *Helena*'s bow back to number 2 turret, and the ship's radio operator remembered being flung into the air by the impact as "the *Helena*'s guns had ceased firing. . . . In that whole room there was but one sound—the soft and stealthy settling of dust disturbed by the torpedo's impact." Then a second torpedo hit. "The explosion slammed us to the deck again," the radio operator recalled. "The light died and for a moment we struggled in darkness to extricate ourselves. Then the battle lights came on, a dim, weird glow though which the shaken dust swam redly in space."[22] This second blast incapacitated the engines.

A third torpedo struck the *Helena* at 0206, and this "insured the failure of the hull, which was well started by the second hit."[23] The *Helena* broke in two, forming a giant V, and the after section quickly sank. But, as bad as this was, Ainsworth was lucky. A Long Lance dented the *St. Louis*'s hull aft of her number 3 mount at 0207 but failed to detonate, and another barely missed the *Honolulu*. Wrapped in layers of dense smoke—a side effect of their flashless powder—the American ships seemed unaware of anything beyond their radar scopes, and the *Helena*'s destruction passed unnoticed even though she sailed in the middle of the column.

As the *Honolulu* steadied on her southeasterly course, her turrets swung to starboard, targeting the *Suzukaze* at 0210 and then, after incorrectly observing hits and explosions, switching to the *Tanikaze* at 0213. Repeated gunnery concussions had jarred the *St. Louis*'s SG, leaving her largely blind. She suffered several other defects, and the dense smoke streaming from her gun barrels hampered visual spotting. She engaged the *Honolulu*'s targets, but did not contribute much to the following action.

While these events unfolded, Yamashiro steamed toward the gunfire. At 0215 Ainsworth came 60 degrees left to an easterly course, and opened fire at the *Amagiri* three minutes later at a range of 11,000 yards south. Yamashiro, in the uncomfortable position of having his T capped, swung starboard to parallel the American column and launched torpedoes toward the enemy. Then 4 six-inch shells smashed the *Amagiri*'s electric power plant and killed ten men. She spewed thick clouds of smoke and at 0221 spun 180 degrees to starboard.

The *Hatsuyuki*, next in line, opened fire at 0218. Shortly thereafter, two American shells tore through her hull without exploding, killing six men and forcing her to engage manual steering. She fell out to the left and headed for Kolombangara's protective shadow. The *Nagatsuki* absorbed one direct hit. She and the last ship in line, the *Satsuki*, circled to starboard inside the *Amagiri*'s track and fled toward the shoreline.

At 0227 Ainsworth swung 150 degrees to starboard, heading west southwest. It was only at this point that he began asking about the *Helena*. At 0232 the *St. Louis* replied that the missing cruiser seemed to be on her port quarter, and the American ships engaged in a lot of TBS chatter as they tried to figure things out. At 0240 Ainsworth bent course to the west northwest and began sweeping seven miles off Kolombangara's shore looking for more targets as "several of his ships whack[ed] away at *Niizuki*'s wreckage (and probably at *Helena*'s bow too) en route."[24]

At 0242 the *Nicholas* launched a half salvo of fish at the *Niizuki*, which was burning just 5,000 yards off her port bow. The *Jenkins* imagined sighting a target to starboard at 0258 and shot five torpedoes into oblivion. By 0305 all American radar screens seemed clear. Ainsworth sent McInerney with the *Nicholas* and *O'Bannon* to scout Vella Gulf and the *Radford* to check Kula Gulf. The rest of the American force executed a 180-degree right turn and pointed their bows toward home. Except for uncertainty about the *Helena*, Ainsworth believed he had fought a perfect action and annihilated an enemy task force consisting of one heavy cruiser, three light cruisers, four destroyers, and four transports. This celebratory mood was broken at 0333, when the *Radford* regretfully reported that she had found the *Helena*'s bow floating stem up, the cruiser's number 50 plainly visible. Ainsworth, anxious to be as far as possible from Shortland and retaliatory air strikes by dawn, detached the *Nicholas* and *Radford* to rescue survivors.

Reports that Vella and Kula Gulfs were clear had been premature. The *Nagatsuki* ran aground just five miles short of Vila at 0246, and the *Satsuki* struggled vainly to pull her free. Meanwhile, the *Suzukaze* and *Tanikaze* ventured back toward Kula Gulf. It had taken the *Suzukaze* nearly three times longer than normal to reload her tubes because her torpedomen had lost their "presence of mind and calmness" working above a fire in an ammunition locker.[25] They proceeded cautiously but "could not find the *Niizuki* nor enemy ships, so they returned to the port," the requirements of honor apparently satisfied.[26] This occurred at 0405.

McInerney's destroyers had heaved to and launched boats to fish *Helena* survivors from the oily water as soon as they discovered the wreckage. When radar registered the presence of the *Suzukaze* and *Tanikaze* nearly 17,000 yards west, the American ships got under way immediately. They returned to their rescue work quickly, however, when the contact receded.

The *Mikazuki* and *Hamakaze* from the first transport group returned to Buin via Blackett Strait after discharging their contingent of men. The *Amagiri*, with Captain Yamashiro aboard, arrived at Vila at 0400, quickly unloaded, and headed north hugging the shoreline. At 0515 the *Amagiri* sailed through the *Niizuki*'s survivors and slowed to commence rescue operations. The *Nicholas* and *Radford*, just a torpedo run away to the northeast, scoped the newcomer at 0519. However, the *Amagiri*'s lookouts had sighted the *Nicholas* a minute before. Yamashiro immediately abandoned the *Niizuki*'s men, including Rear Admiral Akiyama, came to full speed, and continued northwest.

At 0522 the *Nicholas*, standing 7,950 yards from the *Amagiri*, fired five torpedoes to the south from a stopped position. She then kicked in her engines and accelerated to the northeast. The *Radford* added four torpedoes at 0530. The American Mark 15s missed the *Amagiri* both ahead and astern. At 0532 the *Radford* and *Nicholas* altered to a parallel course. The *Radford*'s guns cracked. The *Nicholas* originally contributed star shell, but as the glaring flares burst and slowly drifted to earth behind the target, she likewise fired for effect. The *Amagiri* replied but could not find a target. At 0533, however, she flung five torpedoes toward the Americans. At 0535 a shell detonating amidships destroyed the *Amagiri*'s radio room. Yamashiro turned southwest, trailing smoke. After a Type 93 passed within feet of the *Radford*'s fantail, the Americans came about to present smaller targets and then returned to their rescue work.

The *Amagiri* was unable to return for the *Niizuki*'s men, and approximately 300 of the sunken destroyer's crew perished in Kula Gulf's warm waters. McInerney, thinking he had faced a *Sendai*-class light cruiser and a destroyer, reported both sunk with torpedoes and shell fire. Yamashiro claimed two successful torpedo strikes.

It had been a busy morning, but it was not over yet. The *Hatsuyuki* put into Vila at 0439 and then departed via Blackett Strait, risking the possibility of mines rather than guns. The *Mochizuki* did not leave Vila until 0600. Captain Orita elected to depart via Kula Gulf, logically assuming that because it was nearly dawn, the Americans would all be gone. The *Radford* and *Nicholas* had hardly resumed their mission of mercy when radar alerted them to the *Mochizuki*'s approach. It was light enough to see by this time, and at 0610 the Japanese destroyer opened fire. The Americans, steaming east southeast, replied.

The *Mochizuki* achieved several near misses, but American gunfire once again proved better. A shell damaged the *Mochizuki*'s number one gun at 0613, and another hit her torpedo tubes. She launched a single torpedo at 0615 before scurrying west and eventually returning to Japan for repairs. After this, the American destroyers, their decks crammed with 739 *Helena* survivors and unsure what other surprises might pop out of Kula Gulf, departed for Tulagi at top speed.

The *Satsuki* finally gave up efforts to pull the *Nagatsuki* off the reef and arrived at Vila at 0615. She departed for Buin via Blackett Strait at 0717. Allied aircraft pounded the *Nagatsuki* that day after her cargo of soldiers trekked to Vila. It cost his life, but Admiral Akiyama accomplished his mission, delivering about 1,600 troops and ninety tons of supplies.[27]

Viewed objectively, Ainsworth had fought a decent battle by the standards of 1942; the U.S. Navy announced six Japanese ships were probably sunk and several damaged. However, it was mid-1943. He lost more tonnage than the enemy and failed to accomplish his mission. In fact, the biggest difference between Kula Gulf and the disaster at Tassafaronga was that the torpedo that hit the *St. Louis* failed to explode. Massive applications of gunfire impressed but proved mostly ineffective, as did tightly controlled formations of destroyers tethered to cruisers and excessive reliance on radar. Furthermore, American marksmanship, while better than the enemy's, remained unremarkable. The destroyers shot torpedoes—if at all—in uncoordinated penny packets. Worse, the Americans claimed exaggerated results that led to false appraisals of their tactics and techniques. However, the Japanese suffered from the same disease. They notched one cruiser sunk and one cruiser and three destroyers seriously damaged. At least the U.S. Navy's tactics demonstrated evolution; beside their first operational experiments with radar, the Japanese fought as always.

The fate of the *Jenkins*'s skipper, Cdr. Harry F. Miller, is interesting. Throughout the battle he carefully followed Ainsworth's orders but never fired his guns and indulged in just one low-probability torpedo shot and a wasted salvo. Although he had skippered the *Jenkins* since her commissioning in July 1942, when the destroyer sailed on her next mission a few days later, Miller was not aboard.

Battle of Kolombangara, 13 July 1943

The American offensive against Munda had bogged down by mid-July. In a scenario like Guadalcanal in reverse, separate American columns slowly thrashed through New Georgia's jungles toward the Japanese airfield. Regarding New Georgia as "a key outpost for Bougainville Island, to be secured at all costs," the Japanese stepped up efforts to stall the American drives.[28] On 9 July Vice Admiral Samejima Tomoshige, who replaced Mikawa as 8th Fleet commander on 1 April 1943, sortied with three cruisers and four destroyers and landed 1,200 troops on Kolombangara. He scheduled the delivery of another contingent for the night of 12 July.

Meanwhile, Ainsworth and Merrill took turns steaming up the Slot to cover supply convoys or bombard Japanese positions. Both the American and Japanese sailors were feeling the strain of a fortnight's frenzied operations. To offset recent losses, HMNZS *Leander* reinforced Cruiser Division 9 on 11 July, an assignment that rescued the Kiwi cruiser from a long spell of underutilization. As one crewman

TABLE 8.4. FORCES ENGAGED IN THE BATTLE OF KOLOMBANGARA

Type of Ship	Year Launched	Displacement, Full Load (tons)	Max. Speed (knots)	Guns (number by inch/caliber)	Torpedoes (number of tubes by diameter in inches)	Damage
Allied Cruiser Division 9 (Rear Adm. W.L. Ainsworth)						
Honolulu (F) — CL	1937	12,207	32	15 x 6/47 & 8 x 5/38		D3
St. Louis — CL	1938	12,207	32	15 x 6/47 & 8 x 5/38		D3
Leander (NZ) — CL	1931	9,740	28	8 x 6/50 & 8 x 4/45	8 x 21	D4
Allied Destroyer Squadron 21 (Capt. F.X. McInerney)						
Nicholas (F) — DD	1942	2,924	38	5 x 5/38	10 x 21	
Radford — DD	1942	2,924	38	5 x 5/38	10 x 21	
O'Bannon — DD	1942	2,924	38	5 x 5/38	10 x 21	
Jenkins — DD	1942	2,924	38	5 x 5/38	10 x 21	
Taylor — DD	1942	2,924	38	5 x 5/38	10 x 21	
Allied Destroyer Squadron 12 (Capt. T.J. Ryan)						
Ralph Talbot (F) — DD	1936	2,245	38	4 x 5/38	16 x 21	
Buchanan — DD	1941	2,395	35	5 x 5/38	10 x 21	D1
Woodworth — DD	1941	2,395	35	5 x 5/38	10 x 21	D2
Gwin — DD	1940	2,395	35	5 x 5/38	10 x 21	Sunk
Maury — DD	1938	2,219	35	4 x 5/38	16 x 21	
Japanese Destroyer Squadron 2 (Rear Admiral Izaki Shunji)						
Jintsu (F) — CL	1925	7,100	35	7 x 5.5/50 & 3 x 3.1/40	8 x 24	Sunk

Japanese Destroyer Division 30 Support Group (Captain Orita Tsuneo)							
Mikazuki (F)	APD	1925	1,913	33	2 x 4.7/50	6 x 24	
Japanese Destroyer Division 16 (Captain Yoshima Shimai)							
Yukikaze	DD	1939	2,450	35	6 x 5/50	8 x 24	
Hamakaze	DD	1940	2,450	35	6 x 5/50	8 x 24	
Kiyonami	DD	1942	2,450	35	6 x 5/50	8 x 24	
Yugure	DD	1934	1,650	36	5 x 5/50	9 x 24	

APD—destroyer transport, CL—light cruiser, D1—light or superficial damage (including splinter damage), D2—moderate damage (combat ability not significantly impaired), D3—significant damage (combat or maneuvering ability somewhat impaired), D4—major damage (combat and maneuvering ability significantly impaired or eliminated), DD—destroyer, F—flagship, NZ—New Zealand

Time: 0109–0214
Weather: Passing squalls
Visibility: Mixed, quarter moon
Sea state: Calm
Surprise: None
Mission: Allies—interception based on general intelligence; Japanese—transport

recalled, "Day after day we lay at single anchor in Santos with little to do but look forward to the evening films. . . . American cruisers and destroyer flotillas went out daily to return on most occasions depleted in number, and this was destroying our moral[e]."[29]

On 12 July, when a coast watcher reported ten enemy ships cruising to the south, Halsey ordered Ainsworth, freshly anchored in Purvis Bay, up the Slot again that night. Then Halsey ordered Rear Admiral Turner to supplement Ainsworth's force with every ship he could spare. Halsey meddled in operations to a greater degree than Nimitz or King, who generally trusted or replaced their subordinates.

Turner attached Capt. Thomas J. Ryan's Destroyer Squadron 12. Ryan had time for only a twenty-minute conference before departing for battle. By this point everyone realized that cohesive groups with common doctrine operated more effectively than larger improvised forces; while formations might be standard, things like TBS codes and call signs varied considerably. But Halsey, who "fully appreciated the situation, felt that the advantages to be gained justified the risks involved."[30]

By 1940 hours Ainsworth's force had assumed its circular cruising formation, with five destroyers covering the cruiser column's van and five ringing the rear. A light southwest wind blew over a calm sea, and a quarter gibbous moon hung in a cloudy sky. The Honolulu's spotter flew overhead in a Black Cat, and at 0035 on 13 July, he reported an enemy force twenty-six miles distant and heading southeast. At 0042 Ainsworth ordered his destroyers to assume battle formation. McInerney executed without confusion, but the need to shuffle from a semicircle to a column proved complicated for Ryan's ships. As a result the number two ship, the *Buchanan*, ended up on the starboard quarter of the number four ship, the *Woodworth*. Nonetheless, Ainsworth advanced at twenty-eight knots and ordered McInerney to push ahead at 0048. McInerney reported at 0101 the he "smelled a skunk," and two minutes later the *Nicholas* made visual contact with the Japanese force.[31]

The Japanese commander, Rear Admiral Izaki Shunji speeding southwest twelve miles off Kolombangara at thirty knots, detached the four transport destroyers of Division 22, the *Satsuki*, *Yunagi*, *Matsukaze*, and *Minazuki*. Then, at 0057, he received a seaplane's radioed warning of an enemy force forty miles off Visuvisu.[32] Izaki thus proceeded in "alert cruising disposition," arranging the *Mikazuki*, *Jintsu*, *Yukikaze*, *Hamakaze*, *Kiyonami*, and *Yugure* into column (see Map 8.3). The experienced torpedo crews readied their weapons as the two forces rapidly converged.

At 0106 Ainsworth turned his cruisers 30 degrees right to the west northwest to unmask their main batteries. Then, improving his earlier battle, he released McInerney to attack with torpedoes. Beginning at 0110, the *Nicholas* fired five fish, the *Taylor* launched nine, and the *Radford* loosed five at the excessive range of 10,000 to 11,000 yards. Still, the Japanese had beaten them to the mark. The destroyers launched twenty-two torpedoes. The *Jintsu* launched seven more between 0108 and 0114, even as Izaki bent his column in an 80-degree port turn to a north by northwest heading. This maneuver completely foiled the Americans' initial attack.

At 0111 the *Jintsu*'s searchlight stabbed out. The *Jenkins* had mistakenly turned starboard when Ainsworth ordered a 30-degree turn to port at 0110, which put the American destroyer nearest to the enemy. As the harsh glare from the Japanese spotlight bathed her superstructure, the *Jenkins* snapped off two quick torpedoes and scuttled back into line while the *O'Bannon* and *Taylor* engaged. Within a minute the "big boys" followed suit. The *Honolulu* reported, "At 0111.9 opened 6" radar controlled fire . . . on enemy CL, target #1, bearing 319.2° T, range 10,225 yards."[33] By 0114 the *Honolulu* considered this target eliminated and began the fire and shift routine. She judged target number two sunk by 0115, at which point she engaged target number three.

The rear American destroyers, although badly bunched, aimed their tubes as the lead ships were firing. The *Maury* discharged a half salvo at 0114. The *Buchanan* fired five, and the *Gwin* launched seven about a minute later. As these two squadrons combined to produce the largest American torpedo barrage of the war to date, the American cruisers deluged the *Jintsu* with six-inch shells. The *Leander*, in a surface action for the first time since she chased French warships in June 1941, also released four torpedoes. First, a round stuck the *Jintsu*'s rudder, and then shells plastered her bridge, slaughtering Izaki and his staff. Five minutes later, a flurry of ten or more projectiles punched into her boiler rooms. By this time, the *Jintsu* had skewed to starboard and was burning fiercely as she drifted to a halt.[34]

MAP 8.3. BATTLE OF KOLOMBANGARA, 13 JULY 1943

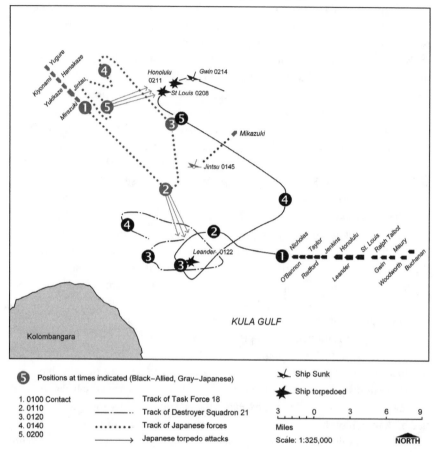

Then the moon, dipping toward the horizon, disappeared behind dense rain clouds. Visibility plummeted, and Ainsworth's battle plan disintegrated. At 0116:5 Ainsworth ordered all his ships to make a simultaneous 180-degree turn to the east northeast. When the execute order went out over TBS, however, several ships did not hear it because the *Honolulu*'s TBS, which had a blind spot aft, began to fade badly. Dense smoke from the Americans' flashless powder baffled lookouts, and as the *Honolulu* turned, the *Leander* loomed suddenly in her path. Both ships abruptly ceased firing, and the *Leander* came hard to port. The *Honolulu* eventually fell in behind the *St. Louis*, and the *Ralph Talbot* had to "back full, maneuver radically, and use whistle signals to narrowly avoid collision with rear destroyers [that] were standing on at 30 knots."[35]

During this confusion torpedoes began to swarm around the American task force. The *Ralph Talbot* witnessed three pass within twenty-five yards of her stern. At 0122 a Long Lance crashed into the *Leander* amidships in the number 1 boiler room and ripped a jagged 600 square foot hole in her port side. The concussion whipped her main mast back and forth and popped the searchlight's shutters, sending an unwanted beam of light shooting skyward. Twenty-eight men died, including several who were swept overboard by the giant water column hurled up by the blast.

Meanwhile, the *Mikazuki* stood by the *Jintsu*, but the other Japanese destroyers dashed into a convenient rain squall that baffled American radar. At 0123 the *Honolulu*'s Black Cat reported these four vessels fleeing northwest, and Ainsworth ordered McInerney: "Go get 'em!"[36] Then the *Honolulu*, now tearing northeast, began shooting at the *Mikazuki*, encouraging the Japanese destroyer transport to make a solitary escape north.

After a bit of confused communication over the TBS, McInerney got his scattered squadron more or less headed in the right direction except for the *Jenkins* and *Radford*, which Ainsworth had detached to stand by the stricken *Leander*. The *Honolulu* checked fire at 0131 and received word of the *Leander*'s distress at 0135. At this time, Ainsworth's radar operators—the *Honolulu* had two SG setups—advised him that their scopes were clear except for the *Jintsu*. Knowing that coast watchers had reported ten enemy ships leaving Shortland and that he had sent McInerney after four, Ainsworth calculated that six Japanese ships had been sunk. At 0138 he broadcast the order to steer due north. Four minutes later, Ainsworth ordered a northwest-by-west heading. The rear destroyers formed column on the *Honolulu*'s port quarter, with the *Gwin* taking the second position, and the *Woodworth, Maury,* and *Buchanan* following in order and all four running at thirty-five knots. The *Ralph Talbot* sailed alone a few thousand yards off the *Honolulu*'s other quarter. Ainsworth clearly intended to fight a battle of annihilation. However, he remained uncertain of McInerney's location.

McInerney had run northwest for ten minutes but saw nothing to chase. Several of his ships launched torpedoes at the *Jintsu*'s burning hulk at 0138, and the division then came about, flinging a few more fish at the same target on the way back. This put McInerney 15,000 yards south of Ainsworth on a reciprocal course, not northwest as the Ainsworth believed. Meanwhile, the *Jintsu* exploded spectacularly at 0145 and broke in two after being clobbered by a torpedo to starboard in the aft engine room. A total of 482 men died.

By 0136 Captain Yoshima Shimai's Division 16 had reloaded torpedoes, and he led his destroyers southeast in search of more action. At 0156 the *Honolulu*'s radar detected the Japanese warships bearing west northwest at a distance of 20,000 yards. The *Honolulu, St. Louis, Ralph Talbot, Gwin, Buchanan,* and *Woodworth* steamed about seven miles ahead of the *Maury* while McInerney's destroyers milled about in the *Leander*'s general vicinity. As the *Maury*'s radar officer remembered, "[T]here were many dozens of pips nearer the center of the PPI. They could be ships or they could be sea return, reflected from high-speed wakes. . . . Here was I, in [the combat information center (CIC)] with the fabulous SG radar in front of me, and I could only tell Captain Sims that I did not know which pip was *Leander*, or even, for sure, which was flagship *Honolulu!*"[37] Ainsworth suffered similar difficulties, reporting later, "The general belief in CIC and Flag Plot was that those ships were our van destroyers returning from their mission against the cripples."[38] Ainsworth tried to radio the as-yet-unidentified contacts, not knowing that the *Honolulu*'s aft radar had already pegged them as skunks. Growing suspicious, the American cruisers fired star shell. This revealed two-stack destroyers in the process of turning away, as if they had just fired torpedoes. Too late, Ainsworth ordered a 60-degree starboard turn to due north.

At 0208, as Ainsworth's ships swung about and before his order to open fire could be executed, lookouts on the *Honolulu* spotted torpedo wakes. Ainsworth maneuvered radically to starboard, but a torpedo slammed into the nearby *St. Louis*'s starboard bow at frame 6. The *Honolulu* successfully dodged several others, but a Long Lance bit a giant chunk from her bow at frame 10 at 0211. Another rammed her stern but failed to explode. At 0214 a tremendous blast shook the *Gwin*, blew her number four mount over the side, and sparked several large fires. In the ensuing pileup the *Buchanan* sideswiped the *Woodworth* and damaged the *Woodworth*'s port propeller, flooding three compartments. A depth charge shook loose and exploded beneath the *Buchanan*'s bow but did little additional damage. The *Ralph Talbot*, the only American vessel to take any offensive action during this catastrophe, ineffectively flung four torpedoes after the fleeing enemy.

Despite severe flooding aft, the *Gwin* valiantly struggled to make Tulagi but had to be scuttled at 0930 the next morning. The *Honolulu* and *St. Louis* both lost their bows. By the end of November after a trip to Mare Island they steamed under Ainsworth's flag once again. The *Leander* remained afloat after an epic struggle. She voyaged to Boston and spent a year in dock.

Except for the *Jintsu*, the Japanese escaped untouched. The transport group slipped into Vila at 0236 and landed 1,200 men. Two Japanese ships then searched for the *Jintsu*'s survivors without luck and cleared Kula Gulf at 0745.[39]

Ainsworth later wrote to Nimitz, "Looking over one's shoulder, one can always see how we should have done differently, and no one knows the fallacy of chasing Jap destroyers with cruisers better than I."[40] During the battle the *Honolulu* and *St. Louis* fired 1,110 and 1,360 six-inch rounds, respectively. The *Leander*, inadvertently providing striking testimony to the capability of the American light cruisers, shot only 160. The admirals remained enchanted by their guns, but Ainsworth fought a much different battle at Kolombangara than he had at Kula Gulf just a week earlier. His destroyers expended thirty-five torpedoes in two large and nearly coordinated attacks, and they fired a dozen more in four small salvos. More than just putting the fish in the water, though, the Americans could claim another torpedo attack success, even if their target had been burning and dead in the water at the time. The U.S. Navy had assembled the ingredients for success; it remained to give them a fair test.

Battle of Vella Gulf, 6–7 August 1943

Exploiting their temporary dominance of the sea lanes surrounding Kolombangara, Japanese destroyers ferried reinforcements to Vila on the nights of 19 July, 22 July, and 1 August. The 8th Fleet designed the 19 July operation to complete the destruction of enemy naval strength in the area. For this purpose Rear Admiral Nishimura led the *Chokai*, *Kumano*, and *Suzuya* and Destroyer Squadron 3, consisting of the *Sendai* and nine destroyers, to the Slot ready to pounce when enemy cruisers showed up. However, the Allies did not cooperate. Rear Admiral Merrill's division lingered in the south, transferring base to Purvis Bay. Likewise, the Australian division under Vice Admiral Crutchley, which had sailed up to stand in for Ainsworth, was unavailable. A Black Cat did spot Nishimura's force, and subsequent air attacks sank the destroyers *Yugure* and *Kiyonami* and damaged the heavy cruiser *Kumano* and the destroyer *Minazuki*. Nishimura's ambush thus proved a costly and embarrassing failure.[41]

Having given up the direct Kula Gulf route to Vila as too risky, the Japanese sent the 22 July and 1 August destroyer transport missions around Vella Lavella Island's Boko Point and down Vella Gulf to thread the mazelike waters of Blackett Strait. There, the destroyers transferred their cargo to barges for transshipment to Vila. On the 1 August mission four Japanese destroyers tangled with fifteen American PT boats, evaded twenty-six torpedoes, successfully unloaded 900 troops and, on the way back, sliced through Lt. Jack Kennedy's *PT109* while dodging four more torpedoes. Japanese commanders thus concluded that PTs did not represent a significant danger to large warships and scheduled a repeat sortie for the night of 6 August with basically the same force carrying 950 troops and fifty-five tons of supplies.

During this relatively quiet period, Rear Adm. Theodore S. Wilkinson replaced Admiral Turner as commander of the Third Amphibious Force and Task Force 31. Wilkinson, formerly Halsey's deputy commander, head of his Annapolis class, and a former destroyer skipper, was open to new ideas on how to crack the nut of Japanese success in night surface actions. On 31 July he sent Cdr. Arleigh A. Burke north with Squadron 12 to hit Kula Gulf. After Burke found the gulf empty, Wilkinson contemplated a destroyer sweep into the hitherto unexplored waters of Vella Gulf. Halsey reassigned Burke on 3 August, so when news of another Tokyo Express arrived, Cdr. Frederick Moosbrugger got the job of penetrating Vella Gulf.[42]

TABLE 8.5. FORCES ENGAGED IN THE BATTLE OF VELLA GULF

Type of Ship	Year Launched	Displacement, Full Load (tons)	Max. Speed (knots)	Guns (number by inch/caliber)	Torpedoes (number of tubes by diameter in inches)	Damage
American Destroyer Division 12 (Cdr. F. Moosbrugger)						
Dunlap (F)	DD	1936	2,103	36	5 x 5/38	12 x 21	
Craven	DD	1938	2,219	35	4 x 5/38	16 x 21	
Maury	DD	1938	2,219	35	4 x 5/38	16 x 21	
American Destroyer Division 15 (Cdr. R. Simpson)						
Lang (F)	DD	1938	2,250	38	4 x 5/38	8 x 21	
Sterett	DD	1938	2,250	38	4 x 5/38	8 x 21	
Stack	DD	1938	2,250	38	4 x 5/38	8 x 21	
Japanese Destroyer Division 4 (Captain Sugiura Kaju)						
Hagikaze (F)	DD	1940	2,450	35	6 x 5/50	8 x 24	Sunk
Arashi	DD	1940	2,450	35	6 x 5/50	8 x 24	Sunk
Kawakaze	DD	1936	1,950	36	5 x 5/50	8 x 24	Sunk
Japanese Destroyer Division 27 (Captain Hara Tameichi)						
Shigure (F)	DD	1935	1,950	36	5 x 5/50	8 x 24	

DD—destroyer, F—flagship
Time: 2341–0017
Weather: Scattered squalls
Visibility: No moon, very dark
Sea state: Calm
Surprise: Americans
Mission: Americans—interception based on general intelligence; Japanese—transport

Moosbrugger enjoyed ample opportunity to meet with Cdr. Rodger W. Simpson and the other destroyer skippers under his command to explain the plan and his tactics, which were adapted from Burke's untested destroyer battle doctrine. This envisioned destroyers operating in two independent formations. Upon making contact with the enemy, the group nearest the enemy would launch torpedoes while the other group crossed the enemy's T and opened fire after the torpedoes struck. The principal variation Moosbrugger introduced reflected the nature of his force. Because Division 15's vessels had surrendered half their original torpedo armament for 40-mm guns, which were the best weapon for barge busting, Simpson's ships would lead the attack if the Americans ran into barges instead of destroyers.

This battle plan made the gunnery admirals uncomfortable on two counts. First, it violated the principle of concentration of force; the occasions when American ships had become separated, like Cape Esperance, the First Battle of Guadalcanal, and Kolombangara, had been unhappy experiences replete with misidentification and friendly fire incidents. Second, guns, not torpedoes, had been the most damaging weapon in every Solomons' surface action.

Moosbrugger departed Purvis Bay at 1130 on 6 August. Seven hours later, as a Japanese force commanded by Captain Sugiura Kaju passed Buki Island, Japanese lookouts spotted an Allied reconnaissance plane ducking into clouds and intercepted a coded message. Sugiura correctly assumed he had been sighted and faced the prospect of a night engagement. Other than that, he lacked specific intelligence.

By 2100 the opposing forces were near their common destination. The Japanese entered Bougainville Strait at thirty knots, and the Americans turned north toward Gizo Strait at sixteen knots. The Japanese sailed in a tight column, with the *Hagikaze* leading the *Arashi, Kawakaze*, and *Shigure*. At 2226 the quarter moon set, darkening a night punctuated by periodic rain squalls. Hardly any wind ruffled the calm sea, however. A member of the *Sterett's* crew remembered, "I stepped out on deck and into the blackest night I ever saw. . . . [T]he feeling of claustrophobia that settled on us became understandable when we realized the clouds were not much higher than the mast."[43]

At 2228 Moosbrugger's two divisions tacked starboard and swept the mouth of Blackett Strait. Finding nothing, they steered north to inspect Kolombangara's west coast. Each division proceeded in column, leaving 500 yards between ships. Moosbrugger sailed ahead and 4,000 yards to port of Simpson. For its part, Sugiura's column was rounding Boko Point to enter Vella Gulf from the north. The *Shigure*, trailing her companions by 1,500 yards, had her torpedo tubes trained to port since to starboard the shores of Vella Lavella showed clear.

The *Dunlap,* leading Moosbrugger's division, made radar contact with the Japanese at 2333. As the first pip resolved into four, Moosbrugger ordered Division 12 to prepare to fire torpedoes port while Simpson's Division 15, originally inshore ready to shoot up barges, swung behind his track and maneuvered to cross the Japanese T. The range dropped rapidly as Moosbrugger adjusted course to put the enemy beam on. At 2341 with the first target bearing 6,300 yards broad off the port bow, Moosbrugger broadcast the order "Execute William."[44] The torpedoes flawlessly swooshed from their tubes at three-second intervals set for thirty-six knots and a run of 4,840 yards to target. With Moosbrugger's ships blending into Kolombangara's dark mass, the usually sharp lookouts aboard the Japanese destroyers missed their danger.

Destroyer Division 12's salvo marked a turning point in American naval surface warfare. The torpedoes carried a new, more powerful warhead filled with Torpex, an enhanced TNT blend, instead of pure TNT, and the MK6 magnetic detonators that had functioned periodically at best, had finally been disabled on Admiral King's permission only the month before. Next, fairly certain the torpedoes were running too deep, Moosbrugger ordered that the depth settings for each weapon be staggered between five and nine feet. The *Maury*, for one, set all eight torpedoes to five feet, which ensured contact with a destroyer drawing twelve to fourteen feet if the aim was true.

With torpedoes away, Moosbrugger immediately had his ships tack 90 degrees to starboard to frustrate any return salvos. Aboard the *Maury*, "each man clutched something solid and held his breath. If the ship was going to be hit by an enemy torpedo, it would be now."[45] As the American fish sped hot and normal, Sugiura, steaming at thirty knots, maintained a steady south-by-southeast course. To starboard, out into the gulf, Japanese lookouts scanned a clear horizon. To port, however, Kolombangara seemed to swallow all light. Then, each of the Japanese vessels began reporting sightings of ambiguous shapes, possibly PT boats, in the murk. Suddenly, the *Shigure*'s lookout shouted, "[W]hite waves! Black objects! . . . several ships headed toward us!"[46] By then it was too late.

The *Shigure*'s Hara, aided by his ship's position well behind the main Japanese force, ordered hard-a-starboard and within the minute fired a countersalvo of eight torpedoes. But at 2345, even before the last of the *Shigure*'s torpedoes smacked the water, a dramatic sequence of closely spaced detonations ripped the night and brought cheers from Moosbrugger's men, who had been nervously counting the seconds to impact. The *Hagikaze* was the first to erupt in a tower of flame. Then a second torpedo struck her engine spaces, dousing the fire, but jarring the *Hagikaze* to a halt. Hara next witnessed a "pillar of fire" spring up amidships on the *Arashi* as a pair of torpedoes smashed into her engine room.[47] A fifth American torpedo bashed the *Kawakaze* just beneath her bridge, detonating a magazine in a giant conflagration.

Moosbrugger's attack, impressive by any standard, with at least five of twenty-two weapons striking targets, could have been better. Another torpedo holed the *Shigure*'s rudder without exploding, and two more passed within twenty yards of the *Shigure* as she swung to starboard in what Hara called the two most "breathtaking minutes" of his life.[48] The *Shigure* made smoke and fled northwest to reload tubes.

As the American torpedoes did their damage, Simpson's division maneuvered athwart Sugiura's course and opened fire at 2347 as the enemy vessels blazed up. The *Kawakaze* lay only 3,000 yards northwest of the approaching Americans and Division 15 initially concentrated on her. One of the *Sterett*'s officers recalled, "At fairly close range, we poured perhaps fifteen salvos into the hulk of that second ship. Each salvo caused further damage and started new fires."[49] The *Stack* added four torpedoes to the barrage, and the *Kawakaze* rolled over and sank at 2352.

At this point Division 12 turned south and joined the gun action three minutes later. The *Arashi* and *Hagikaze* returned fire "raggedly in all directions."[50] The *Maury*'s radar overload relay tripped so her guns fell silent after only five broadsides. At 2357, with two American ships steadily shooting, Simpson countermarched east to take another pass at the burning enemy ships.

The violent onslaught had silenced the *Arashi* and *Hagikaze* by 0000 on 7 August, and Moosbrugger doubled back to the northwest in case any reinforcements entered the gulf, remembering how the Japanese had operated in separate divisions at Kula Gulf and Kolombangara. Meanwhile, the *Shigure*, tubes recharged, returned south. Queries to her flotilla mates met dead air. At 0010 the *Arashi*'s magazine exploded. Seeing this blast and hearing the sounds of an aircraft engine overhead, Hara "decided retreat was honorable."[51]

The *Hagikaze* remained afloat at 0018 despite enduring a concentrated bombardment from both American divisions. At 0021 Simpson's ships fired two more torpedoes each. Three explosions followed, and the *Hagikaze* vanished. With this, American radar displayed empty seas, and this time they reported the truth. At 0035 Division 12 turned south. Burning oil covered the battle area, and the gas fumes inflamed the eyes. Then the *Maury*'s main feed pump failed, prompting Moosbrugger to lead his division home around the north of Kolombangara after ordering Simpson to secure some prisoners. Division 12 fired twenty-four torpedoes and only 173 rounds during the battle. Division 15 contributed ten torpedoes. The *Stack* lost track of her ordnance expenditure, but Simpson's other two ships reported shooting 482 rounds.

Division 15 crisscrossed the battle area for an hour fruitlessly offering rescue to the hundreds of heads bobbing amid the wreckage; 1,210 Japanese died in this battle, and only 310 survived. Sugiura drifted ashore after thirty hours and wandered in the jungle for a week before being rescued. Back in Rabaul the *Shigure*'s crew were taunted with allegations of cowardliness; however, the 250 soldiers she carried "shouted with joy as they staggered down the ramp to solid land."[52]

Vella Gulf was catastrophic for the Japanese, both materially and psychologically. Throughout the twenty months of war with the United States, the Japanese destroyers had never before been bested in a night torpedo action. For the Americans, Vella Gulf marked the divide between effort and success. U.S. Navy destroyers had independently, and deliberately, engaged Japanese surface forces for the first time since the Battle of Balikpapan eighteen months earlier. The American destroyermen regarded their success as vindication of their weapons and proof their ships served best as offensive platforms unencumbered by screening or escort duties. However, while the refined battle plan and naval doctrine employed at Vella Gulf were significant, other factors loomed large in making the American victory possible.

As the U.S. Navy rotated men in and out, a weeding out process gradually lifted competent fighters like Moosbrugger and Simpson to positions of leadership. Officers and crew had seen enough war to sense the flaws in their weapons and ways to offset them. Faulty torpedo detonators were out; flashless powder, flash hiders, and more powerful warheads were in. Then there were the intangibles. The Americans found the Japanese first and occupied the perfect position against a dark shore. Japanese eyes had outperformed American radar many times before Vella Gulf, and if lookouts had seen the Americans even one minute earlier, the results at Vella Gulf could have been different. As events at Tassafaronga had proven and would prove again at Samar, it was possible to have a sound plan, a superior force, and the element of surprise and still suffer a stinging defeat. War offered no guarantees, but Moosbrugger did everything right, all the intangibles worked in his favor, and he was rewarded with one of the war's most complete victories.

CHAPTER 9

Victory in the Solomons, September–November 1943

[The] fortune of war is a fickle wench and . . . results hang by a narrow thread. . . . The Squadron is proud of its accomplishments, but it is also humbly aware that these accomplishments were made possible by a Force beyond its control.
—CAPT. A.A. BURKE, NOVEMBER 1943

In the year between the 7 August 1942 landing on Guadalcanal and the capture of Munda on 4 August 1943, American forces advanced just 200 miles in the Solomons. It seemed the Allied counteroffensive was being impaled on the stakes of Japan's defensive perimeter, and the 12,000 Imperial troops garrisoning the large and mountainous island of Kolombangara sharpened their bayonets anticipating the next move. However, the Americans declined the campaign Japanese commanders wanted. Instead, on 15 August, Admiral Wilkinson landed on the southern end of lightly held Vella Lavella Island, bypassing Kolombangara altogether.

The 17th Army and 8th Fleet agreed that a counterlanding with their available resources would be like "pouring water on a hot stone."[1] They flung three air attacks against the American landing ships and claimed to have sunk four large transports, one cruiser, and one destroyer. In truth, all three air strikes failed to hit even a single ship. The 8th Fleet had become so reduced that Admiral Samejima never considered a surface strike. Instead, he decided to land two infantry companies and some naval construction troops at Horaniu on Vella Lavella's northeastern corner. From there, the navy could maintain communications with Kolombangara using small craft rather than valuable destroyers while concentrating to defend Bougainville (see Map 9.1).

The Japanese flotilla lifting troops to Horaniu consisted of thirteen barges, three motor boats, and six small escorts. Destroyer Squadron 3, now commanded by Rear Admiral Ijuin Matsuji, screened this convoy. Ijuin assumed command on 10 July, and before embarking on what constituted his first major operation, he informed his captains that "our duty is to guard the convoy, not to seek duels. I disapprove of the dogged inflexibility which has proved such a detriment to our navy."[2] He departed Rabaul at 0500 on 17 August, and the convoy pushed off from Buin at 0900 the same day.

MAP 9.1. ADVANCE UP THE SOLOMONS, AUGUST–DECEMBER 1943

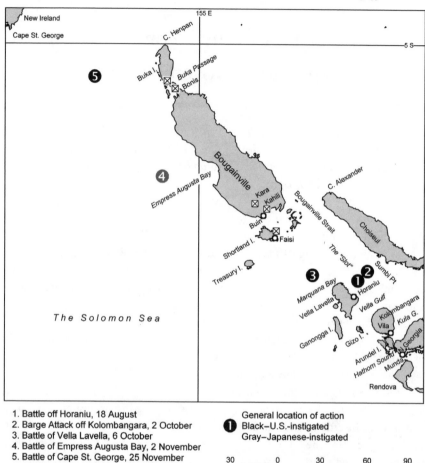

1. Battle off Horaniu, 18 August
2. Barge Attack off Kolombangara, 2 October
3. Battle of Vella Lavella, 6 October
4. Battle of Empress Augusta Bay, 2 November
5. Battle of Cape St. George, 25 November

⊠ Airfield

General location of action
❶ Black–U.S.-instigated
Gray–Japanese-instigated

30 ____ 0 ____ 30 ____ 60 ____ 90
Nautical miles
Scale: 1:2,640,000   NORTH

Wilkinson had just returned to Tulagi when aerial reconnaissance reported the convoy. He immediately dispatched Captain Ryan with the barely refueled Destroyer Division 41 to intercept. Ryan hastened north at thirty-two knots, receiving word from a Black Cat that enemy destroyers were also at sea. Likewise, Japanese scouts spotted Division 41. Ijuin pushed his ships to twenty-eight knots, worried the enemy might maul the vulnerable convoy slowly advancing along Choiseul's coast before he could get there.

At 2300 Ryan passed Visuvisu—once the entry to the battle zone, now a way station—under a clear, bright sky with a waning moon two days past full.

Squalls darkened the northern horizon. Meanwhile, eight Avengers jumped Ijuin as he neared Vella Gulf, but his ships fended them off in a running fight. At 2323 Ryan observed anti-aircraft gunfire ahead in the distance.

Battle off Horaniu, 18 August 1943

As the last Avenger dropped its bombs, Ijuin found himself running east across the mouth of Vella Gulf with Kolombangara's ominous volcano towering ahead. He ordered a 180-degree turn to avoid conditions disconcertingly similar to the devastating ambush suffered in those same waters eleven days before. The Japanese had steamed nearly thirty miles west when, at 0027, the *O'Bannon* reported detecting enemy ships 11.5 miles away bearing northwest. Five minutes later the *Sazanami's* lookouts spotted American ships 16,400 yards to the southeast on a parallel course. Meanwhile the barge convoy plodded south about sixteen miles short of Horaniu.

Ijuin believed the Americans would seek battle before assaulting the barges. Consequently, he dropped the *Sazanami* and *Hamakaze* back, thinking to give the convoy time to scatter by luring the enemy north. Ryan, meanwhile, maneuvered the American ships to launch a surprise torpedo attack. Vella Gulf loomed large in the minds of both commanders, but a replay of that battle was prevented when a Japanese floatplane dropped a blue and white flare over the American destroyers at 0040. With surprise lost, Ryan turned toward the barges milling 15,000 yards east (see Map 9.2).

Now fearing a slaughter more than ever before, Ijuin ordered torpedo action to port. The *Shigure*, following 7,000 yards behind the flagship, fired a salvo at 0046 from 12,500 yards. The *Hamakaze's* Long Lances rumbled out of their tubes at 0050, followed by the *Isokaze's* at 0051, and the *Sazanami's* Type 90s at 0055. As thirty-one torpedoes surged toward the America column, Ryan neatly, if unintentionally, frustrated this attack by detouring around the barges with a simultaneous turn northwest at 0050 and then another north-northwest turn at 0053. Ijuin's original hunch was right; at 0054 Ryan broadcast to his command, "We'll get those barges later."

The *Hamakaze* and *Sazanami* turned south at 0055. The *Shigure* and *Isokaze*, a mile closer to the Americans, began their turns two minutes later. Ryan tacked west at 0056, suffering Ijuin to cross his T. Silhouetted in the moonlight, he was taking a chance, and at 0057 salvos began splashing nearby. Ijuin properly kept his ship's searchlights shuttered and, at ranges between 9,000 and 12,000 yards, Japanese accuracy suffered.

The *Chevalier* launched four torpedoes at the *Shigure* from 9,000 yards at 0059. Ryan then turned north to uncap the T and returned fire. American radar

TABLE 9.1. FORCES ENGAGED IN THE BATTLE OFF HORANIU

Type of Ship	Year Launched	Displacement, Full Load (tons)	Max. Speed (knots)	Guns (number by inch/caliber)	Torpedoes (number of tubes by diameter in inches)	Damage
American Destroyer Division 41 (Capt. T.J. Ryan)						
Nicholas (F) — DD	1942	2,924	38	5 x 5/38	10 x 21	
O'Bannon — DD	1942	2,924	38	5 x 5/38	10 x 21	
Chevalier — DD	1942	2,924	38	5 x 5/38	10 x 21	
Taylor — DD	1942	2,924	38	5 x 5/38	10 x 21	
Japanese Destroyer Squadron 3 (Rear Admiral Ijuin Matsuji) and Destroyer Division 17 (Captain Miyazaki Toshio)						
Sazanami (F) — DD	1931	2,389	33	6 x 5/50	9 x 24	
Hamakaze — DD	1940	2,450	35	6 x 5/50	8 x 24	D1
Isokaze — DD	1939	2,450	35	6 x 5/50	8 x 24	D1
Destroyer Division 27 (Captain Hara Tameichi)						
Shigure — DD	1935	1,950	34	5 x 5/50	8 x 24	

D1—light or superficial damage (including splinter damage), DD—destroyer, F—flagship
Time: 0040–0121
Weather: Squalls, light east-southeasterly breeze
Visibility: Fair, moon two nights past full
Sea state: Calm
Surprise: None
Mission: Americans—interception based on general intelligence; Japanese—transport

outperformed Japanese optics. At 0100 a near miss jolted the *Hamakaze*. As the range dropped to 5,500 yards, rounds whistled over the *Shigure* "kicking up pillars of water and spray." Captain Hara began weaving and ordered smoke, "but no matter which way we turned shells kept falling around us every six or seven seconds with breath-taking, uncanny tempo," he recalled.[3] Finally, the *Shigure* launched four torpedoes and turned northwest to follow Ijuin. Ryan continued north.

As the range opened the *Shigure* and *Isokaze* continued to trade broadsides with Division 41. American accuracy might have seemed uncanny to the Japanese, but Ryan's ships found that the smoke and jinking targets spoiled their aim. By 0111 as the two forces steamed northwest in parallel columns almost 15,000 yards

MAP 9.2. BATTLE OFF HORANIU, 18 AUGUST 1943

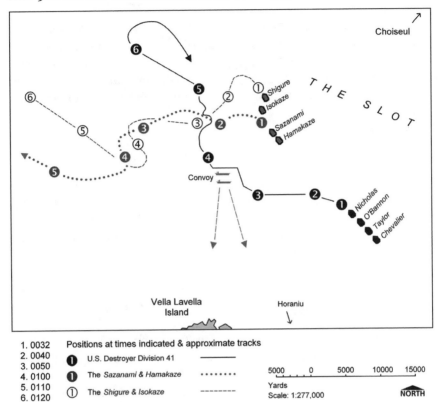

1. 0032	Positions at times indicated & approximate tracks	
2. 0040	● U.S. Destroyer Division 41	———
3. 0050		
4. 0100	● The *Sazanami* & *Hamakaze*	··········
5. 0110		
6. 0120	① The *Shigure* & *Isokaze*	- - - - -

5000   0   5000   10000   15000

Yards
Scale: 1:277,000   NORTH

apart, the *Isokaze* launched her reload torpedoes. A five-inch shell thwacked her three minutes later, which was remarkable shooting considering the range. Then the *Hamakaze*'s radar operator—apparently misreading returns from the barge group—reported that a powerful enemy force was approaching.[4] Reacting to this, Ijuin continued leading his ships northwest at high speed, thus ending the action and leaving the convoy to its fate. He believed the *Shigure*'s last torpedo salvo had sunk one enemy destroyer and that he had scored hits on two other destroyers.[5] Ryan chased until 0121 then turned to go barge hunting.

Division 41 discovered, however, that a large, high-speed warship made a poor platform for snaring small, slow coastal craft. The Japanese convoy had scattered during the forty-minute battle, and Ryan did not locate any targets until 0151. His destroyers bagged one armed barge and the sub chasers *Cha5* and *Cha12*, which weighed 135 tons standard and were armed only with depth charges and a pair of 13.2-mm machine guns. Ryan's ships also drove an MTB ashore. The rest of the

Japanese convoy found refuge along Vella Lavella's north coast and unloaded their troops the next night.[6]

This indecisive battle satisfied no one. Although they expended 3,028 five-inch rounds Ryan's ships only slightly damaged two enemy destroyers and failed to stop the convoy. The Japanese established an important way station that facilitated the evacuation of Kolombangara before being overrun by Americans on 14 September. Ijuin did not distinguish himself in his first fight, but he obtained acceptable results.

Patrolling the Slot

In September 1943 Italy abandoned the Axis coalition. This relieved the Allies of the need to guard against Rome's powerful fleet, and Imperial planners quickly grasped the implications. As one Japanese author later explained, "The greatest effect felt in the Far East as a result of the change on the European front was that it had now become possible for a powerful portion of the British Fleet to reinforce the Indian Ocean area, thus bringing a new threat to bear."[7]

Given the "war trend," Imperial headquarters decided to abandon the central Solomons. This involved evacuating Gizo and the Arundel Islands and concentrating Kolombangara's garrison on the island's north coast to facilitate evacuation. The Japanese navy, lacking the ships to extract so many men in one operation, formed three retreat groups on separate beaches so that discovery of one would not compromise either of the others.

On 20 September a hundred barges chugged out of Buin and methodically voyaged to Sumbi Point, Choiseul, which is thirty-two miles across the Slot from Kolombangara. Ijuin's Squadron 3 covered. For this mission, the squadron included an attack group made up of Ijuin's flagship, the *Akigumo*, and the *Isokaze*, and *Kazagumo*; an escort group with the *Amagiri* and *Yunagi*; a transport group with the *Fumizuki*, *Minazuki*, and *Yayoi*; and a feint group consisting of the *Matsukaze*, *Yugumo*, and *Shigure*. The *Samidare* and *Satsuki* also participated in the operation at various stages.

Admiral Wilkinson knew the Japanese were on the move, but his forces had a lot of water to cover. With the fall of dark Rear Admiral Merrill's Cruiser Division 12 made nightly runs to the north to back up the constantly patrolling U.S. destroyers in case Japanese cruisers intervened. However, as one of the *Montpelier*'s men recorded on 26 September, "We have been very busy for the past 5 days and nights looking for Jap warships in their own backyard but we could not find any. Every day we would leave Tulagi at 4 pm for our trip up the Slot and we would not return until the next day at noon."[8] That night, the *Columbia* narrowly avoided a submarine attack (or an imagined attack). Wilkinson left blockade duty to the destroyers after that.

On the night of 28–29 September Japanese barges moved 1,691 men to Sumbi Point, and destroyers ferried 2,115 Imperial troops directly to Rabaul without interference. On the night of September 29–30 Capt. Frank Walker's Destroyer Squadron 4, consisting of the *Patterson, Foote, Ralph Talbot*, and *McCalla*, headed north. At 2220, after avoiding several air attacks, they found a barge sixteen miles north of Kolombangara. Sent to destroy this enemy craft, the *McCalla* discovered several others and attacked them as well. During this action, the *McCalla*'s gyro malfunctioned, and, upon returning to the American formation, she rammed the *Patterson*. The collision smashed the *Patterson*'s bow and killed three men while injuring ten. The *Patterson*'s bow fell off just forward of Mount 51 as she crept back to Purvis Bay, and she missed six months of action. The *McCalla* required three months of repair.[9]

The next night U.S. Destroyer Division 22, with the *Waller, Eaton, Renshaw*, and *Cony* under Capt. William Cooke, and U.S. Destroyer Division 42, with the *Radford, Saufley*, and *Grayson* under Cdr. A.D. Chandler, drew duty. At 2223 Cooke's force lit into a group of Japanese barges. After a half hour, Merrill's cruisers, which were standing well south, relayed a message that enemy destroyers were moving in from the northwest. Chandler's ships set out to intercept, and Division 22 fell in astern. Enemy forces cluttered the Slot and impeded the American destroyers' progress, however. First, the Americans encountered more barges. Then, bogies began dropping flares and bombs and forced the destroyers to maneuver radically for more than an hour. Three near misses sprayed the *Saufley* with splinters, killing two men and wounding eleven. Ijuin's destroyers likewise failed to engage. A Japanese summary of this action explains, "[S]ince the small craft unit came between our surface forces and the enemy's we lost the opportunity for an engagement."[10]

Kolombangara Evacuation Action, 2–3 October 1943

Time: 2316–0215
Weather: Light breeze, overcast, squalls
Visibility: Dark, no moon
Sea state: Calm
Surprise: None
Mission: Americans—interception based on general intelligence; Japanese—escort and transport

On the night of 2 October Captain Cooke led the *Waller, Eaton*, and *Cony* north, accompanied by the *Ralph Talbot, Taylor*, and *Terry*, which were under the command of Cdr. Harold O. Larson. Larson's ships passed Visuvisu Point at 1800 and went to general quarters. Japanese night flyers began their harassment two hours later, dropping float lights and red, green, and white flares as they neared the Kolombangara-Choiseul passage. Ijuin had nine destroyers at sea, and four of them had proceeded to the evacuation point and loaded wounded, finishing around 2300.

At 2109 the *Ralph Talbot* scoped a barge 4,330 yards away, and Larson's ships filed past, firing in succession. The division repeated this procedure at 2135 and again at 2200. The waters appeared to be full of enemy small craft, giving onlookers the impression of a shooting gallery. The gallery shot back, however, inflicting minor damage on the *Ralph Talbot*.[11]

Larger blips blossomed on the American's PPI scopes at 2315. These signified the four Japanese destroyers departing the beach at high speed. Larson turned to intercept, and his ships launched half salvos of torpedoes at 2325 from 7,500 yards. The Japanese tacked to starboard, though, and this salvo missed. Larson maneuvered for another try, and at 2343 his ships sent fifteen more torpedoes swimming. Again, all missed. Meanwhile, Cooke chased, but "high enemy speed made it impossible to make appreciable advance from a position broad on their starboard quarter."[12]

At midnight the adversaries began swapping broadsides from 8,000 yards as they ran north northwest. Larson broke off two minutes later, but Cooke continued and struck the *Shigure*'s hull with three shells—all duds. The Japanese, thinking they faced three cruisers and three destroyers, fired fourteen torpedoes back at their pursuers. These forced Cooke to turn away at 0019 on 3 October and counter with torpedoes of his own that proved as ineffective as all the earlier salvos.

Four destroyers under Ijuin's direct command observed the action while patrolling the mouth of Vella Gulf, but "since our ships were in a confused tangle [the destroyers] refrained from participating in the action."[13] Afterwards, both U.S. destroyer divisions returned to the passage and continued their barge hunt. Larson's division claimed barge sinkings at 0036, 0116, 0117, 0140, 0158, and 0210. The Japanese account relates, "Tanegashima Transport Group boarded 2,117 soldiers on seventeen barges and later transferred 1,450 soldiers to the destroyers, which joined the group from the attacking squadron. On the way to Sumbi, the transport group was attacked for two hours starting from [0030] by the enemy destroyers and torpedo boats. As a result, five barges sank but the rest arrived safely at Sumbi."[14]

Overall, the Japanese extracted 9,400 men to reinforce Bougainville's garrison. The Americans, tallying enthusiastic claims from various action reports, believed they had slaughtered thousands of soldiers and accounted for forty-six barges. The *Waller*'s skipper, Lt. Cdr. W.T. Dutton, presented a more balanced picture: "Barges are difficult targets to hit and to keep under fire. Once fire is opened they appear to disappear in splashes both visually and in the radar screen.... Frequently after it had appeared that all targets had been destroyed firing would be checked but further illumination a minute later would reveal the continued presence of barges. Whether these were the same or additional barges was very often a matter of doubt."[15]

Battle of Vella Lavella, 6 October 1943

After clearing out Kolombangara, the last significant group of Japanese lingering in the Central Solomons consisted of 589 men stranded on Vella Lavella. These were the personnel inserted to establish the Horaniu base and scattered survivors who washed ashore after the Battle of Vella Gulf. Vice Admiral Samejima ordered Destroyer Squadron 3 to rescue these castaways. Ijuin planned an offensive/defensive operation in which three destroyers would escort landing barges to the area and six destroyers would screen the transports or attack if required. A pickup force of five sub chasers, three MTBs, and four small landing craft sailing independently from Buin would conduct the actual evacuation.

The Japanese destroyers departed Rabaul on the morning of 6 October, and the pickup force left Buin that afternoon. Allied aircraft promptly reported the Japanese movement. Admiral Wilkinson only had Walker's three destroyers available, so he detached Larson's division, consisting of the *Ralph Talbot*, *Taylor*, and *La Vallette*, from convoy duty and ordered the two groups to rendezvous off Vella Lavella's Marquana Bay at 2300 hours on 6 October.

Walker came up the Slot at twenty knots. Larson, having more water to cover, pounded north at thirty knots via the Solomon Sea. At 1900 Japanese aircraft snooped Walker and marked his progress with flares and float lights. As always, the American sailors found this attention unsettling: A member of the *Ralph Talbot*'s crew remembered, "Strange yellowish lights descended and bobbed up and down far out on the water, winking on and off like signal lights with the rise and fall of intervening swells. They gave us the impression of being surrounded by unseen and intangible forces gathering quietly on the dark perimeter of our vision."[16]

Knowing his ships had been spotted, Ijuin split the support group, pushing ahead with Division 10 toward Marquana Bay and ordering Captain Hara's Division 27 and the transport force, consisting of the *Fumizuki*, *Matsukaze*, and *Yunagi*, to meet the pickup unit near Shortland Island and then proceed southeast at nine knots. Ijuin hoped to deceive the enemy about the size of his force and to position Hara to launch a surprise flank attack.

Approaching the bay, Ijuin's ships sighted four enemy destroyers "in the direction of the assembly point. . . . [However] a battle did not develop because the enemy was lost from sight due to a squall that restricted the field of vision."[17] Shortly after, as Hara later related, "groping in the utter darkness and preoccupied with dire thoughts about the enemy's radar controlled guns, Ijuin . . . was handed a message from the radio room."[18] This message was that an American cruiser division and destroyer division were approaching the assembly point so Ijuin ordered the transport force to turn north and Hara's division to join him while he lured the enemy away from the pickup force, which was still en route. At 2210 Hara ordered thirty knots—the maximum speed his hard-used destroyers could muster—and hastened to comply.

TABLE 9.2. FORCES ENGAGED IN THE BATTLE OF VELLA LAVELLA

	Type of Ship	Year Launched	Displacement, Full Load (tons)	Max. Speed (knots)	Guns (number by inch/ caliber)	Torpedoes (number of tubes by diameter in inches)	Damage
American Destroyer Squadron 4 (Capt. F. Walker)							
Selfridge (F)	DD	1936	2,597	37	8 x 5/38	8 x 21	D4
Chevalier	DD	1942	2,924	38	5 x 5/38	10 x 21	Sunk
O'Bannon	DD	1942	2,924	38	5 x 5/38	10 x 21	D3
Japanese Destroyer Squadron 3 (Rear Admiral Ijuin Matsuji) and Destroyer Division 10 (Captain Amano Shigetaka)							
Akigumo (F)	DD	1941	2,480	35	6 x 5/50	8 x 24	
Isokaze	DD	1940	2,450	35	6 x 5/50	8 x 24	
Kazegumo	DD	1941	2,480	35	6 x 5/50	8 x 24	
Yugumo	DD	1941	2,480	35	6 x 5/50	8 x 24	Sunk
Japanese Destroyer Division 27 (Captain Hara Tameichi)							
Shigure (F)	DD	1935	1,950	30	5 x 5/50	8 x 24	
Samidare	DD	1935	1,950	30	5 x 5/50	8 x 24	

D3—significant damage (combat or maneuvering ability somewhat impaired), D4—major damage (combat and maneuvering ability significantly impaired or eliminated), DD—destroyer, F—flagship

Time: 2238–2317

Weather: Scattered squalls

Visibility: Clear with local fogs, quarter moon

Sea state: Calm

Surprise: None

Mission: Americans—interception based on specific intelligence; Japanese—escort and transit

At 2231 Walker detected the transport group fleeing the area, bearing ten miles northwest. He tried to raise Larson on TBS, but Larson remained twenty miles south and beyond range of the ship-to-ship telephone. By 2240 Walker's ships were cutting through the calm sea at thirty knots, steering just north of west. At this point the enemy flickered on the PPI scopes 20,000 yards to the west (see Map 9.3). Although Wilkinson had warned that the Japanese might have as many as nine destroyers, Walker decided to pile in rather than wait. One of the *Chevalier's*

MAP 9.3. BATTLE OF VELLA LAVELLA, 6 OCTOBER 1943

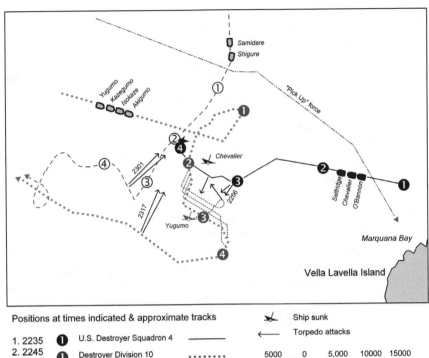

Positions at times indicated & approximate tracks

				Ship sunk
1. 2235	❶	U.S. Destroyer Squadron 4	————	Torpedo attacks
2. 2245	❶	Destroyer Division 10	········	
3. 2255				5000 0 5,000 10000 15000
4. 2305	①	Destroyer Division 27	--------	Yards

Scale: 1:320,000   NORTH

men remembered, "We were going in . . . though it looked like a suicide mission. [Those] Navy skippers were fire-eaters. They wouldn't back down in the face of the whole Jap fleet, regardless of odds."[19]

Ijuin may have been considering the possibility of a sudden eruption of radar-controlled gunfire, such as those that had killed his two immediate predecessors, when, at 2235, with a quarter moon low in the sky and squalls and scattered patches of mist floating over the seascape, he turned Division 10 west to hook up with Hara. As the Japanese destroyers steadied on their new course, the *Kazegumo* reported dark shapes approaching from the east.

By 2240 Ijuin headed south southwest and Hara trailed five miles astern. A dim blue light swung from the *Yugumo*'s stern to guide Hara to the main group. Walker had solid contacts from both Japanese formations but elected to steer toward the larger. The Japanese rear admiral, meanwhile, intended to fire torpedoes as soon as possible, but he mistook destroyers for cruisers and miscalculated the range. When he realized his mistake at 2245, Ijuin ordered a simultaneous 45-degree turn to the southeast. Three minutes later, with the Americans closing at 1,300 yards a minute, he executed a simultaneous 90-degree port turn to the east-southeast. This unfortunate maneuver placed his four ships parallel in echelon, all silhouetted against the setting moon. The *Akigumo* was farthest ahead and most distant from the Americans, followed by the *Isokaze* to port and then the *Kazegumo*. The *Yugumo* was last in line—only 3,300 yards from the *Selfridge*—and she masked the lines of fire of her three companions.

In response to Ijuin's pirouettes Walker steered 40 degrees port to the west southwest, keeping his ships in column, and then west. At 2254 Walker rapped out the order "William!", which signaled his ships to launch torpedoes. As they passed on a reciprocal heading, the three American destroyers sent half salvos, a total of fourteen torpedoes, boiling toward the Japanese. A minute later Walker ordered "Dog," and the bark of artillery ruptured the night.[20]

The *Yugumo*, in the crosshairs of eighteen rapidly firing five-inch guns, spun to port and put eight torpedoes into the water at 2256. The rest of Ijuin's ships turned 90 degrees to starboard when they saw the enemy torpedoes and fell into column. The *Akigumo* and *Kazagumo* snapped off a few salvos during this maneuver.[21] As Ijuin made smoke and presented his stern to the Americans, the *Yugumo* fell behind because at least five shells struck her at 2258, causing her to lose rudder control.

Walker's column began bending northwest to engage the *Shigure* and *Samidare*. Then the *Chevalier* received a report of enemy MTBs and turned to engage this imaginary target with machine guns. At that moment the *Chevalier*'s skipper, Lt. Cdr. G.R. Wilson, reported "two distinct concussions, the first being the explosion of the torpedo and the second, almost simultaneously being Gun 2 magazine." His executive officer, "looking over the [bridge's] twisted wing shield, noticed that there was absolutely nothing left of the ship forward of the bridge and that the ship appeared to be plunging down due to the movement forward."[22]

The *Shigure* and *Samidare* headed southwest until 2259 and then turned sharply northwest, aiming for a good torpedo solution on a course parallel to and ahead of the enemy. At 2301 Hara was satisfied: "We ran some 500 meters in closing the American force before I ordered a left turn and release of torpedoes. It was 30 seconds after 2300. The enemy was 50 degrees to starboard, an ideal torpedo angle, and distance 7,500 meters."[23] The *Shigure* sent eight Type 93s swimming toward the American destroyers, and the *Samidare* put eight more into the water ninety seconds later.

As this barrage streaked toward Walker's reduced formation, the *O'Bannon*, cutting through dense gunpowder smoke, crashed full speed into the *Chevalier*. Lieutenant Commander MacDonald's ship backed clear with a severely warped bow but no casualties. Ijuin, gathering his formation and running south, missed this opportunity and left the *Chevalier*'s men to concentrate on saving their ship.

They began jettisoning all excess weight, including their last five torpedoes. These, the *Chevalier's* crew thoughtfully fired, one-by-one, toward the *Yugumo* burning nearby.

The *Yugumo* exploded anew at 2305 and sank several minutes later. American PT boats rescued seventy-eight of the *Yugumo's* men the next day, and twenty-five of her sailors made it home in a commandeered American lifeboat left behind to benefit any of the *Chevalier's* men still in the water.[24]

Despite the disaster that befell the *Chevalier*, the *Selfridge* raced ahead, her shells straddling the *Shigure*. The time was 2304. The *Shigure* fired back, and she "jerked throughout her length with the sudden deafening roar of her 12.7-cm [five-inch] guns, and the violent muzzle blasts were dazzling and blinding to eyes that had become accustomed to the dark of an ocean night."[25] Then, at 2306.5, the *Selfridge* found herself in torpedo-infested waters. She maneuvered desperately, but a Long Lance launched by the *Shigure* or the *Samidare* clobbered her, blowing away most of her bow.

Larson's group remained twenty minutes out. Shortly before 2313 aircraft warned Ijuin of this new threat. Again mistaking the enemy for cruisers, Ijuin turned northwest and kept going. At 2317 his squadron fired a parting salvo of twenty-four torpedoes at the two American cripples lying 16,000 yards to the northeast, but all of these wandered off-target. Division 27 fell in behind Ijuin, and then the reunited Japanese force collected the destroyer transports, which had been lingering off Shortland, and returned to Rabaul. In this intense twelve-minute action, the *Selfridge* and the *O'Bannon* shot off 390 and 219 five-inch rounds, respectively. The *Selfridge* fired five torpedoes, the *O'Bannon* launched six, and the *Chevalier* loosed ten. The two Japanese divisions launched a total of forty-eight torpedoes. Walker claimed he sank three destroyers and damaged several others. Ijuin tallied two cruisers and three destroyers sunk.

When Larson arrived on the scene, he poked around Marquana Bay until 0020 but missed the barges. Demonstrating their customary stealth, the Japanese small craft made landfall at 0110, loaded evacuees, and slipped away for Buin at 0305.[26]

Following the Japanese withdrawal, the *Chevalier*, which lost fifty-four men, was scuttled by the *LaVallette* with a single torpedo. The *O'Bannon* and the *Selfridge* struggled back to Purvis Bay at ten knots. The *Selfridge* suffered forty-nine killed and missed seven months of action. The *O'Bannon's* repairs and a much-needed overhaul kept her out of service until March 1944.[27]

The Japanese inflicted more damage and successfully completed their mission. Ijuin's strategic battle concept proved sound, as he caught the Americans between two divisions and sank or damaged the entire force. However, he forfeited the opportunity for a greater victory by seeing wolves when he faced only hounds. Walker, on the other hand, attacked head-on despite odds he thought were one to three against him. If Walker had followed Moosbruger's example, his column would have turned 90 degrees right after launching torpedoes rather than plowing into waters teeming with enemy torpedoes. Even after losing two ships, Walker remained relentlessly aggressive. Regardless of the outcome, Walker's conduct, after fourteen months of intense surface combat, demonstrated the U.S Navy's new confidence even in the face of a superior enemy.

Buildup to Bougainville

Japanese forces hunkered down on Bougainville after this battle and awaited the enemy's next move. Rabaul, once an impregnable bastion of offensive might, had become a beleaguered outpost constantly harassed by air raids. However, American losses nearly equaled those suffered by the Japanese, and Nimitz, gathering an armada to launch the long-anticipated Central Pacific drive, withheld reinforcements for Halsey. "Most new construction was being absorbed by the Mediterranean campaign and the U.S. Fifth Fleet."[28] This left the Third Fleet with only one cruiser division and two destroyer squadrons to project sea power into the Northern Solomons. The Combined Fleet, meanwhile, still superior on paper, looked uncertainly toward the Solomons on one hand and the Central Pacific on the other. Admiral Koga Mineichi sortied toward the Marshalls on 17 October, anticipating Nimitz's Central Pacific blow. At the same time Halsey and MacArthur kept Japan's Southeast Area Command occupied with massive air attacks against Rabaul and Buin on 17 and 18 October. With nothing happening in the Central Pacific, Koga rushed back to Truk on 24 October. Three days later, New Zealand troops landed on the Treasury Islands south of Bougainville. At Rabaul Samejima gathered the light cruiser *Nagara* and ten destroyers, but the American transports departed before he could respond.[29]

Following the mid-November 1942 battles off Guadalcanal, the Japanese navy largely withheld its major warships from the Solomon meat grinder. However, with Rabaul directly threatened, Combined Fleet "convinced that this was the last opportunity to take advantage of the strategic situation in the Southeast area, was firmly determined to strike a decisive blow at the enemy's surface strength."[30] Thus *Sentai* 5, under Vice Admiral Omori Sentaro, and Destroyer Squadron 10 reinforced the 8th Fleet on 13 October.

On 31 October Merrill's Task Force 39 supported the impending invasion of Bougainville by flinging 301 tons of ordnance on Buka and then hitting Shortland with 292 tons on the way back. Omori sortied but failed to make contact with the Americans. On 1 November the anticipated blow fell when Wilkinson, leading Task Force 31, landed the 3rd Marine Division at Cape Torokina just north of Bougainville's Empress Augusta Bay. By this time Wilkinson had mastered amphibious shuttle operations. The transports landed their troops and most of the supplies by 1800 hours on the first day and all but four cleared the island.

News of the invasion arrived as Omori was returning to Rabaul from his abortive attempt to intercept Merrill. Combined Fleet saw an opportunity to repeat and perfect the Savo Island victory by smashing the Bougainville beachhead with a counterlanding and sinking the transport fleet, and when Omori returned, Samejima handed him this assignment. Reinforced by Ijuin's Squadron, Omori's ships would escort five destroyer transports carrying 930 men to Empress Augusta Bay, see them ashore, and then destroy the American transports. The commanders held a brief conference, and Omori sailed again at 1700, just six hours after making port.

American aircraft spotted Omori's ships four hours later. The only carriers in the area, the *Saratoga* and *Princeton*, had raided Buka on 1 and 2 November and were refueling to the south. This forced Halsey to order Task Force 39 to cover the Bougainville beachhead, even though only one of the destroyer divisions had refueled from the prior day's operations.

Battle of Empress Augusta Bay, 2 November 1943

Omori's ten warships met the APDs in St. George Channel. American aircraft that had been shadowing the Japanese ships attacked the *Sendai* at 2120. The loss of surprise, along with delays and a report that three battleships, six cruisers, and "many" destroyers had shelled Shortland that morning "led to the conclusion that it would be difficult to make a counterlanding that night." Accordingly, Omori sent the transports back to Rabaul while he got on with the job of "finding and destroying the enemy fleet first."[31]

At 0120 a plane attacked the *Haguro*, opening a side plate and reducing her speed to thirty knots. Nearing Bougainville ten minutes later, the *Haguro*'s scout plane reported sighting an enemy cruiser and three destroyers twenty miles to the south. Omori ordered his ships to make a 180-degree simultaneous turn away from the island while the plane investigated further. After 0200, the scout radioed the promising news that transports crowded the bay, and Omori ordered another 180-degree turn and, at 0225, began steaming straight toward this target. In actuality, the ships seen by the Japanese flyer were the minelayers *Sicard*, *Gamble*, and *Breese* and their escort destroyer, the *Renshaw*; the transports were thirty-five miles south.

Throughout this period the American cruisers of Task Force 39 were steaming north by northwest at the "lowest necessary speed" to reduce wakes and conserve fuel. Merrill reported the conditions as "dark and overcast with occasional patches of blue sky and bright stars peering through low hanging rain clouds. From time to time flashes of heat lighting would show up the ships ahead."[32] On the basis of a

TABLE 9.3. FORCES ENGAGED IN THE BATTLE OF EMPRESS AUGUSTA BAY

Type of Ship	Year Launched	Displacement, Full Load (tons)	Max. Speed (knots)	Guns (number by inch/ caliber)	Torpedoes (number of tubes by diameter in inches)	Damage
American Task Force 39 Cruiser Division 12 (Rear Adm. A.S. Merrill)						
Montpelier (F)	CL	1942	14,131	32	12 x 6/47 & 12 x 5/38	
Cleveland	CL	1941	14,131	32	12 x 6/47 & 12 x 5/38	D1
Columbia	CL	1941	14,131	32	12 x 6/47 & 12 x 5/38	
Denver	CL	1942	14,131	32	12 x 6/47 & 12 x 5/38	D2
American Destroyer Division 45 (Capt. A. Burke)						
Charles Ausburne (F)	DD	1942	2,924	38	5 x 5/38	10 x 21	
Dyson	DD	1942	2,924	38	5 x 5/38	10 x 21	
Stanly	DD	1942	2,924	38	5 x 5/38	10 x 21	
Claxton	DD	1942	2,924	38	5 x 5/38	10 x 21	
American Division 46 (Capt. B. Austin)						
Spence (F)	DD	1942	2,924	38	5 x 5/38	10 x 21	D2
Thatcher	DD	1942	2,924	38	5 x 5/38	10 x 21	D2
Converse	DD	1942	2,924	38	5 x 5/38	10 x 21	
Foote	DD	1942	2,924	38	5 x 5/38	10 x 21	D4

Japanese *Sentai* 5 (Vice Admiral Omori Sentaro)							
Haguro (F)	CA	1928	14,980	30	10 x 8/50 & 8 x 5/40	16 x 24	D2
Myoko	CA	1927	14,980	33	10 x 850 & 8 x 5/40	16 x 24	D1
Japanese Destroyer Squadron 3 (Rear Admiral Ijuin Matsuji)							
Sendai (F)	CL	1922	7,100	35	7 x 5.5/40 & 2 x 5/40	8 x 24	Sunk
Shigure	DD	1935	1,950	33	5 x 5/50	8 x 24	
Samidare	DD	1935	1,950	33	5 x 5/50	8 x 24	D2
Shiratsuyu	DD	1935	1,950	33	5 x 5/50	8 x 24	D2
Japanese Destroyer Squadron 10 (Rear Admiral Osugi Morikazu)							
Agano (F)	CL	1941	8,534	35	6 x 6/50 & 4 x 3/65	8 x 24	
Naganami	DD	1942	2,480	35	6 x 5/50	8 x 24	
Hatsukaze	DD	1939	2,450	35	6 x 5/50	8 x 24	Sunk
Wakatsuki	DD	1942	3,700	33	8 x 3.9/65	4 x 24	

CA—heavy cruiser, CL—light cruiser, D1—light or superficial damage (including splinter damage), D2—moderate damage (combat ability not significantly impaired), D4—major damage (combat and maneuvering ability significantly impaired or eliminated), DD—destroyer, F—flagship

Time: 0245–0539
Weather: Overcast with scattered showers and light southwesterly airs
Visibility: Poor, no moon
Sea state: Gentle southwesterly swells
Surprise: Americans
Mission: Americans—interception based on general intelligence; Japanese—beachhead attack

report received at 2350, Merrill incorrectly believed he had Omori's position fixed and planned to arrive first and fight well offshore. Burke's Destroyer Division 45 led Cruiser Division 12 by 5,000 yards. Capt. B. Austin's Division 46 followed 3,000 yards behind the *Denver*. Burke's ships had refueled, Austin's had not. At 0220 Merrill passed the *Renshaw* and the minelayers, which were clearing the scene.

In the run to contact Omori maintained his formation of three well-separated parallel columns. On the north Ijuin's *Sendai* led the *Shigure*, *Samidare*, and *Shiratsuyu*. Ten thousand yards to starboard sailed the *Myoko* and *Haguro*. The third column, cruising 5,400 yards south of the heavy cruisers, consisted of the *Agano*, *Naganami*, *Hatsukaze*, and *Wakatsuki*. The columns were supposed to be staggered, with the *Sendai* off the *Myoko*'s port bow, but two 180-degree turns had dropped Ijuin's flagship back closer to *Myoko*'s beam and shortened the distance between the formations.

The *Montpelier* scoped Ijuin's force at 0227 while the Japanese were 36,000 yards to the northwest of the Americans. Merrill noted, "Our timing proved to be accurate to the point that we were almost in a 'capping' position when contact was first made."[33] In fact, he was lucky. If Omori had held course and not turned away seeking more information, the Japanese warships would have entered the bay ahead of the Americans and fallen upon the minesweeping group.

Upon contact, Merrill turned due north and implemented his battle plan. The destroyers would attack with torpedoes, and the cruisers would open fire after the torpedoes hit, maintaining ranges greater than 19,000 yards to exploit their radar advantage and because, after nearly two years of war, American intelligence finally recognized the Type 93 torpedo's capabilities. Merrill led the last U.S. cruiser force in the South Pacific, and he wanted to repulse, not annihilate, the enemy without subjecting any of his valuable vessels to unnecessary risk.

At 0231 Burke's destroyers raced north northwest to deliver their torpedoes. At 0239 Merrill realized the enemy sailed in several columns and that the principal targets were probably in the center of the Japanese formation. With Burke already committed, Austin's division and the cruisers countermarched south. This left it for Austin to bear southwest to strike the enemy's main body. However, when Division 46 turned, the *Foote*'s captain, Cdr. Alston Ramsay, misunderstood orders and turned his ship 180 degrees immediately rather than executing a column right to a course of 180 degrees south. This gaffe put the *Foote* far ahead of the *Spence*, "necessitating that she cross our bow and drift aft to take station in column."[34]

At 0245 Austin turned 90 degrees to close on the Japanese heavy cruisers, which bore 25,000 yards to the west. The prospect for a surprise blow from both destroyer divisions looked promising because by 0246 Burke's ships had twenty-five torpedoes streaking toward Ijuin. Burke had ordered the firing of half-salvos, but the *Claxton*'s skipper, Cdr. D. Hamberger, felt Burke would excuse a little extra aggression and fired all ten. Because the *Stanly* had expended five torpedoes against an imagined enemy MTB during the Buka bombardment, however, Hamberger's enthusiasm left Division 45 just ten torpedoes for follow-up attacks. As Burke's division turned away, the *Shigure*'s lookouts spotted their shadows. Division 27's Captain Hara knew what that meant, and he immediately ordered hard right rudder.

As the *Shigure*'s torpedoes whooshed from their tubes, the *Sendai* sheered to starboard. Hara remembered the scene this way: "Turning from watching our own torpedoes . . . I was petrified to see *Sendai* heading straight for my ship! Simultaneously with *Shigure*, the cruiser had also turned right, but in an exceptionally fast and violent manner. I paled to see how close she was."[35] The *Sendai* and *Shigure* missed each other, however, and the close call did not keep Ijuin's flagship from firing eight torpedoes of her own. Merrill, observing this maneuvering, realized Burke's attack would likely fail and did not hesitate. At 0249:5 the *Montpelier's* broadside lit the sky, the streaking arcs of fire aimed at the largest pip in the northern column 19,000 yards away. The other American cruisers also had salvos flying toward the *Sendai* within the next two minutes.

As Merrill's opening salvos flickered on the eastern horizon, Omori turned *Sentai* 5 south and returned fire. The initial Japanese rounds fell 2,000 to 5,000 yards short. The *Agano's* Rear Admiral Osugi Morikazu, in his first sea command after a stint heading the Imperial Japanese Navy's torpedo school, rang up full speed and charged forward. At 0251 Merrill's ships executed a simultaneous turn to the south southwest to maintain range.

Several six-inch shells blasted into the *Sendai's* boiler rooms during the first minutes of the battle, and flames flared in the darkness. More hits jammed the *Sendai's* rudder. At 0252 the *Samidare*, having launched eight torpedoes, turned hard and sideswiped the *Shiratsuyu*. The *Samidare* absorbed 3 five-inch hits immediately after the collision, but these did little additional harm. Ijuin ordered the *Shigure* to come alongside; instead, Hara took his ship to the south in a fruitless search for targets and disappeared from the battle. The *Samidare* and *Shiratsuyu*, however, stood by to assist their burning flagship.

Burke's destroyers made a loop after their torpedo attack, and by 0251 the *Charles Ausburne* and *Dyson* had settled on east-southeasterly heading. The *Stanly* and *Claxton*, however, responding to an order to turn 180 degrees that Merrill intended only for the American light cruisers, made a sharper cut and lost their guide.

By 0256 the *Foote* had cleared the cruisers and rushed to rejoin her division. Austin, racing at thirty-four knots to close for a torpedo attack, changed course to the west at 0300 because his ship "was uncomfortably placed between the fires of both the enemy and our cruisers. . . . Near miss splashes were observed at this time and shells could be heard passing overhead."[36]

Omori's cruisers circled to port and at 0301 settled on a southerly heading. He noted, "U.S. Forces still not definitely fixed in position. *Myoko* fired star shells but were apparently duds."[37] In fact, his stars consistently dropped short, and the misty conditions severely handicapped his lookouts. At this time Merrill was turning north once again and shelling both Omori and Osugi's columns from long range. Also at 0301, a Long Lance—probably one of the *Samidare's*—walloped the *Foote*. The explosion blew away the American destroyer's stern, buckled her main deck, and killed nineteen men. Moreover, she lost way in Merrill's path. The *Montpelier* sighted the *Foote* dead ahead, veered to port, and dispatched a TBS warning to the other cruisers. The *Cleveland* never heard, however, and nearly ran down the damaged destroyer.

MAP 9.4. BATTLE OF EMPRESS AUGUSTA BAY, 2 NOVEMBER 1943

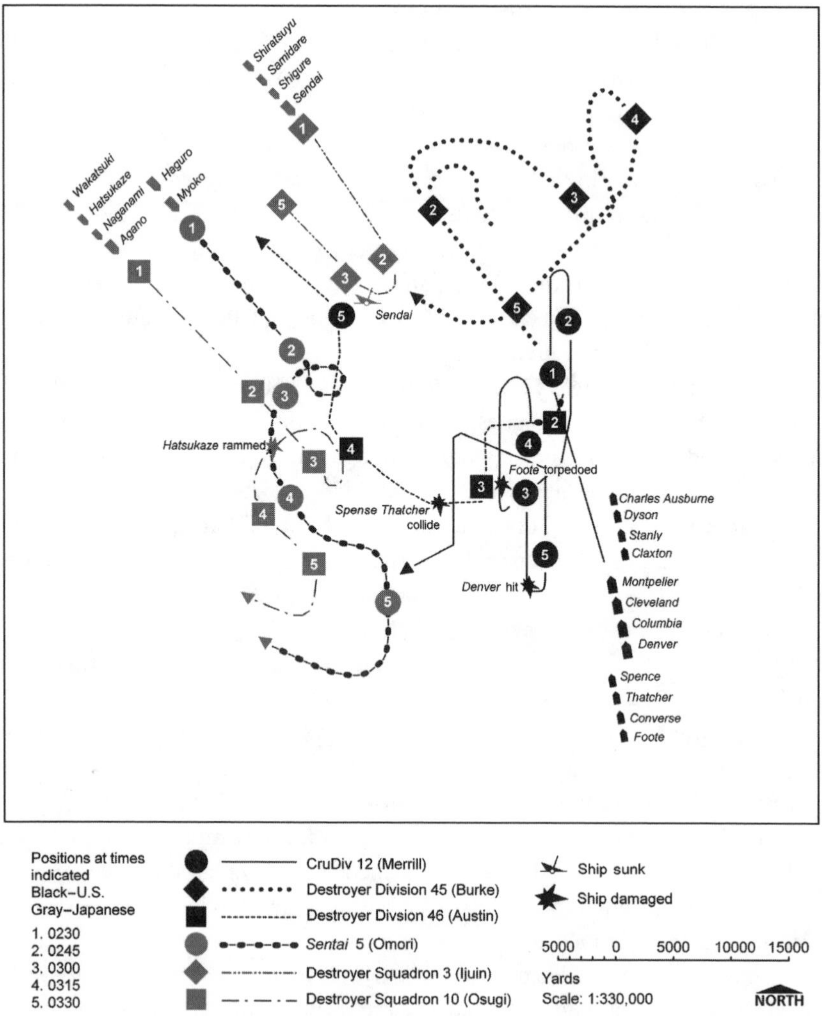

At 0305 Osugi's squadron lay 13,000 yards west of the American cruisers. Because his ships were drawing most of the American gunfire, Osugi reversed course to the west and unwittingly cut across Omori's track. At 0307 the *Myoko* punched into the *Hatsukaze* and sliced through her bow. The *Haguro* barely avoided dealing the *Wakatsuki* a similar fate.

At 0306 Burke's rear destroyers began steaming southeast, in the direction of the American cruisers. At 0308 the *Charles Ausburne* and *Dyson* turned to chase, thinking that their own ships were Japanese vessels threatening the bay. When he discerned the situation, Burke judged it better to concentrate his division before he tried to reengage.

At 0308 as Omori and Osugi likewise sorted themselves out, Merrill directed Austin to attack. Once again, however, misinterpreted orders frustrated American intentions. With shells rumbling overhead and splashing nearby, Austin ordered his ships at 0310 to "stand-by to execute" a turn. The *Thatcher* interpreted this as "execute turn," and so she turned. Heading in opposite directions, the *Spence* and *Thatcher* scraped past each other at thirty knots. The impact knocked the *Thatcher*'s starboard shaft out of line and damaged her upperworks.

The battle had been poorly fought up to this point. The American cruisers had flung prodigious amounts of ordnance, and everyone believed they had inflicted great harm. In fact, only the *Sendai* and *Samidare* had been hit. After twenty minutes, Merrill's cruisers—maneuvering radically at high speed as they were— remained the only force under effective command. Burke was chasing his own tail, and Austin had one ship crippled and two damaged. Ijuin's squadron had scattered. Omori's center and starboard columns played blind man's bluff.

At 0313 the *Myoko* finally pinpointed the enemy's position, and Omori turned his ship twenty degrees to the southeast to close the range. Merrill remembered, "At this time the rain had ceased but a heavy bank of clouds hung over the formation at about 1,500 feet. As the enemy's brilliant star shells broke through, the ceiling of clouds acted as a reflector and enhanced the intensity of the illumination."[38] The Japanese cruisers opened fire at 0315. They followed their shells at 0318 with four torpedoes from the *Myoko* and six from the *Haguro*. Once they had targets, the cruisers' veteran gunners exhibited excellent marksmanship. The *Cleveland*'s report notes that "the enemy error in deflection was so small that . . . the ship steamed through the splashes before they had fallen away."[39]

As the cruisers slugged it out, Austin's destroyers sped north by northwest between the two columns. The *Myoko* spotted the *Spence* at 0315 and shook the American destroyer with a pair of near misses before scoring a solid hit. Although the Japanese shell failed to explode, salt water entering the ship through the hole punched in her side contaminated the *Spence*'s already depleted fuel supply and forced her to reduce speed. The *Spence*'s men plugged the hole with bags of beans. Then, when the range had dropped to 6,000 yards, Austin prepared to unleash torpedoes at the enemy heavy cruisers, but his CIC officer suddenly informed him the ships ahead were friendly. Merrill later lamented the loss of this golden opportunity to strike with thirty torpedoes. He noted, "It seems probable that the many radical changes of course at high speed coupled with the confusion occasioned by the torpedoing of a ship, a collision and a 6-inch hit at the waterline had disoriented Combat Information Center. . . . With no time to investigate . . . the Division Commander immediately swung his flagship to the northward and headed for 'group one' which at the time had him under fire."[40]

Between 0320 and 0325 the *Myoko* and *Haguro* pummeled the *Denver*, scoring hits with shells from three different broadsides. While none of the shells exploded, one did hole the *Denver*, reducing her speed to twenty-eight knots and forcing her out of formation. An eight-inch shell—another dud—penetrated the *Columbia* and came to rest in a sail locker. Another round nicked the *Columbia*'s radar antenna. Merrill was impressed. He later reported, "[The enemy's] 10 gun salvos appeared almost as one enormous splash when seen from the line of fire and the pattern limits in range appeared to be as low as 200 yards. Had the enemy's luck been as good as his shooting we would have suffered severe casualties."[41]

At 0326 Merrill ordered smoke and a 180-degree counterclockwise turn to open the range, which had dropped to 13,000 yards. For their part, the American cruisers scored a total of 6 six-inch and five-inch hits on the *Haguro* between 0310 and 0320, but only two shells exploded, killing one man and wounding five.

Continuing north, Austin's destroyers encountered the *Sendai* at 0328 and sent eight torpedoes streaking toward her, two of which may have hit. The *Sendai* had restored steam, but the jammed rudder kept her circling. She returned the Americans' torpedo salvo with a heavy but ineffective barrage of gunfire while the *Samidare* and *Shiratsuyu* fled northwest. Austin's destroyers gave chase. They fired nineteen more torpedoes, but all missed. Gunfire likewise proved ineffective, even though ranges closed to 3,000 yards.

As Merrill turned into his own smoke at 0327, Omori received reports that torpedoes had blasted the first three American cruisers. His lookouts wishfully interpreted the geysers from misses as explosions, and when the enemy cruisers disappeared from sight, they chalked them up as instantaneously sunk. Claiming victory and not wishing to further tempt fate, Omori ordered his ships to cease firing at 0329 and turned the *Haguro* west at 0333 to terminate the action. After all, Omori later explained, "The analysis of reports indicated that there were at least 7 heavy cruisers and 12 destroyers opposing us."[42]

At 0340 Squadron 10, which had kept to Omori's disengaged side following the *Hatsukaze*'s accident, sent eight torpedoes toward Merrill's cruisers as a parting shot and claimed to have sunk an American ship. As the Japanese withdrew Merrill steamed northwest at 0336, and he returned south at 0342. The American cruisers continued making smoke until 0348.

It was an hour after their initial torpedo attack before Burke's destroyers reappeared on the scene, homing in on the burning *Sendai* at 0349. They then picked up Division 46 on radar and set off in pursuit. Compounding the confusion, Austin's ships scattered after the *Spence* lost suction from earlier damage and fell out of column. Burke reported, "From 0416 to until 0510 we were trying to distinguish our forces from the enemy, with little or no result."[43] Several friendly fire incidents ensued, as the following exchange the destroyer commanders had between 0451 and 0452 illustrates:

Austin: Just showed my fighting lights. Did you identify my lights?
 They're on now.
Burke: They bear 200 degrees from us.
Austin: I think you are the one who shot at us then.
Burke: I'm afraid so too.[44]

At one point Cruiser Division 12 tracked a contact to the northwest. Suspicious it might be friendly, the *Montpelier* fired to miss and asked via TBS if any friendly destroyers had noticed. When no one replied, the *Montpelier* fired for effect. As shells began splashing around her, the *Converse* jumped on the air to tell the *Montpelier* to stop shooting. No damage was done, but the *Converse*'s crew collected a few fragments as souvenirs. In this confusion, the *Samidare*, and *Shiratsuyu* escaped.

At 0457 Merrill ordered the destroyers to rejoin him, but the *Spence* stumbled across the crippled *Hatsukaze*. The U.S. cruisers, questing west for additional targets, likewise found the *Hatsukaze* at 0500. They lobbed some shells at her from 17,500 yards, but scored no hits. Burke's division finished off the *Hatsukaze* at 0539. Heroic damage control kept the *Foote* afloat, and she eventually reached safety at the end of a towline.

Back in Rabaul Omori claimed victory. Admiral Koga showed what he thought of that by reassigning Omori to Osugi's old job at the torpedo school and placing Osugi in command of the navy base at Makassar. A submarine rescued Ijuin who went on to command a convoy group. He died on 24 May 1944 after the USS *Raton* torpedoed his flagship, the corvette *Iki*, off southwest Borneo.[45]

Omori's formation was not unduly complicated, and his maneuvers were not particularly elaborate. In fact, his greatest error was a lack of resolution, breaking off just when he was doing well. Merrill's figure eights were more complicated, and far more risky, than Omori's turnabouts and, fortunately, his cruiser captains executed orders largely without error or miscommunication.[46] Merrill had kept his cruisers safe from Japanese torpedoes, but he also had cause for dissatisfaction. The destroyers turned in a lackluster performance. Burke disappeared for an hour, and Austin suffered one mishap after another and then wandered through the middle of the battle, inflicting little damage except against cripples. About this, Merrill commented, "It is regretted that both destroyer divisions should have attacked the same enemy group. It was intended otherwise."[47]

Once again radar-controlled fire proved largely ineffective except against the first ship targeted, although range, speed, and radical maneuvers also hurt marksmanship. The four cruisers fired 4,591 six-inch and 705 five-inch shells and scored about a dozen hits. During the time Omori's cruisers enjoyed effective illumination, their gunnery proved more accurate. All of the Japanese and many of the American shells that did strike a target were duds.

The landings at Torokina caused a stir at Combined Fleet headquarters as well as at Rabaul. Koga put "the entire mobile surface and air strength of the Combined Fleet under the command . . . of the commander of the Southeast Area Fleet."[48] This involved sending Vice Admiral Kurita's 2nd Fleet, with its seven heavy cruisers and a destroyer squadron, to Rabaul. American aircraft spotted them en route, however, and Halsey sent the *Saratoga* and *Princeton*, now refueled, to attack the base. The carrier strike surprised the Japanese fleet shortly after it entered port and damaged the heavy cruisers *Atago*, *Takao*, *Maya*, and *Mogami*, the light cruisers *Agano* and *Noshiro*, and the destroyer *Fujinami*. Kurita withdrew that same day, aborting the Japanese navy's second and last attempt to apply superior force to the southeast area since Guadalcanal.[49]

Battle of Cape St. George, 25 November 1943

The Japanese army believed that the major base at Buka, just north of Bougainville, formed the true objective of the Allied advance. As one history has described the army's state of mind, "Not only was it feared that the hasty relinquishment of Buka, the last remaining outpost of Rabaul in the Solomons' area, would result in the sudden deterioration of the strategic situation at Rabaul, but also Buka itself was badly needed as a supply base to enable the Buin sector to hold out for an extended period of time."[50] The army pushed to reinforce the garrison, and the navy got the job.

American intelligence revealed that a transport mission to Buka was afoot, and Halsey sent Destroyer Squadron 23 rushing north on 22 November to interdict the strait between Buka and New Ireland. In addition, the admiral dispatched nine PT boats to Buka Passage, the narrow channel separating Buka from Bougainville. Squadron 23 patrolled throughout the night of 23–24 November in vain. They refueled at Hathorn Sound and then returned north the next night. Meanwhile, Captain Kagawa Kiyoto arrived from Rabaul on 24 November at 2300. While the transports slipped into harbor, the *Onami* and *Makinami* waited offshore. At 0024 they encountered PTs and opened fire. The PTs mistook the enemy for Burke's destroyers and withdrew. The transport destroyers loaded 700 aviation personnel—heavy bombing had effectively closed the Buka airfield—and slipped away at 0045 on 25 November bound for Rabaul.

When Squadron 23 had regained the waters midway between Cape St. George and Buka Passage on the direct line to Rabaul, they throttled back to cruise the strait at twenty-three knots. "The night was very dark with no moon. The wind was from the east at force one and the sea . . . presented a tranquil bosom of long, gentle rollers. . . . The sky was overcast with frequent rain squalls moving over the

TABLE 9.4. FORCES ENGAGED IN THE BATTLE OF CAPE ST. GEORGE

Type of Ship	Year Launched	Displacement, Full Load (tons)	Max. Speed (knots)	Guns (number by inch/ caliber)	Torpedoes (number of tubes by diameter in inches)	Damage
American Destroyer Division 45 (Capt. A. Burke)						
Charles Ausburne (F)	DD	1942	2,924	38	5 x 5/38	10 x 21	
Dyson	DD	1942	2,924	38	5 x 5/38	10 x 21	
Claxton	DD	1942	2,924	38	5 x 5/38	10 x 21	
American Destroyer Division 46 (Capt. B. Austin)						
Spence (F)	DD	1942	2,924	38	5 x 5/38	10 x 21	
Converse	DD	1942	2,924	38	5 x 5/38	10 x 21	
Japanese Support Group (Captian Kagawa Kiyoto)						
Onami (F)	DD	1942	2,480	35	6 x 5/50	8 x 24	Sunk
Makinami	DD	1941	2,480	35	6 x 5/50	8 x 24	Sunk
Japanese Transport Group (Captian Yamashiro Katsumori)						
Amagiri (F)	DD	1930	2,389	34	6 x 5/50	8 x 24	
Yugiri	DD	1930	2,389	34	4 x 5/50	8 x 24	Sunk
Uzuki	DD	1925	1,883	33	2 x 4.7/50	6 x 24	D1

D1—light or superficial damage (including splinter damage), DD—destroyer, F—flagship
    Time: 0156–0328
    Weather: Low clouds, scattered squalls, light east-southeasterly breeze
    Visibility: Poor, no moon
    Sea state: Smooth
    Surprise: Americans
    Mission: Americans—interception based on general intelligence; Japanese—escort and transit

area and visibility was about 3,000 yards with binoculars."[51] Division 45 headed
north with Austin's two ships echeloned to starboard 5,000 yards behind. At 0141
the *Dyson's* radar picked up Kagawa's destroyers 22,000 yards away and bearing
northeast. At 0145 Burke turned to close on the Japanese force.

At 0156 with the enemy 5,500 yards away and bearing 50 degrees off the port
bow, Division 45 commenced launching half-salvos for the 4,500-yard, 3.5-minute

run to target. Burke's division fired fifteen torpedoes in all and immediately turned 90 degrees, increasing their speed to thirty knots to avoid counterstrokes. Austin's ships also turned away, but could not fire due to their position and distance from target. At 0159 the *Onami's* lookouts reported the retiring shadows, and thirty seconds later, before Kagawa could react, several torpedoes clobbered his flagship. Amid massive explosions, a fireball shot 300 feet into the sky, and the *Onami* plunged to the bottom with no survivors. Among her dead was Commander Kikkawa who had distinguished himself aboard the *Oshio* at Badung Strait and the *Yudachi* at Guadalcanal. Another torpedo smashed the *Makinami*, but she remained afloat.

Just before his torpedoes struck, Burke picked up Yamashiro's transports on radar as they steamed 13,000 yards to Burke's east northeast. He immediately looped north and ordered Austin to finish the *Makinami*. As Burke departed hell-bent on engaging the new contacts, Division 46 maneuvered to fire torpedoes. The *Converse* let go a half-salvo and observed two explosions. At 0219 a heavy thud shook the *Converse* as if a dud torpedo had struck. Austin immediately turned his division away and then circled to attack with gunfire at 0228. The *Makinami* proved to be remarkably durable. Although the *Converse* reported that "fires immediately broke out over the length of the enemy ship until it was completely outlined," the *Makinami* lasted another half hour. "At 0254 after a series of four major explosions, apparently of individual magazines, the target sank quickly."[52] The *Makinami's* guns had long since been silenced. Twenty-eight survivors drifted ashore on rafts.

When explosions disclosed the presence of danger, Yamashiro immediately swung north northeast with the *Amagiri* leading the *Yugiri* and *Uzuki*. Burke's division chased at thirty-three knots. At 0212 the American commander jinked his ships right 45 degrees to east northeast for sixty seconds before returning to his original course. He claimed this maneuver, which cost him some distance, was based upon a hunch. In fact, the *Yugiri* had launched three torpedoes that detonated in the *Charles Ausburne's* wake. "The explosions were so heavy the ships were badly jarred and the Squadron Commander could not resist the temptation to look at the bow to see whether or not it was still there."[53]

At 0222 the Americans engaged with their forward mounts and fishtailed to bring their rear batteries to bear. The Japanese shot back, managing to score some near misses and drenching the *Claxton's* bridge. Then, at 0225, the Japanese warships veered off in three directions. The *Amagiri* went northwest, the *Yugiri* went north, and the *Uzuki* went north northwest. Burke elected to keep his ships together and pursued the *Yugiri*, which had the largest radar signature. Hoping for a lucky hit, however, the *Dyson* continued to shell the *Uzuki*, as long as she bore, striking the Japanese destroyer once with a dud.

The *Yugiri* enjoyed less luck. Repeated hits chopped at her speed, and by 0256 the Americans had closed range to 8,800 yards. At 0305 a shell exploded in the *Yugiri*'s machinery. The Japanese destroyer skewed about, hurled her remaining torpedoes, and spat defiance with her guns. After an intensive bombardment, and several torpedo attacks, she finally disappeared at 0328 sixty miles east of Cape St. George. A Japanese submarine, *I177*, subsequently rescued 278 crewmen and evacuees. They claimed *Yugiri*'s torpedoes "made a direct hit on one enemy cruiser, starting a large fire," before their ship sank.[54]

Austin's two destroyers hurried north after dispatching the *Makinami*, but Burke's division had chased beyond TBS and radar range. Squadron 23 finally reunited at 0345. At 0405 with New Britain on their radar screens, low on ammunition and fuel, and expecting intensive air attacks from nearby Rabaul come dawn, Burke turned his ships toward home. The squadron anchored in Purvis Bay at 2200 on 25 November.

Although Burke did not prevent the Japanese from landing their reinforcements, or from evacuating the bulk of the aviation personnel, the Americans did sink three enemy destroyers at no loss to themselves and did it in the ideal fashion—with a surprise torpedo attack. On the other hand, Burke underutilized Austin's division. If he had released them to head northwest as Austin had requested and much like Moosbrugger had done with Simpson's division at Vella Gulf, the *Amagiri* and *Uzuki* would, at the very least, have had their best escape route cut off. Two Japanese torpedo attacks that might have turned the results into a draw or even an American defeat failed by a narrow margin. Nonetheless, Burke won an outstanding victory that made a fitting end to a long, arduous naval surface warfare campaign that began so horrifically at Savo Island.

The first of the middle Solomon surface actions occurred in Kula Gulf in March 1943. The next nine were concentrated in the months of July through November 1943. These battles marked the most visible and dramatic steps in the process that rendered Rabaul useless as a Japanese naval base. The campaign demonstrated that airpower alone could not prevent the Japanese from maintaining their island bases. It was the U.S. Navy's persistent and ultimately successful application of sea power that gave the American flyers the bases they required, that choked Japanese sea movements, and that ultimately convinced Japanese commanders they could not prevail regardless of how often they proclaimed the Solomons a decisive battle zone.

In the Solomons, the Japanese admirals, so seduced by the concept of the Decisive Battle, fought a "Decisive Campaign" and never recognized it. They began with superior strength, weapons, doctrine, and position, and they still lost. They hoarded their cruisers and squandered their destroyers. And while repeatedly demonstrating their ability to win individual surface engagements, they proved unable to establish a mutually recognized dominance. In this process, Japan lost the war. Everything that followed—the Central Pacific campaign, the invasion of the Philippines, Iwo Jima, and Okinawa—stood as the consequences of Japan's refusal to acknowledge defeat. Many American, Allied, and Japanese lives were needlessly lost winning what were inevitable victories for the Allies.

CHAPTER 10

The Pacific's Wide Waters, February–August 1944

The [Japanese] have had a taste of what a wallop the American Navy packs and does not like the taste.
— ADM. ERNEST J. KING, 1944

Several elements converged in the autumn of 1943 to produce a sea change in the nature of the Pacific naval war. The balance of resources, which had been in Japan's favor throughout 1942 and level by mid-1943, swung heavily in the direction of the Americans as *Essex*-class carriers, *Iowa*-class battleships, and a plethora of new cruisers and destroyers crowded into Pearl Harbor. American submarines finally began to sink ships in numbers consistent with their intelligence advantages and Japan's pathetic antisubmarine doctrine. American recruitment and training systems were proving robustly capable of supporting the nation's vast accretions of material power with aggressive, high-quality personnel while Japanese systems failed in even greater measure. American leaders had become practiced and confident; Japanese leaders still pursued the chimera of the Decisive Battle and seemed dumbfounded by their inability to counter the relentless American offensive.

The role of the U.S. surface fleet evolved in accordance with the war's new conditions. Along with submarines, airplanes, amphibious forces, and the supply train, surface ships constituted one facet of the American colossus poised to assault Japan's defensive perimeter in the autumn of 1943 (see Map 10.1).

Nimitz unleashed the Central Pacific campaign in November, and the Americans quickly captured Tarawa and Makin in the Gilberts. Admiral Koga sat at Truk and observed. "Somewhat impulsively" he had sent the carrier planes to Rabaul immediately after the Combined Fleet's abortive Wake Island sortie in late October 1943, and there they suffered grievous losses.[1] Without a carrier strike force the rump of Admiral Kurita's 2nd Fleet kept carefully away from American planes and patrolled the lower Marshalls with three heavy cruisers and a few destroyer divisions in late November and early December.

As the New Year opened Japanese power in the Marshalls faded as quickly as it had in the Gilberts. American fast carriers, finally available in numbers that permitted aggressive use, cleared the way for amphibious task forces that seized Kwajalein and Roi Namur in early February. The success of these operations allowed

MAP 10.1. SURFACE ENGAGEMENTS IN THE PACIFIC, FEBRUARY–AUGUST 1944

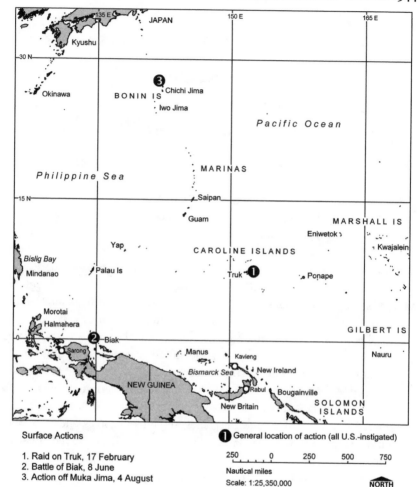

Surface Actions

1. Raid on Truk, 17 February
2. Battle of Biak, 8 June
3. Action off Muka Jima, 4 August

General location of action (all U.S.-instigated)

250   0   250   500   750

Nautical miles

Scale: 1:25,350,000   NORTH

an immediate leap 360 miles forward to Eniwetok Atoll, just 660 miles northeast of Truk, which "for a long while had in the minds of American planners a degree of impregnability rivaled only by Gibraltar."[2]

Raid on Truk, 17 February 1944

Combined Fleet decided to abandon Truk, which had been its headquarters since July 1942, in favor of Palau and to harbor the fleet near Singapore, close to the sources of oil. The U.S. Navy's initial reconnaissance of Truk undertaken on

4 February 1944, produced a report of one battleship, two carriers, ten cruisers, twenty destroyers, and a lagoon packed with shipping. The American flyers just missed the *Yamato* and *Nagato* and their screen, which had departed the day before. When a "sensational rise in the volume of message traffic" indicated American units nearby, Admiral Koga fled Truk aboard the *Musashi* on 10 February, leaving Vice Admiral Kobayashi Masashi in command of 4th Fleet that consisted of just two training cruisers and eight destroyers. Approximately fifty merchant ships and auxiliaries were also left behind.[3] The Truk base went on high alert, but forces stood down on 16 February after a week of quiet.

The U.S. Fifth Fleet's Task Force 58, commanded by Vice Admiral Raymond Spruance, arrived the next day with three fast carrier groups that included a total of five heavy carriers, four light carriers, six battleships, ten cruisers, and twenty-two destroyers. At 0630 the Americans began launching the first of thirty separate attacks. One of the pilots recalled, "Our first sight of Truk was a black curtain of AA. They held it until we got over the target but they weren't too sharp. We surprised them. Their ships were at anchor, dead in the water and that made them duck soup."[4] In fact, a force including the cruiser *Katori*, the destroyers *Maikaze* and *Nowaki*, and the armed merchant cruiser (AMC) *Akagi Maru* (7,387 GRT, 19 knots, 4 six-inch guns) cleared the lagoon's north exit at 0900.

The first report of this exodus reached Spruance at 0942, and he was told that the Japanese had put a carrier and four cruisers to sea. Beginning around 1030 Avengers jumped the Japanese fugitives and sank the *Akagi Maru*, the biggest and slowest target. The American aircraft also hit the *Katori* with a pair of 1,000-pound bombs and damaged *Maikaze*. At 1123 Spruance formed up Task Group 50.9 to chase down the cripples. He steamed west southwest at twenty-five knots until 1210 and then headed due west, keeping well north of the atoll. Coached by carrier planes and undergoing a few nuisance attacks from enemy aircraft along the way, the task group sighted the converted sub chaser *Shonan Maru 15* (355 tons) at 1446, when the vessel was 32,300 yards from the American flagship.

The U.S. destroyers rushed forward and bombarded the *Shonan Maru 15* from 15,000 yards and then spotted the *Katori* to port. At 1516 Spruance ordered Giffen's heavy cruisers, screened by the *Bradford* and *Burns*, to sink the *Katori*. Meanwhile, the *Nowaki* appeared to starboard, standing by the burning *Maikaze*. When the topmasts of the *Iowa* and *New Jersey* rose into view, the *Nowaki* fled west. The *New Jersey* requested permission to engage, but Spruance "did not desire to fire 16″ at light targets."[5]

The two battleships passed the *Shonan Maru 15* as she drifted dead in the water. At 1524 the *New Jersey's* port side five-inch battery opened up from only 1,800 yards away, and the trawler blew up after absorbing twenty-nine shells in thirty seconds. As the *Iowa* passed, all she could see were bits of wreckage and a small boat with one man clinging to the side.

TABLE 10.1. FORCES ENGAGED IN THE RAID ON TRUK

Type of Ship	Year Launched	Displacement, Full Load	Max. Speed (knots)	Guns (number by inch/ caliber)	Torpedoes (number of tubes by diameter in inches)	Damage
American Task Group 50.9 (Vice Adm. R.A. Spruance) and Battleship Division 7 (Rear Adm. O.M. Hustvedt)						
New Jersey (F)	BB	1942	57,540	32	9 x 16/50 & 20 x 5/38	
Iowa	BB	1942	57,540	32	9 x 16/50 & 20 x 5/38	
American Cruiser Division 6 (Rear Adm. R.C. Giffen)						
Minneapolis (F)	CA	1931	12,463	32	8 x 855 & 8 x 5/25	
New Orleans	CA	1931	12,463	32	8 x 8/55 & 8 x 5/25	
American Destroyer Squadron 46 (Cdr. C.F. Espe)						
Izard	DD	1942	2,924	38	5 x 5/38	10 X 21	
Burns	DD	1942	2,924	38	5 x 5/38	10 X 21	
Charrette	DD	1942	2,924	38	5 x 5/38	10 X 21	
Bradford	DD	1942	2,924	38	5 x 5/38	10 X 21	
Japanese						
Katori	CL	1939	6,180	Unknown	4 x 5.5/50 & 6 x 5/40	4 x 24	Sunk
Maikaze	DD	1941	2,450	Unknown	4 x 5/50	8 x 24	Sunk
Nowaki	DD	1939	2,450	35	4 x 5/50	8 x 24	

BB—battleship, CA—heavy cruiser, CL—light cruiser, DD—destroyer, F—flagship
  Time: 0247–1830
  Weather: Overcast, gentle east-northeasterly breeze
  Visibility: Excellent
  Sea state: Short moderate swells
  Surprise: None
  Mission: Americans—interception based on specific intelligence; Japanese—self-defense

The *Burns* and *Bradford* targeted the *Katori* from 17,400 yards, and the *Minneapolis* and *New Orleans* joined this attack at 1523 from 21,000 yards. The Japanese light cruiser replied, but her salvos fell short. The *New Jersey*, meanwhile, shelled the *Maikaze* with her secondary battery from a range of 12,800 yards. The *Iowa* received no orders, but at 1527 Rear Admiral Olaf M. Hustvedt, who occupied that battleship's bridge, gave permission to his gunners to open fire. Between 1531 and 1536 the *Iowa* discharged 8 sixteen-inch salvos at the *Katori* from a mean range of 14,250 yards. The *Iowa*'s secondary battery opened up a minute later. In all, the *Iowa* fired 46 sixteen-inch rounds and 124 five-inch rounds at the *Katori*.

The *Maikaze* and *Katori* launched torpedoes at the battleships rushing down upon them, and one of these streaked between the *New Jersey* and *Iowa* at 1534. The *Iowa* recorded that another passed close down the port side and a third crossed a hundred yards astern. Observing the near misses, Admiral Spruance remarked to his radio intelligence officer, "We better make sure that never happens again!"[6] The *Minneapolis* made a hard turn at 1536 to avoid a fourth and recorded "enemy fire became more accurate. Four enemy shells landed, within a short period, within 50 yards of port beam."[7] But the American cruisers enjoyed good visibility and had "no difficulty in identifying own ship's splashes because of the excellence of the blue dye fired by the *Minneapolis* and the orange dye fired by the *New Orleans*."[8] While the *Minneapolis*'s report does not mention the *Iowa*'s splashes, the battleship claimed straddles and a hit with her fourth salvo.[9]

At 1537 the *Katori*'s bow rose out of the water, and she sank stern first, some guns being served to the end. The *Minneapolis* had expended 204 eight-inch rounds in thirteen minutes on the doomed Japanese cruiser, and the *New Orleans* shot off a similar total.

The *Maikaze* suffered a combined bombardment from the *New Jersey*, *Izard*, and *Charrette* as the Americans raced past as close as 7,000 yards. At 1539 the heavy cruisers, returning to the battle line, laid an eight-inch and several five-inch broadsides on the heavily smoking destroyer. The *Maikaze* rolled over at 1543. The *Iowa* reported that the destroyer left "a large area of burning oil and a towering column of dense black smoke. Her aft mount remained in action until silenced by an explosion near the vessel's stern just before she sank."[10]

Meanwhile, the *Nowaki* had sent a salvo of long-running Type 93 torpedoes toward the American formation. At 1545 the *New Jersey* sheered to starboard without signaling the *Iowa* and fired three of her guns toward the fleeing warship two minutes later at a range of 32,200 yards. The *Iowa* followed the actions of the officer in tactical command and did the same; her initial range was 35,700 yards. Both American ships believed their first broadsides straddled. Then a torpedo streaked across the *Iowa*'s bow. The *Nowaki* steamed into the glare of the sun and, as the range opened, the battleships turned to radar for aiming and spotting.

More straddles followed. Finally, with the range opened to 39,000 yards, Spruance ordered his ships to cease firing, and the lucky Japanese destroyer escaped unharmed. The *New Jersey* fired a total of eighteen rounds in seven salvos, claiming a hit with her fourth. The *Iowa* shot forty rounds in five salvos.

Spruance continued around the atoll, and his force sighted a small patrol vessel on the southwest horizon at 1812. The *Burns* investigated and engaged the sub chaser *Ch24* (460 tons, 16 knots, one 80-mm/.40-caliber gun) at 1839. The little vessel "fought a very game fight and, until she sank [at 1851], was firing her guns rapidly and defiantly."[11] The *Burns* rescued six of the *Ch24*'s men.

This surface action resembled in miniature Nagamo's cruise of March 1942, when carriers and battleships cooperated to sink Allied vessels fleeing Java. Yet, Spruance's ships faced more danger. The *Iowa* and *Minneapolis* both had to dodge torpedoes, and a little carelessness or bad luck might have changed a massacre of Japanese warships into an embarrassment for the Americans.

Throughout the day, U.S. aircraft sank roughly 140,000 tons of shipping, including the auxiliary cruisers *Aikoku Maru* and *Kiyosumi Maru*, the destroyers *Fumizuki* and *Oite*, six tankers, and twenty other ships. Flyers complained about these results, but they achieved the greatest one-day total for sunk shipping during World War II.[12]

The Raid on Truk demonstrated how American admirals were groping to find the best ways for carriers and battleships to cooperate. After the battle one aviator commented, "This is how we can win battles in the future. Teamwork is the answer. We find them and slow them down. The battlewagons close in and pretty soon there aren't any more 'possibles' and 'probables.' They're all 'definitely sunk!'"[13] It was also the first daylight surface action since Komandorski. American gunnery based on optical spotting appeared deceptively effective, keeping in mind two targets were limited in their ability to maneuver. It was the only surface action involving *Iowa*-class battleships, and the *Iowa*'s and *New Jersey*'s final 39,000-yard salvos against the *Nowaki* represented the longest-range broadsides ever fired against an enemy by a ship under way at sea. Both battleships lost their SG radars for short periods when gunfire shock worked vacuum tubes loose from their sockets. The *Iowa*, which fired the most rounds, had the greater difficulties. These would have proved embarrassing in any protracted surface action against a significant foe.

Securing the South Pacific

As the Fifth Fleet executed its part of the Central Pacific offensive, the South Pacific's Third Fleet and the Southwest Pacific's Seventh Fleet continued to pressure the Japanese. By the middle of February 1944 Third Fleet destroyer squadrons were bombarding the enemy's principal bases of Rabaul and Kavieng. The last encounters against enemy warships in the South Pacific occurred on 22 February 1944, when Captain

Burke's Destroyer Squadron 23 embarked on an antishipping sweep of the sea lanes between Kavieng and Truk. The *Charles Ausburne*, *Dyson*, and *Stanly* sank the mine-layer *Natsushima* (450 tons, 19 knots, two 3.1-inch guns) and the netlayer *Kyosei Maru* (556 GRT) seventy-five miles east of Kavieng, and the *Spence* and *Converse* then dispatched the large tug *Nagura* (800 tons, 15 knots) 120 miles to the northwest. Burke rescued seventy-three survivors, an unusually high number.[14]

The Seventh Fleet continued to facilitate General MacArthur's Southwest Pacific drive. As in the Solomons, hard fighting and short advances marked the campaign until the capture of the Admiralty Islands north of New Guinea on 29 February 1944 broke the logjam and frustrated the Japanese army's hopes for a long, bloody campaign. On 22 April 1944 the Seventh Fleet lifted U.S. Army troops all the way to Hollandia in western New Guinea, leapfrogging several enemy divisions. This move stunned the Japanese navy, which was already punch-drunk from a rapid succession of blows along the swollen defensive perimeter. It seemed to Tokyo they had now reached their "fight to the finish" position and that a plan (A-Go) to fight the decisive naval battle was the nation's last hope for victory, or at least a compromise peace. Believing the enemy's intentions were finally clear, Combined Fleet, under its new commander, Admiral Toyoda Soemu, concentrated to fight along the New Guinea–Mindanao axis. Koga had disappeared on 31 March while flying to his new headquarters on Mindanao.[15]

Battle of Biak, 8–9 June 1944

American troops landed on Biak, a large island off western New Guinea, on 27 May 1944. Ugaki called this assault "the most critical crossroad of the war."[16] He feared it would render Operation A-Go impracticable. Although the Japanese army believed Biak lay beyond the new defensive line, Imperial headquarters approved a counterlanding on the night of 4 June with a naval force consisting of a heavy cruiser, a light cruiser, and three destroyers supported by a battleship, two heavy cruisers, and five destroyers. An American submarine detected the Japanese far from their destination, and, following reports of American battleships and carriers off Biak (actually landing ship, tanks [LSTs] and destroyers), Admiral Toyoda postponed the operation. Still hoping a long struggle for Biak would produce conditions favorable to the Decisive Battle, he authorized another try on 7 June.

Rear Admiral Sakonju Naomasa departed Sarong at midnight 7 June with six destroyers, three of which were towing troop barges. The cruisers *Aoba* and *Kinu* from *Sentai* 16 provided distant cover. Allied aircraft quickly spotted the convoy, and at 1245 on 8 June, ten B-25s attacked and sank the *Harusame* and three barges. The U.S. bombers also lightly damaged the *Shiratsuyu*, *Shikinami*, and *Samidare*.[17] Despite this discouraging beginning, Sakonju pressed on. Meanwhile, a Seventh Fleet task force patrolled off Biak, anticipating the arrival of the Japanese ships.

TABLE 10.2. FORCES ENGAGED IN THE BATTLE OF BIAK

Type of Ship		Year Launched	Displacement, Full Load	Max. Speed (knots)	Guns (number by inch/ caliber)	Torpedoes (number of tubes by diameter in inches)	Damage
Allied Task Force 74/75 (Rear Admiral Victor Crutchley)							
Australia (AU) (F)	CA	1927	14,190	29	8 x 8/50 & 8 x 4/45	8 x 21	
Phoenix	CL	1935	12,207	32	15 x 6/47 & 8 x 5/38		
Boise	CL	1935	12,207	32	15 x 6/47 & 8 x 5/38		
Allied Destroyer Division 42 (Cdr. A.E. Jarrell)							
Fletcher (F)	DD	1942	2,924	38	5 x 5/38	10 x 21	
Jenkins	DD	1942	2,924	38	5 x 5/38	10 x 21	
Radford	DD	1942	2,924	38	5 x 5/38	10 x 21	
LaVallette	DD	1942	2,924	38	5 x 5/38	10 x 21	
Allied Destroyer Division 47 (Capt. K.M. McManes)							
Hutchins (F)	DD	1942	2,924	38	5 x 5/38	10 x 21	
Daly	DD	1942	2,924	38	5 x 5/38	10 x 21	
Beale	DD	1942	2,924	38	5 x 5/38	10 x 21	
Abner Read	DD	1942	2,924	38	5 x 5/38	10 x 21	
Allied Destroyer Division 48 (Cdr. J.B. McLean)							
Ammen (F)	DD	1942	2,924	38	5 x 5/38	10 x 21	
Mullany	DD	1942	2,924	38	5 x 5/38	10 x 21	
Trathen	DD	1942	2,924	38	5 x 5/38	10 x 21	
Australian Division (Commander A.E. Buchanan)							
Arunta (F) (AU)	DD	1940	2,519	36	6 x 4.7/45	4 x 21	
Warramunga (AU)	DD	1942	2,519	36	6 x 4.7/45	4 x 21	

Japanese Support Group (Rear Admiral Sakonju Naomasa)							
Shikinami (F)	DD	1929	2,389	34	4 x 5/40	9 x 21	
Shigure	DD	1935	1,950	33	5 x 5/50	8 x 24	D2
Uranami	DD	1928	2,389	34	4 x 5/40	9 x 21	
Transport Group							
Shiratsuyu	DD	1935	2.050	31	4 x 5/50	8 x 24	
Samidare	DD	1935	2.050	31	4 x 5/50	8 x 24	

AU—Australian, CA—heavy cruiser, CL—light cruiser, D2—moderate damage (combat ability not significantly impaired), DD—destroyer, F—flagship
  Time: 2320–0227
  Weather: Overcast, passing showers
  Visibility: Good, moon two days past full
  Sea state: Moderate northwesterly swells
  Surprise: None
  Mission: Allies—interception based on general intelligence; Japanese—transport

At 2200 a search plane alerted Crutchley that Sakonju's ships were sixty miles to the Allies' west northwest and closing at twelve knots. Crutchley continued steaming west at twenty knots in anti-aircraft formation, with Division 42 ahead and the cruisers following in a diamond formation ringed by the other ten destroyers. Believing that the bright moon made a surprise torpedo attack unlikely, Crutchley had arranged his ships so the cruisers could provide gunfire support to the destroyers. He intended to assume battle formation after contact.

At 2320 the *Boise* reported, "Surface gadgets 290 distance 26,000."[18] The *Fletcher* confirmed this contact a minute later. Unfortunately for Crutchley's plans, Sakonju spotted the Allied force at the same time, and the Japanese altered their course to the northeast at 2323 and increased speed, belching clouds of dark smoke. The destroyers launched torpedoes and cast off their barges from behind this screen.

Meanwhile, Crutchley methodically implemented his plan, forming the cruisers into column and sending Division 47 to the van and Division 48 to the rear. He ordered Division 42 to fall back to the cruiser column's port quarter, but Cdr. Albert E. Jarrell noted that the range, 16,100 yards at 2327, was beginning to open. He disregarded Crutchley's instructions and swung his destroyers north at 2328. Three minutes later, he radioed Crutchley, saying, "I could not get your last message. I am moving ahead at 30 knots on [the enemy's] starboard bow. I think he fired torpedoes."[19] With this, Crutchley released Divisions 47 and 48 to join Division 42. It was now eleven minutes after first contract and eight minutes after the enemy had reversed course.

The Allied cruisers worked up to twenty-five knots. At 2340 a torpedo passed behind the *Boise*, causing the Allied column to maneuver and lose more ground. Division 42 began seeing troop barges at the same time. The *Fletcher* passed one so rapidly, her 40-mms couldn't track fast enough to fire. One can imagine the thoughts of the embarked Japanese soldiers watching the American warships tear by in the moonlight. Further back, Cdr. John B. McLean's division began peppering the barges, prompting Jarrell to complain, "You are firing on me. The enemy is 297—18,000 from me." To which McLean responded, "I am not firing on you. Firing on small boats."[20]

The Japanese destroyers separated into two columns. The *Fletcher*'s laconic chronology of times and ranges suggests the slow frustration of the chase: 2352: 19,500; 0000: 18,700; 0015: 17,600.[21] At 0017 the *Fletcher* opened fire with her bow mounts hoping to score a lucky hit or at least to force the enemy to maneuver. Sakonju's ships replied in kind, hoping for a similar result. By 0031, the distance between the *Fletcher* and the Japanese had only dropped to 16,500 yards.

At 0045 Crutchley, seeing no profit in running north at high speed, dropped the cruisers out of the chase and recalled McLean's division. The Australian destroyers backtracked to hunt barges, but were disappointed when they found only one. Jarrell's Division 42 and Capt. Kenmore M. McManes' Division 47 continued north with McManes trailing several thousand yards on Jarrell's starboard quarter. Crutchley gave them until 0230 to force a decision or turn back.

At 0126 Division 42 turned to port, and all four American destroyers flung broadsides toward the enemy, which was now 13,600 yards from the *Fletcher*. The shells were sent in the hope of turning the Japanese to starboard and toward Division 47, and the scheme met with some success. The Americans' PPI scopes registered straddles on the rear Japanese ship, and two of the enemy vessels deviated 50 degrees to starboard. The salvos also provoked more torpedoes from the Japanese.

The exchange and maneuvering brought McManes' ships to within 15,000 yards of the Japanese, and at 0205 Division 47 opened fire. At 0211 lookouts reported an explosion on one of the targets. The Americans had hit the *Shigure* twice, killing seven men and wounding fifteen, but the Japanese destroyer's speed remained unaffected. With the deadline almost upon them, Jarrell and McMannus consulted and finally turned their ships back at 0227. It had been a long frustrating chase. Destroyer Division 42 had fired 631 five-inch rounds, and Division 47 had shot 1,374 rounds, all to little effect. Ironically, most of the barges eventually delivered their troops.

In light of this partial success, Toyoda approved plans to push another reinforcement convoy through to Biak, this time supported by the *Yamato*, the *Musashi*, four heavy cruisers, and eight destroyers, but Nimitz frustrated this plan by orchestrating a massive invasion of Saipan on 15 June. The prospect of heavy bombers over Tokyo outweighed the loss of Biak; thus, the Combined Fleet under Vice Admiral

Ozawa Jisaburo rushed north. As one historian aptly commented about Ozawa's dilemma, "Battles must be fought where the opportunity presents itself, and the opportunity was present in the Philippine Sea after 15 June."[22]

The Japanese got their Decisive Battle in the Philippine Sea on 19 and 20 June, losing three carriers, two tankers, and 395 planes from the Imperial navy's painstakingly restored carrier air groups against American losses of no ships and 130 aircraft. The battle did not lead to the annihilation of Japan's navy like some Americans felt it should have, but the defeat was sufficiently complete to cause one Japanese official to despair, "Hell is on us." The defeat also led to the fall of General Tojo's government.[23] Still, the war perversely continued.

Action off Muka Jima, 4 August 1944

After the conquest of the Marianas, the fast carriers of U.S. Task Force 58 spent the last half of July ravaging the western Caroline Islands. Then, Task Group 58.1 and Task Group 58.3, with four heavy and two light carriers, steamed to the Bonin Islands in response to reports of a Japanese light carrier and heavy concentrations of aircraft there. They arrived south of the chain on 4 August. The expected targets were not present, but at 0800 hours carrier scouts located a Japanese force zigzagging north out of Chichi Jima. This was Convoy 4804, consisting of eight transports and three warships of the 2nd Escort Group.

Beginning at 1000, Task Group 58.1's aircraft attended to the convoy and sank the transports *No 7 Unkai Maru* (2,182 GRT), *Enju Maru* (5,374 GRT), *Tonegawa Maru* (4,996 GRT), and *Shogen Maru* (4,739 GRT). The American planes also damaged the *Hokkai Maru* (8,416 GRT) and all three escorts. Meanwhile, Rear Adm. Joseph J. Clark, overall commander of Task Force 58, formed a surface attack group to finish off the cripples.

At 1241 the attack group, under Rear Adm. Laurance T. Dubose, left the carriers and raced north at thirty knots, cutting between Ototo and Yome Jima. The sun had just set when the first indications of the scattered convoy appeared on the American scopes. Preceding the cruisers, Destroyer Division 91 attacked the *Ryuko Maru* (5,636 GRT) at 1845. The Americans next found the *Matsu* at 1924, and the *Santa Fe* and *Biloxi* were flinging six-inch broadsides at the Japanese destroyer escort within six minutes while the *Oakland* illuminated. During a running gunfight of seventy minutes, the *Matsu* proved a game and evasive opponent, replying accurately to the massed cruiser gunfire. Finally, her hull riddled with six-inch holes, the *Matsu* succumbed to flooding and sank. American destroyers fished six survivors from the water.

Dubose continued north. The *Santa Fe* destroyed a large landing barge, and the rest of the American cruisers ran down the already damaged *Hokkai Maru* at 2145.

TABLE 10.3. FORCES ENGAGED IN THE ACTION OFF MUKA JIMA

Type of Ship	Type of Ship	Year Launched	Displacement, Full Load	Max. Speed (knots)	Guns (number by inch/ caliber)	Torpedoes (number of tubes by diameter in inches)	Damage
American Cruiser Division 13 (Rear Adm. L.T. Dubose)							
Santa Fe (F)	CL	1941	14,131	32	12 x 6/47 & 12 x 5/38		
Biloxi	CL	1941	14,131	32	12 x 6/47 & 12 x 5/38		
Mobile	CL	1941	14,131	32	12 x 6/47 & 12 x 5/38		
Oakland	CL	1941	8,340	32	16 x 5/38	8 x 21	
American Destroyer Division 91 (Cdr. C.F. Espe)							
Ingersoll	DD	1942	2,924	38	5 x 5/38	10 x 21	
Knapp	DD	1942	2,924	38	5 x 5/38	10 x 21	
Cogswell	DD	1942	2,924	38	5 x 5/38	10 x 21	
Japanese 2nd Escort Group (Rear Admiral Takahashi Ichimatsu)							
Matsu (F)	DE	1944	1,530	27	3 x 5/40	4 x 24	Sunk
Kaibokan 4	DC	1944	940	17	2 x 4.7/45		
Kaibokan 12	DC	1944	940	17	2 x 4.7/45		

CL—light cruiser, DC—corvette/sloop, DD—destroyer, DE—destroyer escort, F—flagship
Time: 1845–2145
Weather: n/a
Visibility: n/a
Sea state: n/a
Surprise: None
Mission: Americans—interception based upon specific intelligence; Japanese—escort and transit

At 2200 with no more contacts on their scopes, Dubose's ships circled Muka Jima and headed south. The two Japanese corvettes and a least one cargo ship escaped into the night. Dubose's Cruiser Division 13 shelled Chichi Jima the next day. Alarmed by this raid, Imperial Headquarters allocated the Bonin Islands a steady stream of reinforcements.[24]

Dubose's cruisers were back in action against surface targets on the night of 9 September 1944 off Bislig Bay, when they pounced upon and "demolished" an unescorted convoy of small ships and coastal craft that was proceeding unescorted down the coast of Mindanao. With the United States preparing to invade the Philippine archipelago, the conditions that led to so many surface engagements in the Solomon Islands were about to be repeated.[25]

The Truk and Muka Jima actions illustrated how surface warships magnified the striking power of the carriers. Nevertheless, the Japanese sailored fatalistically on, choking on a deadly brew of heavy carriers, fast battleships, increasingly effective submarines, and practiced amphibious forces that were combining their efforts to fight a wholly new type of warfare—albeit one the Japanese themselves had foreshadowed.

Despite the debacle at the Philippine Sea, Combined Fleet continued to hone its plan for the Decisive Battle, expecting to miraculously reverse the tide of defeat that had been its bitter fate to experience for the best part of two years. The Imperial Japanese Navy retained a powerful surface force, including the world's two largest battleships. In August 1944 the commander of these ships, Admiral Ugaki, wrote, "I looked back at the time of the battle of the Yellow Sea and thought we shouldn't get so downhearted; they had some hard time, too, during the Russo-Japanese War."[26]

CHAPTER 11

European Waters After Operation Torch, June 1944–April 1945

Hitler, as well as the Japanese Emperor, might well have brooded over the tragedy of fatal mistakes and lost opportunities as the year 1944 progressed.

—VIZEADMIRAL FRIEDRICH RUGE

After the Battle of Casablanca in November 1942 the U.S. Navy's surface fleet did not engage an Axis warship larger than a destroyer in European waters during the balance of the Second World War. A U.S. task group that included the *Washington* assisted in protecting the convoys to Murmansk during the summer of 1942, opening the remote possibility of a clash with the German battleship *Tirpitz*, and the *Iowa* spent several weeks guarding the North Atlantic in September 1943, lest the German battle fleet emerge from its Norwegian fjords while the British concentrated their battleships in the Mediterranean for the invasion of Italy. Otherwise, the principal tasks of U.S. surface forces in European waters were to escort shipping, conduct antisubmarine operations, interdict Axis supplies, and conduct amphibious operations. These duties reflected the state of the enemy they faced. When Italy announced its armistice with the Allies on 8 September 1943, the Axis lost its most significant surface force in the European theater.

Despite their decided disadvantage, German warships did tangle with U.S. warships in five engagements that satisfy the criteria for inclusion in this history. Because these actions have been described elsewhere, they receive only cursory treatment here.[1]

The U.S. Navy's surface fleet made its major effort in European waters in support of amphibious attacks in the Mediterranean and then during the ambitious and risky cross-channel attack on Normandy. Germany's remaining surface assets—destroyers, torpedo boats, and MTBs—made strenuous efforts to interfere but lacked the strength to make a difference. German submarines accomplished even less. Following the Normandy landings and the subsequent Allied breakout into France's countryside, Germany retained enclaves in the Channel Islands and at other French ports throughout the war. The Allies, applying lessons learned in the Pacific, contentedly quarantined these pockets of resistance.

The U.S. Navy held responsibility for security in the Gulf of St. Malo and the Channel Islands. During the first weeks of August 1944, while Patton's armies motored into Brittany, the U.S. Navy patrolled the waters of the gulf every night with PT boats supported by destroyers or destroyer escorts, experiencing the vicious coastal war the British had been fighting for four years. The Americans' opposition consisted of German *M*-class minesweepers—capable vessels used as corvettes—and a flotilla of armed trawlers.

On 11–12 August the American destroyer escort *Borum* supporting *PT500* and *PT502* engaged two ships of the 24th German Minesweeper Flotilla off La Corbiere on the southwest coast of Jersey. Following an unsuccessful torpedo attack, heavy gunfire chased the Americans off and damaged two boats. On the night of 13–14 August the *Borum*, the British destroyers *Onslaught* and *Saumarez*, *PT505*, *PT498*, and two British MTBs engaged the large minesweepers *M412*, *M432*, *M442*, and *M452* (all 776 tons, 17 knots, one 4.1-inch gun), which were escorting a merchant vessel off St. Peter Port, Guernsey. *Borum* vectored the PTs toward the German ships. Under heavy fire, the PTs each launched two torpedoes from 1,500 yards, but they missed and the PTs retired undamaged. St. Malo fell to the American Army on 18 August. After that, the German navy kept largely to port, and the U.S. Navy discontinued offensive operations, although patrols using smaller warships like sub chasers and patrol boats continued.

In the Mediterranean Germany held the coastline from the Franco-Spanish border to the stalemated Italian front line south of Rome from October 1943 to June 1944. The German navy's "capital ships" in the area consisted of captured torpedo boats and destroyers, which, combined with a fleet of corvettes, MTBs, barges, gunboats, and armed trawlers, protected a brisk coastal convoy traffic and engaged in offensive missions such as shore bombardment and mining. In general the Allies relied on MTBs, motor gunboats (MGBs), and armed landing craft to harass this traffic and used their larger warships to guard the beachheads and escort shipping. Between June 1944 and August 1944 the German-held shoreline contracted drastically when the Allies finally broke through central Italy to the Gothic Line in the north and invaded southern France. During this summertime operation, U.S. destroyers tangled with German surface units larger than coastal craft.

Early on the morning of 15 August the American destroyer *Somers*, skippered by Cdr. W.C. Hughes, patrolled south of Île du Levant in support of a raiding group on the left flank of the Anvil invasion of southern France, which was scheduled to begin at 0830 that morning. At 0347 two pips appeared on *Somers's* radar screen. Hughes tracked these contacts until it seemed their course would threaten the transports. At 0440, after the ships ignored his challenge, Hughes passed astern and opened fire from 4,750 yards. The intruders were German warships: the *UJ6081* (728 tons, 18 knots, one 3.9-inch gun, two 17.7-inch torpedoes), which was formerly the Italian corvette *Camoscio*, and the *SG21* (917 tons, 20 knots, two 4.1-inch guns) a former French aviso.

The *Somers* belted the *SG21* with her opening salvos and left her ablaze with "numerous explosions forward and aft as ammunition began exploding."[2] The American destroyer then chased down the outgunned *UJ6081* and left her dead in the water by 0520. The *UJ6081* rolled over and sank at 0722. The *SG21* burned and periodically erupted with small explosions until after dawn. The *Somers* expended only 270 rounds and suffered no casualties during this brief, conclusive, and well-fought action.

Two nights later a Naval Special Operations Force consisting of the American destroyer *Endicott*, two British river gunboats, the *Aphis* and *Scarab*, two PT boats, and four motor launches appeared off La Ciotat, halfway between Marseilles and Toulon, to feint a landing. During this operation the corvette *UJ6082*, the ex-Italian *Antilope* and sister to the *UJ6081*, and the large sub chaser *UJ6073* (1,710 GRT, one 3.5-inch gun), formerly the Khedive of Egypt's motor yacht *Nimet Allah*, attacked a small craft at 0545, prompting urgent calls for help. The British gunboats arrived at 0555 to find themselves outmatched and were chased southeast by the aggressive corvettes.

The *Endicott*, skippered by the PT veteran Cdr. John D. Bulkley came on the scene at 0620. She engaged the *UJ6073*, which was the much larger of the two available targets, even though jammed breech blocks had disabled three of the *Endicott*'s four mounts. In the first minutes 2 five-inch shells detonated in the ex-yacht's engine room, and the *UJ6073* quickly lost way. The Germans return fire fell close. One shell penetrated the *Endicott* and caused minor flooding but failed to explode. Using leather mallets to open and close the breech blocks, the *Endicott* continued to close range; at no time was she able to fire a full broadside using all four guns.

The *UJ6073*, listing heavily to port, began to explode at 0648, but the *UJ6082* launched two torpedoes, forcing the *Endicott* to evade. The destroyer replied with two torpedoes of her own. When the *UJ6082* combed the America torpedoes' tracks, she masked her main battery. This allowed the *Endicott* to close to 1,500 yards. At 0702 Bulkey's 20-mm and 40-mm guns raked the corvette's deck. The *UJ6082* gamely returned fire for a few minutes until five-inch rounds exploded near her stack and bridge. The *UJ6082*'s crew started abandoning ship at 0717, and the *Endicott* ceased firing. The *UJ6073* sank at 0709. The *UJ6082* finally capsized at 0830.

In the following weeks the Allies overran southern France, but their resources did not permit an offensive over the Alpine passes into the Italian Po Valley. For this reason, the front line froze east of Monaco along the Franco-Italian border, preserving Germany's enclave on the Ligurian Sea for another eight months.

In October the Allies established a naval Flank Force, Mediterranean that was made up largely of French units and under French command to guard the western portions of this enclave. British and American destroyers and coastal craft based out of Livorno patrolled the eastern flank. These naval forces supported Allied ground units, attacked German shipping, and were harassed in their turn by German coastal and small battle units. Throughout this campaign, German torpedo boats remained remarkably active, as when they shelled Allied positions near the Arno estuary on the night of 30–31 August.

On the evening of 1 October 1944, as the American destroyer *Gleaves* skippered by Cdr. W.M. Klee patrolled off San Remo, Italy, news arrived that Allied aircraft had bombed three vessels off Porta Maurizio further up the coast. Klee decided to head toward Imperia to investigate.

That same evening the *TA24* and *TA29* (both 1,110 tons, 28 knots, two 3.9-inch guns, six 17.7-inch torpedoes), and *TA32* (2,000 tons, 31 knots, four 4.1-inch guns, three 21-inch torpedoes) sailed from Genoa toward San Remo to lay a minefield. The *TA29* and *TA32* were loaded with ninety-eight mines. The German force had just passed Imperia when, at 2313, lookouts spotted a large warship about 11,000 yards southwest. This was the *Gleaves*, which was also tracking the Germans. At 2319 the American destroyer turned parallel, rang up twenty knots, and opened fire.

The first salvo fell only fifty yards from the *TA24*. The Germans maneuvered as the next American salvo sent geysers spouting near the *TA29*. At 2324 the German commander ordered a simultaneous turn to starboard. The *TA29*, her rudder control affected by her cargo of mines, rammed the *TA24*. The German ships managed to separate and retreated toward Genoa, opening fire against the American destroyer at 0235. Klee assumed shore batteries were engaging, and when his radar detected two aircraft only three miles away at 2339, Klee had the *Gleaves* make smoke and head west. The gunfire continued until 2345. At 2348 the *Gleaves* secured from general quarters after expending eighty rounds and eight star shells.

The German torpedo boats made port by 0315. They thought they had fought a French light cruiser. In his report Klee concluded he had attacked three merchant ships. He observed two of them explode while under fire and believed them sunk or seriously damaged. Much more exciting was the encounter later that night with Axis small battle units. The big destroyer had some narrow escapes, sank several boats, and captured an enemy vessel. For this, the commanders of Cruiser Division 8 and the Eight Fleet recommended a slew of medals for the *Gleaves*'s crew.

The German navy retained a sting. In the most unlikely of combat zones, far behind the front line, the final surface action of the war involving the German and U.S. navies occurred on the night of March 8, 1945, when a small German force consisting of the *M412*, *M432*, *M442*, *M452* (all 776 tons, 17 knots, one 4.1-inch gun), and nine other vessels sailed from St. Hélier in the Channel Islands to conduct a commando strike against the mainland port of Granville. En route they encountered the U.S. sub chaser *PC564* (463 tons, 19 knots, one 3-inch gun, one 40-mm gun, two 20-mm guns) and severely damaged her, killing fourteen men and wounding eleven. With this defeat, the product of complacency, the U.S. Navy heightened its vigilance but the Germans did not venture out again before the European war ended two months later.

CHAPTER 12

The Battles of Leyte Gulf, October 1944

We were prepared to fight to the last man, but we wanted to die gloriously.
—Vice Admiral Koyanagi Tomiji

After being defeated in the Battle of the Philippine Sea, the Japanese fleet spent two weeks in home waters adding radar and more anti-aircraft guns. Then the battle line returned to Lingga Roads near Singapore while the carriers remained to flesh out their shattered air groups with a fresh crop of barely trained pilots. The battle fleet spent the summer practicing tactics, "including swift interception, gunnery, long-range torpedo firing—with emphasis still on night battle. It was felt that with radar available to both sides, Japan's pre-radar advantage had been restored."[1]

Japanese commanders anticipated that the Americans would strike the Philippines in November, but they devised four plans to cover all eventualities: *Sho-Ichi-Go* to repel an invasion of the Philippines, *Sho-Ni-Go* to protect Formosa or the Ryukyu Islands, *Sho-San-Go* to guard Japan, and *Sho-Yon-Go* to protect Hokkaido and the Kuriles in the unlikely event that these proved to be the enemy's target. The *Sho* plans were intended to get the big guns of the navy's battleships and cruisers—so carefully preserved through nearly three years of warfare—where they could do decisive damage. This was something the Imperial Japanese Navy had not accomplished since Guadalcanal.[2]

American planners faced the much happier problem of determining where and when to apply massive offensive force. King favored an invasion of Formosa, while MacArthur insisted upon a push to recapture the Philippines. However, the Joint Chiefs of Staff postponed making a decision until well into September. Washington finally declared that MacArthur could attack Leyte in late December. Then, when the Third Fleet encountered artificially light resistance in the Philippines during a mid-September raid, Admiral Halsey recommended an immediate thrust to the archipelago's heart; this would shorten the road to victory by two invasions and several months. The Joint Chiefs of Staff, emboldened by the ease of their recent victories, accepted this idea with little consideration.[3]

Setting a 20 October invasion date, American planners worried about Japan's ability to feed air reinforcements into the Philippines via Okinawa and Formosa. To forestall such traffic, Task Force 38 attacked Okinawa on 10 October, and Formosa two days later. Combined Fleet mistook Halsey's massive raid as a prelude to invasion and activated the aerial component of *Sho-Ni-Go*. The Air Battle of Formosa that followed cost the Japanese hundreds of aircraft; the Americans estimated 650, but the Japanese admitted to 330.[4] Imperial headquarters uncritically accepted the battle results claimed by its aviators and announced a great victory: "Twelve enemy ships—cruisers and above—had been sunk and another twenty-three enemy ships had been otherwise destroyed." While Ugaki cautioned that "we mustn't kid [ourselves] by exaggerating the results achieved," he still estimated Japanese counterattacks sank three carriers and three other ships.[5] Toyoda even dispatched Vice Admiral Shima Kiyohide's 5th Fleet to chase down Halsey's remnants. Actually, despite their supreme effort, Japanese aviators only crippled two cruisers and lightly damaged two carriers.

On 17 and 18 October the Seventh Fleet landed a U.S. Army Ranger battalion on Homonhan, Suluan, and Dinagat Islands outside of Leyte Gulf to destroy enemy installations in advance of the main operation. In response Toyoda activated the naval portion of *Sho-Ichi-Go*. This plan called for five forces to strike or distract the American invasion fleet. The composition of these five groups was as follows:

First Strike Force—Located at Lingga Roads and under the command of Vice Admiral Kurita, this force contained five battleships, ten heavy cruisers, two light cruisers, and fifteen destroyers.

Second Strike Force—Located at Lingga Roads and under the command of Vice Admiral Nishimura, this force was made up of two battleships, one heavy cruiser, and four destroyers.

Third Strike Force—Located in Japanese home waters and under the command of Vice Admiral Shima, this force contained two heavy cruisers, one light cruiser, and six destroyers.

Mobile Force—Located in Japanese home waters and under the command of Vice Admiral Ozawa, this force was made up of one aircraft carrier, three light carriers, two battleship/carriers, three light cruisers, and seven destroyers.

Transport Unit—Vice Admiral Sakonju Naomasa commanded this unit, which consisted of one heavy cruiser, one light cruiser, one destroyer, and four destroyer-transports.

Japan's armada steaming toward Leyte represented an overwhelming force by any standard, except one—the American Third and Seventh Fleets (see Table 12.1). Commanded by Vice Admiral Kinkaid, the Seventh Fleet had the task of transporting the U.S. Army's invasion force and seeing it safely ashore. It included old battleships and escort carriers generously supported by cruisers, destroyers, and a full complement of auxiliaries. Admiral Halsey's Third Fleet, consisting of four fast carrier task groups, had the less-straightforward mission of protecting the landing and, if the opportunity arose, taking offensive action against the Japanese fleet. Because of interservice tensions the invasion had no overall commander: Kinkaid reported to MacArthur and Halsey to Nimitz.

TABLE 12.1. FORCES COMMITTED DURING THE BATTLES OF LEYTE GULF

Type	Japanese	U.S. Seventh Fleet	U.S. Third Fleet	Ratio of Japanese Ships to the Total of U.S. Ships from the Seventh and Third Fleets
Battleships	9a	6	6	75%
Carriers	4	18	17	11%
Cruisers	21	11b	14	84%
Destroyer types	38	105c	57	23%
Total	72	140	94	31%

Note. These totals do not include vessels in the transport units or subtract losses suffered during the Japanese and Americans' approaches to Leyte.
a. The Japanese battleship count includes two hybrid battleship/carriers that did not carry aircraft.
b. Two Australian cruisers sailed with the Americans at Leyte, and these are included in this total.
c. Two Australian destroyers sailed with the Americans, and these are also counted here.

The First and Second Strike Forces sailed north and arrived at Brunei Bay on 20 October. Much to the disgust of Japan's warriors, Combined Fleet had decided to commit its battle line to sink transports, not other warships. However, "[d]isturbed at the idea of hurling our attack force in wherever the enemy attempted to land instead of using it in a decisive engagement," Kurita, like Halsey, wrangled permission to attack enemy carriers if the opportunity arose.[6] The plan required Kurita to sail north of Palawan Island, through the central Philippines, and then debouch into the Philippine Sea via San Bernardino Strait. Ozawa's carriers, meanwhile, carrying only 108 aircraft after their semitrained air crews had been squandered in the abortive battle for Formosa, would dazzle Halsey with their flight decks and lure the Third Fleet north, leaving Leyte Gulf unguarded. This would theoretically allow Kurita a free passage. Nishimura would take the direct route past Mindanao into Leyte Gulf via Surigao Strait. Shima's ships, coming from Japan, would follow Nishimura. Despite the emphasis on night combat training, these fleets would reunite on the morning of 25 October and ravage the American transports and auxiliaries hopefully crowding Leyte Gulf.

MAP 12.1. THE BATTLES OF LEYTE GULF: APPROACH TO BATTLE

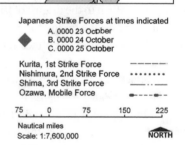
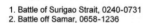

1. Battle of Surigao Strait, 0240-0731
2. Battle off Samar, 0658-1236
3. Battle off Cape Engaño, 1625-2059
4. Destruction of the *Nowaki*, 0054-0135 26 October

❶ General location of action
Black–U.S.-instigated
Gray–Japanese-instigated

◀ TF 38 Task Group locations 0800 24 October
and united 3rd Fleet 0000 25 October

Japanese Strike Forces at times indicated
◆ A. 0000 23 October
B. 0000 24 October
C. 0000 25 October

Kurita, 1st Strike Force   –––––––
Nishimura, 2nd Strike Force ● ● ● ● ● ● ●
Shima, 3rd Strike Force   –– ·· ––
Ozawa, Mobile Force   ●––––●–

75   0   75   150   225

Nautical miles
Scale: 1:7,600,000   **NORTH**

The fate of these forces in their approach to battle varied considerably. Ozawa steamed south on the afternoon of 20 October. He wanted to be found, and Halsey wanted to discover the flattops. Ironically, though, by midday on 24 October Ozawa's whereabouts remained a mystery to Task Force 38. Nishimura departed Brunei Bay at 1500 on 22 October. Task Group 38.4 scouts delivered one extreme-range air attack at 0918 on 24 October that lightly damaged the *Fuso* and *Shigure*.

After that, Nishimura continued unmolested all the way to Surigao Strait. Shima's force was likewise spotted but not attacked.

Kurita's strike force suffered a brutal transit. First the U.S. submarines *Darter* and *Dace* spied his long column of warships off Palawan at 0116 on 23 October. The subs sank the *Maya* and Kurita's flagship, *Atago*, forcing Kurita to swim for five minutes before he was hauled aboard a destroyer. They also severely damaged the *Takeo*. This thrust *Sentai* 1's Vice Admiral Ugaki into temporary command, and he generously detached two destroyers to escort the *Takeo* back to Brunei Bay.[7] Kurita transferred to the *Yamato*, and the fleet continued.

Kurita was recovering from dengue fever, and being dunked did nothing for his physical condition. The admiral had lost a portion of his staff along with his ship, and being forced to rub elbows on the *Yamato* bothered both Kurita and Ugaki.

Halsey now had Kurita's position fixed. He had sent Task Group 38.1 to Ulithi to refuel, but starting midmorning 24 October, Task Groups 38.2 and 38.4 swarmed the First Strike Force with air attacks. Task Group 38.3 was itself the object of Japanese air strikes from Luzon and lost the light carrier *Princeton*, the first fast carrier sunk since the *Hornet* in October 1942. This prevented Task Group 38.3, the most northerly group, from conducting searches that may have found Ozawa, and from adding its full strength against Kurita.

During five American raids the *Yamato* and *Nagato* absorbed two bombs each, and the *Nagato* lost turret number 4 and four secondary guns. The American flyers also lightly damaged the *Tone* and the destroyers *Kiyoshimo*, *Fujinami*, and *Uranami*. A torpedo-damaged shaft forced the *Myoko* to retreat. The super battleship *Musashi* represented Kurita's worse loss, however. After absorbing six torpedoes the *Musashi* dropped out of formation and eventually succumbed to twenty torpedoes and seventeen bomb hits.[8]

Meanwhile, a frustrated Ozawa, "convinced that the luring operation could only succeed if the enemy were given a physical demonstration of the proximity of his force," closed to 150 miles of Task Group 38.3 and launched a fifty-six plane strike.[9] Halsey finally located the Japanese carriers at 1730 and quickly made the fateful decision to sail north with all three task groups, leaving San Bernardino Strait, the narrow passage through which Kurita needed to sail, unguarded. In Halsey's eyes, "Third Fleet would not stand passively waiting around to see whether the battered enemy would venture through the strait. That would be like watching a rathole. There were ships to be hit that had not been hit. The carriers!"[10] Based on excited and exaggerated reports filed by his pilots, Halsey believed Kurita's force was too battered to constitute a serious threat. Even worse, he issued ambiguous orders that led Kinkaid, Nimitz, and King to all assume he had detached Vice Admiral Lee's battle line, Task Force 34, to cover the strait. Remarkably, Ozawa gauged Halsey's actions better than Halsey's fellow Americans.

Battle of Surigao Strait, 25 October 1944

By the morning of 24 October Kinkaid knew that at least two Japanese forces were steaming his way. Assuming Lee's Task Force 34 had the northern threat covered, Kinkaid focused on Surigao Strait as the point of attack. With his designated battle commander Rear Adm. Jesse Oldendorf, Kinkaid choreographed a massive ambush to greet the enemy. He stationed thirty-nine PT boats at intervals along the strait's southern approaches and into the Mindanao Sea and assigned six battleships, eight cruisers, and twenty-eight destroyers to patrol the upper strait and plug its northern exit. Kinkaid's chief of staff remembered, "We were not at all concerned as to the outcome of an encounter with the oncoming forces of the Jap Fleet. As a matter of fact we rather relished the idea of taking part in a major naval battle."[11]

Kinkaid's one worry was a shortage of ordnance. The Seventh Fleet had been bombarding Japanese positions on Leyte for four days, and some of the American destroyers had expended up to 80 percent of their five-inch ammunition. The number of AP rounds available aboard the battleships ranged from a low of 200 on the *West Virginia* to a high of 396 on the *Tennessee*. High-capacity (HC) stocks varied from seventy-eight on the *California* to 543 on the *Mississippi*. In total, the six battleships possessed 1,637 rounds of AP and 1,602 rounds of HC.

Nishimura, meanwhile, had some appreciation of what awaited him, having launched a floatplane to scout Leyte Gulf on the morning of 24 October. At 2030 hours he radioed Kurita his intention to charge into the gulf at 0400 hours and then sent *Mogami* and three destroyers ahead to scout the way. He arbitrarily advanced his planned time of arrival by three hours. Given the air attacks that had delayed Kurita, Nishimura's blow against the Americans would now be struck far too early to permit the joint action originally envisioned in the Japanese plan.

Nishimura's motives for scrapping the original timetable have inspired speculation. Kurita considered the *Fuso* and *Yamashiro* too old and too slow to operate with his force; this lent their independent employment the appearance of a decoy force much like Ozawa's carriers. Although such a mission was never stated, Nishimura may have taken it as implied. One Japanese author has written, "On this point I have interrogated admirals who were well acquainted with Nishimura. They were agreed that Nishimura had determined to push toward Leyte Gulf at all cost in order to lessen the pressure that [the] enemy could bring to bear on Kurita."[12]

While still deep in the Mindanao Sea, Nishimura's scouting group slipped past PT Section 1. At 2236 however, the American patrol torpedo boats spotted the Second Strike Force's main body as it passed Bohol Island (see Map 12.1). The *Shigure* damaged *PT152* and *PT130*, but the section reported their sighting, and word of the Japanese approach reached Oldendorf two hours later. Section 3 sighted the

TABLE 12.2. FORCES ENGAGED IN THE BATTLE OF SURIGAO STRAIT

Type of Ship	Year Launched	Displacement, Full Load	Max. Speed (knots)	Guns (number by inch/ caliber)	Torpedoes (number of tubes by diameter in inches)	Damage
American (Rear Adm. J. Oldendorf) BATTLE LINE American Battleship Division 1 (Rear Adm. R.G. Weyler)						
Mississippi (F)	BB	1917	36,157	21	12 x 14/50 & 6 x 5/51		
West Virginia	BB	1921	40,396	21	8 x 16/45 & 16 x 5/38		
Maryland	BB	1920	40,350	21	8 x 16/45 & 12 x 5/25		
American Battleship Division 2 (Rear Adm. T.E. Chandler)						
Tennessee (F)	BB	1919	40,354	20	12 x 14/50 & 16 x 5/38		
California	BB	1919	40,354	20	12 x 14/50 & 16 x 5/38		
Pennsylvania	BB	1915	38,659	22	12 x 14/45 & 16 x 5/38		
American Destroyer Squadron X-ray (Cdr. M.H. Hubbard)						
Claxton (F)	DD	1943	2,924	38	5 x 5/38	10 x 21	
Cony	DD	1943	2,924	38	5 x 5/38	10 x 21	
Thorn	DD	1943	2,924	38	5 x 5/38	10 x 21	
Aulick	DD	1943	2,924	38	5 x 5/38	10 x 21	
Sigourney	DD	1943	2,924	38	5 x 5/38	10 x 21	
Welles	DD	1943	2,924	38	5 x 5/38	10 x 21	

LEFT (EAST) FLANK							
American Cruiser Division 4, (Oldendorf)							
Louisville (F)	CA	1930	13,910	32	9 x 8/55 & 8 x 5/25		
Portland	CA	1932	15,002	32	9 x 8/55 & 8 x 5/25		
Minneapolis	CA	1933	13,719	32	9 x 8/55 & 8 x 5/25		
American Cruiser Division 12 (Rear Adm. R.W. Hayler)							
Denver	CL	1942	14,144	32	12 x 6/47 & 12 x 5/38		
Columbia	CL	1941	14,144	32	12 x 6/47 & 12 x 5/38		
American Destroyer Squadron 56 (Capt. R.M. Smoot)							
Newcomb (F)	DD	1943	2,924	38	5 x 5/38	10 x 21	
Albert W. Grant	DD	1943	2,924	38	5 x 5/38	10 x 21	D4
Richard P. Leary	DD	1943	2,924	38	5 x 5/38	10 x 21	
Robinson	DD	1943	2,924	38	5 x 5/38	10 x 21	
Halford	DD	1943	2,924	38	5 x 5/38	10 x 21	
Bryant	DD	1943	2,924	38	5 x 5/38	10 x 21	
Heywood L. Edwards	DD	1943	2,924	38	5 x 5/38	10 x 21	
Bennion	DD	1943	2,924	38	5 x 5/38	10 x 21	
Leutze	DD	1943	2,924	38	5 x 5/38	10 x 21	
RIGHT (WEST) FLANK							
American Cruiser Division 15 (Rear Adm. R.S. Berkey)							
Phoenix (F)	CL	1938	13,430	32	15 x 6/47 & 8 x 5/25		
Boise	CL	1936	13,430	32	15 x 6/47 & 8 x 5/25		
Shropshire (AU)	CA	1928	14,580	32	8 x 8/50 & 8 x 4/45	8 x 21	

American Destroyer Squadron 24 (Capt. K.M. McManes)								
Hutchins (F)	DD	1943	2,924	38	5 x 5/38	10 x 21	
Daly	DD	1943	2,924	38	5 x 5/38	10 x 21	
Bache	DD	1943	2,924	38	5 x 5/38	10 x 21	
Killen	DD	1943	2,924	38	5 x 5/38	10 x 21	
Beale	DD	1943	2,924	38	5 x 5/38	10 x 21	
Arunta (AU)	DD	1940	2,710	36	6 x 4.7/45	4 x 21	
PICKET GROUP **American Destroyer Squadron 54 (Capt. J.G. Coward)**								
Remey (F)	DD	1943	2,924	38	5 x 5/38	10 x 21	
McGowan	DD	1943	2,924	38	5 x 5/38	10 x 21	
Melvin	DD	1943	2,924	38	5 x 5/38	10 x 21	
McDermut	DD	1943	2,924	38	5 x 5/38	10 x 21	
Monssen	DD	1943	2,924	38	5 x 5/38	10 x 21	
SECOND STRIKE FORCE **Japanese Sentai 2 (Vice Admiral Nishimura Shoji)**								
Yamashiro	BB	1915	39,154	24	12 x 14/35 & 14 x 6/50		Sunk
Fuso	BB	1914	39,154	24	12 x 14/35 & 14 x 6/50		Sunk
Japanese Sentai 5 (Captain Toma Ryo)								
Mogami (F)	CA	1934	13,670	35	6 x 8/50 & 8 x 5/40	12 x 24	D4
Shigure	DD	1935	1,950	30	5 x 5/50	8 x 24	D2
Japanese Destroyer Division 4 (Captain Takahashi Kameshirou)								
Michishio (F)	DD	1941	2,635	35	4 x 5/50	8 x 24	Sunk
Asagumo	DD	1941	2,635	35	4 x 5/50	8 x 24	Sunk
Yamagumo	DD	1941	2,635	35	4 x 5/50	8 x 24	Sunk

THIRD STRIKE FORCE Japanese *Sentai* 21 (Vice Admiral Shima Kiyohide)							
Nachi (F)	CA	1927	14,743	33	10 x 8/50 & 8 x 5/40	16 x 24	D2
Ashigara	CA	1927	14,743	33	10 x 8/50 & 8 x 5/40	16 x 24	
Japanese Destroyer Squadron 1 (Rear Admiral Kimura Masatomi)							
Abukuma (F)	CL	1923	6,050	33	5 x 5.5/50 & 2 x 5/40	8 x 24	D4
Japanese Destroyer Division 7 (Commander Iwagami Juichi)							
Akebono (F)	DD	1930	2,389	34	4 x 5/50	9 x 24	
Ushio	DD	1930	2,389	34	4 x 5/50	9 x 24	
Japanese Destroyer Division 18 (Captain Inoue Yoshio)							
Shiranuhi (F)	DD	1938	2,450	35	4 x 5/50	8 x 24	
Kasumi	DD	1937	2,330	34	4 x 5/50	8 x 24	
Japanese Destroyer Division 21 (Captain Ishii Hisashi)							
Wakaba (F)	DD	1934	2,066	33	4 x 5/50	8 x 24	
Hatsushimo	DD	1934	2,066	33	4 x 5/50	8 x 24	

AU—Australian, BB—battleship, CA—heavy cruiser, CL—light cruiser, D2—moderate damage (combat ability not significantly impaired), D4—major damage (combat and maneuvering ability significantly impaired or eliminated), DD—destroyer, F—flagship

Time: 0240–0731
Weather: Light northeasterly breeze, occasional squalls
Visibility: Moonset 0006, variable from excellent to poor
Sea state: Slight
Surprise: None
Mission: Americans-self defense; Japanese—beachhead attack

Mogami's group southwest of Limasawa Island at 2350. The Americans got two torpedoes into the water before searchlights and gunfire chased them off. Nishimura reunited his force ten miles southwest of Limasawa Island at 0040 for the run up the strait. The *Michishio* led, followed by the *Asagumo*. Forty-four hundred yards behind came the *Yamashiro*. The *Shigure* and *Yamagumo* flanked the battleship, and the *Fuso* and *Mogami* followed at 1,100-yard intervals.

PTs pestered the Japanese as they rounded Panaon Island, but the large warships easily brushed them aside. However, the PTs' reports of engaging the enemy permitted Oldendorf to track the Japanese ships' progress up the strait.

Intermittent visibility bothered Nishimura more than the PTs at this point. The moon had set in an overcast sky. Rain squalls periodically cut vision to less than 5,000 yards, and radar could barely indicate the shoreline. Despite these conditions the *Shigure*'s lookouts reported shapes 9,000 yards ahead at 0256. The distance was actually closer to 15,000 yards, and the contacts were the first layer of the American force waiting to greet Nishimura, Capt. Jesse G. Coward's Destroyer Squadron 54.

Coward, *Sterett*'s former skipper and a veteran of the First Battle of Guadalcanal, had turned south at 0230, leaving the *Mertz* and *McNair* behind in case the enemy tried to sneak east of Dinagat Island. The *Remey, McGowan,* and *Melvin*, under Coward's direct command, headed down the eastern side of the Strait, and Cdr. Richard H. Phillips led the *McDermut* and *Monssen* along the west shore. At 0240 scopes began to blossom with pips. Although Coward intended to hammer the enemy with a coordinated torpedo attack from two directions, he struggled with ambiguous radar returns and thus approached Nishimura from near mid-channel, giving his ships a difficult bow-on shot. Then, at 0258, as one of the *Melvin*'s crew remembered, "A blueish light shot through the darkness in a long arc, swept off the leading destroyer and steadied on our black-and-gray outline for 45 seconds."[13]

Under searchlight illumination, each second seemed like ten, but, in fact, the *Yamashiro*'s initial sweep—made in response to the *Shigure*'s report—lasted thirty seconds and revealed nothing as the Americans remained beyond the light's range. Not knowing this, Coward authorized his captains to attack. The *Remey*'s intended target was the *Fuso*, but the range to the *Yamashiro* (12,000 yards) and the *Yamagumo*'s bearing were used as the principal references. Because of malfunctions the *Remey* discharged only eight torpedoes that ran astern of the *Yamagumo*. The *McGowan* launched a full salvo of ten at the *Fuso*, but she also confused her target's range with the *Yamashiro* and likewise missed astern. Moreover, the *McGowan*'s torpedo flash deflectors malfunctioned, and Japanese observers noticed the red flickers of light. The *Melvin* got both range and bearing correct and, although she miscalculated the *Fuso*'s speed, one of the *Melvin*'s nine torpedoes (one misfired) hit.

The *Yamashiro*'s searchlight snapped back on at 0301, and star shells burst overhead with a yellow radiance. Coward's ships immediately countermarched and belched a thick screen of funnel smoke. The *Yamashiro*'s first broadside fell 200 yards short of target, but each tightly bunched salvo splashed progressively closer. Japanese shells straddled the *Remey* at 0303 as the Americans destroyers zigzagged at flank speed and headed for the strait between Hibuson and Dinagat Islands.

The *Shigure*'s skipper, Commander Nishino Shigeru, was sure the enemy had not fired torpedoes. Perhaps Nishimura felt the same, because he continued on course. Or, as a torpedo expert, he may have calculated that the target angle and range made any hits unlikely. In either event, a series of explosions caused by the *Melvin*'s torpedo staggered the *Fuso* at 0308, and she sheered to starboard as her speed dropped rapidly. Nishimura, his attention focused ahead, missed this event. The *Fuso* apparently lost communications because she did not report her plight. The *Mogami*, which steered around the stricken battleship, likewise failed to report this catastrophe, perhaps assuming Nishimura must know.

Delayed by some tricky maneuvers required to navigate through the battle line, Phillips' two destroyers lagged six miles behind Coward's. Phillips continued south on the Leyte side, acquired the enemy on radar at 0256, and received Coward's target designations at 0258. Three minutes later Phillips overheard TBS chatter indicating Coward's attack had commenced. Only then did Philips realize the distance between the two sections made a simultaneous attack impossible; nonetheless, he pressed on, adjusting course to reach a proper firing position while hoping to confuse any enemy counterattacks. Shells began splashing around Phillips' ships at 0308.

At 0302, noting that the destroyer attacks seemed to be meeting little resistance, Rear Adm. Russell S. Berkey released Destroyer Squadron 24, under Captain McManes, ahead of the time originally planned by Oldendorf, to sally south along the Leyte shore behind Phillips.[14]

At 0310 ten torpedoes from each of Phillips' ships flew from their tubes. The range to the Japanese was 9,000 yards, and the angles to target were excellent, at 298 degrees and 290 degrees, respectively. It was at this time that the *Michishio's* Captain Takahashi Kameshirou ordered his division to assume battle position. Because the *Shigure* had already begun to pull into column, this only affected the *Yamagumo* on the starboard wing. Meanwhile, Phillips immediately turned to starboard. The Japanese searchlights blinked on again, and Japanese gunfire increased in intensity. Nishino recorded that "some of the ships opened fire on the new forces, but due to the poor visibility they were unable to sight the target very well; and although *Shigure* attempted to aim by radar, we could not differentiate between the ships and the land, we just got one merged reaction on the screen. We fired regardless."[15] Then Phillips encountered three PT boats. When he heard one asking permission to attack, he jumped on the PT net to squelch that plan and retreated close inshore.

Faced by Phillips' torpedo attack Nishimura ordered emergency simultaneous ship turns of 90 degrees to starboard. But he came back north just ninety seconds later. Rather than take his ships out of danger, however, Nishimura's maneuvering offset the miscalculations of speed and bearing made by Phillips' destroyers. With "stunning suddenness," three torpedoes slammed into the *Yamagumo*, and she immediately exploded in a blast seen twenty miles north. A fourth torpedo crippled the *Michishio*, and a fifth sheered off the *Asagumo's* bow.[16] The *McDermut* was the agent of this, the most effective salvo fired by an American destroyer during the war. In addition, one of the *Monssen's* torpedoes hit the *Yamashiro*, temporarily slowing the old Japanese battleship.

Shima's Third Strike Force, advancing about forty miles astern of Nishimura, possessed little intelligence of the situation. Indeed, Shima originally believed he would force Surigao Strait alone and only learned of Nishimura's involvement while en route. After correcting a dead reckoning error and nearly running into Panaon Island, Shima prepared to lead his ships into the Strait.

Squadron 54's effective foray damaged all but two of Nishimura's ships, and more was coming. McManes, who had suffered the frustration of a long stern chase at the Battle of Biak, modified his orders to attack close inshore off the enemy's port beam, and devised the aggressive notion of sailing past Nishimura to cut off the Japanese line of retreat. To carry out this ad hoc plan, McManes divided Squadron 24, taking the *Hutchins, Daly,* and *Bache* with him and sending HMAS *Arunta*, skippered by Commander A.E. Buchanan, across the strait with the *Killen* and *Beale* to strike from the eastern side.

McManes intended to launch a scissors attack from the Japanese port quarter and starboard bow. However, Buchanan did not consider sailing across the enemy's nose prudent and instead followed McManes to a favorable position off the enemy's port bow.[17] At 0323 the *Arunta* dispatched four torpedoes toward the *Shigure* from a range of 6,500 yards. The Australian destroyer then turned north making smoke. The *Killen* followed the *Arunta*'s lead, launching five torpedoes at the *Yamashiro* at 0324 from a range of 8,700 yards. Finally, the *Beale* flung five torpedoes toward the *Shigure* from 6,800 yards. At 0324 the *Shigure* came about, and every torpedo aimed at her ran wide. At 0328 the *Killen* pitched two more torpedoes at the *Yamashiro*. At 0331 the Japanese illuminated and opened fire.

The *Shigure* headed south until 0330, passing the *Yamashiro*, which she believed was the *Fuso*, and then the *Mogami* three minutes later. Nishino was concerned as to *Yamashiro*'s whereabouts and sought orders. Then he reversed course again. These maneuvers confused the radar picture and enhanced the *Shigure*'s security. While this was happening, Shima's ships had advanced into the lower strait. At 0325, a torpedo fired by *PT137* crippled the *Abukuma*. Leaving the cruiser to fend for herself, Shima continued north.

On the *Yamashiro*'s lofty bridge Nishimura reported his view of the action at 0330 with a dispatch radioed to Kurita and Shima: "Enemy destroyers and torpedo boats present on both sides of the northern entrance to Surigao Strait. Two of our destroyers torpedoed and drifting. The *Yamashiro* sustained one torpedo hit but no impediment to battle cruising." The vice admiral clearly remained ignorant of the *Fuso*'s and the *Yamagumo*'s fates.

Buchanan's ships endured a hot time during their retreat. At this point in the battle, Nishimura's flagship was only 12,000 yards east southeast of the *Arunta*, and Japanese broadsides straddled both the *Beale* and the *Arunta*. Then, at 0334 one torpedo from the *Killen*'s first salvo jolted the *Yamashiro*, temporarily cutting the battleship's speed to five knots.

Just before Nishimura issued his battle report, the *Hutchins*, McManes' flagship, came abeam of the enemy. At 0329, hearing Buchanan's torpedoes were away and believing he had obtained a good attack position, McManes broadcast, "Coming left to north, fire your fish when you wish."[18] The *Hutchins* then launched a half-salvo at the *Shigure* from a range of 8,200 yards. The *Hutchins* continued her wide turn and by 0333 was pointed south once again.

McManes' subordinate destroyers followed their leader's evolutions with difficulty and suffered extra distractions when the *Daly* reported two wakes, probably from torpedoes loosed by the *Asagumo*, crossing her bow. The *Daly*, on course north by northwest, uncorked a half-salvo against the *Mogami* at 0335 from a range of 10,700 yards. The *Bache* targeted the *Shigure* a minute later from a range of 10,200 yards. These were all long shots made at low speed settings, and all fifteen of these American torpedoes missed. Both destroyers then turned south to follow their flagship, which had drawn 4,400 yards ahead of the *Daly*.

Confused by the *Shigure*'s temporary turn about and McManes' plunge south ahead of schedule, Oldendorf worried that the enemy might be retiring, and he urgently queried Coward and McManes about this. Unable to visualize the situation, he concluded another destroyer squadron needed to attack, and he duly ordered Capt. Roland M. Smoot's Destroyer Squadron 56 to get the big boys at 0335.

As Oldendorf worried, McManes instigated a gunnery action. At 0341 the *Hutchins* turned northeast and engaged the *Asagumo* from 12,000 yards while the *Daly* and *Bache* ganged up on the *Michishio*. Buchanan reversed course at 0341 to lend a hand. McManes' ships reported many explosions and three torpedo hits. In fact, they only added to the *Michishio*'s misery. The *Yamashiro* and *Asagumo* answered this attack, but, while their shells splashed nearby, none connected.

At 0344 three explosions ripped the night, followed by a single blast that overpowered them all. Twenty-five miles north observers aboard the *Mississippi* reported "flames reaching above the mastheads."[19] Standing on the *Nachi*'s bridge far to the south, Vice Admiral Shima saw "a blinding blossom of light that seemed to fill the entire strait."[20] Apparently, flames burning uncontrolled had penetrated the *Fuso*'s vitals and detonated a magazine. The ship broke into two sections, both fiercely ablaze, and continued drifting on the racing current.

At 0349 Berkey ordered McManes to retire to clear the line of fire. At this point the *Hutchins* was heading northeast and tracking the *Asagumo*. The *Daly* and *Bache* remained 5,000 yards farther south, pounding the hapless *Michishio*. The *Hutchins* shot her last five torpedoes at the *Asagumo* from a range of 6,200 yards. These missed their intended target, but at least one plowed into the *Michishio*. She exploded in a blast observed by Kinkaid twenty miles north.

At 0350 the *Yamashiro* steamed north northeast at fifteen knots. She had suffered two torpedo hits but no gunnery damage. The *Shigure* kept pace a thousand yards off her starboard quarter, and the *Mogami* followed several thousand yards south. Racing north at twenty-eight knots, Vice Admiral Shima had now entered the strait. He then spotted the *Fuso*'s two halves off his starboard bow, a sight about which he later remarked, "Although we knew they were Japanese vessels on fire we did not bother with them, just progressed."[21] In fact, he assumed one wreck was the *Fuso* and the other was the *Yamashiro*. These were hardly encouraging thoughts.

Smoot's nine ships, meanwhile, steered south in three sections. He planned a coordinated torpedo attack with Section 1—the *Newcomb, Richard P. Leary*, and *Albert W. Grant*—striking the enemy's starboard bow; Section 2—the *Bryant, Halford*, and *Robinson*—hitting from the east flank; and Section 3—the *Bennion, Leutze*, and *Heywood L. Edwards*—striking from the west flank.

Oldendorf's Left Flank cruisers loitered at five knots back and forth across the top of the strait, 3,000 yards south of the battleships. The rear admiral studied the plots and noted Nishimura's continued advance at an estimated sixteen knots. By this point the range to the enemy from his flagship, the *Louisville*, had dropped to roughly 16,000 yards. Although he would have preferred to wait for Smoot to complete his attack, Oldendorf ordered his cruisers to open fire at 0351. The *Louisville*'s guns erupted immediately, blinding Oldendorf, who occupied the flag bridge. The *Minneapolis, Denver*, and *Columbia* promptly followed. On the right flank the *Boise* took this as implied permission to join the fray, as did the *Phoenix* a few moments later. The Left Flank's *Portland* did not fire until 0352. The Right Flank's HMAS *Shropshire*'s fire control could not acquire targets beyond 15,500 yards, so the Australian ship was forced to wait.

From the *McDermut*'s perspective the bombardment seemed quite a sight: "Crimson streaks of light flash[ed] across the sky from north to south like meteors. . . . A throaty rumble like distant thunder felt more than heard rolled in from the north."[22] As the cruisers lit the night, the *Hutchins* continued to pump shells into the *Yamashiro* until 0352, when McManus' flagship turned northwest and engaged the *Mogami*, which was 6,500 yards away. The *Bache* and *Daly*, judging the *Michishio* finished, also targeted the *Mogami*. By not seeking the shoreline as ordered, however, Squadron 24 created problems for the several CICs tracking them as enemy ships.

At 0353 the *West Virginia*'s giant rifles thundered into action, sending 2,240-pound sixteen-inch shells in an arching flight of 11.25 miles toward the *Yamashiro*. It had been nearly two years since battleships had exchanged salvos in the Pacific and ten months since the last capital ship duel in European waters. Ironically, five of the six American battleships present had been sunk or damaged at Pearl Harbor. The American battle line proceeded east with the *West Virginia* in front and bearing 12,000 yards north northwest of Hibuson Island. Then came the *Maryland, Mississippi, Tennessee, California*, and *Pennsylvania*. Three ships, the *West Virginia*,

Tennessee, and *California,* had the new Mark VIII radar fire control systems, while the others employed the older, less accurate Mark III.

The heavies had watched the enemy approach on radar for half an hour. They had also witnessed three major explosions down the strait, and they worried the battle would end before their opportunity to participate arrived. Oldendorf had originally suggested the battleships maintain a speed of five knots. However, such large vessels were sluggish at low speed, and Rear Adm. R.G. Weyler, the battleship commander, ordered fifteen knots so as to be better able to comb the tracks of any enemy torpedoes that might appear.

The first problem to befall the American battle line arose even before five of the six battleships had opened fire. At 0354 the *Mississippi* informed Weyler that her forward turrets were trained too far aft to bear. In reply, Weyler ordered simultaneous turns thirty degrees to starboard to improve the bearing and close range. In fact, the *Mississippi's* turrets were in director control. They had "the best firing solution ever seen" by the plotting room officer when Weyler ordered her to switch targets and "take the big one," according to one of the *Mississippi's* officers. Her director control radar could not pinpoint this target and, in the course of sweeping back and forth, the turrets followed. At one point the gunnery officer on the bridge received the report that the forward turrets were back against their stops and could not train any further aft. Consequently, he asked the captain to change course to bring the turrets to bear. The *Mississippi's* track chart confirms this change of course was unnecessary, at least at the time.[23]

The other battleships opened fire one by one as they settled on targets. The presence of Squadrons 24 and 56 complicated the process, however. At 0353 the *California* warned, "Believe those three little ones out in front are friendly trying to get over to the shore line."[24] She engaged at 0355 from 20,400 yards in any event, and the *Tennessee* did likewise a minute later. Both U.S. battleships targeted the *Yamashiro.* The *Maryland* started shooting at 0359, ranging on the geysers thrown up by the shells of the other ships. The *Mississippi's* and *Pennsylvania's* Mark III directors fumbled for a solution, and their guns remained silent.

As the first shells from the American battle line began rocketing overhead, Smoot's ships accelerated to twenty-five knots. His center section had fallen slightly behind while maneuvering around Oldendorf's cruisers. Section 2 on the east side, however, enjoyed an approach to the Japanese that was nearly free of interference, and each destroyer fired five torpedoes between 0354 and 0359 at ranges between 8,400 and 9,000 yards. The *Halford* sent her fish swimming at medium speed and a depth of six feet. The selected target had stopped. Unsure if it was a cruiser or battleship, the *Halford* nonetheless claimed several hits. In fact, all the torpedoes fired by this section missed due to a combination of long range and bad angles. Moreover, the *Bryant's* captain misunderstood orders and fired early. The Japanese barrage intensified, forcing their withdrawal west of Hibuson Island, rather than east as intended.

Shells began splashing near the *Yamashiro* at 0352. Observers aboard the American destroyers and the *Shigure* and *Mogami* witnessed the Japanese battleship taking terrific punishment. Nishimura queried the *Fuso* about her speed and hoped for support on the basis of a message from the *Shigure* that indicated the destroyer was following the *Fuso*; Nishino still had the two ships confused. The *Fuso* did not answer, of course, and at 0356 the *Yamashiro*'s bow swung west as her heavy guns roared back. The *Shropshire* saw 2 fourteen-inch shells splash short and another four fly close overhead. According to *Shropshire*'s crewmen, the Japanese shells passed through the rigging, and the "sound of rushing air was not only dramatic but downright frightening."[25] The *Columbia*, plainly silhouetted by the battleships' gun flashes, "observed large caliber shells falling close aboard the stern of the ship" beginning at 0359.[26] She counted fourteen heavy salvos, five of which straddled. The *Minneapolis* and *Denver* also reported straddles.

The *Mogami*, meanwhile, turned to port at 0353. Her radar was not returning any worthwhile information, so her skipper, Captain Toma Ryo, decided to aim torpedoes at the twinkling flashes of the enemy line. By this point, however, McManes' three destroyers had begun hitting the *Mogami* from astern, and by 0356 the Americans' gunfire had ignited several blazes on the Japanese ship. Toma flashed a recognition signal, which instigated more gunfire. With the enemy now ahead of him and behind him, and the flagship burning from stem to stern, Toma tacked south, increased speed, and began making smoke. At 0401 the *Mogami* ejected four Long Lances on a long run north.

Then, observing that the "big one" was getting plenty of attention, the *Portland*, which was the only ship in the U.S. battle line to distribute fire, ranged in on the Japanese cruiser. At 0402 a pair of eight-inch shells slammed into the *Mogami*'s bridge and slaughtered Toma and his officers. More hits disabled all but one of the *Mogami*'s engines and the steering mechanism. She was out of control, burning, and losing speed when, at 0404, all fire against her suddenly ceased.

The *Shigure*'s radar signature was too small to draw attention, but being only a thousand yards off the *Yamashiro*'s starboard beam, numerous near misses and an eight-inch hit rocked her and concussions damaged her gyrocompass and radio. Nishino endured a few minutes of this hell before hastening south. Although the Left Flank cruisers lay only 12,000 yards ahead, he did not fire torpedoes.

Smoot's Section 3, attacking from the Leyte side, faced heavier counterfire during their approach and consequently began launching long-range half-salvos of torpedoes at the *Shigure* and *Yamashiro* between 0357 and 0359. Of these fifteen torpedoes, one from the *Bennion* may have hit the *Yamashiro*. Smoot's center section pressed in the closest. The *Newcomb* began launching a half-salvo at

0404 from 6,900 yards as she turned west. The *Richard P. Leary*, which had fallen behind, experienced two misfires and only discharged three torpedoes. The *Albert P. Grant* hurled five torpedoes. All of Section 3's ships had their fish away within a minute of each other.

The *Newcomb* achieved one hit on the *Yamashiro*, and possibly two if the *Bennion* missed. The others ran errant, largely because the forest of geysers surrounding the *Yamashiro* confused American fire control radars. Moreover, the *Yamashiro's* secondary batteries hammered away at the onrushing destroyers. As the *Albert W. Grant* turned, the *Louisville's* eager five-inch gunners likewise threw salvos her way. Fortunately, all of the friendly fire missed the *Albert W. Grant*.

At 0402 Oldendorf suggested that the American battleships alter course to west, which Weyler duly ordered. However, the *California* misunderstood the order to turn 150 degrees to starboard as an order to turn 15 degrees. The *Mississippi's* officer of the deck recalled, "I walked out to the starboard wing of the bridge to check the other ships' movements. At this point I received my biggest thrill of the night because the *California*, which originally had been astern of us . . . was cutting across our bow." The two ships missed each other by the width of a "coat of paint."[27] The *California* discharged two more salvos before she corrected her error and fell in behind the *Tennessee* at 0407, blocking the *Tennessee's* and *Mississippi's* lines of fire.

At 0405 a torpedo, probably fired by the *Bennion* at 0359, struck the *Yamashiro*. Nonetheless, providing a remarkable contrast to her sister, the *Yamashiro* worked back up to twelve knots. Fires smoldered along her length, punctuated by periodic explosions, but she fought back, straddling the *Denver* and *Minneapolis* at 0406 and hitting the *Albert W. Grant*. Just then a six-inch shell fired by the *Denver* walloped the *Albert W. Grant* from the other side, disabling her aft mounts. More shells followed within a minute, and at 0408 the *Albert W. Grant* expended her last torpedoes lest she sink with weapons in her tubes. Smoot radioed Oldendorf that the battle line had his squadron under fire.

At 0409 Oldendorf ordered the battleships to cease firing. During sixteen minutes the *West Virginia* had expended ninety-three main battery rounds, and the *Tennessee* had fired sixty-nine. The *California* had hurled sixty-three, and the *Maryland* forty-eight. The *Mississippi* finally found a target and discharged the final salvo of nine rounds at a range of nearly 20,000 yards. The *Pennsylvania*, much to her crew's frustration, never fired at all.

As the big guns fell silent, the *Yamashiro* turned south, and it seemed she might escape. Then one of the *Newcomb's* torpedoes detonated against the old ship's hull. Somehow, the *Yamashiro* increased speed to sixteen knots, but she capsized at 0419 and sank rapidly with few survivors. On the American side, only the *Albert W. Grant* suffered damage, taking twenty-two hits, the majority from the *Denver*. *Albert W. Grant*'s ship's history related that "Fires broke out, and the ship lost steering control and all power. Thirty-eight men were killed and 104 were wounded."[28] The *Newcomb* eventually towed the crippled destroyer out of danger. She returned to service in March 1945.

At 0413 the *Richard P. Leary* spotted the torpedoes the *Mogami* had launched twelve minutes before, and Weyler, his fears seemingly realized, ordered the *Mississippi*, *Maryland*, and *West Virginia* to turn north. Rear Adm. T.E. Chandler's division, still confused by the *California*'s failure to maintain formation, continued on course. At 0419 Oldendorf finally radioed permission to reengage, but all targets had vanished.

During this action Shima continued north at high speed, his cruisers preceding the destroyers. He could hear the rumble of gunfire, but he saw only flashes diffused by smoke. Then, a sudden silence fell. Five minutes later, the *Shigure* emerged from the gloom. Nishino blinkered a challenge and exchanged calls with the *Nachi*. He reported steering problems and continued south. Then the *Nachi*'s radar indicated a contact 13,000 yards north. Shima immediately ordered *Sentai* 21 to turn east and prepare to fire torpedoes as Destroyer Division 18 passed and continued north.

While the Third Strike Force was engrossed in this process, the *Mogami* appeared, heavily on fire. Shima steered to avoid this apparition, assuming she was dead in the water. At 0427 sixteen Long Lances plopped into the strait to run north, several ending up on Hibuson Island. Meanwhile, the *Mogami*, inexpertly helmed by her chief quartermaster, crept south. By the time Shima realized the *Mogami* had headway it was too late. The *Mogami* rammed the *Nachi* at 0430, knocking a large hole in the *Nachi*'s bow and causing flooding and a loss of speed. Shima immediately steered south at five knots to assess the situation and decided, based upon the *Nachi*'s damage and the condition of Nishimura's survivors, to abort his mission. He signaled, "This force has concluded its attack and is retiring from the battle area to plan subsequent action."[29]

Destroyer Division 18 could see Hibuson Island through breaks in the smoke when they turned east at 0430 trying to find the contacts Shima had reported. But it seemed the entire American fleet had vanished. At 0435 the Japanese destroyers received the admiral's order to retire and complied with alacrity. Their torpedoes remained in their tubes. Far to the south, the *Asagumo* had shored up her bow and at 0445 she turned north to follow Shima into action.[30]

Oldendorf, meanwhile, had received reports from his PTs that a second enemy group was penetrating the strait, and the *Denver*'s radar showed three large contacts fourteen to seventeen miles south. At 0432 the American commander ordered a torpedo charge by his last six destroyers, Division X-Ray, which had been screening the battleships. A minute later, he ordered the Left Flank cruisers to form up and start south as well. However, it took nearly twenty minutes to get started. Oldendorf then directed Division 56, less the *Newcomb* and *Albert W. Grant*, to fall in. Division X-Ray, an improvised unit with an inexperienced commander, did not clear the battleships until after 0500, and even then the *Thorn* and *Sigourney* trailed far behind. Finally, Berkey decided to take his cruisers down the strait to support Oldendorf, if needed. Weyler thus found his battleships alone.

As the Americans slowly sorted themselves out, Shima's ships scurried south at eighteen knots. He ordered Nishimura's survivors to follow, but the *Mogami* could only manage fifteen knots, and by 0530 she trailed 3,000 yards off the *Ashigara's* starboard quarter. The *Asagumo* lagged off Shima's port quarter by 6,000 yards, and the *Shigure* had retreated independently ahead of *Nachi*.

The sky was beginning to lighten when the *Portland* surprised the *Mogami* at 0529 by straddling her from 19,500 yards. The heavily damaged cruiser maneuvered to confuse this attack while making recognition signals, believing, once again, that friendly ships were responsible. Shima saw the gun flashes but left the *Mogami* to her fate. In the space of ten minutes another ten shells clobbered the unfortunate cruiser, as the *Denver* joined in at 0531, followed by the *Louisville* and *Columbia* from a range of 21,200 yards. The *Columbia's* skipper remarked that his target "was completely ablaze and burning worse than the *Arizona* burned at Pearl Harbor."[31] The *Asagumo* escaped notice until 0533, when the *Minneapolis* flung an eight-inch broadside and hit her astern, sparking a severe fire and slowing her from fourteen to seven knots. Her captain, Commander Shibayama Kazuo, was thankful when the *Minneapolis* almost immediately switched to target the *Mogami*. Meanwhile, the *Louisville* sank the *Fuso's* bow section.

At 0537, concerned that *Mogami* had discharged torpedoes, Oldendorf turned his cruisers north and ceased fire two minutes later. The *Mogami* had been the target of 197 eight-inch shells and 356 six-inch shells during this brief period. Among her pursuers, supplies of AP shell had fallen to critical levels. The *Minneapolis* had only fifteen rounds remaining, while the *Denver* retained 113 six-inch AP rounds—just enough for ninety seconds of rapid fire. Still heading north, Oldendorf ordered his ships into an anti-air cruising formation, fearing enemy air attacks with the coming of dawn at 0630. He did not swing south until 0618.

This caution granted the *Mogami* another reprieve, and she remained combative enough to repel a PT attack at 0605. By 0610 the *Mogami* had even regained contact with Shima. The *Shigure* ignored orders to fall in behind the *Nachi* and led the retreat at twenty-four knots. The *Asagumo* continued to burn, and Commander Shibayama prepared to abandon ship. By this time the brave *Asagumo* was battling *PT323*. The American boat fired two torpedoes at the drifting target and missed, but scored with a third at 0705. Then Division X-Ray's *Cony* found the *Asagumo* and opened fire. Seven other destroyers, as well as the *Denver* and *Columbia*, also congregated. The *Denver* did not engage, but the *Colombia* expended 103 AP rounds and the destroyers joined in the bombardment. At 0721 the *Asagumo*, returning fire to the end, rolled over and sank.

PT boats witnessed Shima's withdrawal and fruitlessly expended three torpedoes at the cost of one PT heavily damaged. Then, at 0727 Oldendorf received a message that enemy battleships had engaged the Seventh Fleet's escort carriers off Samar, and he turned north at 0737, leaving a pair of destroyers to guard the strait. Oldendorf formed an emergency task force consisting of the *California*, *Tennessee*, and *Pennsylvania*, which were the three battleships with the most AP ammunition remaining, three heavy cruisers, and twenty destroyers carrying 165 torpedoes to assist the beleaguered carriers, if ordered.

U.S. Army planes bombed the *Mogami* at 0915 and scored several hits. The Japanese ship finally lost all power but remained afloat. The *Akebono* eventually torpedoed this tough ship, which had also survived massive damage at the Battle of Midway, at 1307. B-24s punished the *Abukuma* southwest of Negros at 1242, and carrier planes hit the *Shiranuhi* at 1500. Otherwise, Shima escaped.[32]

Surigao Strait enjoys fame as the last battleship-versus-battleship action. It is easy to criticize Nishimura's conduct, and many have done so.[33] But given his mission, Oldendorf's preparations, and the battle zone's narrow waters, Nishimura faced a hopeless situation. Compounding these disadvantages, Japanese forces operated as if sadly out of practice. The famous acuity of their lookouts was absent, communications were abysmal, and Nishimura's ships and Shima's acted as cobelligerents rather than units of the same navy. The *Shigure* and Shima's destroyers retreated from battle with full loads of torpedoes! The *Mogami* persisted in believing friendly ships had her under fire.

On the other hand, Oldendorf took no chances. His ships and men, who had little reason to expect a surface engagement when they arrived on station, and who were largely facing enemy gunfire for the first time, performed with courage, aggression, and an acceptable level of competence and served him well. That this was no fluke was even more convincingly demonstrated that same day in the waters off Samar by the jeep carriers and their escorts, which had even less reason to believe they would ever see the smoke of enemy guns fired in anger against them.

Battle off Samar, 25 October 1944

Reeling from the pressure of Task Force 38's air attacks, Kurita ordered the ships of the First Strike Force to reverse course at 1500 on 24 October. The Japanese mood was "anger and anguish" over the lack of friendly air support.[34] Nonetheless, Kurita turned his ships east once again at 1714. Two hours later Combined Fleet exhorted, "Trust in Heaven's assistance. All units attack." Unsurprisingly, as a Japanese historian has noted, "Kurita's staff greeted this tardy order with jeering remarks. It would have been more realistic to say: 'Believing in annihilation, resume the attack.'"[35] Before even reaching the intended battle zone the First Strike Force had lost one battleship, four cruisers, and four destroyers—either sunk or turned back—and had two battleships, one cruiser, and three destroyers damaged. Yet, Kurita still commanded a powerful force. Strung out in a long column, sailing in moonlight filtering through a cloudy sky, the strike force penetrated San Bernardino Strait even as Halsey tore north after Ozawa.

At 0035 hours on 25 October, Kurita's ships debouched one by one from the narrow strait into an empty Philippine Sea (see Map 12.2). The suspicious vice admiral cushioned himself with twenty miles of sea room before turning south southeast in a night scouting formation of six columns from port to starboard: Destroyer Squadron 10, *Sentai 7, Sentai 3,* a composite formation of *Sentai 4* and *Sentai 5's* two survivors, *Sentai 1,* and, last, Destroyer Squadron 2.

The sun rose at 0627, revealing a sky replete with dark clouds and scattered squalls. Kurita ordered an anti-aircraft formation in preparation for the expected aerial onslaught. Lookouts scanned the horizon. Then, an excited call of masts to the south came from the *Yamato's* towering crow's nest. This was quickly followed by a report of the sighting of the boxy shape of carriers. The time was 0644. Kurita radioed Combined Fleet, saying, "By Heaven-sent opportunity, we are dashing to attack the enemy carriers. Our first objective is to destroy the flight decks and then the task force."[36]

Kinkaid's back door was banging in the wind. Rear Adm. T.L. Sprague commanded three escort carrier groups nicknamed "Taffys" after their radio call signals. The Taffys were deployed in the Philippine Sea, presumably far from any surface threat. Kurita had stumbled upon Taffy 3, Task Group 77.4, which was commanded by Rear Adm. Clifton A. F. Sprague, who was no relation to T. L. Sprague. The six escort carriers, three destroyers, and four destroyer escorts in Taffy 3 cruised farthest north, directly in Kurita's path.

Japanese voices on the radio net and dark puffs of smoke marking anti-aircraft fire to the northwest gave the Americans their first intimations of danger. Then a plane on antisubmarine patrol reported a sighting of four enemy battleships, eight cruisers, and a host of destroyers. On the *Fanshaw Bay's* bridge Sprague thought, "Now, there's some screwy young aviator reporting part of our own forces. . . . [U]ndoubtedly he's just spotted some of Admiral Halsey's fast battleships."[37] But at 0657, after the pilot insisted that the ships had the distinctive Japanese pagoda masts, Sprague ordered Taffy 3 to steer due east, sufficiently into the wind to permit the carriers to launch aircraft while working up to full speed and making smoke. Within a minute of this order, the accuracy of the pilot's report was confirmed when yellow, red, and blue geysers began erupting astern of Taffy 3.

TABLE 12.3. FORCES ENGAGED IN THE BATTLE OFF SAMAR

Type of Ship	Year Launched	Displacement, Full Load	Max. Speed (knots)	Guns (number by inch/caliber)	Torpedoes (number of tubes by diameter in inches)	Damage
American Task Group 77.4.3 (Rear Adm. C.A.F. Sprague) and Carrier Division 25 (C.A.F. Sprague)						
Fanshaw Bay (F)	CVE	1943	10,902	17	1 x 5/38		D2
Kitkun Bay	CVE	1943	10,902	17	1 x 5/38		D1
White Plains	CVE	1943	10,902	17	1 x 5/38		D2
St. Lo	CVE	1943	10,902	17	1 x 5/38		
American Division 26 (Rear Adm. R.A. Ofstie)						
Kalinin Bay (F)	CVE	1943	10,902	17	1 x 5/38		D3
Gambier Bay	CVE	1943	10,902	17	1 x 5/38		Sunk
American Screen (Cdr. W.D. Thomas)						
Hoel (F)	DD	1942	2,924	38	5 x 5/38	10 x 21	Sunk
Johnston	DD	1943	2,924	38	5 x 5/38	10 x 21	Sunk
Heermann	DD	1942	2,924	38	5 x 5/38	10 x 21	D2
Dennis	DE	1943	1,811	24	2 x 5/38	3 x 21	D2
John C. Butler	DE	1943	1,811	24	2 x 5/38	3 x 21	
Raymond	DE	1943	1,811	24	2 x 5/38	3 x 21	
Samuel B. Roberts	DE	1943	1,811	24	2 x 5/38	3 x 21	Sunk

Japanese First Strike Force (Vice Admiral Kurita Takeo) and *Sentai* 1 (Vice Admiral Ugaki Matome)							
Yamato (F)	BB	1940	69,990	26	9 x 18.1/45 & 12 x 6.1/60		D1
Nagato	BB	1919	42,753	24	6 x 16.1/45 & 14 x 5.5/50		
Japanese *Sentai* 3 (Vice Admiral Suzuki Yoshio)							
Haruna	BB	1913	36,400	25	8 x 14/45 & 14 x 6/50		
Kongo	BB	1913	36,400	30	8 x 14/45 & 14 x 6/50		
Japanese *Sentai* 4/5 composite							
Haguro	CA	1925	14,743	35	10 x 8/50 & 8 x 5/40	8 x 24	D2a
Chokai	CA	1928	14,604	35	10 x 8/50 & 8 x 5/40	8 x 24	Sunka
Japanese *Sentai* 7 (Vice Admiral Shiraishi Kazutaka)							
Kumano (F)	CA	1936	13,668	35	10 x 8/50 & 8 x 5/40	12 x 24	Sunk
Suzuya	CA	1934	13,668	35	10 x 8/50 & 8 x 5/40	12 x 24	Sunka
Chikuma	CA	1937	15,200	35	8 x 8/50 & 8 x 5/40	12 x 24	Sunka
Tone	CA	1937	15,200	35	8 x 8/50 & 8 x 5/40	12 x 24	
Japanese Destroyer Squadron 2 (Rear Admiral Hayakawa Mikio)							
Noshiro	CL	1942	8,534	35	6 x 6/50 & 4 x 3/65	8 x 24	D1
Shimakaze	DD	1942	3,000	39	4 x 5/50	15 x 24	
Fujinami	DD	1943	2,480	35	4 x 5/50	8 x 24	
Hayashimo	DD	1943	2,480	35	4 x 5/50	8 x 24	
Kishinami	DD	1943	2,480	35	4 x 5/50	8 x 24	
Okinami	DD	1943	2,480	35	4 x 5/50	8 x 24	

Asashimo	DD	1943	2,480	35	4 x 5/50	8 x 24	
Hamanami	DD	1943	2,480	35	4 x 5/50	8 x 24	
Japanese Destroyer Squadron 10 (Rear Admiral Kimura Susumu)							
Yahagi	CL	1942	8,534	35	6 x 6/50 & 4 x 3/65	8 x 24	D2
Urakaze	DD	1939	2,450	35	4 x 5/50	8 x 24	
Yukikaze	DD	1940	2,450	35	4 x 5/50	8 x 24	
Isokaze	DD	1940	2,450	35	4 x 5/50	8 x 24	
Nowaki	DD	1940	2,450	35	4 x 5/50	8 x 24	

a Damage inflicted by aircraft
BB—battleship, CA—heavy cruiser, CL—light cruiser, CVE—escort aircraft carrier, D1—light or superficial damage (including splinter damage), D2—moderate damage (combat ability not significantly impaired), DD—destroyer, DE—destroyer escort, F—flagship
 Time: 0658–1236
 Weather: Overcast, occasional squalls, northeasterly wind
 Visibility: Mixed, overcast, hazy
 Sea state: Slight swells
 Surprise: Japanese
 Mission: Americans-self defense; Japanese—beachhead attack

Sprague and Kurita faced problems beyond the purview of normal training and tactics. The only other time a functional aircraft carrier had faced enemy surface gunfire had occurred more than four years before, when two German battleships sank HMS *Glorious*. On that occasion the *Glorious* hesitated twenty minutes before going to action stations and never managed to launch a plane in her own defense.[38]

Sprague possessed a keener sense of the threat facing him and reacted promptly, decisively, and correctly. He advertised his peril and begged for help in plain language. Sprague needed to prevent the Japanese from piling into Leyte Gulf, to avoid encirclement, and, hopefully, to draw the Japanese toward Oldendorf's heavy ships. In short, Sprague had a set of impossible objectives.

Kurita believed he had surprised fleet carriers, cruisers, destroyers, and, perhaps, a battleship. After the pain American aircraft had inflicted on his ships the day before, Kurita's first priority was to perforate flight decks. The question was how to do this. Kurita later said his "intention was to reduce the range, keeping to windward of the American forces."[39] He regarded the weather gauge as critical because staying upwind would prevent the American carriers from turning into the wind to conduct air operations.

MAP 12.2. BATTLES OF SURIGAO STRAIT AND SAMAR, SITUATION 0700,
25 OCTOBER 1944

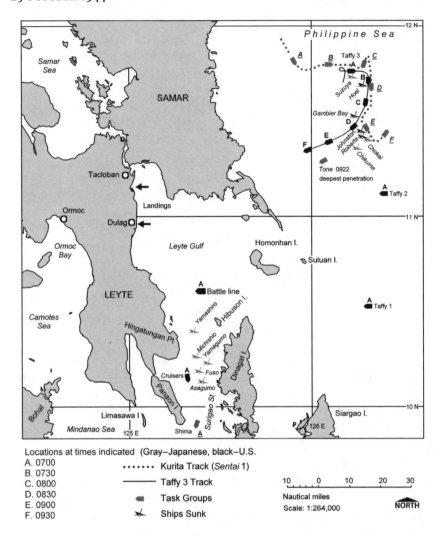

Locations at times indicated (Gray–Japanese, black–U.S.)
A. 0700
B. 0730   ⋯⋯⋯ Kurita Track (*Sentai* 1)
C. 0800   ——— Taffy 3 Track
D. 0830   ◄█ Task Groups
E. 0900   ✕╱ Ships Sunk
F. 0930

10   0   10   20   30

Nautical miles
Scale: 1:264,000   NORTH

Accordingly, Kurita steered his ships east at 0653, had them open fire at 0658,
and ordered a general attack at 0703, granting every division permission to
fight individually. An American historian has criticized, "That was the fatal error.
Kurita should have formed battle line . . . which would have allowed his superior
fire power to count, and he should have committed light forces immediately for
torpedo attack. But complete surprise seems to have deprived the admiral of all

power of decision and the result was a helter-skelter battle."[40] Kurita's chief of staff offered a kinder interpretation: "In a pursuit the only essential is to close the gap as rapidly as possible and concentrate fire upon the enemy. Admiral Kurita did not therefore adopt the usual deployment procedures but instantly ordered, General attack."[41]

From Sprague's perspective Kurita's initial charge seemed effective. Towering geysers straddled the *White Plains* three times at 0704. Water splashed pilots in open cockpits waiting to take off, and the escort carrier temporarily lost steering control. Sprague asserted that "at this point it did not appear that any of our ships could survive another five minutes of the heavy-caliber fire being received."[42] At 0706 Sprague ordered his destroyers to counterattack. At the same time a thick squall loomed in the path of the little carriers. He steered into the rain seeking temporary refuge.

As the carriers fled, the destroyers hastened to comply with Sprague's order. The *Hoel* abandoned her task of making smoke, and the *Johnston*, which had been zigzagging between the Japanese columns and the carriers, immediately turned to close. Her skipper, Cdr. Earnest Evans, did not wait for the division commander, Cdr. William D. Thomas aboard the *Hoel*, to take the lead. The *Heermann*, originally Taffy 3's point ship, cut back through the formation to join up.

Meanwhile, Sprague was bending his course from east to southeast, thinking to steer toward Oldendorf's battleships. After ten minutes the escort carriers emerged from the squall, steaming at 17.5 knots. The *Johnston* advanced west northwest through a forest of multicolored geysers, trading salvos with the *Kumano* while being repeatedly straddled but never touched. Evans, expected such luck could not last and so, at 0720, "to insure being within torpedo range and to insure being able to fire our torpedoes even though this heavy fire should put the ship out of action before the range had closed" he launched ten torpedoes set to run 10,000 yards at low speed.[43] With fish running hot, straight, and normal, the *Johnston* "whipped around immediately and began retiring behind a heavy smoke screen."[44]

Overhead, Taffy 3's hastily launched aircraft began to annoy the Japanese, dropping light bombs and depth charges, making strafing runs, and even just buzzing the enemy in ones, twos, and threes. The American flyers inflicted a blow at 0724, when a near miss off the *Suzuya*'s fantail knocked a propeller shaft out of alignment and cut the cruiser's speed to twenty-three knots.

As the *Suzuya* fell behind, a heavy explosion rocked the *Kumano*. One of the *Johnston's* torpedoes impacted at 0727 and nearly severed her bow. The crippled cruiser veered away at fourteen knots. Following this success, the *Kongo* found the elusive *Johnston's* range and clobbered the American destroyer with 3 fourteen-inch shells. Another trio of six-inch rounds struck within thirty seconds. The *Johnston* reported this blow as coming at 0730.[45] The rapid succession of hits destroyed the *Johnston*'s after engine room and steering engine and cut power to three guns. Then the squall engulfed Evan's battered ship, allowing her to undertake emergency repairs.

By this time the *Hoel* was charging through the same squall, with the *Heermann* about 7,000 yards back. The *Raymond, John C. Butler*, and *Dennis*, hastening to the engaged side, clustered off the *Fanshaw Bay*'s starboard bow and made smoke as the carriers now swerved to a southerly heading. The *Samuel B. Roberts*, however, tacked northeast on her own.

The destroyer escorts carried just three torpedoes, and their crews had limited surface combat training. The *Samuel B. Roberts* demonstrated this deficiency when she and the *Heermann* crossed paths and nearly collided. The *Samuel B. Roberts*'s skipper, Lt. Cdr. Robert W. Copeland, unsure what to do, decided to follow the *Heermann* toward the enemy fleet.

Near the end of her approach and even before the *Samuel B. Roberts* and *Heermann* almost crashed, a shell smashed into the *Hoel*'s bridge, destroying her communications. She discharged five torpedoes at the *Kongo* from a range of 9,000 yards a few minutes later. Then more misery followed, as enemy projectiles slammed into her after fireroom and engine room and knocked out her steering control and power to her aft mounts. The *Hoel* slowly began to drift toward the *Kongo* until, powered by one engine and steering by hand, she reestablished control. Fortunately for the *Hoel*'s men the *Kongo* had veered sharply to port to avoid the destroyer's fish.

The damaged *Johnston*, radar dangling from her yardarm, was retreating east southeast when the *Samuel B. Roberts* sailed past. Evans decided to follow and support the destroyer escort with his two remaining guns. The *Raymond* and *Dennis*, maintaining station several thousand yards northwest of the escort carriers, came in range of the enemy and opened fire at 0730 and 0740, respectively.

The small carriers turned south shortly before 0730 and then veered to south by southwest. Kurita, however, perched on the *Yamato*'s bridge, had a spotty view. He knew he had the Americans fleeing in confusion. But he complained the smoke was a "very serious trouble" and "exceedingly well used tactically" and that his enemy's zigzagging "made it difficult to get the range."[46] He maintained an easterly course even as Sprague plunged south and, distracted by the American destroyers, the volume of Japanese fire against the carriers slackened.

Kurita's four undamaged heavy cruisers split into two groups: the *Haguro* leading the *Chokai*, and the *Tone* leading the *Chikuma*. The *Kongo* sailed roughly parallel to the cruisers, while the *Yamato* and *Nagato* trailed to starboard with the *Haruna* nearby. Damage suffered the day before had reduced the *Haruna*'s speed, forcing her and the *Kongo* to operate independently. The two destroyer squadrons followed on either quarter of *Sentai* 1.

When the ring of flattops emerged from the squall, however, Japanese aim improved. Kurita ordered his cruisers to pursue east by southeast at top speed. Kinkaid had already denied Sprague permission to flee directly into Leyte Gulf. Running short of options, Sprague ordered his escort carriers to commence firing their solitary five-inch guns and the destroyer escorts to form up and attack.

When Sprague gave this order, the fleet destroyers remained engaged. The *Heermann*, racing to close on the *Hoel*, did not appreciate the flagship's damaged condition and had to reverse engines at 0749 to avoid a collision. After this close call, the *Hoel*, steering by hand with the torpedo officer perched atop number two mount, sent five torpedoes streaking toward the *Haguro*. Within a few minutes the *Heermann* shot seven more at the same target while sniping at the *Chikuma* with her guns. The *Heermann* then spotted the Japanese battleships and closed on the *Haruna*, firing her last three torpedoes at this imposing target from only 4,400 yards. Return fire from the cruisers and battleship never touched the *Heermann*, and she retired at 0803, incorrectly claiming a torpedo hit on the *Haruna*.

The *Hoel* also tried to rejoin the carriers, but running on only one engine, she could not pull away from the Japanese, who were now veering east by southeast. As a result, the *Hoel* remained caught between the *Kongo* on her port beam and the Japanese cruisers on her starboard quarter.

The *Samuel B. Roberts* sailed through a sea lashed with smoke and haze, holding fire and taking advantage of her low profile. Copeland instructed his chief engineer, "As soon as we fire our fish, I will ring up flank speed and I want you to hook on everything you've got. Don't worry about your reduction gears or your boilers or anything because there's all hell being thrown at us up here."[47] The *Samuel B. Roberts* closed to within 4,000 yards of the *Chokai* before a shell snagged her mast and rigging. Considering this a sign, Copeland emptied his tubes at the cruiser, wheeled around, and plunged into his own smoke, making twenty-eight knots. The time was shortly after 0800. The *Samuel B. Roberts* reported a hit, but, in fact, she missed.

The *Raymond* approached the *Haguro* and discharged her three torpedoes at 0756 from 6,000 yards. The *Raymond* incorrectly claimed a hit and retreated as the *Haguro* flung fifteen broadsides at her, missing with every one. The *Dennis* likewise dashed forward and launched torpedoes from 8,000 yards at the *Tone* at 0759. Simultaneously, the *Tone* was deflecting an air attack that caused her to drop behind the *Chikuma*. The *Dennis* headed west southwest and traded broadsides with the *Chikuma* from 0802 to 0809 before plunging into the smoke and joining the *Heermann, Johnston*, and *Samuel B. Roberts* on Taffy 3's port quarter. These torpedo strikes reaped their greatest benefit at 0754, when the *Yamato* spotted tracks foaming in her direction. Kurita ordered a turn to the non-engaged side and, as Vice Admiral Ugaki criticized, "this caused us a lot of trouble afterward because we were caught between four torpedoes on the starboard and two on the port, and enemy slow-speed torpedoes running parallel to *Yamato* with 26 knots didn't permit her to turn for a pretty long time."[48] For ten minutes the giant battleship was forced "to speed away from the enemy."[49]

Meanwhile the six escort carriers fled southwest, vomiting smoke and banging away with their five-inch guns. The *Kalinin Bay* and *Gambier Bay* occupied the exposed rear positions on the windward side. The *Gambier Bay*'s Capt. Walter Vieweg wrote, "These cruisers then to the northeast were in an excellent position and without opposition to pour in a rather heavy fire upon the *Gambier Bay* and the *Kitkun Bay*. . . . However, their fire was somewhat inaccurate, not very fast, salvos were about a minute or a minute and a half apart and they did not fire a particularly large salvo, they fired four gun salvos. . . . Their spotting was rather methodical and enabled us to dodge salvos."[50]

Nonetheless, at 0750 a battleship shell punctured the *Kalinin Bay*'s hangar deck and tore through her thin hull. Eleven more shells followed, igniting small fires even as water flooded in. At the same time 4 eight-inch shells plunged into the *Fanshaw Bay*'s forward flight deck. They penetrated into the lower deck spaces and passed right out. Two near misses off the *Fanshaw Bay*'s port bow peppered her stem with splinters. The *Gambier Bay* suffered her first hit at 0810, when the *Chikuma* found her range. At this same time the *Yamato* finally turned around after a run north that "felt like a month" to Vice Admiral Ugaki and cost *Sentai* 1 and Destroyer Squadron 10 some 15,000 yards.[51]

Sprague's carriers had survived seventy minutes under the guns of the enemy fleet. Except for the luckless *Hoel*, the destroyers had concentrated on Taffy 3's exposed northern and western sides. The Japanese columns had become widely separated, but the surviving cruisers, now led by the *Chikuma*, were starting to advance on Taffy 3's port quarter. The *Kongo* and *Haruna* flanked the cruisers, while Destroyer Squadron 2 had eschewed the *Yamato*'s coattails and commenced a charge on the Americans' starboard quarter. The *Haguro*, however, suffered a direct hit from a 100-pound bomb on her number 2 turret around 0800—0825 by her records—and suffered thirty men killed. This caused the *Haguro* to fall back.[52]

Taffy 2 almost got sucked into this fight. The small American group turned northeast into the wind and toward the enemy at 0754 and launched all available strike aircraft. Because many of Taffy 2's bombers were already conducting routine missions, this represented less than half the potential strength. Taffy 2 then fled southeast until 0805 when the carriers turned to launch fighters.

At this time the *Haruna* and *Kongo* sighted Taffy 2's masts 35,000 yards distant and advised Kurita that more carriers lay in the offing. Taffy 2 continued southeast until 0833 when, decks replenished with more aircraft from the hangers, it turned a third time and launched sixteen Avengers and eight Wildcats. The range to the two Japanese battleships quickly shortened, and by 0841 the *Haruna*, which had veered furthest east, was lobbing salvos toward Taffy 2's destroyers.

The main danger continued to stalk Taffy 3, however. The *Chikuma* shelled the *Gambier Bay* beginning at 0810. A near miss holed the escort carrier at 0820 and flooded her engine room. As her speed dropped to eleven knots, the *Gambier Bay* fell behind the American formation, and the *Haguro* and *Chokai* concentrated their batteries against her from 10,000 yards. Captain Vieweg wrote, "We were being hit probably every other minute. The hits that went through the upper structure did very little damage since the shells did not explode inside the ship. However, those shells which hit either just short or below the water line did explode. . . . At about 0850 with the ship helpless in the water and with this division of cruisers passing close by. . . . I ordered the ship abandoned."[53]

At 0826 with the situation rapidly deteriorating Sprague ordered the *Dennis* and *John C. Butler* on the starboard quarter to swing around and tackle the *Chikuma*. They joined the *Raymond*, which was already engaged in a hot firefight with the *Tone*. Although the *John C. Butler* still had torpedoes, she could not get into a firing position. Nonetheless, the combined efforts of the American escorts at least forced the Japanese cruisers to divide fire.

To the north the *Hoel* had survived amidst the enemy's warships by "fish-tailing and chasing salvos."[54] Her two surviving guns fired 500 rounds, and she was the target of hundreds in return. The *Hoel*'s time ran out at 0830, when an eight-inch shell detonated in her engine spaces. As the battered destroyer drifted to a stop with her Number 1 magazine ablaze, Cdr. Leon Kintberger ordered his crew to abandon ship. The time was 0835. A *Hoel* survivor remembered, "I threw open the starboard escape hatch and crawled through a pile of bodies and body parts to the main deck. I looked around in shock and disbelief at the condition of the ship."[55]

As the battle entered its third hour, damage to both sides accumulated. At 0850 an eight-inch shell punched through the *Dennis* without exploding, but fragments sliced cables and shorted out her forward gun. At 0900 another shell detonated on the *Dennis*'s after 40-mm director and disabled her aft gun. With only machine guns left, she retired into a smoke screen laid by the *John C. Butler*.

The *John C. Butler* and *Raymond* escaped the day unharmed, but the *Samuel B. Roberts* did not. She guarded the flotilla's port quarter, blasting away at the *Chikuma*. At 0851 a brace of eight-inch shells rattled through the *Samuel B. Roberts*'s forward fireroom and exited, leaving gaping holes in her side. As her speed dropped to seventeen knots, more shells walloped the crippled destroyer escort. Then, at 0900 several fourteen-inch rounds exploded alongside and ripped her hull open. The *Samuel B. Roberts* went dead in the water, and Copeland ordered his crew to abandon ship ten minutes later. Eighty-nine men died. She had fired 608 five-inch rounds from her two guns. As Copeland remembered, this included, "Five-inch blind loaded and plugged, 5-inch AA, 5-inch common, 5-inch AP, 5-inch star shells, 5-inch proximity fuse, just whatever came up the ammunition hoist."[56]

The *Johnston* emerged from "a heavy smoke screen" to see *Heermann* "on a collision course ... at a distance of about two hundred yards." The *Heermann* had just careened through the formation at flank speed and had nearly been rammed by the *Fanshaw Bay*. Both ships backed full and, according to the *Johnston*, averted disaster "by the narrowest possible margin."[57] Almost immediately thereafter, Evans engaged the *Kongo* from 7,000 yards and then tried to distract the *Chikuma* from the *Gambier Bay*.

The *Heermann* joined her sister in this unequal contest. A pair of eight-inch shells from the same salvo pierced the *Heermann*, killing four men on the bridge. The shells exited without exploding but caused moderate flooding forward. The *Heermann* escaped further damage when an aerial torpedo clobbered the *Chikuma* at 0853 and forced the Japanese ship to turn away with a damaged rudder and propeller.

Meanwhile, Kinkaid monitored the situation. He worried that undamaged Japanese forces in the Mindanao Sea might make another attempt to force Surigao Strait, but there were other considerations: Kinkaid's chief of staff remembered, "When the time came (and there was no time to lose) to order Oldendorf out of the gulf to engage ... Kinkaid hesitated and questioned whether he should risk the destruction of battleships and cruisers, which take a long time and are expensive to build to protect CVEs that were rapidly being built by the hundreds."[58]

Kinkaid finally released Oldendorf at 0850. Five minutes later, the gallant *Hoel* rolled to port and slid into the deep waters stern first. Only 86 men from her crew of 349 survived after spending several days in the water. The *Gambier Bay* also sank at 0907, but her survivors numbered nearly 800. The *St. Lo* and *Kalinin Bay* reported numerous straddles, some as near as twenty yards, and two shells struck the *Fanshaw Bay* forward at 0858. The carriers, however, gained a small measure of revenge by hitting the *Chokai* with their five-inch guns. Then, at 0905 a dive bomber surprised the *Chokai*, planting a 500-pound projectile in the forward machinery room. She went dead in the water, burning fiercely.

The *Johnston*, meanwhile, turned to confront Destroyer Squadron 10, which was charging forward on Taffy 3's starboard quarter. At 0905 the *Johnston* traded salvos with the *Yahagi* from 7,000 yards, hitting the Japanese ship forward and damaging a stateroom as the cruiser released seven Long Lances. As Kimura's flagship sheered sharply north, the *Johnson* turned her guns on the *Urakaze*, the second ship in line. This destroyer and then the *Isokaze*, *Yukikaze*, and *Nowaki*, all launched their Type 93s and turned 90 degrees to starboard following the *Yahagi*.

With their torpedoes running, the destroyers circled back to the southeast and plastered the *Johnston*. Shells ravaged the doomed American vessel, silencing her last guns and shredding her bridge. At 0945 Evans, "bandaged and bloody, his uniform in shreds—conning from the fantail because her bridge had been utterly destroyed," ordered his men over the side.[59] Of the Johnston's complement of 327 men, 186 died, including 92 who were alive in the water when she sank. Reportedly, a Japanese officer saluted as his destroyer steamed past the Johnston's wreckage.[60]

The Haguro and Tone were now pressing the carriers most closely. Sprague steered west by southwest as both Japanese cruisers attacked from less than 8,000 yards off his port beam. Shells foamed the water around the White Plains, and repeated shocks knocked her starboard engine out of alignment. Another round exploded alongside the White Plains and damaged her below the waterline. Shards of steel from near misses perforated the Kitkun Bay. The Kalinin Bay also absorbed more damage. Sprague had about exhausted his options, with the Johnston, Hoel, and Samuel B. Roberts sunk or sinking, the Dennis without weapons, the John C. Butler short of ammunition, and the Heermann damaged. Nonetheless, at 0910 he issued another call for his escorts to attack.

Twenty-five thousand yards north of Sprague, Kurita likewise considered his situation unsatisfactory. At 0911 he ordered the Japanese ships to "[c]ease actions, come north with me 20 knots."[61] At 0920 Squadron 10's torpedoes appeared, running parallel to the American flattops. Some exploded prematurely. Sprague later remembered, "At 0925, my mind was occupied with dodging torpedoes, when near the bridge I heard one of the signalmen yell, 'God damn it, boys, they're getting away!' I could not believe my eyes, but it looked as if the whole Japanese fleet was indeed retiring."[62]

Like Halsey's decision to leave San Bernardino Strait unprotected, Kurita's order to concentrate and reorganize his scattered force has sparked controversy. A staff officer summarized the reasons underlying Kurita's action this way: "First, fuel; second, we had poor communications with our cruisers and couldn't see what they were doing; third, we intercepted a message which called for reinforcements and the reply indicated reinforcement of planes not before one or two hours."[63]

Kurita still intended to storm Leyte Gulf, however. The initial round had, by his assessment, been relatively productive. At 1000 hours he reported to Toyoda, "Definitely sunk: two aircraft carriers (of which one is regular large type carrier) two heavy cruisers and some destroyers. Definitely hit: One or two carriers."[64] Meanwhile, he lost two more cruisers. The Fujinami rescued the Chokai's crew and sank the stricken ship with a torpedo at 0930. The Nowaki took off the Chikuma's men and likewise scuttled her. At 1055 the Japanese commander, his fleet collected, looped southwest, and steered toward Leyte once again. During this period air attacks continued. At 1050 thirty planes attacked the Suzuya. She took a torpedo at 1100 and sank at 1230.[65]

By 1150 Kurita had learned of Nishimura's fate and believed, based upon misinformation from Manila, that an enemy task force was maneuvering thirty miles to the northeast and that the Seventh Fleet had massed sixty miles to the southeast. On the basis of radio intercepts, Kurita anticipated a large air strike. If he continued toward Leyte, he reasoned, "We would fall into a very hard fight, being concentrically attacked by many planes on a sea narrow as a pond." Moreover, "it was probably that there would no ships left in the bay even if we rushed in."[66] These rationalizations formed the true kernel of Kurita's decision to terminate his Leyte dash.

As an alternative, he decided to "decisively attack" the force reported to be to the northeast and then retire through San Bernardino Strait. In fact, the northern force was imaginary; the report of it was probably based on a sighting of Kurita's own ships. Later, he described his decision a "mistake of exhaustion."[67] It had been three days since he had enjoyed any sleep.

On the way north 147 aircraft from Task Group 38.1, recalled by Halsey, delivered two extreme-range attacks on Kurita's ships but failed to inflict further damage. Taffy 3, however, remained exposed to a new and frightening weapon: Kamikaze suicide bombers. During the rest of the day Kamikazes sank the *St. Lo*, inflicted major damage on the *Kalinin Bay*, *Santee*, and *Suwannee*, and caused minor harm to the *Kitkun Bay* and *White Plains*.[68]

During the Battle off Samar, American destroyer attacks compelled the Japanese to take evasive action. This compounded the confusion caused by smoke and aerial strikes and helped foil Kurita's offensive. The Japanese only admitted to one surface torpedo hit against the *Kumano*, and damage inflicted by gunfire fell far short of American claims, but the final results of the battle were self-evident and ultimately in the Americans' favor. The destroyer escorts of Taffy 3 were second-line units. They held relatively safe assignments. Draftees and reserve officers crewed them, with a leavening of about 15 percent regulars. Nonetheless, when confronted with a life-and-death situation, the destroyer escorts and their crews responded in a fashion that impressed even their enemies. In the process, they were instrumental in averting what would have been a shocking setback for the Americans.

Battle off Cape Engaño, 25 October 1944

The third action fought on 25 October consisted of a series of Third Fleet air strikes against Ozawa's decoy force and surface attacks against a Japanese cripple and ships engaged in rescue operations by an American force of cruisers and destroyers.

Ozawa's force operated in two groups. The first consisted of the carrier *Zuikaku*, the light carrier *Zuiho*, the light cruisers *Oyodo* and *Tama*, the destroyers *Hatsuzuki*, *Wakatsuki*, *Kuwa*, and *Akizuki*, and the battleship/carrier *Ise*. This group was

TABLE 12.4. FORCES ENGAGED IN THE BATTLE OFF CAPE ENGAÑO

	Type of Ship	Year Launched	Displacement, Full Load	Max. Speed (knots)	Guns (number by inch/caliber)	Torpedoes (number of tubes by diameter in inches)	Damage
American Cruiser Division 6 (Rear Adm. L.T. DuBose)							
Santa Fe (F)	CL	1942	14,131	32	12 x 6/47 & 12 x 5/38		
Mobile	CL	1942	14,131	32	12 x 6/47 & 12 x 5/38		
American Cruiser Division 13 (Rear Adm. C.T. Joy)							
Wichita (F)	CA	1937	13,015	33	9 x 8/55 & 8 x 5/38		
New Orleans	CA	1933	12,463	32	9 x 8/56 & 8 x 5/25		
American Destroyer Squadron 50 (Capt. E.R. Wilkerson)							
Clarence K. Bronson (F)	DD	1943	2,924	38	5 x 5/38	10 x 21	
Cotton	DD	1943	2,924	38	5 x 5/38	10 x 21	
Dortch	DD	1943	2,924	38	5 x 5/38	10 x 21	
Healy	DD	1943	2,924	38	5 x 5/38	10 x 21	
American Destroyer Squadron 55 (Capt. C.R. Todd)							
Porterfield	DD	1943	2,924	38	5 x 5/38	10 x 21	
Callaghan	DD	1943	2,924	38	5 x 5/38	10 x 21	
American Destroyer Division 100 (Capt. W.J. Miller)							
Cogswell (F)	DD	1943	2,924	38	5 x 5/38	10 x 21	
Caperton	DD	1943	2,924	38	5 x 5/38	10 x 21	

Ingersoll	DD	1943	2,924	38	5 x 5/38	10 x 21	
Knapp	DD	1943	2,924	38	5 x 5/38	10 x 21	
Bagley	DD	1936	2,245	38	4 x 5/38	16 x 21	
Patterson	DD	1937	2,245	38	4 x 5/38	16 x 21	
Japanese							
Chiyoda	CV	1937	15,100	0	8 x 5/40		Sunk
Isuzu	CL	1921	6,100	33	6 x 5/40	4 x 24	
Japanese Destroyer Division 61 (Captain Amano Shigetake)							
Hatsuzuki (F)	DD	1942	3,700	33	8 x 3.9/65	4 x 24	Sunk
Wakatsuki	DD	1942	3,700	33	8 x 3.9/65	4 x 24	
Kuwa	DE	1944	1.506	27	3 x 5/40	4 x 24	

CA—heavy cruiser, CL—light cruiser, CV—aircraft carrier, DD—destroyer, DE—destroyer escort, F—flagship
   Time: 1625–2059
   Weather: Overcast, light east-northeasterly breeze
   Visibility: Good
   Sea state: Slight
   Surprise: Americans
   Mission: Americans—interception based on specific intelligence; Japanese—self-defense

followed by the light carriers *Chitose* and *Chiyoda*, the battleship/carrier *Hyuga*, the light cruiser *Isuzu*, and the destroyers *Maki, Sugi, Kiri,* and *Shimotsuki.*

The first American air strike against Ozawa's ships lasted from 0721 to 0759 and involved 130 planes. This foray damaged the *Zuikaku, Ise,* and *Oyodo* and sank the *Akizuki.* At 0822 Halsey received a report that Taffy 3 was under surface attack. He was "surprised, but not greatly alarmed."[69] Task Force 38's second attack by thirty-six planes started at 0945 and yielded hits on the *Chiyoda* and *Tama.* Meanwhile, Halsey continued to receive increasingly desperate pleas for help from Kinkaid. Halsey directed the still distant Task Group 38.1, on its way back to the battle zone to assist Kindaid and continued to concentrate on pounding Ozawa's decoy fleet. Then, at 0952, a query from Nimitz arrived. Its content reflected the confusion shared by Seventh Fleet, Nimitz, and King regarding Halsey's actions and his orders and read: "Where is Task Force 34?" Task Force 34 was Lee's battle line, which everyone assumed had been guarding San Bernardino Strait. Taking this for a reprimand, a tired Halsey, "plucked off his cap, hurled it to the deck, and broke into sobs."[70] He had intended to surge north with Task Force 34 to harvest Japanese cripples. Instead, Halsey turned Task Force 34 south at 1115, leaving Vice Adm. Marc Mitscher, commanding Task Force 38, to finish the battle.

The third strike went in at 1310. Two hundred planes damaged the *Zuiho* and put three torpedoes into the *Zuikaku*, which sank at 1414. At 1420 Mitscher ordered Rear Admiral DuBose with Cruiser Divisions 6 and 13, a pale shadow of Task Force 34, to start north in hunt of cripples. In part, he based this order on reports that the hybrid battleships had departed the scene, which would reduce the danger to the U.S. cruisers. The fourth strike of forty aircraft followed shortly after and managed four near misses on the *Ise*. However, the *Zuiho* sank from accumulated damage at 1526.

Led by the *Santa Fe*, the *Mobile*, *Wichita*, and *New Orleans* proceeded in column, with the destroyers on either quarter. As the Americans sped north, they encountered the *Chiyoda* wallowing without power and the *Isuzu* standing by. The *Wichita* engaged at 1625 from 19,000 yards as *Isuzu* fled. Aboard the *Wichita*, a telephone talker on the flag bridge recalled, "It was just like target practice. . . . It appeared that every salvo plunged into the *Chiyoda* and simply disappeared. Occasionally I would see an orange ball, which indicated an explosion."[71] The Japanese carrier returned a few ragged, ineffective salvos before capsizing and sinking at 1655. There were no survivors.

The fifth American air strike, which began at 1710, was the largest, consisting of five deck loads. But many pilots were exhausted by this time. They targeted the *Ise* and *Hyuga*, near-missing the first thirty-four times and the second seven times. The sixth and final strike of thirty-six planes arrived at 1800. It scored a few near misses.[72]

At this time the *Porterfield* and *Callaghan* joined DuBose with Squadron 55's Capt. Carlton R. Todd, who assumed command of the destroyers. Todd formed four groups of three destroyers each and stationed two groups on either quarter of the cruiser column while DuBose continued north, coached on by the *Essex's* night fighters.

At 1833 the *Wichita's* radar registered contacts 35,200 yards to north, and the American cruisers surprised the *Hatsuzuki*, *Wakatsuki*, and *Kuwa* at 1854 as the Japanese ships were fishing the *Zuikaku's* and *Zuiho's* survivors from the water. The light cruisers opened fire on the *Hatsuzuki* at 1852, while the heavy cruisers were supposed to target the more-distant *Wakatsuki* and *Kuma*. The *Wichita* tried a salvo at 1900 but, at 28,200 yards, the range proved excessive.[73] A running fight then developed as the Japanese fled and the American cruisers worked up to thirty knots.

At 1911 a shell stuck the *Hatsuzuki*, provoking her to simulate a torpedo attack and lay smoke. When the American maneuvered to avoid the phantom fish, the *Hatsuzuki* swung back to the north. The *Hatsuzuki* repeated its feint several times as the *Wakatsuki* and *Kuma* escaped.

The *Cogswell*, *Ingersoll*, and *Caperton* pulled ahead of the cruisers at 1929 to make their own torpedo attack, but it took forty minutes before they fired half-salvos from

6,800 yards. All missed. At 2026 an impatient DuBose radioed Rear Adm. Charles T. Joy, saying, "As we get in to 10,000 yards open up and please sink that ship."[74] The *Hatsuzuki* was, in any case, clearly doomed. A *Wichita* crewman remembered, "Our light cruisers were really firing rapid fire at the *Hatsuzuki* when I was watching her. It seemed like that was a continuous stream of fire coming from their four turrets."[75] An official report states the *Hatsuzuki* was "literally punched to pieces." Nonetheless, she fought back, straddling the *Santa Fe* and showering the *Wichita* with splinters and wounding one American. American observers variously identified the pugnacious Japanese destroyer as an *Aoba*-class heavy cruiser and an *Agano*-class light cruiser. The one point of agreement among the Americans, as stated in the *Wichita*'s report, was that the "ability of the ship to absorb punishment . . . indicates a ship larger than a destroyer."[76]

Altogether, the *Santa Fe* fired 954 six-inch round, 972 five-inch rounds, and 104 star shells during this engagement. The *Mobile* added 779 six-inch shells. The *New Orleans* expended 35 percent of her AP rounds, and the *Wichita* 22 percent, which broke out as 148 eight-inch rounds against the *Chiyoda* and 173 against the *Hatsuzuki*.[77] The *Hatsuzuki* finally succumbed to all this metal at 2059. Twenty-five men, seventeen from the carriers, made it to Formosa after two weeks in an open boat, but no one else survived.

The Americans continued north, but, with the destroyers running short of fuel, DuBose turned back at 2130. He did not know that Ozawa, responding to the *Hatsuzuki*'s pleas for help, had been sailing toward the Americans with the *Ise*, *Hyuga*, *Oyodo*, and *Shimotsuki* since 2041, hoping to salvage something by sinking the enemy cruisers in a night action.

Destruction of the *Nowaki* off San Bernardino Strait, 26 October 1944

Halsey led an abbreviated version of Task Force 34 south on the evening of 25 October, steaming through a sea of hubris and arriving three hours too late to block Kurita's exit from the Philippine Sea. He had the battleships *Iowa* and *New Jersey*, the light cruisers *Biloxi*, *Vincennes*, and *Miami*, and the eight destroyers of Squadron 53. Like Kurita's decision to turn north, Halsey had reasons for dividing his task force three times until, at the end, he retained a force inferior to his potential foe. Also like Kurita's reasons, Halsey's require much explanation. It is best to say they did not matter because he was too late, as confirmed at midnight by a seaplane pilot, who reported the presence of fourteen enemy ships in the strait steaming west: "Stragglers and cripples, in numbers and locations not comprehensively established, appeared to be the only possible victims of TG 34.5."[78]

TABLE 12.5. FORCES ENGAGED IN THE DESTRUCTION OF THE *NOWAKI*

	Type of Ship	Year Launched	Displacement, Full Load	Max. Speed (knots)	Guns (number by inch/caliber)	Torpedoes (number of tubes by diameter in inches)	Damage
American Cruiser Division 14 (Rear Adm. F. Whiting)							
Vincennes (F)	CL	1943	14,131	32	12 x 6/47 & 12 x 5/38		
Biloxi	CL	1943	14,131	32	12 x 6/47 & 12 x 5/38		
Miami	CL	1942	14,131	32	12 x 6/47 & 12 x 5/38		
Owen	DD	1943	2,924	38	5 x 5/38	10 x 21	
Miller	DD	1943	2,924	38	5 x 5/38	10 x 21	
Japanese (Commander Moriya Setsuji)							
Nowaki	DD	1940	2,450	35	4 x 5/50	8 x 24	Sunk

CL—light cruiser, DD—destroyer, F—flagship
Time: 0054–0135
Weather: Forty percent overcast, occasional squalls, moderate breeze
Visibility: Moonless and dark
Sea state: Moderate
Surprise: Americans
Mission: Americans—interception based on general intelligence; Japanese—transit

The *Nowaki* had fallen behind while rescuing the *Chikuma*'s survivors. She hastened north with 1,100 men crowded aboard, as Halsey, sitting in the *New Jersey*'s darkened bridge, sent the *Lewis Hancock* twelve miles ahead to scout. When the destroyer reported a contact at 0028, Halsey dispatched Rear Adm. Francis Whiting's Cruiser Division 14 and a pair of destroyers to get the *Nowaki* while the rest of his force stayed clear.

The American cruisers surprised the *Nowaki* at 0054 with a four-minute outburst of rapid fire from 18,300 yards. They then stopped to measure the damage inflicted. During this pause the *Biloxi*, the middle ship in the American column, missed an order to come 40 degrees to port and nearly collided with the *Miami*, the rear ship. When Whiting saw the *Nowaki* was still making ten knots, he ordered another dousing at 0101. The Americans destroyers joined in on this barrage four minutes later from a range of 11,000 yards.

The *Nowaki* began burning at 0106 and skewed to a stop. In two short bombardments the *Miami* expended 399 six-inch rounds. Whiting led the cruisers away after ordering the destroyers to "polish him off."[79] The *Owen* shot a half-salvo of torpedoes from 4,400 yards and missed. Both U.S. destroyers then closed to point-blank range and hosed the *Nowaki* with five-inch shells. At 0132, "the Japanese ship suffered a massive explosion that sent debris hundred of feet into the air and lit up the entire battle area."[80] She sank three minutes later, and not one of the thousand-plus men jammed aboard the Japanese destroyer survived.

The Americans observed only a few random salvos from the enemy ship toward the end of the action. Highlighting the continuing problem of target identification, the *Miami's* gunnery officer observed, "Reports of identification by ships of the engaging group scaled downward from a *Fuso* class BB though various cruiser types to DD classes ranging through 4, 3, 2 and 1 gun mounts forward."[81] This was the only contribution the guns of the Third Fleet made against the enemy's main force in the largest battle in naval history. It fell far short of what Halsey could have and should have accomplished.

One must question Japanese capabilities by this stage of the war. Throughout the conflict there had been insufficient fuel for routine training. The authors of a history of the *Musashi* commented that, "The crew of the *Musashi* underwent rigorous daily training [but] most of the drills were performed with both ships (the *Yamato* also) tied to their buoys."[82] The *Musashi's* crew, among others, got drunk the night before departing Brunei Bay on 22 October. A chasm divided the brave words and lofty goals of the navy's commanders and the fleet's actual performance. Perhaps cynicism explained the ennui that marked the performance of several Japanese warships such as the *Shigure* and which stood in such contrast to the aggression of American skippers like McManes and Evans.

Overall, the U.S. Navy fought the Battles of Leyte Gulf with largely inexperienced ships and men. Action report after action report notes the need for more training and more practice. They also contain comments like, "In this, the ship's first action against enemy surface craft, the Commanding officer is pleased to note the exemplary conduct of all hands."[83] While experienced ships and men provided stiffening, the U.S. Navy won the tactical action—decisively—with a system and a doctrine. This, not the count of ships sunk or damaged, represented the true triumph of American arms and of the surface fleet. Had Kurita pursued a more aggressive course, it would have been the battle the Japanese admirals all claimed they wanted, an opportunity to die gloriously.

Chapter 13

Final Actions, December 1944–January 1945

As a naval officer of Japan, I never thought to try to save my own life while my warship was still afloat.
—Lieutenant Matsunaga Ichiro

A prominent historian has noted that a decisive naval victory "was supposed to enable the victor to 'control the seas,' to cut off the enemy's seaborne supplies and reinforcements. . . . That was what strategists in both the U.S. and Japan had long believed."[1] But following the battles of Surigao Strait and Samar, the Americans did not control the seas around Leyte. In fact, Japanese commanders believed their forces had inflicted horrendous damage to the enemy in the air battle of Formosa, in the surface action off Samar, and from kamikazes. The normally skeptical Ugaki recorded on 31 October, "An army reconnaissance . . . brought splendid news that no enemy plane was sighted either on land or in the air at Tacloban, and there were only one battleship and three cruisers or destroyers in the roads; the rest were sixty to seventy sunken transports reclining in the water."[2] The confidence this false intelligence fostered led to the conclusion that "the opportunity to annihilate enemy [was] at hand" and to the formal order to fight the decisive ground battle on Leyte.[3]

Between 23 October and 11 December, nine convoys and many barge runs delivered 45,000 troops and 10,000 tons of matériel to Leyte's Ormoc Bay, an effort that would have guaranteed victory at Guadalcanal.[4] Following hard on the heels of the cataclysmic naval battles of 25 October, this remarkable achievement was one reason the Imperial Japanese Navy did not immediately realize it had been so roundly defeated.

The U.S. Navy, meanwhile, neglected its Solomon lessons and failed to blockade Leyte with warships, expecting airpower could do the job. But Leyte's airfields proved inadequate, the weather was atrocious, and, after their extended operations, the fast carriers needed to resupply and rest their pilots. Staging fresh planes in from Formosa, the Japanese often gained local air superiority. Finally, the Seventh Fleet reorganized on 29 October and sent all but three battleships, four cruisers, and thirteen destroyers back to Ulithi. Fearing mines and feeling pinched for resources, Rear Admiral Weyler, who commanded this force, concentrated on defensive operations and did not venture major warships into the Camotes Sea west of Leyte. Moreover, kamikazes continued to wreak havoc, sinking one destroyer and damaging three

MAP 13.1. FINAL ACTIONS, DECEMBER 1944–JANUARY 1945

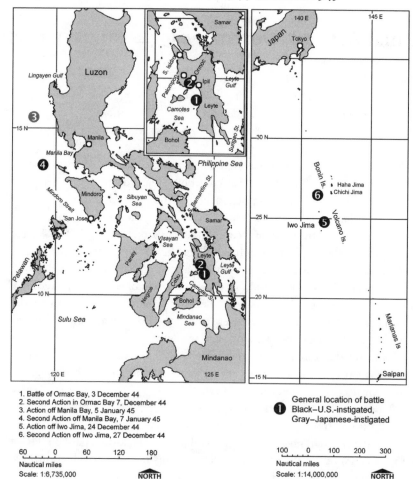

1. Battle of Ormac Bay, 3 December 44
2. Second Action in Ormac Bay 7, December 44
3. Action off Manila Bay, 5 January 45
4. Second Action off Manila Bay, 7 January 45
5. Action off Iwo Jima, 24 December 44
6. Second Action off Iwo Jima, 27 December 44

General location of battle
❶ Black–U.S.-instigated,
Gray–Japanese-instigated

60   0   60   120   180
Nautical miles
Scale: 1:6,735,000   ▲NORTH

100   0   100   200   300
Nautical miles
Scale: 1:14,000,000   ▲NORTH

carriers and five destroyers between 29 October and 1 November. Task Force 38, refueled and rearmed, partially restored the situation on 5 and 6 November with massive strikes against enemy airfields on Luzon, but by this time the U.S. Army faced a protracted campaign on Leyte.[5]

Japan's first major Ormoc convoy of six destroyers, four escorts, and four transports landed 11,000 troops on 1 November. Barges and light vessels poured in fresh soldiers nightly through the first part of November. On 9 November another large operation delivered 2,600 troops and 6,600 tons of supplies. However, on this convoy's return trip to Manila, U.S. Army air strikes force sank three transports and a corvette.

Disaster struck the Japanese on 11 November, when Task Force 38 returned, in part due to MacArthur's growing frustration with the situation. A 347-plane strike overwhelmed a convoy of five transports carrying 10,000 troops and sank every one, as well as four destroyers and a minesweeper. These results led to the reports that the "only men to arrive at Leyte were those men who swam to shore."[6] Ironically, Vice Admiral Kurita had sortied from Brunei on 9 November with the *Yamato*, *Nagato*, *Haruna*, a cruiser, and four destroyers to support this doomed operation, but Halsey missed him again.

Elements of Task Force 38 hit targets in and around Luzon on 13, 14, 19, and 25 November, but the Japanese persisted in their reinforcement efforts. American minesweepers finally cleared the Camotes Strait on 27 November, and destroyer divisions began patrolling the approaches to Ormoc Bay on a nightly basis. On 28 November the *Waller*, *Saufley*, *Renshaw*, and *Pringle* combined to sink the sub chaser *Ch53* (442 tons, 16 knots, one 3.1-inch/.40-caliber gun) off Ormoc.[7] On the night of 1–2 December four destroyers reported the destruction of one transport, and PT boats reported the destruction of another. The Japanese army transports *SS10* and *SS14* disappeared that night and were the likely victims.[8]

Battle of Ormoc Bay, 3 December 1944

On the afternoon of 2 December American flyers reported sightings of four Japanese transports and one escort en route to Ormoc. Weyler ordered the freshly arrived Destroyer Division 120, which consisted of new "super" destroyers of the *Sumner* class, to intercept. The third echelon of Convoy TA7 slipped into Ormoc Bay on 2 December and began off-loading late that evening. Cdr. John C. Zahm's destroyer division had a rougher voyage. Japanese floatplane bombers and night fighters were out in force, and a tight timeframe forced Zahm's ships to steam at thirty knots. A bright moon, a calm sea, and their foaming wakes combined to make them easily visible from the sky during their 160-mile passage into the Camotes Sea. A bomb near-missed the *Allen M. Sumner's* starboard bow at 2308, spraying the ship with fragments and wounding eleven men. From that time on, bogies continuously haunted her radar.

Although an American Blackcat pilot reported that Ormoc Bay was empty, Zahm decided to press on, and Division 120 entered the bay just a few minutes before midnight. The flagship *Allen M. Sumner* sailed on the left flank, the *Cooper* occupied the center, and the *Moale* took the right, with intervals of 1,500 yards between ships. The formation was intended to maximize the Americans' heavy forward armament and present a smaller target. Japanese planes continued to harass the destroyers, and the racket of AA guns broadcast the American approach.

TABLE 13.1 FORCES ENGAGED IN THE BATTLE OF ORMOC BAY

	Type of Ship	Year Launched	Displacement, Full Load (tons)	Max. Speed (knots)	Guns (number by inch/ caliber)	Torpedoes (number of tubes by diameter in inches)	Damage
American Destroyer Division 120 (Cdr. J.C. Zahm)							
Allen M. Sumner (F)	DD	1943	3,218	36	6 x 5/38	10 x 21	D1
Cooper	DD	1943	3,218	36	6 x 5/38	10 x 21	Sunk
Moale	DD	1943	3,218	36	6 x 5/38	10 x 21	D1
Japanese Escort Squadron 31							
Take	DE	1944	1.506	27	3 x 5/40	4 x 24	D2
Kuwa	DE	1944	1.506	27	3 x 5/40	4 x 24	Sunk
T9	APD	1944	1,800	22	2 x 5/40		
T140	LST	1944	1,010	13	1 x 3.1/40		
T159	LST	1944	1,010	13	1 x 3.1/40		

APD—destroyer transport, D1—light or superficial damage (including splinter damage), D2—moderate damage (combat ability not significantly impaired), DD—destroyer, DE—destroyer escort, F—flagship, LST—landing ship, tank
    Time: 0003–0032 Weather: Partial overcast, light airs
    Visibility: Good, full moon, slight haze
    Sea state: Calm
    Surprise: None
    Mission: Americans—interception based on general intelligence; Japanese—escort and transit

At 2355 the *Allen M. Sumner*'s radar registered a contact 20,000 yards to the north. As the pip separated from shore, the Americans identified it as a vessel and then as two enemy ships, one to the northwest heading south and the other closer to the beach. At 0005 Zahm ordered his ships to "Execute dog" on the approaching contact, which proved to be the *Take*.[9] The *Moale* engaged the *Take* from a range of 7,500 yards, and the *Allen M. Sumner* and *Cooper* targeted the *Kuwa* from 9,000 and 12,000 yards, respectively (see Map 13.2). The *Cooper*'s first salvo fell short, but she claimed hits with the second; the *Allen M. Sumner* considered her third broadside effective. The *Cooper* believed she hit a "large destroyer," while the *Allen M. Sumner* described it as a "small transport."[10] In any case, American shellfire severely punished the *Kuwa*.

MAP 13.2. BATTLE OF ORMOC BAY, 3 DECEMBER 1944

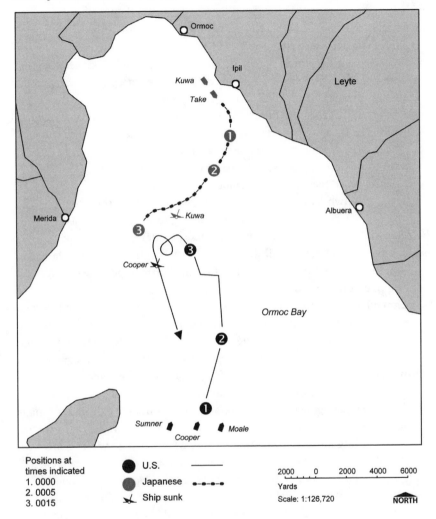

The Japanese destroyer escorts replied, and their volleys of five-inch rounds were supplemented by streams of bullets from the dozens of 25-mm guns arming the landing ships and by aircraft dropping down to strafe the three destroyers. The response was so intense that the Americans imagined MTBs were attacking from either beam. A sailor aboard the *Allen M. Sumner* described the scene: "The night began to light up like a huge fireworks display from the red and green tracers going in all directions, from ships and shore installations burning and exploding in multi-colored fireballs, and from winks of fire coming from the many guns firing at us."[11]

The violent opposition disrupted Zahm's neat formation. The *Allen M. Sumner* turned west at 0008 to put some distance between herself and the enemy guns; three minutes later she veered sharply north. Meanwhile, the *"Moale* had commenced emergency maneuvers to avoid torpedoes that might have been fired and to confuse reported bogies."[12] In the process she cut in front of the *Cooper* and forced her sister ship to abruptly hold fire. After the *Moale* moved on the *Cooper* engaged the *Take*, but the Japanese ship already had torpedoes swimming. A Long Lance clobbered the *Cooper* amidships at 0013. The force of the explosion knocked the large destroyer 45 degrees to starboard. Her last salvo ricocheted off the water, and she then jackknifed and sunk in just thirty seconds. One hundred ninety-one of the *Cooper's* men perished.

At the same time the *Kuwa*, torn apart by the intense American barrage, followed the *Cooper* to the bottom of Ormoc Bay.

Zahm, meanwhile, turned to clear the area and clarify the situation. The *Allen M. Sumner* and *Moale* continued shooting to port as they fled the bay. The *Allen M. Sumner* had used up her flashless powder, and the smokeless day powder emitted a great yellow flash that blinded her gunners and drew Japanese fire. Nonetheless, the Americans hit the *Take*, inflicting moderate damage and disabling one of her engines.

Zahm queried the *Moale* as to the *Cooper's* whereabouts at 0022 and learned that the *Cooper* had been torpedoed. At 0025 Zahm swung back to help, but when the *Moale* clarified that she had seen the *Cooper* sink, Zahm judged a rescue attempt to be too risky. As the *Moale's* captain reported, "The strike was designed as an offensive; however, there was a strong feeling of being on the defensive throughout."[13] At 0032 Zahm began the journey home.

Division 120 expended moderate amounts of ammunition during this half-hour battle, with the *Cooper* firing 300–400 shells, the *Allen M. Sumner* expending 842 (including air engagements), and the *Moale* firing 550. The *Allen M. Sumner* suffered minor damage from aerial attacks and one small-caliber shell during the surface action. Three rounds struck the *Moale* and damaged her after torpedo mount and holed her hull above the waterline. In addition, a Japanese strafing run killed two of the *Moale's* men and wounded twenty-two others. Many near misses peppered both the American survivors with splinters. The *Allen M. Sumner* welded more than forty patches over holes in the ship's bow that ranged from "the size of a dime to that of a bowling ball."[14]

Three hours after the Americans departed, the Japanese convoy weighted anchor. The *Take* limped along on one engine, but the landing ships escaped major harm. Drifting in the bay, the *Cooper's* survivors observed the Japanese departure. Seaplanes were able to rescue some of the *Cooper's* men, and they subsequently described the landing vessels as submarines. These erroneous reports led to the belief that the *Cooper* had fallen victim to a sub ambush.

The unsatisfactory outcome of this battle for the Americans was determined by new ships, green crews, bright moonlight, and bad positioning, with the last probably being the greatest factor. As the *Allen M. Sumner's* action report relates, "Enemy planes and shore batteries could see us but we could not see them due to the dark land background."[15] These were the conditions that led to the loss of the last U.S. warship in a surface action against the Japanese.

Second Action in Ormoc Bay, 12 December 1944

Continuing Japanese resistance on Leyte and the Americans' failure to gain air superiority caused the invasion of Mindoro, the campaign's next advance, to be postponed ten days. While largely unwelcome, at least this setback freed up shipping that the U.S. Army used to transport a newly arrived division directly into Ormoc Bay. The objective was to quickly end resistance by slamming shut the "enemy's back door."[16] The Japanese reacted violently with massive kamikaze strikes that crashed three destroyers, a destroyer transport, and a landing ship, medium (LSM). The American troops, which came ashore north of Albuera, experienced heavy resistance, and had to fight their way into Ormoc, which they reached on 10 December.[17]

Despite the seemingly hopeless situation a Japanese brigade attempted to reach Palompon on 7 December, but air strikes forced it ashore at San Isidro on Leyte's northwestern tip. The last Japanese transport operation to Leyte, TA9, left Manila on 9 December with "great expectations," carrying 3,000 troops in three transports and a Special Naval Landing Force equipped with amphibious tanks embarked on the *T140* and *T159*.[18] The convoy's escort force included the destroyers *Yuzuki*, *Uzuki*, and *Kiri* and the sub chasers *Cha17* and *Cha37*.

U.S. Army airplanes jumped the Japanese transports off Palompon on the afternoon of 11 December, hitting two of them and driving the third—accompanied by the sub chasers—into Palompon. While the *Uzuki* rescued survivors, Captain Sawamura Seiji entered Ormoc Bay with the *Yuzuki*, *Kiri*, *T140*, and *T159*.

At the same time thirteen American LSMs and landing craft, infantry (LCIs) and Destroyer Squadron 4—the flagship *Caldwell* followed by the *Reid*, *Conyngham*, *Smith*, *Coghlan*, and *Edwards*—under Capt. J.F. Newman steamed for the same destination. While the Americans were en route, two Japanese aircraft crashed into the *Reid* and secondary explosions detonated her after magazine. She sank with heavy loss of life. After detaching two LSMs and a destroyer for a subsidiary operation south of Ormoc, the balance of the American force headed for Ipil.

Sawamura arrived first, but American troops greeted and sank one landing barge that attempted to dock at Ormoc's pier. Sawamura moved west to the mouth of the Pagsangahan River, where the transports beached and disgorged the naval troops and their four tanks. This provoked a firefight with U.S. troops ashore, who

TABLE 13.2. FORCES ENGAGED DURING THE SECOND ACTION IN ORMOC BAY

Type of Ship	Year Launched	Displacement, Full Load (tons)	Max. Speed (knots)	Guns (number by inch/ caliber)	Torpedoes (number of tubes by diameter in inches)	Damage
American (Lt. Cdr. B.B. Cheatham)						
Coghlan	DD	1943	3,218	36	6 x 5/38	10 x 21	
Japanese Destroyer Division 30 (Captain Sawamura Seiji)						
Yuzuki (F)	APD	1927	1,913	37	2 x 4.7/45	4 x 24	
Kiri	DE	1944	1,506	27	3 x 5/40	4 x 24	
T140	LST	1944	1,010	13	1 x 3.1/40		D2
T159	LST	1944	1,010	13	1 x 3.1/40		Sunk

APD—destroyer transport, D2—moderate damage (combat ability not significantly impaired), DD—destroyer, DE—destroyer escort, F—flagship, LST—landing ship, tank
  Time: 0155–0217
  Weather: Scattered squalls, light breeze
  Visibility: Poor
  Sea state: Calm
  Surprise: Both
  Mission: Americans—amphibious attack; Japanese—amphibious attack

employed tank destroyers emplaced 1,000 yards up the beach and artillery from further inland. The Army forces claimed that "enemy vessel attempted to pull out to sea, but after proceeding less than fifty yards it burst into flames and sank. About 150 men, two tanks, a number of rifles, mortars, and machine guns, and a quantity of ammunition had been unloaded before the vessel sank, but most of the supplies, including four ammunition trucks, had been destroyed by American fire while the vessel was unloading."[19]

Meanwhile, Newman's squadron entered the bay. Lookouts noted "flares" on the beach, then a large searchlight illuminated the *Caldwell* and *Coghlan*. The *Caldwell* was straddled by what seemed to be fire from shore batteries, and the destroyers turned south seeking maneuvering room. At 0155 on 12 December the Japanese ships began to depart. Operating to the east southeast off Ipil the *Coghlan*'s radar detected three pips. She turned toward the contacts and opened fire from 14,000 yards. Because her fire control radar could not distinguish the targets from the land, the *Coghlan* used "the regular shore bombardment set-up." Closing to 6,000 yards the *Coghlan* shifted to full-radar controlled fire against the third target because, according to the ship's report, "At no time could target be seen visually, though flashes of bursting projectiles would indicate hits on a solid object."[20]

At 0213 the *Coghlan* claimed one enemy ship sunk. This may have been the *T159*, which foundered off the beach. The *T140* suffered damage but managed to pull away and, with the two destroyers, flee the bay. Sawamura believed he was facing cruisers. Lt. Cdr. B.B. Cheatham ordered his gunners aboard the *Coghlan* to cease firing at 0217 and reported that one vessel was departing at high speed. At 0427, as the American convoy gathered to leave, the *Coghlan* detected a small surface contact and opened fire again for eight minutes until the contact withdrew north in an apparently damaged condition. During the two incidents, the *Coghlan* fired a total of 221 five-inch common rounds and eight star shells and did not notice any return fire.

Sawamura rounded the peninsula and landed more troops at Palompon, where the *Uzuki* fell victim to *PT490* and *PT492*. The American boats spotted the enemy destroyers, idled in until they were just 1,000 yards from their target, and released six torpedoes. One exploded beneath the *Uzuki*'s bridge, and a second detonated amidships, "sending oil, water, and debris hundred of feet in the air."[21] The *Yuzuki* didn't survive the night either. Marine aircraft caught and sank her in the Visayan Sea.

After this unusual episode the hard pressed Japanese defenders of Leyte received no more help. On Christmas Day 1944, MacArthur declared the island secured except for "minor mopping up," adding it was "perhaps the greatest defeat in military annals of the Japanese Army."[22] Resistance to the Americans, however, persisted until 8 May 1945.

From Leyte to Luzon

American troops next landed at San Jose on the lightly held island of Mindoro on 15 December. This 200-mile leap caught the enemy by surprise. Kamikaze attacks sank five LSTs and five transports over the next three days. Ugaki observed, "This is considered to be the very time for the surface force to make a successful thrusting attack."[23] Combined Fleet shared his view, and Japanese surface forces proceeded to demonstrate their continued ability to surprise the enemy.

On 26 December a "penetration" unit that included the heavy cruiser *Ashigara*, the light cruiser *Oyodo*, and the destroyers *Kasumi*, *Kiyoshimo*, *Asashimo*, *Kaya*, *Sugi*, and *Kashi* sallied from Cam Ranh Bay. An American flyer spotted the Japanese force 160 miles short of Mindoro, and the pilot mistook the *Ashigara* for the *Yamato*. This prompted a frantic response from the Americans, but with the Seventh Fleet's major warships at Leyte Gulf, aircraft and PT boats were all Kinkaid had to meet the threat. In any event, the Japanese brushed past defending PTs while subjecting them to "intense and accurate fire" and then conducted an anticlimactic and largely harmless forty-minute bombardment of Mindoro.[24] Air attacks had damaged the *Kiyoshimo* and while they were withdrawing shortly after midnight, a pair of PTs encountered the Japanese raiders. *PT221* launched two torpedoes and reported, "a bright orange-red flash on the third ship in line, followed by the sound of a heavy explosion." The target was the *Kiyoshimo*, which quickly sank. By the time Kinkaid had rushed four cruisers and eight destroyers to the scene, the enemy was nearly 700 miles away.[25]

With Mindoro secured, Luzon lay open to MacArthur and the Seventh Fleet. During 2–8 January, American task groups bound for Lingayen Gulf sailed from Leyte Gulf to meet off the projected beachhead. Most of the Japanese opposition to these movements came from kamikazes, who exacted a terrible toll. The loss of life and shipping caused by the suicide attacks was so high that Oldendorf felt it necessary to warn Kinkaid that the whole operation might need to be reconsidered.

Preparations for the Luzon invasion continued, however. The Imperial Japanese Navy retained six battleships, and the American admirals also feared a Leyte style intervention. However, the only Japanese surface forces to interfere with the Seventh Fleet turned out to be a pair of destroyer escorts.

Action off Manila Bay, 5 January 1945

At 1430 a minesweeping and hydrographic group of eighty-five vessels steaming slowly north to Lingayen Gulf received a report from the group's combat air patrol (CAP) that two enemy ships had departed Manila Bay. Commander Iwagami Juichi may have been attempting to reach Cape St. Jacques, Vietnam. If this was his intent, his timing was peculiar, as he ventured out during the day and on a course calculated to intercept a large, slow, and vulnerable armada of enemy auxiliaries protected only by the destroyer *Bennion*, the sloop HMAS *Warrego*, and the frigate HMAS *Gascoyne*. Large numbers of Japanese aircraft were aloft, so Iwagami presumably possessed some knowledge of his enemy's movements and strength.

Informed that Japanese warships, originally reported to be cruisers, were approaching, one of the *Warrego*'s men recalled, "The report didn't make us very happy as none of us could outgun a cruiser."[26] Nonetheless, the *Bennion* reversed course at 1537, and at 1540 her skipper, Cdr. R.H. Holmes, ordered the Australians to follow. The American destroyer made radar contact with the Japanese at 1548 at a range of 23,300 yards. Two minutes later, the *Bennion* sighted the enemy on the southeast horizon. As the *Gascoyne* fell in astern, the *Bennion* slowed to the frigate's top speed of twenty knots. Iwagami's destroyers noted warships coming their way—likely mistaking their shapes for a cruiser and destroyers—and immediately put about for Manila. They flung a salvo at 1557 from 18,700 yards and commenced laying both funnel and chemical smoke several minutes later. The *Bennion* fired her first ranging salvos at 1558. The *Gascoyne* shot a broadside at 1603, which the CAP, spotting overhead, reported as about a mile short.

TABLE 13.3. FORCES ENGAGED IN THE ACTION OFF MANILA BAY

	Type of Ship	Year Launched	Displacement, Full Load (tons)	Max. Speed (knots)	Guns (number by inch/caliber)	Torpedoes (number of tubes by diameter in inches)	Damage
				Allied (Cdr. R.H. Holmes)			
Bennion (F)	DD	1943	2,924	38	5 x 5/38	10 x 21	
Warrego (AU)	PS	1940	1,510	17	3 x 4.7/45		
Gascoyne (AU)	FF	1943	2,180	20	2 x 4/45		
			Japanese Destroyer Division 52 (Commander Iwagami Juichi)				
Hinoki (F)	DE	1944	1.506	27	3 x 5/40	4 x 24	
Momi	DE	1944	1.506	27	3 x 5/40	4 x 24	

AU—Australian, DD—destroyer, DE—destroyer escort, F—flagship, FF—frigate, PS—sloop
Time: 1550–1640
Weather: 5/10 clouds, light northeasterly breeze
Visibility: Excellent
Sea state: Slight
Surprise: None
Mission: Americans—escort and transit; Japanese—transit (?)

At 1611 Holmes decided to increase speed because the range was slowly open-ing and because he wanted to drive the enemy toward Oldendorf's powerful Task Group 77.2 to the south. At 1624 the *Bennion* resumed firing with her forward guns, this time at a range of 17,400 yards. The Japanese zigzagged to chase salvos as the Australian ships slowly faded from the action. By 1636 the *Bennion*'s range had dropped to 14,300 yards. Holmes observed enemy shells splashing between 500 and 1,000 yards short on the starboard beam. He periodically swerved to unleash salvos from all five of his guns, and when the CAP reported, "You almost got him" at 1637, he commenced "rapid continuous fire from all 5" guns."[27]

The CAP observed splashes surrounding the trailing Japanese destroyer. By this time, however, the *Bennion* had chased thirty miles from the convoy she was responsible for protecting. At 1640, hearing that a large enemy air strike was inbound, Holmes broke off and left it to Task Group 77.2's aircraft to continue the hunt. The *Bennion* expended 349 rounds during her forty minutes of action. The escort carriers of Task Group 77.2 launched sixteen torpedo bombers and nineteen fighters, which sank the *Momi* and damaged the *Hinoki*. The surviving Japanese ship limped back to Manila.²⁸

The landing at Luzon was scheduled to begin on 9 January, but Rear Admiral Oldendorf commenced the preinvasion bombardment on 6 January, a costly day that saw a strike by the "largest and most deadly group of suicide planes encountered during the operation."²⁹ Kamikazes sank one warship and damaged eleven more, including two battleships.³⁰

Second Action off Manila Bay, 7 January 1945

After undergoing emergency repairs at Manila, the *Hinoki* again attempted to escape on 7 January. She emerged about two hours after dark, but once again ran into traffic streaming north in conjunction with the scheduled American invasion. This time, it was Destroyer Squadron 23 escorting transport group 78.1.

At 2115 the *Charles Ausburne* picked up a radar contact at 40,000 yards, but "due to very poor quality of pip and its erratic behavior," the ship's Capt. T.B. Dugan did not consider it a legitimate contact.³¹ The pip persisted, however, and Dugan turned to investigate at 2217, increasing speed from nine knots to twenty-five. At 2226 the *Charles Ausburne* lofted a star shell east by northeast and revealed the *Hinoki*'s silhouette 10,000 yards off and heading west by northwest.

Upon being spotted, Iwagami steered the *Hinoki* 100 degrees to starboard and fired torpedoes. These missed, in part because the Americans were undertaking radical course changes due to "an uneasy feeling that a submarine or submarines might have been accompanying the surface unit being engaged."³² At 2235 the *Charles Ausburne* observed a broadside hit the Japanese destroyer squarely, and the *Hinoki*'s speed immediately dropped. The *Braine* assumed illumination duties as the flagship pumped salvos from all five guns at six-second intervals.

The *Hinoki* returned fire, and many Japanese shells fell within twenty to thirty yards of the *Charles Ausburne*. This prompted Dugan to observe, "The enemy's deflection was fair to excellent, and his range estimate accurate, but fortunately not good enough. *Ausburne* was lucky in not receiving any hits."³³ Iwagami could not say the same. Damage to the *Hinoki* accrued as the range closed to 1,100 yards.

The *Charles Ausburne* raked her target, and the *Hinoki* sank at 2255, shooting her machine guns to the end. "As she went down," Dugan wrote, "her small arms ammunition was exploding causing brilliant tracers to light up the sky, after which there was silence. . . . Only a strong smell of diesel oil remained."³⁴

Earlier that day news from the American Naval Group, China that a "major Japanese surface force" was at sea west of Kyushu caused a minor panic in Seventh Fleet headquarters. On 12 January, after being reminded that the many ships lent by the Pacific Fleet to the Seventh Fleet had to be returned, MacArthur wrote

TABLE 13.4. FORCES ENGAGED IN THE SECOND ACTION OFF MANILA BAY

	Type of Ship	Year Launched	Displacement, Full Load (tons)	Max. Speed (knots)	Guns (number by inch/caliber)	Torpedoes (number of tubes by diameter in inches)	Damage
American Destroyer Squadron 23 (Capt. T.B. Dugan)							
Charles Ausburne (F)	DD	1943	2,924	38	5 x 5/38	10 x 21	
Braine	DD	1943	2,924	38	5 x 5/38	10 x 21	
Shaw	DD	1935	2,103	36	5 x 5/38	12 x 21	
Russell	DD	1938	2,313	35	5 x 5/38	8 x 21	
Japanese Destroyer Division 52 (Commander Iwagami Juichi)							
Hinoki	DE	1944	1.506	27	3 x 5/40	4 x 24	Sunk

DD—destroyer, DE—destroyer escort, F—flagship
Time: 2115–2255
Weather: Clear, light northeasterly airs
Visibility: Poor
Sea state: Slight
Surprise: None
Mission: Americans—interception based on general intelligence; Japanese—transit

Nimitz that "to withdraw the Third Fleet and the elements which have temporarily augmented the Seventh Fleet will completely expose Lingayen to naval surface attack and would plainly invite disaster."[35] In response to MacArthur's concerns, Nimitz juggled his allocations and allowed the Seventh Fleet to keep four battleships and a host of cruisers and destroyers to deal with the threat of Japan's surviving battleships. Moreover, Halsey camped north of Luzon during the Lingayen operation hoping the enemy would venture out, but again he was doomed to disappointment.

Throughout the balance of the Philippine campaign, the Japanese navy's surface fleet avoided contact. However, in an interesting demonstration of attitudes and capabilities toward the end of the war, the Seventh Fleet received intelligence early in February 1945 that the hybrid battleship/carriers *Ise* and *Hyuga* would be deploying from Singapore to home waters. Admiral Berkey, "the racehorse of the Seventh Fleet," suggested intercepting them at night with light cruisers and destroyers. Kinkaid rejected this proposal on the basis that the Fifth Air Force and a host of Pacific Fleet submarines could do the job. However, American aircraft missed the enemy due to weather, and the submarines never got in position to attack. The *Ise* and *Hyuga* were probably lucky Kinkaid reined in Berkey.[36]

Action off Iwo Jima, 24 December 1944

As the tide of war washed against the Japanese home islands, American cruiser–destroyer forces continued to raid enemy bases and sweep shipping routes. On two occasions these actions resulted in one-sided surface engagements against Japanese warships larger than 500 tons. On several other occasions small warships and convoys fell victim to the surface fleet.

The Bonin campaign commenced with a decision in October 1944 to capture Iwo Jima as an emergency B-29 airstrip. From December 1944 to February 1945 the Navy conducted five surface bombardments of the island, in addition to nearly daily air raids, to clear the way for the assault and suppress air attacks against Saipan's B-29 base. Rear Adm. Alan E. Smith's Cruiser Division 5 with heavy cruisers *Chester*, *Pensacola*, and *Salt Lake City* and six destroyers led the first raid on 8 December 1944, shelling Iwo Jima's airfields and shore batteries. On 22 December Smith sailed for an encore.

TABLE 13.5. FORCES ENGAGED IN THE ACTION OFF IWO JIMA

Type of Ship	Year Launched	Displacement, Full Load (tons)	Max. Speed (knots)	Guns (number by inch/caliber)	Torpedoes (number of tubes by diameter in inches)	Damage
American Task Unit 94.9.3 (Cdr. J.P. Craft Jr.)						
Roe (F)	DD	1939	2,313	35	5 x 5/38	8 x 21	
Case	DD	1935	2,103	36	4 x 5/38	12 x 21	
Japanese						
T8	APD	1944	1,800	22	2 x 5/40		Sunk

APD—destroyer transport, DD—destroyer, F—flagship
Time: 1503–1600
Weather: Overcast, fresh northeasterly breeze
Visibility: Fair
Sea state: Moderate crests
Surprise: None
Mission: Americans—shore bombardment; Japanese—transit

The second bombardment of Iwo Jima commenced at 1300 on 24 December. After just twenty minutes American flyers reported a destroyer fleeing north, and Rear Admiral Smith sent the *Case* and *Roe* after it. The two destroyers swung north by northeast at 1324 and worked up to thirty-three knots. Their quarry was the fast destroyer-transport *T8*, which was loaded with troops she had been delivering to the island.

A spotter buzzed overhead and guided the Americans. As they closed Cdr. J.P. Craft Jr. sent the *Case* to port and kept the *Roe* on a direct course to the target. At 1503 the enemy came into view while still 20,000 yards away (see Map 13.3). The *Case* opened fire at 1522 after the range had closed to 14,600 yards, and the *Roe* followed suit shortly after. The *T8* immediately commenced violent evasive maneuvers. With the spotter's assistance, however, the American destroyers made good shooting. The *Case*'s action report reflects this: "Target was effectively hit with these early salvos and his speed was quickly reduced to 14 knots, permitting *Roe* and *Case* to close range rapidly."[37]

The *T8* fought back, shooting a total of twenty-four salvos between 1535 and 1552. The nearest she came to doing damage was a round that splashed fifteen yards short of the *Case*. At 1549 the *T8* cut to starboard of the *Roe* blocking the *Case*'s line of fire for several minutes. Craft then announced on the TBS he was going to ram, but he later refrained from taking this drastic and unnecessary step.

At 1552 the *Case*, her decks crowded with spectators watching the action, reported seeing torpedoes in the water even though the *T8* carried no such weapons. The *Case* swung sharply to port to avoid the imaginary torpedoes. By this time the *Roe* had closed to within several hundred yards of the Japanese, and shells from both the American ships were consistently detonating on target. The Japanese transport sank at 1559 about forty miles south of Hara Jima. Both the *Case* and the *Roe* attempted to "pick up prisoners." Craft, nervous about his proximity to Chichi Jima, noted that his only regret was that he did not use a torpedo to more quickly sink the *T8* to expedite withdrawal from "enemy waters."[38]

This was a successful action by any measure, but Craft's decision to split his force was unusual. In their after action assessments, the *Case*'s skipper, Cdr. R.S. Willey, wrote, "[T]actical concentration of the two destroyers upon reaching surface target would have been a better decision than to split up." To which Craft made the testy endorsement that "[n]o advantage is seen in maintaining *Roe* and *Case* in close proximity." He argued that a widely divided formation complicated the enemy commander's defense.[39] It is difficult to accept Craft's reasoning. The commander of the *T8* would have had to divide his fire even if the destroyers fought in formation, and the other problems would not have arisen.

While Craft's unit chased the Japanese APD, the bombarding American destroyers found enemy shipping in Iwo Jima's boat basin. The *Dunlap* claimed several hits on an LST, probably the landing ship *T157*, which was lost that day.[40]

MAP 13.3. ACTION OFF IWO JIMA, 24 DECEMBER 1944

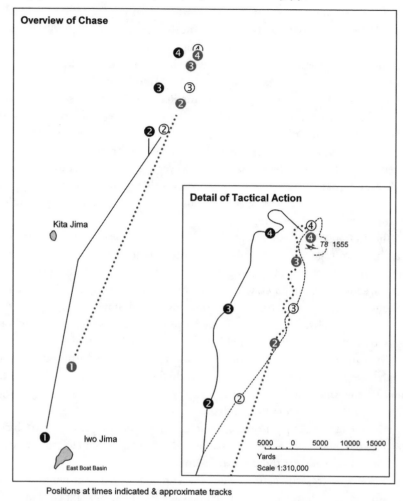

Second Action off Iwo Jima, 27 December 1944

Despite Rear Admiral Smith's Christmas Eve bombardment, Japanese aircraft raided Saipan the next day, provoking a return visit by the American surface ships three days later. At 1220 as Cruiser Division 5 approached their bombardment stations, the *Chester* reported sighting a destroyer on the island's east side. Capt. H.P. Smith

TABLE 13.6. FORCES ENGAGED IN THE SECOND ACTION OFF IWO JIMA

Type of Ship	Year Launched	Displacement, Full Load (tons)	Max. Speed (knots)	Guns (number by inch/caliber)	Torpedoes (number of tubes by diameter in inches)	Damage
American Task Unit 94.9.2 (Capt. H.P. Smith)						
Dunlap (F) — DD	1936	2,103	36	4 x 5/38	12 x 21	D1
Fanning — DD	1936	2,103	36	4 x 5/38	12 x 21	
Cummings — DD	1935	2,103	36	4 x 5/38	12 x 21	
Japanese						
T7 — APD	1944	1,800	22	2 x 5/40		Sunk
T132 — LST	1944	1,010	13	1 x 3.1/40		Sunk

APD—destroyer transport, D1—light or superficial damage (including splinter damage), DD—destroyer, F—flagship, LST—landing ship, tank

Time: 1256–1454
Weather: n/a
Visibility: n/a
Sea state: n/a
Surprise: Americans
Mission: Americans—shore bombardment; Japanese—transit

led the ships of Task Unit 94.9.2 around to investigate. At 1257 they encountered *T7* anchored southwest of the boat basin, and they opened fire a minute later.

At 1305 the *Dunlap* and *Fanning* went to twenty-five knots and headed west southwest to close the basin, which contained more enemy shipping, including at least two large landing ships. The *Dunlap* observed straddles around the *T7* at 1306 and commenced firing rapidly from a range of 7,700 yards. The *T7* had been raising steam, but after a shell punched a large hole in her hull, she swung toward shore and ran aground. Shortly thereafter, the American observers spotted an LST, "painted light green, beached with ramp down about 1,500 yards northeast of present target, evidently surprised in act of unloading."[41]

The American destroyers divided their fire between the *T7* and the landing craft. Shore batteries entered the action, and a shell burst over the *Dunlap* at 1320, disabling her TBS antenna. Dust, smoke, and spray degraded visibility as Smith's ships engaged the shore batteries as well as the previous targets and other small boats. Cease fire sounded at 1440. Observers reported the *T7* down at the stern—

her after part a "mass of tangled and twisted iron."[42] At 1454 the *T132* exploded violently, sending a tall column of smoke billowing into the sky. The Americans left another landing ship smoldering.

Final Patrols

On 5 January Cruiser Division 5 returned with six destroyers. This time they raided Chichi Jima and Haha Jima as well as Iwo Jima. Operating ahead of the division as a radar picket, the *Fanning* encountered the landing ship *T107* at 0206. The *Fanning* engaged fifty miles west southwest of Chichi Jima and left the smaller craft crippled. Later, the *Fanning* and the *Dunlap* teamed up to sink the *T107*.

During the 5 January bombardment a mine badly damaged the *David W. Taylor*, and a shore battery perforated the *Fanning* with three light-caliber shells. Later, the *Dunlap, Cummings, Ellet,* and *Roe* dispatched the *T154* fifteen miles south of Iwo Jima. This campaign's final bombardment by surface ships occurred on 24 January, when Rear Adm. Oscar C. Badger brought the *Indiana* along with Cruiser Division 5 to the area. By coincidence, a small Japanese convoy had arrived that morning, and the *Dunlap* and *Fanning* destroyed the transport *Yoneyama Maru* (584 GRT) and the auxiliary minesweepers *Keinan Maru* (316 GRT) and *Showa Maru 7* (264 GRT) twenty-five miles southeast of the island.

After the bloody assault on Iwo Jima that began on 19 February and continued into April, destroyers continued to patrol off Chichi Jima and Haha Jima. The American ships occasionally encountered and sank Japanese shipping and auxiliary warships, as on 19 June 1945 when the *Dunlap* fired torpedoes at a pair of luggers that were en route to Chichi Jima to evacuate civilians and then sank them with gunfire after the torpedoes missed. She also bagged a cargo ship that afternoon and rescued fifty-two survivors.[43]

On 26 June 1945, in another example of late war surface engagements, the old cruisers *Richmond* and *Concord* and the destroyers *Bearss, John Hood, Jarvis,* and *Porter* sailed from Attu and penetrated the Okhotsk Sea east of the Kurile Islands. The destroyers shot up a convoy and sank the small escorts *Cha73, Cha206,* and *Cha209* (all 273 tons, 11 knots, one 25-mm) and the guard boat *No.2 Kusunoki Maru* south of Onekotan.[44]

Along with these normal duties, American destroyers found themselves taking up the never-envisioned and extremely hazardous task of serving as early warning pickets and attracting kamikazes away from the transports of the Okinawa invasion fleet. During the Okinawa campaign the Japanese navy also conducted its last major surface foray. On 6 April 1945, the *Yamato,* escorted by a light cruiser and eight destroyers, left the Inland Sea and headed for Okinawa. Hundreds of American carrier aircraft intercepted the *Yamato* and her escorts long before the Japanese had any chance to engage U.S. surface forces and sank the battleship, the cruiser, and four destroyers. The Japanese lost 3,665 men in this disaster, while the Americans lost only ten aircraft.

The *Yamato's* sortie came with four months remaining in the war. Although Japan remained pugnacious and the Imperial navy retained enough surface assets in home waters to assemble a respectable strike force until at least July 1945, the navy never again attempted to dispute the American advance in such a fashion. The simple reason is they could not. Japan imported no fuel oil after the first quarter of 1945, and domestic production for the year was about 34,000 tons.[45] The *Yamato* force, to cite the most apt example, consumed about 40 tons of fuel each hour cruising at economic speeds and up to 200 tons per hour when at battle speeds. Japan still had to maintain communications with Korea and China, and there was no fuel to spare for surface warfare.[46]

Ironically Japan's last surface naval engagement was not even in the Pacific Ocean, and it was not against the U.S. Navy. It occurred on 16 May 1945, when the battered veteran *Haguro* ran afoul of the British navy's Destroyer Flotilla 24 during an abortive attempt to maintain communications with the Andaman Islands. The meeting resulted in the torpedoing and loss of the *Haguro*.[47]

Conclusion

I think myself the power above us nodded on that day when the Argives put to sea in their fast sailing ships, with death aboard and doom for Trojans.

—HOMER, ILIAD II, 325–328

This book began with two questions: How did the U.S. Navy achieve such success in World War II, and what role did the surface fleet play in securing that success?

To answer the second question this book analyzed the U.S. Navy's surface actions, focusing especially on the Pacific theater. It examined how surface warships fought, why they fought, and what the larger implications of their battles were, particularly in the East Indies, the Solomon Islands, and the Philippines. It demonstrated that the guns and torpedoes of the surface fleet made major contributions to America's victory by playing decisive roles at critical junctures in the war. It refuted the widely held notion that the attack on Pearl Harbor suddenly rendered the battleships, guns, and torpedoes of the fleet obsolete and that naval aviation and submarines subsequently dominated the Pacific War.

From this analysis, an answer to the first question emerges. Success came from the effective integration of the Navy's air, amphibious, logistical, submarine, and surface components. Success came also from the U.S. Navy's abilities to improve its war-fighting techniques based upon experience and to appreciate its failures and accomplishments with greater intellectual honesty than the Japanese viewed their own fallacies and deeds. U.S. industrial might and the ability of the American military to recruit, train, and promote outstanding personnel were also critical factors. None of these elements alone won the war, but together they proved insurmountable. The history of the U.S. fleet's surface engagements illustrates all aspects of this winning formula in action.

The surface fleet faced great odds and suffered defeat in the East Indies. In the process, however, it demonstrated the will to struggle to the bitter end. In the Solomons the surface fleet fought a campaign of sixteen months and met the Japanese in eighteen surface actions. A comparison between Savo Island, the first action, and Empress Augusta Bay, the penultimate, is illuminating because in each case the Japanese sailed on the identical mission of disrupting an American amphibious landing. The Imperial navy surprised an unprepared enemy at Savo and inflicted a massive defeat. At Empress Augusta Bay, a waiting, confident U.S. naval force sent the Japanese packing.

In the Philippines the surface fleet proved crucial even after submarines had resolved their major problems and fast carriers had reached their height of power and range. It is instructive that in January 1945 General MacArthur petitioned Admiral Nimitz to keep the Pacific Fleet's divisions of old battleships to protect his amphibious fleets from the Japanese navy's battleships because, as he saw at Leyte Gulf, airpower and submarine power alone could not be trusted to do the job. The Navy itself concluded in March 1945:

> Actions covering this period illustrate most perfectly the potency of air power. On the other hand, they also illustrate the inadequacy of air power against armored and well armed units unless the attacks be unremittent. . . . The afternoon attacks of 24 October should have prevented the enemy from coming out through San Bernardino Straits but they did not prevent this. . . . On the other hand, our own surface vessels made short work of the enemy fleet attempting to enter Southern Leyte Gulf and we sustained very little damage in this action. It would therefore seem that, whenever possible, use should be made of our armored ships to sink enemy armored ships.[1]

World War II sparked a period of rapid evolution. It saw the introduction of many weapons that are used today, such as cruise missiles, jet aircraft, and assault rifles. One of the war's fascinating aspects is the study of how organizations adapted new technologies to the solution of old problems. The examination of the surface fleet's actions reveals this evolution in process. It shows how radar, for example, went from being a distrusted novelty to where the lack of this gear "gave all hands a feeling of being blindfolded."[2] The actions of the surface fleet highlighted the human component to the Navy's success. The old-salt professionals of the Asiatic Fleet did not lack for aggression or courage in 1942. Despite the Navy's massive expansion, those qualities were not diluted, as the Seventh Fleet's men and officers demonstrated in October 1944. Commanders and officers had to perform to certain standards, and the Navy proved ruthless in enforcing those standards—sometimes arbitrarily—sometimes unjustly, but on the whole effectively.

Lessons learned from the battles detailed in this book are as important today as they were six decades ago. Nowhere is this more true than in the area of intelligence. It is important to know what the enemy plans to do, but in many cases, it is more important to know what you have done. To illustrate this, consider Figure 14.1, which shows how in four surface actions fought at Guadalcanal, the U.S. Navy

FIGURE 14.1. CLAIMS OF SHIPS SUNK AND ACTUAL SINKINGS:
SOLOMON ISLANDS BATTLES, OCTOBER–NOVEMBER 1942

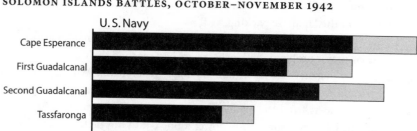

claimed it sank nineteen enemy warships. Actually, it accounted for seven. The Japanese claimed sixteen and got nine.

Such exaggerations prevented commanders from making realistic assessments of their performance and sugarcoated mistakes. As the war progressed, Americans claims came to more closely correspond to reality while Japanese claims grew increasingly fantastic.

According to one American intelligence officer, the Japanese commanders' penchant for overstating their achievements grew out of a lack of good management and concern with saving face. "The Japanese apparently had no organization capable of assessing reports based on combat observations. The bombastic style of their action reports suggests that it would have taken great courage for any Japanese administrative organization to attempt such assessment, but without it, plans and decisions were apt to be based on dangerously fictitious values."[3]

Prewar planners also made dangerously fictitious assumptions about their weapons. The Japanese expected to win battles with long-range torpedo barrages. The Americans expected to begin scoring effective hits with their battleship rifles within five minutes, even when firing at extreme range. Combat proved these expectations to be wildly optimistic. In fact, the weapons and ordnance both the U.S. and Japanese navies took to war suffered from serious defects. The reluctance to acknowledge and correct for these defects cost lives and battles.

Blind adherence to doctrine was a problem at least as great as having no doctrine at all. Pearl Harbor shattered the U.S. Navy's prewar doctrine of fighting a decisive action with the battle line. Slowly, after a diet of steady defeat, the Navy developed a new understanding of how to fight with their surface warships and use them to secure sea power. The Japanese, on the other hand, had their prewar surface warfare doctrine apparently vindicated in battle after battle. However, as the U.S. Navy's doctrine evolved, the Japanese Navy found itself without a response. An apt analysis of this Japanese strategic weakness reads, "In the interwar period it [the Imperial navy] prepared itself, in terms of doctrine, weaponry, and ship construction, to fight the battle it planned to win, but this translated itself differently to the point that the Imperial Navy was only able to fight the battle it planned to win. . . . Unfortunately for the Kaigun, the battle that presented itself was not one that the Imperial Navy had anticipated."[4]

This assessment does not subtract from the legendary persistence the men of the Imperial Japanese Navy displayed in both the bright and the dark days of their long war. Nor does it in any way diminish the dogged dedication of American sailors who lost their lives to gain the victories later historians have decreed to have been inevitable. In fact, the conduct of the naval war between Japan and the United States confirmed an intellectual problem articulated by the Prussian Field Marshall Helmuth von Moltke: "No battle plan ever survives contract with the enemy." One of war's greatest fallacies is the belief that the enemy will act according to one's own plans. Or, expressed slightly differently, the fallacy is to fight the war one plans to fight rather than the war that is. Confronted with confusion and uncertainty, unanticipated defeats, and shattered plans, the U.S. Navy proved more agile than the Japanese Imperial Navy. The evolution of America surface combat doctrine was one of the clearest examples of this agility. To the end, the Japanese took the opposite tack and tried to make the problem fit their solution—sometimes brilliantly, but ultimately ineffectually.

Finally, surface combat was quick and confusing, and few men had a chance to practice the art, much less master it. In that aspect, it proved far different from land or air operations, where a squad leader or fighter pilot could expect to see action repeatedly and (hopefully) learn from experience. Surface combat occurred suddenly, often without warning, and generally to men who had no experience of it. The relative ease of the U.S. Navy's victories from mid-1943 on indicates that the Americans successfully institutionalized knowledge about how to fight and applied it operationally. This proved to be one of the U.S. surface fleet's great accomplishments.

The history of the war waged by the U.S. Navy's surface fleet can serve as a cautionary parable as well as a guide. It is dangerous to assume that when engaged in a conflict against conventional or asymmetric enemies, the nation and its military hold the same virtues of swift adaptability and intellectual honesty demonstrated by the Navy three generations past. Instead the Navy's accomplishments need to be periodically reevaluated in the light of contemporary conditions and beliefs. Otherwise, these lessons will be lost or become submerged in popular mythology, and we will have truly squandered the heritage of heroes.

Appendix and Statistical Analysis

CONVERSIONS

1 nautical mile = 2,205 yards, 1,852 meters, or 1.151 statute miles
1 knot = 1.852 km/hour or 1.151 miles/hour
1 yard = .9144 meter
1 inch = 2.54 centimeters

MISSION DEFINITIONS

Amphibious attack—Ships attacked while supporting the landing of troops on an enemy-controlled coast.

Beachhead attack—Ships at sea to attack enemy shipping supporting an amphibious assault.

Escort and transit—Ships engaged while escorting other vessels in transit.

Interception based upon general intelligence—Ships at sea to attack a specific target whose location has been inferred or estimated.

Interception based upon specific intelligence—Ships at sea to attack a specific target whose location was known.

Offensive and sea superiority patrol without specific intelligence—Ships at sea in enemy or disputed waters to deny the enemy their use.

Self-defense—Ships unexpectedly attacked when not otherwise engaged on a mission.

Shore bombardment—Ships attacked while at sea to bombard targets ashore.

Transit—Ships engaged when in transit from one point to another.

Transport—Ships engaged while acting as transports.

STATISTICAL ANALYSIS

The U.S. Navy fought forty-nine surface actions during World War II involving warships displacing more than 500 tons. The majority of these actions were in the Pacific/East Indies theater. Figure A.1 shows where these actions occurred. The gray portion of every bar represents engagements fought in open waters, and the black portion shows the number of actions fought in waters where nearby land could affect operations.

FIGURE A.1. U.S. NAVY'S SURFACE ENGAGEMENTS BY LOCATION
AND ENVIRONMENT

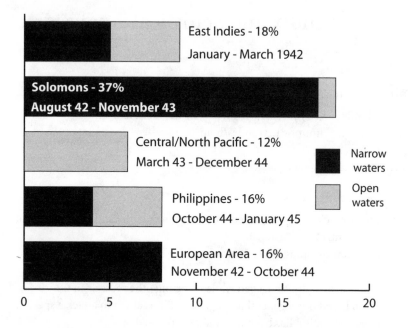

Because the Pacific and European wars were so different in character, the remaining analysis considers only engagements against the Japanese navy. Figure A.2 shows the number of battles the U.S. Navy fought in each year of the war. The gray portion of each bar reflects the number of day actions, and the black portion indicates night actions.

FIGURE A.2. U.S. NAVY'S SURFACE ENGAGEMENTS IN THE PACIFIC
BY YEAR AND TIME OF DAY

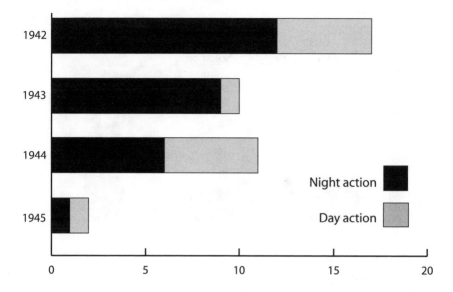

Forty percent of all actions occurred in 1942. From the start of the war most actions took place at night, but the U.S. Navy fought in some of the war's largest day actions, including Java Sea, Casablanca, Komandorski, and Samar. Figure A.3 shows the number of battles fought in each of the forty-five months the war in the Pacific lasted.

FIGURE A.3. U.S. NAVY'S SURFACE ENGAGEMENTS IN THE PACIFIC
BY MONTH

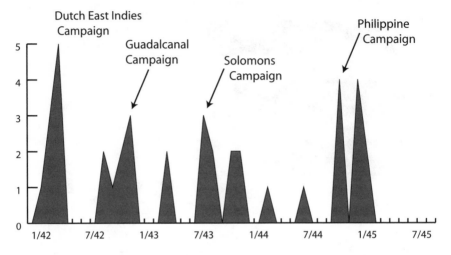

The events that provoked the most engagements were Japan's invasion of the Dutch East Indies (eight), the struggle for Guadalcanal (eight), the conquest of the Upper Solomons (ten), and the liberation of the Philippines (eight). Months of intense activity were interspaced with periods of little activity. Only two surface actions occurred in the ten months from December 1943 to September 1944.

An objective in most sea battles is to inflict harm on the enemy. Figure A.4 shows the damage suffered by the Allied and Japanese navies in the surface engagements described in this book.

FIGURE A.4. LARGE U.S. AND JAPANESE WARSHIPS SUNK AND DAMAGED IN SURFACE ENGAGEMENTS IN THE PACIFIC IN 1942 AND 1943–45 BY TYPE OF SHIP

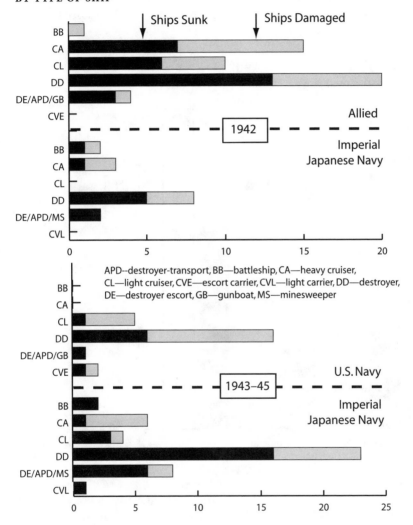

The abbreviation (BB, CA, etc.) identifies the type of warship represented by each bar. The black portion of each bar shows ships sunk, and the gray portion represents ships suffering significant damage. In these battles the Allies, including the Dutch and British, had thirty-eight major warships sunk and thirty-six damaged. The Japanese also had thirty-eight major warships sunk, but only twenty-one damaged. What is remarkable about these losses is their distribution. The top half of the figure shows losses incurred in 1942, and the bottom represents the period 1943–45. After the Battle of Tassafaronga the U.S. Navy dramatically reversed its fortunes. The Allies suffered 68 percent of their losses in 1942; the Japanese suffered 75 percent of their losses in 1943–45. Figure A.5 identifies which weapons caused the damage show in Figure A.4.

FIGURE A.5. PERCENT OF U.S. AND JAPANESE WARSHIPS SUNK OR SEVERELY DAMAGED BY CAUSE

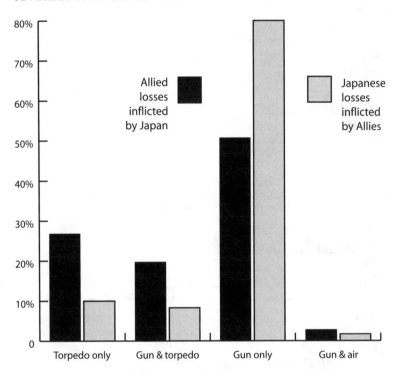

The black bars represent Allied warships, and the gray bars indicate Japanese warships. Twenty-seven percent of the losses and damage suffered by Allied warships were caused by Japanese torpedoes, which is a percentage remarkably similar to that obtained by the German navy against Allied warships (26 percent). Allied torpedoes, on the other hand, caused just 10 percent of all Japanese losses and damage. The category of Allied gunnery accounted for 80 percent of all damage inflicted. Except for the Battle of Samar, none of the surface engagements between U.S. and Japanese warships involved significant aerial intervention.

Notes

Preface

1. Clark G. Reynolds, *The Fast Carriers: The Forging of an Air Navy* (Annapolis: Naval Institute Press, 1992), 22.
2. Martin Middlebrook and Patrick Mahoney, *Battleship: The Loss of the* Prince of Wales *and the* Repulse (London: Penguin, 2001), 322.

Chapter 1. The Navy That Went to War

1. Thomas C. Hone and Trent Hone, *Battle Line: The United States Navy, 1919–1939* (Annapolis: Naval Institute Press, 2006), 68. This work gives a good overview of Mahon's impact and of the treaties of the 1920s and 1930s.
2. Donald M. Goldstein and Katherine V. Dillon, *Pearl Harbor Papers: Inside the Japanese Plans* (Dulles, VA: Brassey's), 319.
3. Trent Hone, "The Evolution of Fleet Tactical Doctrine in the U.S. Navy, 1922–1941," *The Journal of Military History* 67 (October 2003), 1121.
4. Norman Friedman, "The American 5-inch/38 Dual Purpose Gun," *Warship* 7 (1978), 171.
5. United States Navy, World War II Action and Operational Reports, 1941–1947, Commander Task Force 64, 3 November 1943, (College Park, MD: Modern Military Records, Textual Archives Service Division, National Archives and Records Administration), 37.
6. Norman Friedman, *U.S. Naval Weapons* (London: Conway Maritime Press, 1983), 58.
7. Carl Schaniel (China Lake Naval Weapons Center), interviews with the author, 2005.
8. Edward Latimer Beach, *The United States Navy: A 200-Year History* (Boston: Houghton Mifflin, 1990), 460; Frank Uhlig Jr., *How Navies Fight: The US Navy and its Allies* (Annapolis: Naval Institute Press, 1994), 139.
9. David C. Evans and Mark R. Peattie, *Kaigun: Strategy, Tactics, and Technology in the Imperial Japanese Navy, 1887–1941* (Annapolis: Naval Institute Press, 1994), 415.
10. Edwin P. Hoyt, *How They Won the War in the Pacific: Nimitz and His Admirals* (New York: The Lyons Press, 2000), 348.
11. John Prados, *Combined Fleet Decoded: The Secret History of American Intelligence and the Japanese Navy in World War II* (New York: Random House, 1995), 70 for 1941 comparisons, and page 443 for Japanese staffing throughout the war. The growth of U.S. Pacific Fleet intelligence operations is detailed on page 408 of Prados's work.
12. Evans and Peattie, *Kaigun*, 416.

13. General Headquarters Far East Command, Allied Translator and Interpreter Section, *The Japanese Version of the Black Chamber* (Doc. No. 64718) (January 1951), 20.

14. Evans and Peattie, *Kaigun*, 401.

15. Fuel consumption data are extracted from Robert Gardiner, ed., *Conway's All the World's Fighting Ships 1922–1946* (Annapolis: Naval Institute Press, 1986); M.J. Whitley, *Destroyers of World War Two* (Annapolis: Naval Institute Press, 1988); M.J. Whitley, *Cruisers of World War Two* (Annapolis: Naval Institute Press, 1995); and Hansgeorge Jentschura, Dieter Jung, and Peter Mickel, *Warships of the Imperial Japanese Navy, 1869–1945* (Annapolis: Naval Institute Press, 1986).

16. Jon Parshall, "Oil and Japanese Strategy in the Solomons: A Postulate," Imperial Japanese Navy Page, http://www.combinedfleet.com/guadoil1.htm.

17. Thomas B. Buell, *Master of Sea Power: A Biography of Fleet Admiral Ernest J. King* (Boston: Little Brown and Company, 1980), 125.

18. Gerald E. Wheeler, *Kinkaid of the Seventh Fleet: A Biography of Admiral Thomas C. Kinkaid, U.S. Navy* (Washington DC: Naval Historical Center, Department of the Navy, 1995), 151.

19. John Ellis, *World War II: A Statistical Survey* (New York: Facts on File, 1995), 328.

20. Beach, *United States Navy*, xix.

21. Evans and Peattie, *Kaigun*, 402.

22. Ibid., 404.

23. Ibid., 405.

24. Donald M. Goldstein and Katherine V. Dillon, *The Pacific War Papers: Japanese Documents of World War II* (Washington, DC: Potomac Books, 2004), 18.

25. Prados, *Combined Fleet Decoded*, 62.

CHAPTER 2. OLD SHIPS, FAULTY AMMUNITION, IRON MEN: THE EAST INDIES I

1. Duane Schultz, *The Last Battle Station: The Story of the USS* Houston (New York: St. Martin's Press, 1985), 71.

2. U.S. Armed Forces Far East, History Division, *Netherlands East Indies Naval Invasion Operations, December 1941–March 1942*. Japanese Monographs Series 101 (Washington, DC: U.S. Army, 1953), 10.

3. James Leutze, *A Different Kind of Victory: A Biography of Admiral Thomas C. Hart* (Annapolis: Naval Institute Press, 1981), 270.

4. Japanese National Institute for Defense Studies, Military History Department, *Naval Operations in Southwest Area*. War History Series (*Senshi Sosho*) 26 (Tokyo: Asagumo Shinbunsha, 1969), 199.

5. S.E. Smith, ed., *The United States Navy in World War II* (New York: Quill, 1966), 75.

6. John J.A. Michel, *Mr. Michel's War: From Manila to Mukden; An American Navy Officer's War with the Japanese* (Novato, CA: Presidio, 1998), 45.

7. U.S. Armed Forces Far East, History Division, *Netherlands East Indies*, 27.

8. Smith, *United States Navy*, 76.

9. Japanese National Institute for Defense Studies, *Naval Operations in Southwest Area*, 200.

10. United States Navy, World War II Action and Operational Reports, USS *Pope*, 24 January 1942, 3.

11. Office of Naval Intelligence, Publications Branch, *The Java Sea Campaign* (Suitland, MD: U.S. Department of the Navy, July 1943), 22.

12. This version is from the USS *John D. Ford*'s action report. See United States Navy, World War II Action and Operational Reports, USS *John D. Ford*, 24 January 1942. Other accounts assert it was shoal water that caused the flagship's sudden maneuver.

13. Smith, *United States Navy*, 76.

14. Motome Ugaki, *Fading Victory: The Diary of Admiral Matome Ugaki, 1941–45*, ed. Donald M. Goldstein and Katherine V. Dillon, trans. Masataka Chihaya (Pittsburgh: University of Pittsburgh Press, 1991), 77.

15. Samuel Eliot Morison, *History of United States Naval Operations in World War II*, vol. III, *Rising Sun in the Pacific, 1931–April 1942* (Boston: Little, Brown, 1984), 290.

16. Vincent P. O'Hara, *The German Fleet at War, 1939–1945* (Annapolis: Naval Institute Press, 2004), 32–40.

17. Robert J. Cressman, *The Official Chronology of the U.S. Navy in World War II* (Annapolis: Naval Institute Press, 2000), 73.

18. Daiji Watanabe, "Island Sea Battle by *Michishio* of the 8th Destroyer Division," private translation, 5.

19. H.E. Eccles, The Java Sea Battle, Bates Papers, Naval War College Library, Series II, Box 15, Folder 15, 8.

20. Japanese National Institute for Defense Studies, *Naval Operations in Southwest Area*, 328.

21. Accounts of this portion of the action are unclear. Some sources state that the *de Ruyter* and *Oshio* exchanged salvos. This book follows the account in Japanese National Institute for Defense Studies, *Naval Operations in Southwest Area*.

22. Apparently, the smoke was unintended: A crew member fell against the MAKE SMOKE button. See Prados, *Combined Fleet*, 256.

23. United States Navy, World War II Action and Operational Reports, USS *Pope*, 20 February 1942, Enc. A, 2.

24. Michel, *Michel's War*, 62.

25. United States Navy, World War II Action and Operational Reports, USS *Pope*, 20 February 1942, Enc. A, 3.

26. Michel, *Mr. Michel's War*, 62.

27. Japanese National Institute for Defense Studies, *Naval Operations in Southwest Area*, 329.

28. Ibid.
29. Eccles, Java Sea Battle, 11.
30. Ibid.
31. Watanabe, "Bali Island Sea Battle," 8.
32. Henk Visser, "The Dockyard at Surabaya and the Capsizing of HNLMS *Krakatau*," *Warship 2006* (2006): 147.
33. Watanabe, "Bali Island Sea Battle," 9.
34. United States Strategic Bombing Survey, *Interrogations of Japanese Officials* (OPNAV-P-03-100) (Washington, DC: Government Printing Office, 1946), 84.
35. U.S. Armed Forces Far East, History Division, *Netherlands East Indies*, 49.
36. Ray Parkin, *Out of the Smoke* (New York: William Morrow, 1960), 212–13.
37. David A. Thomas, *The Battle of the Java Sea* (London: Andre Deutsch, 1968), 158.
38. United States Navy, World War II Action and Operational Reports, USS *John D. Edwards*, 4 March 1942, Paragraph 6.
39. American historians unfairly disparage Doorman. "Unsure of orders, the American destroyers finally operated in a fog of confusion. For another hitch in the operation, the quick turnabout in Soerbaja channel cost the Striking Force a destroyer reinforcement." Theodore Roscoe, *United States Destroyer Operations in World War II* (Annapolis: Naval Institute Press, 1953), 102. W.G. Winslow, *The Ghost that Died at Sunda Strait.* (Annapolis: Naval Institute Press, 1994), 112, wrote, "Without a battle plan we raced hell-bent to engage the enemy, guided only by a vague and laconic directive." Morison, *Rising Sun*, 342–43, more subtly criticizes that Doorman had no time to issue an operation plan because of the "quick turnaround at Surabaya." In fact, Doorman's haste was well justified. Allied fighters attacked the *Naka*'s spotters at 1418 and 1430, but without luck. This indicates that the Japanese floatplanes could have been neutralized, which would have given Doorman the advantage of surprise.
40. Japanese National Institute for Defense Studies, *Naval Operations in Southwest Area*, 451.
41. "Battle of the Java Sea, 27th February 1942," *London Gazette*, July 6, 1948. "Aunt Sally" means anyone who is the target of abuse. The expression comes from an old English game in which rocks are thrown at a wooden head stuck on a pole (Aunt Sally) with the object of breaking a pipe stuck in its mouth.
42. John Toland, *But Not in Shame: The Six Months after Pearl Harbor* (New York: Random House, 1961), 233.
43. W.E. Johns and R.A. Kelly, *No Surrender* (London: W.H. Allen, 1989), 58.
44. W.G. Winslow, *The Fleet the Gods Forgot: The U.S. Asiatic Fleet in World War II* (Annapolis: Naval Institute Press, 1994), 118.
45. Abraham van der Moer, "He Who Sees First Lives Longest," Naval History 8 (July/August 1994), 39.
46. Thomas, *Battle of the Java Sea*, 194.

47. "Battle of the Java Sea," *London Gazette*.

48. Tameichi Hara, *Japanese Destroyer Captain* (New York: Ballantine, 1961), 82.

49. United States Navy, World War II Action and Operational Reports, USS *John D. Edwards*, 4 March 1942, 9.

50. Japanese Navy Action Records, *Jintsu*, CL, Japanese Navy Records, Operational Archives Branch, Naval Historical Center, Washington, DC.

CHAPTER 3. JAVA AFTERMATH: THE EAST INDIES II

1. Parkin, *Out of the Smoke*, 240.

2. Ibid., 243.

3. Schultz, *Last Battle Station*, 166.

4. H.P. Willmott, *Empires in the Balance: Japanese and Allied Pacific Strategies to April 1942* (Annapolis: Naval Institute Press, 1982), 336.

5. Dwight R. Messimer, *Pawns of War: The Loss of the USS* Langley *and the USS* Pecos (Annapolis: Naval Institute Press, 1983), 30. The meeting between Helfrich, Glassford, and Palliser is described in Toland, *But Not in Shame*, 256, and quoted from Glassford's report in Morison, *Rising Sun*, 376-7.

6. Schultz, *Last Battle Station*, 171.

7. G. Hermon Gill, *Royal Australian Navy, 1939-1942* (Adelaide: Griffin Press, 1957), 620.

8. Japanese National Institute for Defense Studies, *Naval Operations in Southwest Area*, 484.

9. Alan Payne, "The Battle of Sunda Strait," *Naval History* 6 (Spring 1992), 32.

10. United States Navy, World War II Action and Operational Reports, USS *Houston*, Log, Enc. 11.

11. Gill, *Royal Australian Navy, 1939-1942*, 620.

12. Roland McKie, *The Survivors* (Indianapolis: Bobbs-Merrill Company, 1953), 221.

13. United States Navy, World War II Action and Operational Reports, USS *Houston*, Log, Enc. 11.

14. Japanese National Institute for Defense Studies, *Naval Operations in Southwest Area*, 485.

15. Japanese Navy Action Records, *Natori*, CL, 1.

16. Schultz, *Last Battle Station*, 175.

17. Japanese National Institute for Defense Studies, *Naval Operations in Southwest Area*, 487.

18. Ibid., 488.

19. United States Navy, World War II Action and Operational Reports, USS *Houston*, Log, Enc. 11.

20. Japanese National Institute for Defense Studies, *Naval Operations in Southwest Area*, 489.

21. Ibid., 493.

22. F.C. van Oosten, *The Battle of the Java Sea* (Annapolis: Naval Institute Press, 1976), 63–4.

23. Ecceles, "Java Sea Battle," 23.

24. Ibid., 24.

25. United States Navy, World War II Action and Operational Reports, USS *Pope*, 1 March 1942, Part II.B.

26. Michel, *Mr. Michel's War*, 74.

27. United States Navy, World War II Action and Operational Reports, USS *Pope*, 1 March 1942, Part III.A.

28. Johns and Kelly, *No Surrender*, 65.

29. Michel, *Mr. Michel's War*, 77.

30. United States Navy, World War II Action and Operational Reports, USS *Pope*, 1 March 1942, Part III.A.

31. Clay Blair, *Silent Victory: The U.S. Submarine War Against Japan* (New York: Bantam, 1976), 91.

32. Messimer, *Pawns of War*, 100 states that these pilots and mechanics were intended to fight as infantry. This seems incredible.

33. Japanese National Institute for Defense Studies, *Naval Operations in Southwest Area*, 494.

34. Don Kehn Jr., correspondence with author, April 19, 2006.

35. Japanese National Institute for Defense Studies, *Naval Operations in Southwest Area*, 513.

CHAPTER 4. FALTERING COUNTEROFFENSIVE: GUADALCANAL, AUGUST-OCTOBER 1942

1. Buell, *Master of Sea Power*, 218.

2. See Samuel Eliot Morison, *History of United States Naval Operations in World War II*, vol. V, *The Struggle for Guadalcanal, August 1942–February 1943* (Boston: Little, Brown, 1966), 27–8 for a criticism of Fletcher's action, and John B. Lundstrom, *Black Shoe Carrier Admiral: Frank Jack Fletcher at Coral Sea, Midway, and Guadalcanal* (Annapolis: Naval Institute Press, 2006), 368–83 for a defense.

3. David C. Evans, ed., *The Japanese Navy in World War II: In the Words of Former Japanese Naval Officers* (Annapolis: Naval Institute Press, 1986), 223.

4. Ibid., 227.

5. Books have been written explaining how the Allies missed Mikawa's approach. See, for example, Denis Warner, Peggy Warner, and Sadao Seno, *Disaster in the Pacific: New Light on the Battle of Savo Island* (Annapolis: Naval Institute Press, 1992).

6. Richard B. Frank, *Guadalcanal: The Definitive Account of the Landmark Battle* (New York: Penguin, 1990), 97.

7. George C. Dyer, *The Amphibians Came to Conquer: The Story of Admiral Richmond Kelly Turner* (Washington, DC: Naval Historical Center, 1972), 374.

8. Evans, *Japanese Navy*, 230.

9. Ibid., 232.

10. Ibid., 233.

11. G. Hermon Gill, *Royal Australian Navy, 1942–1945* (Adelaide: Griffin Press, 1968), 154.

12. Richard W. Bates, *The Battle of Savo Island, August 9th, 1942: Strategical and Tactical Analysis* (Newport, RI: Naval War College, 1950), 114.

13. Some accounts state Mikawa ordered this action. See Bates, *Battle of Savo Island*, 117 for a discussion.

14. Evans and Peattie, *Kaigun*, 277.

15. Morison, *The Struggle for Guadalcanal*, 37.

16. Gill, *Royal Australian Navy, 1942–1945*, 143–4.

17. Crutchley, Morison, and some of the HMAS *Canberra* survivors believe a torpedo sank her. Morison, *Struggle for Guadalcanal*, 54. Many sources cite two torpedo hits on the starboard beam. Other survivors, the Australian Board of Admiralty investigation, and the Naval War College concluded the *Canberra* was sunk by gunfire alone. Loxton and Coulthard-Clark have argued that the USS *Bagley* accidentally torpedoed the *Canberra*. Bruce Loxton and Chris Coulthard-Clark, *The Shame of Savo: Anatomy of a Naval Disaster* (Annapolis: Naval Institute Press, 1997), 191–205.

18. Japanese Navy Action Records, *Yubari*, CL, 2.

19. Bates, *Battle of Savo Island*, 119.

20. The subsequent inquiry "found censure definitely warranted only for Captain Bode." Frank, *Guadalcanal*, 122. Bode committed suicide rather than face a general court-martial.

21. Office of Naval Intelligence, Publications Branch, *The Battle of Savo Island* (Suitland, MD: U.S. Department of the Navy, November 1943), 19.

22. Evans, *Japanese Navy*, 236.

23. Office of Naval Intelligence, Publications Branch, *Battle of Savo Island*, 21.

24. Richard F. Newcomb, *Savo* (New York: Bantam, 1963), 94.

25. Office of Naval Intelligence, Publications Branch, *Battle of Savo Island*, 27.

26. Roscoe, *United States Destroyer Operations*, 172.

27. Bates, *Battle of Savo Island*, 299.

28. Eric Lacroix and Linton Wells II, *Japanese Cruisers of the Pacific War* (Annapolis: Naval Institute Press, 1997), 307.

29. Ugaki, *Fading Victory*, 180.

30. Buell, *Master of Sea Power*, 222.

31. Frank, *Guadalcanal*, 146.

32. United States Navy, World War II Action and Operational Reports, USS *Blue*, 22 August 1942, 2.

33. Morison, *Struggle for Guadalcanal*, 81.

34. "But as the tropical twilight performed its quick fadeout and the pall of night fell on Iron-bottom Sound, Allied ships cleared out like frightened children running home from a graveyard. . . . Then the Japanese took over." Morison, *Struggle for Guadalcanal*, 114.

35. U.S. Armed Forces Far East, History Division, *Southeast Naval Operations Part I, May 42–Feb. 1943.* Japanese Monographs Series 98 (Washington, DC: U.S. Army, 1949), 19.

36. United States Navy, World War II Action and Operational Reports, USS *Gregory*, 5 September 1942, 1.

37. Frank, *Guadalcanal*, 212.

38. Evans, *Japanese Navy*, 179.

39. U.S. Armed Forces Far East, History Division, *Southeast Naval Operations Part I*, 24.

40. Morison, *Struggle for Guadalcanal*, 147.

41. John B. Lundstrom, *The First Team and the Guadalcanal Campaign*, (Annapolis: Naval Institute Press, 2005), 295.

42. Office of Naval Intelligence, Publications Branch, *Battle of Cape Esperance* (Suitland, MD: U.S. Department of the Navy, November 1943), 4.

43. Ibid., 47.

44. Roy Boehm, Boatswain's Mate 3rd Class Roy Boehm's USS *Duncan* DD 485 Experiences, USS Duncan Reunion Association, http://www.ussduncan.org/capesper_page3.htm.

45. Ibid.

46. Charles Cook, *The Battle of Cape Esperance: Encounter at Guadalcanal* (Annapolis: Naval Institute Press, 1992), 62.

47. Japanese National Institute for Defense Studies, Military History Department, *Naval Operations in Southeast Area, 2,* War History Series (*Senshi Sosho*) 83 (Tokyo: Asagumo Shinbunsha, 1975), 195; Morison, *Struggle for Guadalcanal*, 162.

48. Office of Naval Intelligence, Publications Branch, *Battle of Cape Esperance*, 25–26.

49. Frank, *Guadalcanal*, 309–10.

50. U.S. Armed Forces Far East, History Division, *Southeast Naval Operations Part I*, 32.

51. Morison, *Struggle for Guadalcanal*, 176.

52. Naval Historical Center, *Dictionary of American Naval Fighting Ships*, vol. VIII (Washington, DC: Government Printing Office, 1959–1991), 555.

53. David M. Armstrong, The Battle of Sealark Channel, David M. Armstrong Papers, East Carolina Manuscript Collection, J.Y. Joyner Library, Collection No. 555, 8.

54. United States Navy, World War II Action and Operational Reports, USS *Trever*, Action Report, 2.

55. Armstrong, Battle of Sealark Channel, 14.

56. Naval Historical Center, *Dictionary*, vol. VIII, 556.

57. Armstrong, Battle of Sealark Channel, 17.

58. Frank, *Guadalcanal*, 359.

59. Ugaki, *Fading Victory*, 258.

60. For accounts of this battle see Frank, *Guadalcanal*, 379–403; Morison, *Struggle for Guadalcanal*, 207–24; and Lundstrom, *First Team and the Guadalcanal Campaign*, Chapters 19–22.

61. Edwin B. Hooper, Some Recollection of World War II, 1971–1978, 9, Oral History Program, U.S. Naval Institute.

CHAPTER 5. THE TURN OF THE TIDE: GUADALCANAL, NOVEMBER 1942

1. U.S. Armed Forces Far East, History Division, *Southeast Naval Operations Part I*, 45.
2. Frank, *Guadalcanal*, 427.
3. Hara, *Destroyer Captain*, 135.
4. Ibid., 138.
5. J.E. Bennett, "Callaghan Was Calm and Collected at Guadalcanal," *Shipmate* 59 (April 1996), 18.
6. Abe's summary report is quoted in Ugaki, *Fading Victory*, 272.
7. Bennett, "Callaghan Was Calm," 19.
8. Hara, *Destroyer Captain*, 142.
9. Frank, *Guadalcanal*, 438.
10. This occurred at 0151 according to Japanese National Institute for Defense Studies, Military History Department, *Naval Operations in Southeast Asia*, 2, 364. The times given in different sources do not agree.
11. Eric Hammel, *Guadalcanal: Decision at Sea: The Naval Battle of Guadalcanal, November 13–15, 1942* (Pacifica, CA: Pacifica Military History, 1999), 167.
12. Office of Naval Intelligence, Publications Branch, *Naval Battle of Guadalcanal 11–15 November 1942* (Suitland, MD: U.S. Department of the Navy, February 1944), 19. The time at which this order was given is variously reported as between 0148 and 0152.
13. United States Navy, World War II Action and Operational Reports, *O'Bannon* 12–13 November 1942, 2.
14. Japanese Navy Action Records, *Nagara*, CL, 1.
15. United States Navy, World War II Action and Operational Reports, USS *Atlanta* 12–13 November 1942, enclosure B "List of Hits Received." Grace credits the *Hiei* with these hits on the *Atlanta* and states the crew misjudged their size because, being special rounds, they did far less damage than would normally be expected from a fourteen-inch shell. The hits could also have been six-inch rounds from the *Hiei's* secondary battery. J.W. Grace, *The Naval Battle of Guadalcanal: Night Action 13 November 1942* (Annapolis: Naval Institute Press, 1999). Grace's argument is supported by the *Nagara's* action record which records only nine rounds being fired at this time in the battle.
16. Hammel, *Guadalcanal: Decision at Sea*, 168. Frank argues in *Guadalcanal* that the *San Francisco* fired the shell that struck Scott down based on the locations of the *Atlanta* and the *San Francisco*.
17. Japanese National Institute for Defense Studies, *Naval Operations in Southeast Area*, 2, 366.
18. Stephen Howarth, *The Fighting Ships of the Rising Sun: The Drama of the Imperial Japanese Navy, 1895–1945* (New York: Atheneum, 1983), 313.

19. Hara, *Destroyer Captain*, 143.

20. Commander Hara's *Destroyer Captain* is the most accessible Japanese account of these events available in English and is often cited. Hara describes firing eight torpedoes and reloading his tubes in five minutes, a process that normally required up to a half hour. It is more likely that he only fired four torpedoes at this time.

21. Bruce McCandless, "The *San Francisco* Story," *Proceedings* 84 (November 1958), 41; Grace, *Naval Battle of Guadalcanal*, 75.

22. McCandless, "San Francisco Story," 43.

23. William Thomas Generous Jr., *Sweet Pea at War: A History of USS* Portland (Lexington, KY: University of Kentucky Press, 2003), 88.

24. The person who wrote the *Juneau's* action report, the ship's medical officer, had a poor picture of the overall battle, and only ten men survived her subsequent torpedoing by the Japanese submarine *I-26*.

25. Hara, *Destroyer Captain*, 149.

26. United States Navy, World War II Action and Operational Reports, USS *Fletcher*, 12–13 November 1942, 4(d).

27. Ibid., 4(g).

28. Hara, *Destroyer Captain*, 152.

29. Japanese National Institute for Defense Studies, Military History Department, *Naval Operations in Southeast Area*, 2, 370–1; Grace, *Naval Battle of Guadalcanal*, 123–6; Frank, *Guadalcanal*, 451–5.

30. United States Navy, *War Plans CINCPAC Files. Admiral Nimitz Command Summary, Running Estimate and Summary* (Grey Book); United States Navy, World War II Action and Operational Reports, *Portland* to Commander South Pacific, 17 November 1942.

31. Kondo wrote this assessment after the war. See "Some Opinions Concerning the War," in Goldstein and Dillon, *Pacific War Papers*, 317.

32. Ukagi, *Fading Victory*, 267.

33. See Lacroix and Wells, *Japanese Cruisers*, 311. These authors assert that the *Chokai* also fired 381 rounds during this bombardment.

34. Frank, *Guadalcanal*, 467.

35. Ugaki, *Fading Victory*, 270.

36. Kondo, "Some Opinions Concerning the War," 315, in Goldstein and Dillon, *Pacific War Papers*.

37. Morison, *Struggle for Guadalcanal*, 273. "Ching" was Lee's Naval Academy nickname. The "big boss" was Maj. Gen. Alexander A. Vandegrift, who was a personal friend of Lee's. There are several versions of this famous exchange.

38. United States Navy, World War II Action and Operational Reports, USS *South Dakota*, 14–15 November 1942, 5; USS *Washington*, 14–15 November 1942, 8.

39. Japanese Navy Action Records, *Sendai*, CL, 5.

40. Office of Naval Intelligence, Publications Branch, *Naval Battle of Guadalcanal*, 67.

41. The number of torpedoes fired in this salvo is unclear. Three of the five Japanese ships involved had been present at the First Battle of Guadalcanal and had expended torpedoes that night as well.

42. Hooper, Some Recollections of World War II.

43. United States Navy, World War II Action and Operational Reports, USS *South Dakota*, 14–15 November 1942, 22.

44. Japanese Navy Action Records, *Nagara*, CL, 2.

45. Japanese National Institute for Defense Studies, *Naval Operations in Southeast Area*, 2, 390.

46. Japanese Navy Action Records, *Kirishima*, BB, 1.

47. Ivan Musicant, *Battleship at War: The Epic Story of the USS* Washington (New York: Avon, 1986), 126.

48. Quoted in C.W. Kilpatrick, *Naval Night Battles of the Solomons* (New York: Exposition Press, 1987), 130.

49. Japanese National Institute for Defense Studies, *Naval Operations in Southeast Area*, 2, 392.

50. Hooper, Some Recollections of World War II, 9.

51. United States Navy, World War II Action and Operational Reports, USS *South Dakota*, 14–15 November 1942, 3.

52. Ibid., 10.

53. Ibid., 11.

54. United States Navy, World War II Action and Operational Reports, USS *Washington*, 14–15 November 1942, 11.

55. Japanese Navy Action Records, *Nagara*, CL, 2.

56. Ugaki, *Fading Victory*, 276.

57. Naval Historical Center, *Dictionary*, vol. IV, 308.

58. Quoted in Hoyt, *How They Won*, 185.

59. Ibid., 187.

60. Kondo, "Some Opinions Concerning the War," 316, in Goldstein and Dillon, *Pacific War Papers*.

61. U.S. Armed Forces Far East, History Division, *Southeast Naval Operations Part I*, 49.

62. Wheeler, *Kinkaid*, 283.

63. See, for example, Morison, *Struggle for Guadalcanal*, 301: "Ever since the summer of 1941, Destroyer Squadron 2 under Tanaka's command had steamed together in peacetime exercise and wartime operations."

64. Russell S. Crenshaw, *The Battle of Tassafaronga* (Baltimore: Nautical & Aviation Publishing, 1995), 33.

65. Evans, *Japanese Navy*, 200.

66. Kilpatrick, *Naval Night Battles*, 145.

67. Frank, *Guadalcanal*, 508.

68. Crenshaw, *Battle of Tassafaronga*, 52.

69. Evans, *Japanese Navy*, 200.

70. Morison, *Struggle for Guadalcanal*, 303.

71. Crenshaw, *Battle of Tassafaronga*, 90.

72. United States Navy, Bureau of Ships, Summary of War Damage to U.S. Battleships, Carriers, Cruisers, Destroyers and Destroyer Escorts: 17 October 1941 to 9 October 1945, USS *New Orleans*, Torpedo Damage, Lunga Point, 30 November 1942, 7.

73. Evans, *Japanese Navy*, 201.

74. Crenshaw, *Battle of Tassafaronga*, 189.

75. Frank, *Guadalcanal*, 514–5; Kilpatrick, *Naval Night Battles*, 152–3.

76. Ugaki, *Fading Victory*, 302.

77. See Frank, *Guadalcanal*, 582–97, for a good summary of Japan's evacuation from Guadalcanal.

CHAPTER 6. AFRICA: CASABLANCA, NOVEMBER 1942

1. Michael Howard, *The Mediterranean Strategy in the Second World War* (London: Greenhill, 1993), 31.

2. There is a need to expand the English language coverage of the French navy's activities between June 1940 and November 1942, especially from the French perspective. Paul Auphan and Jacques Mordal, *The French Navy in World War II* (Westport, CT: Greenwood Press, 1976) and Anthony Heckstall-Smith, *The Fleet that Faced Both Ways* (London: Anthony Blond, 1963) are both dated, and Charles W. Koburger Jr., *The Cyrano Fleet: France and Its Navy, 1940–1942* (New York: Praeger, 1989) lacks detail.

3. George F. Howe, *Northwest Africa: Seizing the Initiative in the West* (Washington, DC: Government Printing Office, 1957), 40.

4. Amiral Henri and Jean Queguiner Darrieus, *Historique de la Marine française 1922–1942* (St Malo: l'Ancre de Marine, 1996), 338. Most English sources state the *Jean Bart* fired first.

5. Samuel Eliot Morison, *History of United States Naval Operations in World War II*, vol. II, *Operations in North African Waters, October 1942–June 1943* (Boston: Little, Brown, 1984), 97.

6. Heckstall-Smith, *Fleet That Faced Both Ways*, 201.

7. Auphan and Mordal, *The French Navy in World War II*, 230.

8. Morison, *Operations in North African Waters*, 97.

9. Rick Atkinson, *An Army at Dawn: The War in North Africa, 1942–1943* (New York: Henry Holt and Company, 2002), 134.

10. United States Navy, World War II Action and Operational Reports, USS *Massachusetts*, 8 November 1942, 7.

11. Ibid.

12. Barbara Brooks Tomblin, *With Utmost Spirit: Allied Naval Operations in the Mediterranean, 1942–1945* (Lexington, KY: University of Kentucky Press, 2004), 35.

13. Quoted in Atkinson, *Army at Dawn*, 133.

14. Morison, *Operations in North African Waters*, 105.

15. United States Navy, World War II Action and Operational Reports, USS *Wichita*, 8 November 1942, 8.

16. Ibid.

17. Tomblin, *Utmost Spirit*, 49.

18. Ibid.

CHAPTER 7. ALASKA: KOMANDORSKI, MARCH 1943

1. Quoted in Roscoe, *United States Destroyer Operations*, 150.

2. United States Strategic Bombing Survey, *Interrogations*, 303.

3. Prados, *Combined Fleet*, 470.

4. Ibid.

5. During the battle the Americans used Pearl Harbor time (Z–10) which was plus three hours (and minus one day) from local time. The Japanese, as always, used Tokyo time, (Z+10).

6. United States Strategic Bombing Survey, *Interrogations*, 209.

7. W.J. Holmes, *Double-edged Secrets: U.S. Naval Intelligence Operations in the Pacific During World War II* (Annapolis: Naval Institute Press, 1979), 133.

8. Office of Naval Intelligence, Publications Branch, *The Aleutians Campaign* (Suitland, MD: U.S. Department of the Navy, May 1945), 46.

9. United States Strategic Bombing Survey, *Interrogations*, 99.

10. The Japanese attributed these hits to six-inch or five-inch shells. Lacroix and Well, *Japanese Cruisers*, 316. The *Nachi*'s Action Record, 2, however, makes no mention of the size of these shells.

11. The *Salt Lake City*'s action report states this shell hit on the port side below the water-line. The version related in this book is taken from Samuel Eliot Morison, *History of United States Naval Operations in World War II*, vol. VII, *Aleutians, Gilberts and Marshalls, June 1942–April 1944* (Boston: Little, Brown, 1982), 30. Morison states he confirmed his version with other crew members.

12. United States Strategic Bombing Survey, *Interrogations*, 99.

13. Ibid.

14. Office of Naval Intelligence, Publications Branch, *Aleutians Campaign*, 56.

15. Smith, *United States Navy*, 665.

16. Roscoe, *United States Destroyer Operations*, 160.

17. Ibid., 161.

18. United States Strategic Bombing Survey, *Interrogations*, 100.

19. Ibid., 112.

20. Andrieu D'Albas, *Death of a Navy: Japanese Naval Action in World War II* (New York: Devin-Adair, 1957), 274.

21. See Masataka Chihaya, "The Withdrawal from Kiska" in Evans, *The Japanese Navy*, 245–77, for an account of the Japanese evacuation. Morison, *Aleutians, Gilberts and Marshalls*, 62–4 describes the thrust against empty Kiska.

INTERMEZZO. SUNDAY, 7 MARCH 1943

1. U.S. Armed Forces Far East History Division, *Southeast Naval Operations, Part II, February–October 1943*. Japanese Monographs Series 99. (Washington, DC: U.S. Army, 1947, 4.
2. United States Navy, *War Plans*, Cominch to Cincpac, Comsopac, 30 November 1942.
3. United States Navy, *War Plans*, Daily Summary 7 March, 1943.
4. United States Navy, *War Plans*, ICPOA Estimate 16 February 1943.

CHAPTER 8. ADVANCE UP THE SOLOMONS, MARCH–AUGUST 1943

1. H.P. Willmott, *The War with Japan: The Period of Balance, May 1942–October 1943* (Wilmington, DE: SR Books, 2002), 157.
2. U.S. Armed Forces Far East, History Division, *Southeast Naval Operation*, Part II, 8.
3. Fletcher Pratt, *Night Work: The Story of Task Force 39* (New York: H. Holt and Company, 1946), 44.
4. United States Navy, World War II Action and Operational Reports, USS *Waller*, 5 March 1943, 3.
5. Ibid.
6. Kilpatrick, *Naval Night Battles*, 176.
7. Pratt, *Night Work*, 50.
8. United States Strategic Bombing Survey, *Interrogations*, 142.
9. U.S. Armed Forces Far East, History Division, *Southeast Naval Operations, Part II*, 19.
10. Japanese aviators reported sinking one cruiser, two destroyers, and nineteen transports during I Operation raids. The actual count was a destroyer, a corvette, a tanker, and two transports. Also, Japanese flyers claimed to have definitely downed 156 aircraft and to have probably destroyed another fifty-six while only losing sixty-one planes themselves. See Ugaki, *Fading Victory*, 329 and Holmes, *Double Edged Secrets*, 134.
11. Arnold S. Lott, *Most Dangerous Sea: A History of Mine Warfare and an Account of U.S. Navy Mine Warfare Operations in World War II and Korea* (Annapolis: Naval Institute Press, 1959), 97.
12. U.S. Armed Forces Far East, History Division, *Southeast Naval Operations, Part II*, 26–28.
13. Joseph H. Wellings, "The Night *Strong* Was Sunk," *Shipmate* 40 (July/August 1977), 24–25.
14. The Japanese National Institute for Defense Studies, *Naval Operations in Southeast Area*, 2, 228, asserts the contact was only five kilometers away.
15. United States Navy, World War II Action and Operational Reports, USS *O'Bannon*, 6 July 1943, 2.

16. United States Navy, World War II Action and Operational Reports, USS *Honolulu*, 6 July 1943, TBS Log, 1.

17. Ibid.

18. United States Navy, World War II Action and Operational Reports, USS *Honolulu*, 6 July 1943, Gunnery Report, 1.

19. United States Navy, World War II Action and Operational Reports, USS *Helena*, 6 July 1943, 2–3.

20. United States Navy, World War II Action and Operational Reports, USS *O'Bannon*, 6 July 1943, 2.

21. United States Navy, World War II Action and Operational Reports, USS *Honolulu*, 6 July 1943, Gunnery Report, 5.

22. Smith, *United States Navy*, 454.

23. United States Navy, World War II Action and Operational Reports, USS *Helena*, War Damage Report, 11.

24. Samuel Eliot Morrison, *History of United States Naval Operations in World War II*, vol. VI, *Breaking the Bismarcks Barrier, 22 July 1942–1 May 1944* (Boston: Little, Brown, 1988), 169.

25. Ibid., 172.

26. Japanese National Institute for Defense Studies, *Naval Operations in Southeast Area*, 2, 230.

27. For general accounts of this action see Paul S. Dull, *A Battle History of the Imperial Japanese Navy (1941–1945)* (Annapolis: Naval Institute Press, 1982), 274–6; Morison, *Bismarcks Barrier*, 161–75; Kilpatrick, *Naval Night Battles*, 183–94; and Russell S. Crenshaw Jr., *South Pacific Destroyer: The Battle for the Solomons from Savo Island to Vella Gulf* (Annapolis: Naval Institute Press, 1998), 132–45.

28. U.S. Armed Forces Far East, History Division, *Southeast Naval Operations, Part II*, 32.

29. Jack S. Harker, *Well Done Leander* (Auckland: Collins, 1971), 295.

30. Quoted in S.D. Waters, *The Royal New Zealand Navy* (Wellington: War History Branch, 1956), 318.

31. United States Navy, World War II Action and Operational Reports, USS *Ralph Talbot*, 12 July 1943, TBS Log, 1.

32. Japanese National Institute for Defense Studies, *Naval Operations in Southeast Area*, 2, 245. The *Yukikaze's* Captain Yoshima Shimai claimed the Japanese possessed a radar detection device that "positively determined the presence of the enemy two hours before we met him." However, Shimai's remarks are inconsistent with the technology available, and the aerial sighting was probably Rear Admiral Izaki Shunji's best indication of the American presence. See Waters, *Royal New Zealand Navy*, 319, and United States Naval Technical Mission to Japan, *Japanese Radar Counter-measures and Visual Signal Display Equipment* (Report E-07), http://www.fischer-tropsch.org/primary_documents/gvt_reports/USNAVY/USNTMJ%20Reports/USNTMJ_toc.htm.

33. United States Navy, World War II Action and Operational Reports, USS *Honolulu*, 12 July 1943, Gunnery Report, 1.

34. Lacroix and Wells, *Japanese Cruisers*, 433.

35. United States Navy, World War II Action and Operational Reports, USS *Ralph Talbot*, 12 July 1943, 2.

36. Morison, *Bismarcks Barrier*, 186.

37. Crenshaw, *South Pacific Destroyer*, 174.

38. United States Navy, World War II Action and Operational Reports, USS *Honolulu*, 12 July 1943, Enc. A, 2.

39. See Morison, *Bismarcks Barrier*, 190, and Chenshaw, *South Pacific Destroyer*, 180–9, for accounts of the Battle of Kolombangara's aftermath.

40. Roscoe, *United States Destroyer Operations*, 232.

41. U.S. Armed Forces Far East, History Division, *Southeast Naval Operations, Part II, February–October 1943*, Japanese Monographs Series 99 (Washington, DC: U.S. Army, 1947), 36–7.

42. See Crenshaw, *South Pacific Destroyer*, 197–201, and U.S. Armed Forces Far East, History Division, *Southeast Naval Operations, Part II*, 43.

43. C. Raymond Calhoun, *Tin Can Sailor: Life Aboard the USS* Sterett, *1939–1945* (Annapolis: Naval Institute Press, 2000), 120.

44. Kilpatrick, *Naval Night Battles*, 213.

45. Crenshaw, *South Pacific Destroyer*, 211.

46. Hara, *Destroyer Captain*, 188.

47. Ibid., 189.

48. Ibid.

49. Calhoun, *Tin Can Sailor*, 123.

50. Morison, *Bismarcks Barrier*, 219.

51. Hara, *Destroyer Captain*, 191.

52. Ibid., 193.

CHAPTER 9. VICTORY IN THE SOLOMONS, SEPTEMBER–NOVEMBER 1943

1. U.S. Armed Forces Far East, History Division, *Southeast Naval Operations, Part II*, 48.

2. Hara, *Destroyer Captain*, 195.

3. Kilpatrick, *Naval Night Battles*, 222; Hara, *Destroyer Captain*, 199.

4. Prados, *Combined Fleet Decoded*, 501.

5. Japanese National Institute for Defense Studies, *Naval Operations in Southeast Area*, 2, 267.

6. Ibid.; Morison, *Bismarcks Barrier*, 236.

7. U.S. Armed Forces Far East, History Division, *Southeast Naval Operations, Part III, Oct. 43–Feb. 44*, Japanese Monographs Series 100 (Washington, DC: U.S. Army, 1947), 1.

8. James J. Fahey, *Pacific War Diary, 1942–1945: The Secret Diary of an American Sailor* (New York: Zebra, 1984), 52.

9. United States Navy, World War II Action and Operational Reports, USS *Ralph Talbot*, 29 September–3 October 1943, A-2; Japanese National Institute for Defense Studies, *Naval Operations in Southeast Area*, 2, 297–9; Roscoe, *Destroyer Operations*, 237.

10. U.S. Armed Forces Far East, History Division, *Southeast Naval Operations, Part II*, 53.

11. United States Navy, World War II Action and Operational Reports, USS *Ralph Talbot*, 29 September–3 October 1943, A-2.

12. United States Navy, World War II Action and Operational Reports, USS *Waller*, 1–3 October 1943, 5.

13. U.S. Armed Forces Far East, History Division, *Southeast Naval Operations, Part II*, 53.

14. Japanese National Institute for Defense Studies, *Naval Operations in Southeast Area*, 2, 301.

15. United States Navy, World War II Action and Operational Reports, USS *Waller*, 1–3 October 1943, 7.

16. R.H. Roupe, "Hell and High Water," Destroyer History, http://www.destroyerhistory.org/fletcherclass/usschevalier/roupe.html.

17. U.S. Armed Forces Far East, History Division, *Southeast Naval Operations, Part II*, 56.

18. Hara, *Destroyer Captain*, 216.

19. Roupe, "Hell and High Water."

20. Kilpatrick, *Naval Night Battles*, 230.

21. Japanese National Institute for Defense Studies, *Naval Operations in Southeast Area*, 2, 83. Most sources state that only the *Yugumo* and *Kazegumo* fired at this time. For example, "*Kazegumo* got in a couple of salvos on the turn, but *Isokaze* and *Akigumo* were as yet unable to fire a shot." Roscoe, *Destroyer Operations*, 241.

22. United States Navy, World War II Action and Operational Reports, USS *Chevalier*, 6 October 1943, Executive Officer's Report.

23. Hara, *Destroyer Captain*, 223.

24. Morison, *Bismarcks Barrier*, 251.

25. Hara, *Destroyer Captain*, 223.

26. Morison, *Bismarcks Barrier*, 251.

27. Kilpatrick, *Naval Night Battles*, 233.

28. E.B. Potter, *Bull Halsey* (Annapolis: Naval Institute Press, 2003), 250.

29. U.S. Armed Forces Far East, History Division, *Southeast Naval Operations, Part III*, 10.

30. Ibid., 13.

31. Ibid., 14.

32. United States Navy, World War II Action and Operational Reports, Commander Task Force 39, 3 November 1943, 15.

33. Ibid., 17.

34. United States Navy, World War II Action and Operational Reports, USS *Spence*, 1–2 November 1943, 3.

35. Hara, *Destroyer Captain*, 233.

36. United States Navy, World War II Action and Operational Reports, USS *Spence*, 1–2 November 1943, 3.

37. United States Strategic Bombing Survey, *Interrogations*, 338.

38. United States Navy, World War II Action and Operational Reports, Commander Task Force 39, 3 November 1943, 25.

39. United States Navy, World War II Action and Operational Reports, USS *Cleveland*, 1–2 November 1943, 9.

40. United States Navy, World War II Action and Operational Reports, Commander Task Force 39, 3 November 1943, 21.

41. Ibid., 18.

42. United States Strategic Bombing Survey, *Interrogations*, 340.

43. United States Navy, World War II Action and Operational Reports, USS *Charles Ausburne*, 1–2 November 1943, 3.

44. Ibid., TBS Log.

45. See Imperial Japanese Navy, http://homepage2.nifty.com/nishidah/e/index.htm, for the subsequent assignments of Admirals Omori, Osugi, and Ijuin; also Morison, *Bismarcks Barrier*, 322.

46. The *Foote*, *Cleveland*, *Thatcher*, *Stanly*, and *Claxton* all missed or misinterpreted orders at some point in the battle. If any of the cruisers had failed to execute Merrill's radical maneuvers as ordered, the results could have been catastrophic.

47. United States Navy, World War II Action and Operational Reports, Commander Task Force 39, 3 November 1943, 21.

48. U.S. Armed Forces Far East, History Division, *Southeast Naval Operations, Part III*, 13.

49. Morison, *Bismarcks Barrier*, 323–30.

50. U.S. Armed Forces Far East, History Division, *Southeast Naval Operations, Part III*, 31.

51. Ken Jones, *Destroyer Squadron 23: Combat Exploits of Arleigh Burke's Gallant Force* (Annapolis: Naval Institute Press, 1997), 249.

52. United States Navy, World War II Action and Operational Reports, USS *Converse*, 24–25 November 1943, 4.

53. Roscoe, *Destroyer Operations*, 266.

54. U.S. Armed Forces Far East, History Division, *Southeast Naval Operations, Part III*, 32.

CHAPTER 10. THE PACIFIC'S WIDE WATERS, FEBRUARY–AUGUST 1944

1. Evans, *Japanese Navy*, 295.

2. Thomas Parrish, ed., *The Simon and Schuster Encyclopedia of World War II* (New York: Simon and Schuster, 1978), 636.

3. Prados, *Combined Fleet Decoded*, 535.

4. Reynolds, *Fast Carriers*, 138.

5. United States Navy, World War II Action and Operational Reports, USS *New Jersey*, 16–17 February 1944, 5.

6. United States Navy, World War II Action and Operational Reports, USS *Iowa*, 16–17 February 1944, 8; Prados, *Combined Fleet Decoded*, 538.

7. United States Navy, World War II Action and Operational Reports, USS *Minneapolis*, 16–17 February 1944, 7.

8. Ibid., 9.

9. United States Navy, World War II Action and Operational Reports, USS *Iowa*, 16–17 February 1944, 7.

10. Ibid., 9.

11. United States Navy, World War II Action and Operational Reports, USS *Minneapolis*, 16–17 February 1944, 13.

12. The two-day total of shipping sunk was 200,000 tons. See Marc Bernstein, "Hail Storm at Truk," *Naval History* 8 (January/February 1994), 24.

13. Reynolds, *Fast Carriers*, 138.

14. Cressman, *Official Chronology*, 213.

15. See Prados, *Combined Fleet Decoded*, 549–50.

16. Ugaki, *Fading Victory*, 376.

17. Dull, *Battle History of the Imperial Japanese Navy*, 302.

18. Gill, *Royal Australian Navy 1942–1945*, 431.

19. United States Navy, World War II Action and Operational Reports, USS *Fletcher*, 8–9 June 1944, TBS Log.

20. Ibid.

21. United States Navy, World War II Action and Operational Reports, USS *Fletcher*, 8–9 June 1944, Chronological Account of Action.

22. Dull, *Battle History of the Imperial Japanese Navy*, 303.

23. William T. Y'Blood, *Red Sun Setting: The Battle of the Philippine Sea* (Annapolis: Naval Institute Press, 1989), 211.

24. Samuel Eliot Morison, *History of United States Naval Operations in World War II*, vol. VIII, *New Guinea and the Marianas, March 1944–August 1944* (Boston: Little, Brown, 1984), 367; Reynolds, *Fast Carriers*, 243; Cressman, *Official Chronology*, 245; *Matsu* Tabular Record of Movement, Imperial Japanese Navy Page, http://www.combinedfleet.com/matsu_t.htm.

25. Cressman, *Official Chronology*, 252.

26. Ugaki, *Fading Victory*, 440.

CHAPTER 11. EUROPEAN WATERS AFTER OPERATION TORCH, JUNE 1944–APRIL 1945

1. See O'Hara, *German Fleet at War*.

2. United States Navy, World War II Action and Operational Reports, USS *Somers*, 15 August 1944, 5.

CHAPTER 12. THE BATTLES OF LEYTE GULF, OCTOBER 1944

1. Masanori Ito, *The End of the Imperial Japanese Navy* (New York: Jove, 1986), 120.

2. H.P. Willmott, *The Battle of Leyte Gulf: The Last Fleet Action* (Bloomington, IN: Indiana University Press, 2005), 47.

3. Hoyt, *How They Won the War*, 420–22; Samuel Eliot Morison, *History of United States Naval Operations in World War II,* vol. XII, *Leyte: June 1944–January 1945* (Boston: Little Brown, 1974), 55–65.

4. See United States Strategic Bombing Survey (Pacific), *The Campaigns of the Pacific War* (Washington, DC: Government Printing Office, 1946), 283; Evans, *Japanese Navy*, 351–2.

5. Ugaki, *Fading Victory*, 474.

6. Evans, *Japanese Navy*, 351; Akira Yoshimura, *Battleship Musashi: The Making and Sinking of the World's Biggest Battleship*, trans. Vincent Murphy (Tokyo: Kodansha International, 1999), 358.

7. These ships were crowded with survivors. See Willmott, *Battle of Leyte Gulf*, 102.

8. Yoshimura, *Battleship Musashi*, 159–65.

9. *Reports of General MacArthur*, 2 vols. (Tokyo: Department of the Army, General Headquarters Far East Command, 1950), vol. II, 389.

10. Carl Solberg, *Decision and Dissent: With Halsey at Leyte Gulf* (Annapolis: Naval Institute Press, 1995), 117.

11. Wheeler, *Kinkaid*, 399.

12. Ito, *Japanese Navy*, 142–43.

13. Smith, Torpedo Run, Bates Papers, Naval War College Library, Series II, Box 15, Folder 13, 3.

14. Trent Hone, "Triumph of U.S. Navy Night Fighting," *Naval History* 20 (October 2006), 55.

15. United States Strategic Bombing Survey, *Interrogations*, 347.

16. Robert W. Bates, *The Battle of Leyte Gulf, October 1944: Strategical and Tactical Analysis*, vol. 5, *Battle of Surigao Strait, October 24th–25th* (Newport, RI: Naval War College, 1953–1958), 328.

17. When operating ships other than carriers jointly, the senior officer, whether Australian or American, commanded the group. In this case Buchanan had seniority.

18. Bates, *Battle of Leyte Gulf*, 427.

19. James D. Hornfischer, *The Last Stand of the Tin Can Sailors* (New York: Bantam, 2004), 109.

20. John Toland, *The Rising Sun: The Decline and Fall of the Japanese Empire* (New York: Bantam, 1981), 636.

21. United States Strategic Bombing Survey, *Interrogations*, 240.

22. Thomas J. Cutler, *The Battle of Leyte Gulf: 23–26 1944* (New York: Pocket Books, 1994), 219.

23. Paul Barnes, *USS Mississippi: View From a Battleship's Bridge* (unpublished manuscript, 1993), 30.

24. United States Navy, World War II Action and Operational Reports, USS *California*, 25 October 1944, 13.

25. Stan Nichols, "HMAS *Shropshire*, Often Unheralded, but the Most Successful Warship in the Royal Australian Navy During World War II," H.M.A.S. *Shropshire*, http://www.hmasshropshire.com/speech.htm.

26. United States Navy, World War II Action and Operational Reports, USS *Columbia* 25 October 1944, 4.

27. Barnes, *USS* Mississippi, 32.

28. Naval Historical Center, *Dictionary*, vol. I, 151.

29. Morison, *Leyte*, 233.

30. Cutler, *Battle of Leyte Gulf*, 226-29.

31. United States Navy, World War II Action and Operational Reports, USS *Columbia*, 25 October 1944, 5.

32. Cutler, *Battle of Leyte Gulf*, 230-31.

33. A typical assessment reads, "Of Nishimura the most charitable verdict is that his skill was inversely proportionate to his courage." James A. Field, *The Japanese at Leyte Gulf: The Shō Operation* (London: Princeton University Press, 1947), 139.

34. Ito, *Imperial Japanese Navy*, 132.

35. Ibid., 140.

36. Ibid. 161.

37. C.A.F. Sprague, "They Had Us on the Ropes," *American Magazine*, April 1945, http://www.bosamar.com/reading/ropes.html.

38. O'Hara, *German Fleet*, 57.

39. United States Strategic Bombing Survey, *Interrogations*, 41.

40. Morison, *Leyte*, 250.

41. Evans, *Japanese Navy*, 367.

42. Morison, *Leyte*, 253.

43. United States Navy, World War II Action and Operational Reports, USS *Johnston*, 25 October 1944, Part II.

44. Robert C. Hagen, "We Asked for the Jap Fleet," *American Magazine*, April 1945. http://www.ussjohnston-hoel.bigstep.com/generic56.html;$sessionid$JFCVRXAAAANNH TZENUKJPQWPERWRJPXo.

45. United States Navy, World War II Action and Operational Reports, USS *Johnson*, 25 October 1944, Part II.

46. United States Strategic Bombing Survey, *Interrogations*, 43.

47. Robert Jon Cox, *The Battle off Samar: Taffy III at Leyte Gulf* (San Diego, CA: Ivy Alba Press, 2003), 92.

48. Ugaki, *Fading Victory*, 493.

49. U.S. Armed Forces Far East, History Division, *Philippines Area Naval Operations, Part II, Oct.-Dec. 1944*, Japanese Monographs Series 84 (Washington, DC: U.S. Army, 1947), 60.

50. United States Navy, World War II Action and Operational Reports, USS *Gambier Bay*, 25 October 1944.

51. Ugaki, *Fading Victory*, 493.

52. Lacroix and Wells, *Japanese Cruisers*, 349.

53. United States Navy, World War II Action and Operational Reports, USS *Gambier Bay*, 25 October 1944.

54. United States Navy, World War II Action and Operational Reports, USS *Hoel*, 25 October 1944.

55. Cox, *Battle off Samar*, 107.

56. Ibid., 108.

57. United States Navy, World War II Action and Operational Reports, USS *Johnston*, 25 October 1944.

58. Wheeler, *Kinkaid*, 402.

59. Thomas J. Cutler, "Lest We Forget: Ernest E. Evans," *Proceedings* 132 (March 2006), 94.

60. This famous incident is best described in Cutler, *Battle of Leyte Gulf*, 280.

61. Dull, *Imperial Japanese Navy*, 326.

62. Sprague, "They Had Us on the Ropes."

63. United States Strategic Bombing Survey, *Interrogations*, 173.

64. United States Strategic Bombing Survey, *Campaigns of the Pacific War*, 304.

65. Ibid. Also see Morison, *Leyte*, 296–300.

66. U.S. Armed Forces Far East, History Division, *Philippines Area Naval Operations, Part II*, 65.

67. Evan Thomas, "Understanding Kurita's 'Mysterious Retreat.'" *Naval History* 18 (October 2004), 26.

68. Morison, *Leyte*, 300–03; Cutler, *Battle of Leyte Gulf*, 303–09.

69. Potter, *Bull Halsey*, 301.

70. Ibid. Halsey received the message with its terminal padding, a nonsense phase intended as a security measure, still inserted. The nonsense portion followed the code "RR." Thus, the message as handed to him read: "Where is, repeat, where is Task Force 34? RR The World Wonders." See Willmott, *Leyte Gulf*, 194, for a most penetrating criticism of Halsey's reaction to this message.

71. Louis H. Parker, USS *Wichita*, 25 October 1944, http://www.j-aircraft.org/smf/index.php#3 (accessed August 7, 2005).

72. For a fuller account of the aerial attacks see Morison, *Leyte*, 322–38.

73. United States Navy, World War II Action and Operational Reports, USS *Wichita*, 25 October 1944, 8.

74. United States Navy, World War II Action and Operational Reports, USS *Wichita*, 25 October 1944, 22.

75. Parker, USS *Wichita*.

76. United States Navy, World War II Action and Operational Reports, USS *Wichita*, 25 October 1944, Performance of Own Ordnance Material and Equipment, 1–2.

77. Willmott, *Battle of Leyte Gulf*, 365 (n276).

78. United States Navy, World War II Action and Operational Reports, USS *Miami*, 26 October 1944, 2.

79. Ibid., 4.

80. Willmott, *Battle of Leyte Gulf*, 216.

81. United States Navy, World War II Action and Operational Reports, USS *Miami*, 26 October 1944, 8.

82. Yoshimura, *Battleship* Musashi, 136.

83. United States Navy, World War II Action and Operational Reports, USS *Miami*, 26 October 1944, 6.

Chapter 13. Final Actions, December 1944–January 1945

1. Ronald H. Spector, *Eagle Against the Sun: The American War with Japan* (New York: The Free Press, 1985), 511.

2. Ugaki, *Fading Victory*, 503.

3. *Reports of General MacArthur*, vol 2, 380.

4. Morison, *Leyte*, 351.

5. Ibid., 343–9.

6. Prados, *Combined Fleet Decoded*, 693–4; see *Reports of General MacArthur*, vol 2, 415–6 for specifics on this operation.

7. Jentschura et al., 217; Morison, *Leyte*, 369, states the victim was an unidentified submarine.

8. Morison, *Leyte*, 369–70.

9. United States Navy, World War II Action and Operational Reports, Commander Destroyer Division 120, 3 December 1944, paragraph 5.

10. United States Navy, World War II Action and Operational Reports, USS *Cooper*, 3 December 1944, Part I; USS *Sumner*, 3 December 1944, Part I.

11. Eugene George Anderson, "Nightmare in Ormoc Bay," USS *Allen M. Sumner* (DD-692), http://www.dd-692.com/nightmare.htm.

12. United States Navy, World War II Action and Operational Reports, USS *Moale*, 3 December 1944, Part II.

13. Ibid., Part V.

14. Anderson, Eugene George, "Nightmare in Ormoc Bay."

15. United States Navy, World War II Action and Operational Reports, USS *Sumner*, 3 December 1944, Part V.

16. *Reports of General MacArthur*, vol 1, 234.

17. See Morison, *Leyte*, 375–85 for an overview of this operation.

18. U.S. Armed Forces Far East, History Division, *Philippines Area Naval Operations, Part II*, 109.

19. M. Hamlin Cannon, *United States Army in World War II The War in the Pacific, Leyte: The Return to the Philippines* (Washington DC: Office of the Chief of Military History, Department of the Army, 1993), 317–18.

20. United States Navy, World War II Action and Operational Reports, USS *Coghlan*, 12 December 1944, 7.

21. Robert J. Bulkley Jr., *At Close Quarters: PT Boats in the United States Navy* (Annapolis: Naval Institute Press, 2003), 400.

22. *Reports of General MacArthur*, vol 1, 236–17.

23. Ugaki, *Fading Victory*, 529.

24. Bulkley, *At Close Quarters*, 407.

25. Ibid., 408. For a good overview of this action see John Prados, "Mindoro's Desperate Hours," *MHQ: The Quarterly Journal of Military History* 8 (Autumn 1995), 90–101.

26. J.O. Campbell, "Red Jealousy; Opee; Leave & Learn; Philippine Survey; Ambition," in *H.M.A.S. Mk. IV: The R.A.N.'s Fourth Book* (Sydney, Australia: Royal Australian Navy, 1945), http://www.diggerhistory2.info/ran/1945/chapter05.htm.

27. United States Navy, World War II Action and Operational Reports, USS *Bennion* 5 January, 1945, Part II, 2.

28. Samuel Eliot Morison, *History of United States Naval Operations in World War II*, Vol. XIII, *The Liberation of the Philippines, Luzon, Mindanao, the Visayas 1944–1945* (Boston: Little, Brown, 1984), 102.

29. *Reports of General MacArthur*, vol 1, 256.

30. Morison, *Liberation of the Philippines*, 110.

31. United States Navy, World War II Action and Operational Reports, USS *Charles Ausburne*, 9 January 1945, 1.

32. Ibid., 3.

33. Ibid.

34. Ibid., 4.

35. Wheeler, *Kinkaid*, 422.

36. Morison, *Liberation of the Philippines*, 284.

37. United States Navy, World War II Action and Operational Reports, USS *Case*, 24 December 1944, 3.

38. Ibid., First Endorsement.

39. Ibid., 7 and First Endorsement.

40. United States Navy, World War II Action and Operational Reports, USS *Dunlap*, 24–27 December 1944, Part II, 3.

41. Ibid., 4.

42. Ibid., 10.

43. For a outline of operations in the Bonin Islands see Cressman, *Official Chronology*, 286, 290, 328; Roscoe, *United States Destroyer Operations*, 517–18.

44. Cressman, *Official Chronology*, 330; Roscoe, *United States Destroyer Operations*, 518.

45. General Headquarters Far East Command, Allied Translator and Interpreter Section, *Stockpiling of Liquid Fuel in Japan* (1953), Appendix, Table 2.

46. This is a calculated approximation based on economical and battle speeds and fuel storage capacity. The *Yamato*, for example, had a storage capacity of 6,300 tons of fuel oil. She could steam 8,600 miles at nineteen knots. This is roughly fourteen tons per hour. At battle speeds of twenty-seven knots she could steam 4,100 miles while consuming more than forty tons per hour. See Jentschura et al., *Warships of the Imperial Japanese Navy* for storage and consumption data.

47. See O'Hara, "The Royal Navy's Revenge," *World War II* (May 2006), 50–6.

CONCLUSION

1. United States Navy, *Battle Experience: Battle of Leyte Gulf*, March 1945, 97.

2. United States Navy, World War II Action and Operational Reports, USS *South Dakota*, 14–15 November 1942, 22.

3. Holmes, *Double-edged Secrets*, 190.

4. Willmott, *War with Japan*, 140.

Bibliography

PRIMARY SOURCES AND OFFICIAL PUBLICATIONS

Bates Papers. Naval War College Library.

Bates, Richard W. *The Battle of Leyte Gulf, October 1944: Strategical and Tactical Analysis*. Vol. 5. *Battle of Surigao Strait, October 24th–25th*. Newport, RI: Naval War College, 1953–1958. Available at http://www.ibiblio.org/hyperwar/USN/rep/Leyte/NWC-5.pdf (accessed August 18, 2006).

———. *The Battle of Savo Island, August 9th, 1942: Strategical and Tactical Analysis*. Newport, RI: Naval War College, 1950. Available at http://www.ibiblio.org/hyperwar/PTO/Hell/NWC-Savo.pdf (accessed August 18, 2006).

Bounds, James. USS *Helena*. 13 November 1942 and 13 July 1943. Interview with the author. August 17, 2005.

David M. Armstrong Papers. East Carolina Manuscript Collection, J. Y. Joyner Library.

General Headquarters Far East Command, Allied Translator and Interpreter Section. *The Japanese Version of the Black Chamber* (Doc. No. 64718). January 1951.

———. *Stockpiling of Liquid Fuel in Japan*. March 1953.

Hooper, Edwin B. The Reminiscences of Vice Admiral Edwin B. Hooper. Oral History Program, U.S. Naval Institute, Annapolis, 1978.

———. Some Recollections of World War II. Unpublished paper, 1964.

Japanese National Institute for Defense Studies, Military History Department. *Naval Operations in Southwest Area*. War History Series (*Senshi Sosho*) 26. Tokyo: Asagumo Shinbunsha, 1969.

———. *Naval Operations in Southeast Area, 2*. War History Series (*Senshi Sosho*) 83. Tokyo: Asagumo Shinbunsha, 1975.

———. *Naval Operations in Southeast Area, 3*. War History Series (*Senshi Sosho*) 96. Tokyo: Asagumo Shinbunsha, 1976.

Japanese Navy Action Records. *Haguro*, CA. Japanese Navy Records, Operational Archives Branch, Naval Historical Center, Washington, D.C.

———. *Jintsu*, CL.

———. *Kirishima*, BB.

———. *Nachi*, CA.

———. *Nagara*, CL.

———. *Naka*, CL.

———. *Natori*, CL.

———. *Sendai*, CL.

———. *Yubari*, CL.

Joint Intelligence Center, Pacific Ocean Areas. *Battle Lesson Learned in the Greater East Asia War (Torpedoes)*. Volume VI. Translation of Captured Japanese Document. Honolulu, HI, 1944.

LaGesse, Lewis. USS *Salt Lake City*, 26 March 1943. Oral history.

Naval Historical Center. *Dictionary of American Naval Fighting Ships*. 8 Vols. Washington, D.C.: Government Printing Office, 1959–1991.

Office of Naval Intelligence, Publications Branch. *The Aleutians Campaign*. Suitland, MD: U.S. Department of the Navy, May 1945. Transcription available online at http://www.ibiblio.org/hyperwar/USN/USN-CN-Aleutians.html (accessed August 17, 2006).

———. *The Battle of Cape Esperance 11 October 1942*. Suitland, MD: U.S. Department of the Navy, November 1943. Transcription available at http://www.ibiblio.org/hyperwar/USN/USN-CN-Esperance/index.html (accessed August 17, 2006).

———. *The Battle of Savo Island 9 August 1942*. Suitland, MD: U.S. Department of the Navy, November 1943. Transcription available at http://www.ibiblio.org/hyperwar/USN/USN-CN-Savo/index.html (accessed August 17, 2006).

———. *The Java Sea Campaign*. Suitland, MD: U.S. Department of the Navy, July 1943. Transcription available online at http://www.ibiblio.org/hyperwar/USN/USN-CN-Java/index.html (accessed August 17, 2006).

———. *Naval Battle of Guadalcanal 11–15 November 1942*. Suitland, MD: U.S. Department of the Navy, February 1944. Transcription available online at http://ftp.ibiblio.org/hyperwar//USN/USN-CN-Guadalcanal/USN-CN-Guadalcanal-fwd.html (accessed August 17, 2006).

Reports of General MacArthur. 2 vols. Tokyo: Department of the Army, General Headquarters Far East Command, 1950.

Schaniel, Carl. China Lake Naval Weapons Center. Interviews with the author, 2005.

U.S. Armed Forces Far East. History Division. *The "A-GO" Operations, May–June 1944*. Japanese Monographs Series 90. Washington, DC: U.S. Army, 1947.

———. *Aleutian Naval Operation, March 1942–February 1943*. Japanese Monographs Series 88. Washington, DC: U.S. Army, 1952.

———. *The Burma and Andaman Invasion Naval Operations, March–April 1942*. Japanese Monographs Series 79. Washington, DC: U.S. Army, 1953.

———. *Eastern New Guinea Invasion Operations, March–September 1942*. Japanese Monographs Series 96. Washington, DC: U.S. Army, 1947.

——. *The Imperial Japanese Navy in World War II, 1941–1945*. Japanese Monographs Series 116. Washington, DC: U.S. Army, 1952.

——. *Inner South Seas Islands Area Naval Operations, Part I, Gilbert Islands Operations, November 1941–November 1943*. Japanese Monographs Series 161. Washington, DC: U.S. Army, 1952.

——. *Midway Operations, May–June 1944*. Japanese Monographs Series 93. Washington, DC: U.S. Army, 1947.

——. *Netherlands East Indies Naval Invasion Operations, December 1941–March 1942*. Japanese Monographs Series 101. Washington, DC: U.S. Army, 1953.

——. *Philippines Area Naval Operations, Part II, October–December 1944*. Japanese Monographs Series 84. Washington, DC: U.S. Army, 1947.

——. *Southeast Naval Operations, Part I, May 1942–February 1943*. Japanese Monographs Series 98. Washington, DC: U.S. Army, 1949.

——. *Southeast Naval Operations, Part II, February–October 1943*. Japanese Monographs Series 99. Washington, DC: U.S. Army, 1947.

——. *Southeast Naval Operations, Part III, October 1943–February 1944*. Japanese Monographs Series 100. Washington, DC: U.S. Army, 1947.

——. *Western New Guinea and North of Australia Area Naval Operations April–September 1944*. Japanese Monographs Series 87. Washington, DC: U.S. Army, 1947.

United States Navy. *Battle Experience: Battle of Leyte Gulf*. March 1945.

——. *Gunnery Doctrine and Instructions Battleships, U.S. Pacific Fleet*. 1944.

——. *Gunnery Doctrine and Standard Fire Control Procedures, Cruisers Pacific Fleet*. 1943.

——. *Navy Department Communiqués: December 10, 1941–May 24, 1945*. 1946.

——. *War Instructions, United States Navy*. November 1944.

——. *War Plans CINCPAC Files. Admiral Nimitz Command Summary, Running Estimate and Summary* (Grey Book).

United States Navy. World War II Action and Operational Reports, 1941–1947. USS *Barker*. 21–23 January 1942. College Park, MD: Modern Military Records, Textual Archives Service Division, National Archives and Records Administration.

——. USS *John D. Ford*. 24 January 1942.

——. USS *Pope*. 24 January 1942.

——. USS *John D. Edwards*. 20 February 1942.

——. USS *Pope*. 20 February 1942.

——. USS *Stewart*. 20 February 1942.

——. USS *John D. Ford*. 27 February 1942.

————. USS *Pope*. 1 March 1942.

————. USS *John D. Edwards*. Recommendations. 4 March 1942.

————. USS *Blue*. 22 August 1942.

————. USS *Gregory*. 5 September 1942.

————. USS *Trever*. 25 October 1942.

————. USS *Zane*. 25 October 1942.

————. USS *Augusta*. 8 November 1942.

————. USS *Ludlow*. 8 November 1942.

————. USS *Massachusetts*. 8 November 1942.

————. USS *Swanson*. 8 November 1942.

————. USS *Wichita*. 8 November 1942.

————. USS *Atlanta*. 12–13 November 1942.

————. USS *Fletcher*. 12–13 November, 1942.

————. USS *Juneau*. 12–13 November 1942.

————. USS *O'Bannon*. 12–13 November 1942.

————. Commander Task Force 64. 14–15 November 1942.

————. USS *South Dakota*. 14–15 November 1942.

————. USS *Washington*. 14–15 November 1942.

————. USS *Portland* to Commander South Pacific. 17 November 1942.

————. USS *Montpelier*. 5 March 1943.

————. USS *Waller*. 5 March 1943.

————. USS *Honolulu*. 4 July 1943.

————. USS *Helena*. 6 July 1943.

————. USS *Honolulu*. 6 July 1943.

————. USS *Nicholas*. 6 July 1943.

————. USS *O'Bannon*. 6 July 1943.

————. USS *Honolulu*. 12 July 1943.

————. USS *Ralph Talbot*. 12 July 1943.

————. USS *Ralph Talbot*. 29 September–3 October 1943.

————. USS *Waller*. 1–3 October 1943.

————. USS *Chevalier*. 6 October 1943.

————. USS *Charles Ausburne*. 1–2 November 1943.

————. USS *Cleveland*. 1–2 November 1943.

————. USS *Columbia*. 1–2 November 1943.

————. USS *Denver*. 1–2 November 1943.

————. USS *Montpelier*. 1–2 November 1943.

————. USS *Spence*. 1–2 November 1943.

————. Commander Task Force 39. 3 November 1943.

————. USS *Converse*. 24–25 November 1943.

————. USS *Iowa*. 16–17 February 1944.

———. USS *Minneapolis*. 16–17 February 1944.

———. USS *New Jersey*. 16–17 February 1944.

———. USS *Fletcher*. 8–9 June 1944.

———. USS *Somers*. 15 August 1944.

———. USS *Endicott*. 17 August 1944.

———. USS *Benson*. 30 September–2 October 1944.

———. USS *Gleaves*. 1–2 October 1944.

———. Commander Task Force 77. 25 October 1944.

———. USS *California*. 25 October 1944.

———. USS *Claxton*. 25 October 1944.

———. USS *Columbia*. 25 October 1944.

———. USS *Denver*. 25 October 1944

———. USS *Gambier Bay*. 25 October 1944.

———. USS *Halford*. 25 October 1944.

———. USS *Hoel*. 25 October 1944.

———. USS *Johnson*. 25 October 1944.

———. USS *Mobile*. 25 October 1944.

———. USS *Newcomb*. 25 October 1944.

———. USS *Portland*. 25 October 1944.

———. USS *West Virginia*. 25 October 1944.

———. USS *Wichita*. 25 October 1944.

———. USS *Miami*. 26 October 1944.

———. Commander Destroyer Division 120. 3 December 1944.

———. USS *Allen M. Sumner*. 3 December 1944.

———. USS *Cooper*. 3 December 1944.

———. USS *Moale*. 3 December 1944.

———. USS *Coghlan*. 12 December 1944.

———. USS *Case*. 24 December 1944.

———. USS *Dunlap*. 27 December 1944.

———. USS *Bennion*. 7 January 1945.

———. USS *Charles Ausburne*. 9 January 1945.

———. USS *PC564*. 8–9 March 1945.

———. USS *Houston*. Statements of Survivors and Reconstructed Log. 9 September 1945.

United States Navy, Bureau of Ships. *Summary of War Damage to U.S. Battleships, Carriers, Cruisers, Destroyers and Destroyer Escorts: 17 October 1941 to 9 October 1945* (4 Volumes). Available at http://www.dcfp.navy.mil/cgi-bin/WarSummary.cgi (accessed August 18, 2006).

———. USS *Helena*. Loss in Action, Kula Gulf, Solomon Islands. 6 July 1943.

———. USS *Honolulu*. Torpedo Damage. 12–13 July 1943.

———. USS *Minneapolis*. Torpedo Damage Battle of Lunga Point. 30 November 1942.

———. USS *New Orleans*. Torpedo Damage, Lunga Point. 30 November 1942.

———. USS *Quincy*, USS *Astoria* and USS *Vincennes* Report of Loss in Action, 9 August 1942.

———. USS *Salt Lake City*. Gunfire Damage Bering Sea. 26 March 1943.

———. USS *San Francisco*. Gunfire Damage. 12–13 November 1942.

———. USS *South Dakota*. Gunfire Damage, Battle of Guadalcanal. 13 November 1942.

———. USS *Sterett*. Gunfire Damage, Battle of Guadalcanal. 13 November 1942.

United States Strategic Bombing Survey (Pacific). *The Campaigns of the Pacific War*. Washington, DC: Government Printing Office, 1946.

———. *Interrogations of Japanese Officials* (OPNAV-P-03-100). Washington, DC: Government Printing Office, 1946.

United States Technical Mission to Japan. *Summary Report*. November 1946.

United States War Department. *FM 30–50. Recognition Pictorial Manual of Naval Vessels, Supplement No. 1*. September 1943.

Watanabe, Daiji. "Bali Island Sea Battle by *Michishio* of the 8th Destroyer Division." Private translation.

SECONDARY SOURCES
BOOKS

Agawa, Hiroyuki. *The Reluctant Admiral: Yamamoto and the Imperial Navy*. Tokyo: Kodansha International, 1985.

Atkinson, Rick. *An Army at Dawn: The War in North Africa, 1942–1943*. New York: Henry Holt and Company, 2002.

Auphan, Paul, and Jacques Mordal. *The French Navy in World War II*. Westport, CT: Greenwood Press, 1976.

Barnes, Paul. *USS* Mississippi: *View from a Battleship's Bridge*. Unpublished manuscript, 1993.

Barnett, Correlli. *Engage the Enemy More Closely: The Royal Navy in the Second World War*. New York: W.W. Norton, 1991.

Beach, Edward Latimer. *The United States Navy: A 200-Year History*. Boston: Houghton Mifflin, 1990.

Bell, Frederick J. *Condition Red: Destroyer Action in the South Pacific*. New York: Longmans, Green and Co., 1944.

Blair, Clay. *Silent Victory: The U.S. Submarine War Against Japan*. New York: Bantam, 1976.

Boyd, Carl, and Akihiko Yoshida. *The Japanese Submarine Force and World War II*. Annapolis: Naval Institute Press, 1995.

Brown, David. *Warship Loses of WWII*. Annapolis: Naval Institute Press, 1995.

Buell, Thomas B. *Master of Sea Power: A Biography of Fleet Admiral Ernest J. King*. Boston: Little Brown and Company, 1980.

Bulkley, Robert J. Jr. *At Close Quarters: PT Boats in the United States Navy*. Annapolis: Naval Institute Press, 2003.

Calhoun, C. Raymond. *Tin Can Sailor: Life Aboard the USS* Sterett, *1939–1945*. Annapolis: Naval Institute Press, 2000.

Campbell, J.O. "Red Jealousy; Opee; Leave & Learn; Philippine Survey; Ambition." *H.M.A.S. Mk. IV: The R.A.N.'s Fourth Book*. Sydney, Australia: Royal Australian Navy, 1945. Available at http://www.diggerhistory2. info/ran/1945/chapter05.htm.

Campbell, John. *Naval Weapons of World War II*. Annapolis: Naval Institute Press, 2002.

Cannon, M. Hamlin. *United States Army in World War II The War in the Pacific. Leyte: The Return to the Philippines*. Washington, DC: Office of the Chief of Military History, Department of the Army, 1993.

Churchill, Winston S. *The Second World War Volume II: Their Finest Hour*. Houghton Mifflin: Boston, 1949.

———. *Volume III: The Grand Alliance*. Houghton Mifflin: Boston, 1950.

———. *Volume IV: The Hinge of Fate*. Houghton Mifflin: Boston, 1950.

Cook, Charles. *The Battle of Cape Esperance: Encounter at Guadalcanal*. Annapolis: Naval Institute Press, 1992.

Coombe, Jack D. *Derailing the Tokyo Express: The Naval Battles for the Solomon Islands that Sealed Japan's Fate*. Harrisburg, PA: Stackpole, 1991.

Costello, John. *The Pacific War*. New York: Rawson, Wade, 1981.

Cox, Robert Jon. *The Battle off Samar: Taffy III at Leyte Gulf*. San Diego: Ivy Alba Press, 2003.

Crenshaw, Russell S. Jr. *The Battle of Tassafaronga*. Baltimore: Nautical & Aviation Publishing, 1995.

———. *South Pacific Destroyer: The Battle for the Solomons from Savo Island to Vella Gulf*. Annapolis: Naval Institute Press, 1998.

Cressman, Robert J. *The Official Chronology of the U.S. Navy in World War II*. Annapolis: Naval Institute Press, 2000.

Cutler, Thomas J. *The Battle of Leyte Gulf: 23–26 October 1944*. New York: Pocket Books, 1994.

———. *A Sailor's History of the U.S. Navy*. Annapolis: Naval Institute Press, 2005.

D'Albas, Andrieu. *Death of a Navy: Japanese Naval Action in World War II*. New York: Devin-Adair, 1957.

Darrieus, Amiral Henri, and Jean Queguiner. *Historique de la Marine française 1922–1942*. St Malo: l'Ancre de Marine, 1996.

Dear, I.C.B., ed. *The Oxford Companion to World War II*. New York: Oxford University Press, 1995.

Dulin, Robert O. Jr., and William H. Garzke Jr. *Battleships: United States Battleships in World War II*. Annapolis: Naval Institute Press, 1976.

Dull, Paul S. *A Battle History of the Imperial Japanese Navy (1941–1945)*. Annapolis: Naval Institute Press, 1982.

Dunnigan, James F., and Albert A. Nofi. *Pacific War Encyclopedia*. New York: Checkmark Books, 1998.

——. *Victory at Sea: World War II in the Pacific*. New York: William Morrow, 1995.

Dyer, George C. *The Amphibians Came to Conquer: The Story of Admiral Richmond Kelly Turner*. Washington, DC: Naval Historical Center, 1972.

Ellis, John. *World War II: A Statistical Survey*. New York: Facts on File, 1995.

Evans, David C., ed. *The Japanese Navy in World War II: In the Words of Former Japanese Naval Officers*. Annapolis: Naval Institute Press, 1986.

Evans, David C., and Mark R. Peattie. *Kaigun: Strategy, Tactics, and Technology in the Imperial Japanese Navy, 1887–1941*. Annapolis: Naval Institute Press, 1994.

Fahey, James J. *Pacific War Diary, 1942–1945: The Secret Diary of an American Sailor*. New York: Zebra, 1984.

Field, James A. *The Japanese at Leyte Gulf: The Shō Operation*. London: Princeton University Press, 1947.

Frank, Richard B. *Guadalcanal: The Definitive Account of the Landmark Battle*. New York: Penguin, 1990.

Friedman, Norman. *U.S. Aircraft Carriers: An Illustrated Design History*. Annapolis: Naval Institute Press, 1989.

——. *U.S. Battleships: An Illustrated Design History*. Annapolis: Naval Institute Press, 1985.

——. *U.S. Cruisers: An Illustrated Design History*. Annapolis: Naval Institute Press, 1989.

——. *U.S. Destroyers: An Illustrated Design History*. Annapolis: Naval Institute Press, 1982.

——. *U.S. Naval Weapons*. London: Conway Maritime Press, 1983.

Gardiner, Robert, ed. *Conway's All the World's Fighting Ships 1906–1921*. Annapolis: Naval Institute Press, 1986.

——. *Conway's All the World's Fighting Ships 1922–1946*. New York: Mayflower 1980.

Garfield, Brian. *The Thousand Mile War: World War II in Alaska and the Aleutians*. New York: Bantam, 1982.

Generous, William Thomas Jr. *Sweet Pea at War: A History of USS Portland*. Lexington, KY: University of Kentucky Press, 2003.

Gill, G. Hermon. *Royal Australian Navy, 1939–1942*. Adelaide: Griffin Press, 1957.

———. *Royal Australian Navy, 1942–1945*. Adelaide: Griffin Press, 1968.

Goldstein, Donald M., and Katherine V. Dillon. *The Pacific War Papers: Japanese Documents of World War II*. Washington, D.C.: Potomac Books, 2004.

———. *The Pearl Harbor Papers: Inside the Japanese Plans*. Dulles, VA: Brassey's, 2000.

Grace, James W. *The Naval Battle of Guadalcanal: Night Action 13 November 1942*. Annapolis: Naval Institute Press, 1999.

Green, Jack. *War at Sea: Pearl Harbor to Midway*. New York: Gallery Books, 1988.

Grove, Eric. *Sea Battles in Close Up World War II, Volume Two*. Annapolis: Naval Institute Press, 1993.

Hammel, Eric. *Guadalcanal: Decision at Sea: The Naval Battle of Guadalcanal, November 13–15, 1942*. Pacifica, CA: Pacifica Military History, 1999.

Hara, Tameichi. *Japanese Destroyer Captain*. With Fred Saito and Roger Peneau. New York: Ballantine, 1961.

Harker, Jack S. *Well Done Leander*. Auckland: Collins, 1971.

Heal, S.C. *Ugly Ducklings: Japan's WWII Liberty Ship Equivalents of World War II*. Annapolis: Naval Institute Press, 2003.

Heckstall-Smith, Anthony. *The Fleet that Faced Both Ways*. London: Anthony Blond, 1963.

Hocking, Charles. *Dictionary of Disasters at Sea During the Age of Steam: Including Sailing Ships and Ships of War Lost in Action, 1824–1962*. London: Lloyd's Register of Shipping, 1969.

Holmes, W.J. *Double-edged Secrets: U.S. Naval Intelligence Operations in the Pacific During World War II*. Annapolis: Naval Institute Press, 1979.

Hone, Thomas C., and Trent Hone. *Battle Line: The United States Navy, 1919–1939*. Annapolis: Naval Institute Press, 2006.

Hornfischer, James D. *The Last Stand of the Tin Can Sailors*. New York: Bantam, 2004.

Howard, Michael. *The Mediterranean Strategy in the Second World War*. London: Greenhill, 1993.

Howarth, Stephen. *The Fighting Ships of the Rising Sun: The Drama of the Imperial Japanese Navy, 1895–1945*. New York: Atheneum, 1983.

Howe, George F. *Northwest Africa: Seizing the Initiative in the West*. Washington, DC: Government Printing Office, 1957.

Hoyt, Edwin P. *The Battle of Leyte Gulf*. New York: Jove, 1985.

———. *How They Won the War in the Pacific: Nimitz and His Admirals*. New York: The Lyons Press, 2000.

Ienaga, Saburo. *The Pacific War 1931–1945*. New York: Pantheon Books, 1978.

Ito, Masanori. *The End of the Imperial Japanese Navy*. New York: Jove, 1986.

Jentschura, Hansgeorge, Dieter Jung, and Peter Mickel. *Warships of the Imperial Japanese Navy, 1869–1945*. Annapolis: Naval Institute Press, 1986.

Johns, W.E., and R.A. Kelly. *No Surrender*. London: W.H. Allen, 1989.

Jones, Ken. *Destroyer Squadron 23: Combat Exploits of Arleigh Burke's Gallant Force*. Annapolis: Naval Institute Press, 1997.

Jordan, Roger. *The World's Merchant Fleets 1939*. Annapolis: Naval Institute Press, 1999.

Karig, Walter, Russell L. Harris, and Frank A. Manson. *Battle Report: The End of an Empire*. New York: Rinehart and Company, 1948.

Karig, Walter, and Eric Purdon. *Battle Report: Pacific War: Middle Phase*. New York: Rinehart and Company, 1946.

Keegan, John. *The Times Atlas of the Second World War*. New York: Harper & Row, 1989.

Kemp, Paul. *Friend or Foe: Friendly Fire at Sea 1939–1945*. London: Leo Cooper, 1995.

Kemp, P.K. *Key to Victory: The Triumph of British Sea Power in WWII*. Boston: Little, Brown, 1957.

Kilpatrick, C.W. *Naval Night Battles of the Solomons*. New York: Exposition Press, 1987.

Koburger, Charles W. Jr. *The Cyrano Fleet: France and Its Navy, 1940–1942*. New York: Praeger, 1989.

Krug, Hans-Joachim et al. *Reluctant Allies: German–Japanese Naval Relations in World War II*. Annapolis: Naval Institute Press, 2001.

Kukui, Shizuo. *The Japanese Navy at the End of WW2*. Old Greenwich, CT.: We, Inc.

Lacroix, Eric and Linton Wells II. *Japanese Cruisers of the Pacific War*. Annapolis: Naval Institute Press, 1997.

Langtree, Christopher. *The Kellys: British J, K & N Class Destroyers of World War II*. Annapolis: Naval Institute Press, 2002.

Leutze, James. *A Different Kind of Victory: A Biography of Admiral Thomas C. Hart*. Annapolis: Naval Institute Press, 1981.

Lorelli, John A. *The Battle of the Komandorski Islands*. Annapolis: Naval Institute Press, 1981.

Lott, Arnold S. *Most Dangerous Sea: A History of Mine Warfare and an Account of U.S. Navy Mine Warfare Operations in World War II and Korea*. Annapolis: Naval Institute Press, 1959.

Loxton, Bruce, and Chris Coulthard-Clark. *The Shame of Savo: Anatomy of a Naval Disaster*. Annapolis: Naval Institute Press, 1997.

Lundstrom, John B. *Black Shoe Carrier Admiral: Frank Jack Fletcher at Coral Sea, Midway, and Guadalcanal*. Annapolis: Naval Institute Press, 2006.

———. *The First Team and the Guadalcanal Campaign*. Annapolis: Naval Institute Press, 2005.

Mahan, A.T. *The Influence of Sea Power Upon History, 1660–1783*. Boston: Little, Brown and Company, 1918.

Mason, John T. *The Atlantic War Remembered: An Oral History Collection*. Annapolis: Naval Institute Press, 1990.

———. *The Pacific War Remembered: An Oral History Collection*. Annapolis: Naval Institute Press, 1986.

McKie, Ronald. *The Survivors*. Indianapolis: Bobbs-Merrill Company, 1953.

Messimer, Dwight R. *Pawns of War: The Loss of the USS Langley and the USS Pecos*. Annapolis: Naval Institute Press, 1983.

Michel, John J.A. *Mr. Michel's War: From Manila to Mukden; An American Navy Officer's War with the Japanese*. Novato, CA: Presidio, 1998.

Middlebrook, Martin, and Patrick Mahoney. *Battleship: The Loss of the* Prince of Wales *and the* Repulse. London: Penguin, 2001.

Miller, Edward S. *War Plan Orange: The U.S. Strategy to Defeat Japan 1897–1945*. Annapolis: Naval Institute Press, 1991.

Miller, John Jr. *Guadalcanal: The First Offensive*. New York: Barnes and Noble Books, 1995.

Miller, Nathan. *The War at Sea: A Naval History of WWII*. New York: Scribner, 1995.

Mollo, Andrew. *The Armed Forces of World War II: Uniforms, Insignia and Organization*. New York: Crown, 1981.

Morison, Samuel Eliot.

———. *History of United States Naval Operations in World War II*. 15 vols. Vol. I, *The Battle of the Atlantic 1939–1943*. Boston: Little, Brown, 1984.

———. Vol. II, *Operations in North African Waters, October 1942–June 1943*. Boston: Little, Brown, 1984.

———. Vol. III, *The Rising Sun in the Pacific, 1931–April 1942*. Boston: Little, Brown, 1984.

———. Vol. IV, *Coral Sea, Midway and Submarine Operations, May 1942–August 1942*. Boston: Little, Brown, 1974.

———. Vol. V, *The Struggle for Guadalcanal, August 1942–February 1943*. Boston: Little, Brown, 1966.

———. Vol. VI, *Breaking the Bismarcks Barrier, 22 July 1942–1 May 1944*. Boston: Little, Brown, 1988.

———. Vol. VII, *Aleutians, Gilberts and Marshalls, June 1942–April 1944*. Boston: Little, Brown, 1982.

———. Vol. VIII, *New Guinea and the Marianas, March 1944–August 1944*. Boston: Little, Brown, 1984.

———. Vol. IX, *Sicily–Salerno–Anzio, January 1943–June 1944*. Boston: Little, Brown, 1990.

———. Vol. X, *The Atlantic Battle Won, May 1943–May 1945.* Boston: Little, Brown, 1982.

———. Vol. XI, *The Invasion of France and Germany, 1944–1945.* Boston: Little, Brown, 1974.

———. Vol. XII, *Leyte, June 1945–January 1945.* Boston: Little, Brown, 1974.

———. Vol. XIII, *The Liberation of the Philippines, Luzon, Mindanao, the Visayas, 1944–1945.* Boston: Little, Brown, 1984.

———. Vol. XIV, *Victory in the Pacific 1945.* Boston: Little, Brown, 1975.

———. Vol. XV, *Supplement and General Index.* Boston: Little, Brown, 1962.

———. *The Two Ocean War.* Boston: Little, Brown, 1963.

Musicant, Ivan. *Battleship at War: The Epic Story of the USS* Washington. New York: Avon, 1986.

Newcomb, Richard F. *Savo.* New York: Bantam, 1963.

O'Hara, Vincent P. *The German Fleet at War, 1939–1945.* Annapolis: Naval Institute Press, 2004.

Okumiya, Masatake, Jiro Horikoshi, and Martin Caidin. *Zero.* New York: ibooks, 2002.

Parillo, Mark P. *The Japanese Merchant Marine in World War II.* Annapolis: Naval Institute Press, 1993.

Parkin, Ray. *Out of the Smoke.* New York: William Morrow, 1960.

Parrish, Thomas, ed. *The Simon and Schuster Encyclopedia of World War II.* New York: Simon and Schuster, 1978.

Polmar, Norman, and Samuel Loring Morison. *PT Boats at War World War II to Vietnam.* Osceola, WI: MBI, 1999.

Poolman, Kenneth. *The Winning Edge: Naval Technology in Action 1939–1945.* Annapolis: Naval Institute Press, 1997.

Potter, E.B. *Bull Halsey.* Annapolis: Naval Institute Press, 2003.

———. *Nimitz.* Annapolis: Naval Institute Press, 1976.

Prados, John. *Combined Fleet Decoded: The Secret History of American Intelligence and the Japanese Navy in World War II.* New York: Random House, 1995.

Pratt, Fletcher. *Night Work: The Story of Task Force 39.* New York: H. Holt and Company, 1946.

Preston, Anthony. *Navies of World War II.* London: Bison, 1976.

Reilly, John C. Jr. *United States Navy Destroyers of World War II.* Poole, Dorset: Blandford Press, 1983.

Reynolds, Clark G. *The Fast Carriers: The Forging of an Air Navy.* Annapolis: Naval Institute Press, 1992.

Rohwer, J., and G. Hummelchen. *Chronology of the War at Sea 1939–1945.* Annapolis: Naval Institute Press, 1992.

———. *Allied Submarine Attacks of World War II.* Annapolis: Naval Institute Press, 1997.

——. *Axis Submarine Successes of World War II*. Annapolis: Naval Institute Press, 1999.

Rohwer, Jergen. *War at Sea 1939–1945*. Annapolis: Naval Institute Press, 1996.

Roscoe, Theodore. *United States Destroyer Operations in World War II*. Annapolis: Naval Institute Press, 1953.

Rose, Lisle A. *The Ship That Held the Line: The USS Hornet and the First Year of the Pacific War*. Annapolis: Naval Institute Press, 1995.

Roskill, S.W. *The War at Sea 1939–1945*. Vol. I. *The Defensive*. London: HMSO, 1954.

——. Vol. II. *The Period of Balance*. London: HMSO, 1956.

——. Vol. III. *The Offensive, Part I*. London: HMSO, 1960.

——. Vol. III. *The Offensive, Part II*. Nashville: Battery Press, 1994.

——. *White Ensign*. Annapolis: Naval Institute Press, 1960.

Sadkovich, James J., ed. *Reevaluating Major Naval Combatants of World War II*. New York: Greenwood Press, 1990.

Sauer, Howard. *The Last Big-Gun Naval Battle: The Battle of Surigao Strait*. Palo Alto, CA: Glencannon Press, 1999.

Schultz, Duane. *The Last Battle Station: The Story of the USS Houston*. New York: St. Martin's Press, 1985.

Smith, S.E., ed. *The United States Navy in World War II*. New York: Quill, 1966.

Solberg, Carl. *Decision and Dissent: With Halsey at Leyte Gulf*. Annapolis: Naval Institute Press, 1995.

Spector, Ronald H. *Eagle Against the Sun: The American War with Japan*. New York: The Free Press, 1985.

——. *At War at Sea*. New York: Penguin Viking, 2001.

Spurr, Russell. *A Glorious Way to Die: The Kamikaze Mission of the Battleship Yamato, April 1945*. New York: Newmarket Press, 1982.

Stafford, Edward P. *Little Ship, Big War*. New York: Jove, 1985.

Stevens, David, ed. *The Royal Australian Navy in World War II*. St. Leonards, Australia: Allen & Unwin, 1996.

Stewart, Adrian. *The Battle of Leyte Gulf*. New York: Charles Scribner's Sons, 1980.

Taylor, Theodore. *The Magnificent Mitscher*. Annapolis: Naval Institute Press, 1991.

Thomas, David A. *Battle of the Java Sea*. London: Andre Deutsch, 1968.

——. *Japan's War at Sea, Pearl Harbor to the Coral Sea*. London: Andre Deutsch, 1978.

Toland, John. *But Not in Shame: The Six Months after Pearl Harbor*. New York: Random House, 1961.

——. *The Rising Sun: The Decline and Fall of the Japanese Empire*. New York: Bantam, 1981.

Tomblin, Barbara Brooks. *With Utmost Spirit: Allied Naval Operations in the Mediterranean, 1942–1945.* Lexington, KY: University of Kentucky Press, 2004.

Ugaki, Matome. *Fading Victory: The Diary of Admiral Matome Ugaki, 1941–45.* Edited by Donald M. Goldstein and Katherine V. Dillon. Translated by Masataka Chihaya. Pittsburgh: University of Pittsburgh Press, 1991.

Uhlig, Frank Jr. *How Navies Fight: The US Navy and Its Allies.* Annapolis: Naval Institute Press, 1994.

Van der Vat, Dan. *The Pacific Campaign: The U.S.–Japanese Naval War 1941–1945.* New York: Touchstone, 1991.

Van Oosten, F. C. *The Battle of the Java Sea.* Annapolis: Naval Institute Press, 1976.

Warner, Denis, Peggy Warner, and Sadao Seno. *Disaster in the Pacific: New Light on the Battle of Savo Island.* Annapolis: Naval Institute Press, 1992.

Waters, S.D. *The Royal New Zealand Navy.* Wellington: War History Branch, 1956.

Watts, Anthony J., and Brian G. Gordon. *The Imperial Japanese Navy.* New York: Doubleday, 1971.

Wheeler, Gerald E. *Kinkaid of the Seventh Fleet: A Biography of Admiral Thomas C. Kinkaid, U.S. Navy.* Washington DC: Naval Historical Center, Department of the Navy, 1995.

Whitley, M.J. *Battleships of World War Two.* Annapolis: Naval Institute Press, 1998.

———. *Cruisers of World War Two.* Annapolis: Naval Institute Press, 1995.

———. *Destroyers of World War Two.* Annapolis: Naval Institute Press, 1988.

Wildenberg, Thomas. *Grey Steel and Black Oil: Fast Tankers and Replenishment at Sea in the U.S. Navy, 1912–1995.* Annapolis: Naval Institute Press, 1996.

———. *The Battle of Leyte Gulf: The Last Fleet Action.* Bloomington, IN: Indiana University Press, 2005.

Willmott, H.P. *Empires in the Balance: Japanese and Allied Pacific Strategies to April 1942.* Annapolis: Naval Institute Press, 1982.

———. *The War with Japan: The Period of Balance, May 1942–October 1943.* Wilmington, DE: SR Books, 2002.

Winslow, W.G. *The Fleet the Gods Forgot: The U.S. Asiatic Fleet in World War II.* Annapolis: Naval Institute Press, 1994.

———. *The Ghost that Died at Sunda Strait.* Annapolis: Naval Institute Press, 1994.

Worth, Richard. *Fleets of World War II.* Cambridge: Da Capo, 2001.

Y'Blood, William T. *Red Sun Setting: The Battle of the Philippine Sea.* Annapolis: Naval Institute Press, 1989.

Yoshimura, Akira. *Battleship Musashi: The Making and Sinking of the World's Biggest Battleship.* Translated by Vincent Murphy. Tokyo: Kodansha International, 1999.

———. *Zero Fighter.* Trans. Retsu Kaiho and Michael Gregson. Westport, CT: Praeger, 1996.

ARTICLES

Bernstein, Marc D. "Hail Storm at Truk." *Naval History* 8 (January/February 1994): 17–24.

———. "Tin Cans Raid Balikpapan." *Proceedings* 129 (April 2003): 80–3.

Bennett, J.E. "Callaghan Was Calm and Collected at Guadalcanal." *Shipmate* 59 (April 1996): 17–9.

Buell, Harold L. "The Enigma of Admiral Frank Jack Fletcher." *Naval History* 17 (February 2003): 50–1.

Chase, Jean L. "A Grasshopper Survives Samar." *Naval History* 18 (October 2004): 16–21.

Chew, John L., and Charles Lee Lewis. "Some Shall Escape." *Proceedings* 71 (August 1945): 887–903.

Clemens, Martin. "Awaiting the 'Fleet Majestical.'" *Naval History* 12 (November/December 1998): 56–61.

Conlin, Carter B. "USS *Houston* (CA30)—Pride of the Asiatic Fleet." *Shipmate* 59 (March 1996): 19, 40.

Cutler, Thomas J. "Lest We Forget: Ernest E. Evans." *Proceedings* 132 (March 2006): 94.

Date, John C. "Leyte: HMAS *Shropshire* and HMAS *Arunta* in the Battle of Surigao Strait." *Naval Historical Review* 19 (March 1988).

DePalma, Arthur R. "Japanese Naval Nightmare." *World War II* (February 2001): 50–56.

Dickson, David W. "Naval Tactics . . . an Introduction." *Warship International* 3 (1976): 168–76.

Feuer, A.B. "The End of the Asiatic Fleet Part I." *Pacific War* 3 (2004): 3–6.

———. "The End of the Asiatic Fleet Part II." *Pacific War* 4 (2004): 17–9.

Frank, Richard B. ". . . Nailed the Colors to the Mast." *Naval History* 6 (Winter 1992): 6–12.

Franken, Daniel J. "Strike One, Task One." *Naval History* 6 (Fall 1992): 6–10.

Friedman, Norman. "The American 5-inch/38 Dual Purpose Gun." *Warship* 7 (1978): 171–77.

Fuquea, David C. "Task Force One: The Wasted Assets of the United States Pacific Battleship Fleet, 1942." *The Journal of Military History* 67 (October 1997): 707–34.

Hagen, Robert C. "We Asked for the Jap Fleet." *American Magazine*, April 1945. http://www.ussjohnston-hoel.bigstep.com/generic56.html;$sessionid$JF CVRXAAAANNHTZENUKJPQWPERWRJPX0.

Harrington, Skip Wild. "The Mystery of USS *Edsall*." *Shipmate* 43 (January/February 1980): 26–8.

Harvey, A.D. "Army Air Force and Navy Air Force: Japanese Aviation and the Opening Phase of the War in the Far East." *War in History* 6(2) (1999): 174–204.

Hone, Trent. "The Evolution of Fleet Tactical Doctrine in the U.S. Navy, 1922–1941." *The Journal of Military History* 67 (October 2003): 1107–48.

———. "Triumph of U.S. Navy Night Fighting." *Naval History* 20 (October 2006): 52–9.

Itani, Jiro et al. "Japanese Oxygen Torpedoes and Fire Control Systems." *Warship 1991*: 121–33.

Jackson, Erwin. "Trapped in a Typhoon." *Naval History* 18 (December 2004): 50–4.

Jones, William. "The *Helena* at Guadalcanal." *Naval History* 6 (Winter 1992): 30–1.

Klar, John W. "World War II Operational History of USS *Stewart* (DD-224)." *Warship International* 24(2) (1989): 139–59.

Lacouture, John. "Disaster at Savo Island. *Naval History* 6 (Fall 1992): 11–5.

Lacroix, E. "The Development of the 'A Class' Cruisers in the Imperial Japanese Navy, Part I. *Warship International* 14(4) (1979): 329–62.

———. "The Development of the 'A Class' Cruisers in the Imperial Japanese Navy, Part III. *Warship International* 15(1) (1979): 41–62.

Lengerer, Hans. "The Japanese Super Battleship Strategy." *Warship VII* (1983): 30–9, 88–96, 161–69.

Levy, James P. "The Race for the Decisive Weapon." *Naval War College Review* 58 (Winter 2005): 137–50.

London Gazette. "Battle of the Java Sea, 27th February 1942," July 6, 1948, supplement.

———. "Loss of H.M. Ships Prince of Wales and Repulse," February 20, 1948, supplement.

"Loss of *Little* and *Gregory*." *The Green Dragons: Newsletter of the American APD Corporation*. San Diego, CA.

Lundstrom, John B. "Frank Jack Fletcher Got a Bum Rap." *Naval History* 6 (Summer 1992): 22–7.

———. "Frank Jack Fletcher Got a Bum Rap." *Naval History* 6 (Fall 1992): 22–8.

Makin, Norman J.O. "*Perth* Died Bravely." *Naval Historical Review* 5 (June 1974): 12–4.

Marsh, Robert M. "Tactics Rule at Empress Augusta Bay." *Naval History* 17 (December 2003): 42–7.

McCandless, Bruce. "The *San Francisco* Story." *Proceedings* 84 (November 1958): 34–52.

Miles, Lion, Kelly Long, and Geary Dixie. "A Ship to Remember: USS *Edsall* (DD219)." *China Gunboatman*. September 2002:

Morss, Strafford. "*Iowa* vs. *Yamato*: Another View." *Warship International* 21(2) (1986): 118–36.

Mullin, Daniel J. "Balikpapan, 1942." *Shipmate* 47 (January/February 1984): 18–20.

O'Dell, Robert. "Rediscovering the Asiatic Fleet." *Naval History* 12 (November/December 1998): 40–2.

O'Hara, Vincent P. "A Most Remarkable Effort: The Battle of Balikpapan." *Pacific War* 8 (2005): 3–7.

———. "The Royal Navy's Revenge." *World War II* (May 2006): 50–6.

Payne, Alan. "The Battle of Sunda Strait." *Naval History* 6 (Spring 1992): 30–4.

Prados, John. "Mindoro's Desperate Hours." *MHQ: The Quarterly Journal of Military History* 8 (Autumn 1995): 90–101.

Ransom, Harry H. "The Battleship Meets the Airplane." *Military Affairs* 23 (Spring 1959): 21–7.

Roudman, Hyman. "The Evolution of New Fleet Tactics." *Military Affairs* 7 (Winter 1943): 197–201.

Sprague, C.A.F. "They Had Us on the Ropes." *American Magazine*, April 1945. http://www.bosamar.com/reading/ropes.html.

Strope, Walmer Elton. "The Decisive Battle of the Pacific War." *Proceedings* 72 (May 1946): 627–41.

Swan, W.N. "A Century of Japanese Intelligence (Four Parts)." *Naval Historical Review* 5–6 (September 1974, December 1974, March 1975, June 1975).

Sweetman, Jack. "Great Sea Battles of World War II." *Naval History* 9 (May 1995): 6–57.

Thomas, Evan. "Understanding Kurita's 'Mysterious Retreat.'" *Naval History* 18 (October 2004): 22–6.

Thornton, Tim. "The Sinking of the Yamato." *Warship XII* (1989): 145–55.

Till, Geoffrey. "Midway: The Decisive Battle?" *Naval History* 12 (November/December 1998): 40–2.

Valle, James E. "What If?" *Naval History* 19 (December 2005): 34–8.

Van der Moer, Abraham. "He Who Sees First Lives Longest." *Naval History* 8 (July/August 1994): 35–40.

Visser, Henk. "The Dockyard at Surabaya and the Capsizing of HNLMS *Krakatau*." *Warship 2006* (2006): 144–7.

Wellings, Joseph H. "The Night *Strong* Was Sunk." *Shipmate* 40 (July/August 1977): 23–6.

Williams, Gordon B. "A Dip in Iron Bottom Sound." *Shipmate* 54 (May 1991): 23–4.

Willmott, H. P. "Guadalcanal: The Naval Campaign." *Joint Force Quarterly* 2 (Autumn 1993): 98–106.

Wylie, J. C. "Captain Hoover: Right or Wrong?" *Naval History* 6 (Winter 1992): 28–9.

Zingheim, Karl J. "A Duel in the Gloom." *Pacific War* 1 (2004): 21–2.

INTERNET

Anderson, Eugene George. "Nightmare in Ormoc Bay." USS *Allen M. Sumner* (DD-692). http://www.dd-692.com/nightmare.htm.

Battle off Samar. Taffy III at Leyte Gulf. http://www.bosamar.com.

Boehm, Roy. Boatswain's Mate 3rd Class Roy Boehm's USS *Duncan* DD 485 Experiences. USS Duncan Reunion Association. http://www.ussduncan. org/capesper_page3.htm.

Destroyer History. http://www.destroyerhistory.org/destroyers/introduction.html.

Destroyers Online. http://www.destroyersonline.com.

Guidry, John Rodney. Interview: USS *Alden*. 27 February–1 March 1942. By Carl Hasbrink, March 2000. Netherlands East Indies, 1941–1942. http://www. geocities.com/dutcheastindies/guidry.html

Hyperwar: A Hypertext History of World War II. http://www.ibiblio.org/hyperwar.

Imperial Japanese Navy. http://homepage2.nifty.com/nishidah/e/index.htm.

Imperial Japanese Navy Page. http://www.combinedfleet.com.

Naval Weapons, Naval Technology and Naval Reunions. http://www.navweaps.com.

Netherlands East Indies, 1941–1942. http://www.geocities.com/dutcheastindies.

Nichols, Stan. "HMAS *Shropshire*, Often Unheralded, but the Most Successful Warship in the Royal Australian Navy During World War II." H.M.A.S. *Shropshire*. http://www.hmasshropshire.com/speech.htm.

The Pacific War: The U.S. Navy. http://www.microworks.net/pacific.

Parker, Louis H. USS *Wichita*, 25 October 1944. http://www.j-aircraft.org/smf/ index.php#3 (accessed August 7, 2005).

Parshall, Jon. "Oil and Japanese Strategy in the Solomons: A Postulate." Imperial Japanese Navy Page. http://www.combinedfleet.com/guadoil1.htm.

Roupe, R.H. "Hell and High Water." Destroyer History. http://www. destroyerhistory.org/fletcherclass/usschevalier/roupe.html

Royal Netherlands Navy Warships of World War II. http://www. netherlandsnavy.nl.

United States Technical Mission to Japan. http://www.fischer-tropsch.org/ primary_documents/gvt_reports/USNAVY/USNTMJ%20Reports/ USNTMJ_toc.htm.

Index

Page numbers followed by an *f*, *t*, or *m* indicate figures, tables, and maps, respectively.

About the Author

Vincent P. O'Hara is a naval historian and researcher. His work has appeared in many periodicals and annuals including *Warship, World War II Quarterly, MHQ, STORIA Militare,* and *World War II.* He is the author of *German Fleet at War,* also published by the Naval Institute Press. O'Hara received his history degree from the University of California, Berkeley. He resides in Chula Vista, California, with his wife and son.

The Naval Institute Press is the book-publishing arm of the U.S. Naval Institute, a private, nonprofit, membership society for sea service professionals and others who share an interest in naval and maritime affairs. Established in 1873 at the U.S. Naval Academy in Annapolis, Maryland, where its offices remain today, the Naval Institute has members worldwide.

Members of the Naval Institute support the education programs of the society and receive the influential monthly magazine *Proceedings* and discounts on fine nautical prints and on ship and aircraft photos. They also have access to the transcripts of the Institute's Oral History Program and get discounted admission to any of the Institute-sponsored seminars offered around the country. Discounts are also available to the colorful bimonthly magazine *Naval History*.

The Naval Institute's book-publishing program, begun in 1898 with basic guides to naval practices, has broadened its scope to include books of more general interest. Now the Naval Institute Press publishes about seventy titles each year, ranging from how-to books on boating and navigation to battle histories, biographies, ship and aircraft guides, and novels. Institute members receive significant discounts on the Press's more than eight hundred books in print.

Full-time students are eligible for special half-price membership rates. Life memberships are also available.

For a free catalog describing Naval Institute Press books currently available, and for further information about subscribing to *Naval History* magazine or about joining the U.S. Naval Institute, please write to:

Member Services
U.S. Naval Institute
291 Wood Road
Annapolis, MD 21402-5034
Telephone: (800) 233-8764
Fax: (410) 571-1703
Web address: www.navalinstitute.org